Managing Quality in Architecture

A Handbook for Creators of the Built Environment

Also by Charles Nelson:

TQM and ISO 9000 for Architects and Designers
Risk Management for Design Professionals

Managing Quality in Architecture

A Handbook for Creators of the Built Environment

Charles Nelson, AIA, FRAIA

Foreword by **Eugene Hopkins**, FAIA

ELSEVIER

AMSTERDAM • BOSTON • HEIDELBERG • LONDON • NEW YORK • OXFORD
PARIS • SAN DIEGO • SAN FRANCISCO • SINGAPORE • SYDNEY • TOKYO
Architectural Press is an imprint of Elsevier

Architectural Press

Architectural Press is an imprint of Elsevier
Linacre House, Jordan Hill, Oxford OX2 8DP, UK
30 Corporate Drive, Suite 400, Burlington MA 01803, USA

First edition 2006

British Library Cataloguing in Publication Data
A catalogue record for this book is available from the British Library

Library of Congress Cataloging-in-Publication Data
A catalog record for this book is available from the Library of Congress

ISBN-13: 978-0-75-066818-7
ISBN-10: 0-75-066818-0

For information on all Architectural Press publications visit our website at www.books.elsevier.com

Printed and bound in the United States of America

Contents

Dedication

To Jennifer

Preface

Mies: 'Less is more'

Quality management has all the earmarks of an oxymoron – no wonder design professionals are suspicious of the concept!

Quality is an idea, an approach, a theory. The hallmarks of any theory are simplicity, brevity and tidyness. Mies got his down to an enduring three short words. Einstein's is even more durable, and – at just five characters – probably has set an unbreakable record.

By contrast, management is about people. Therefore, management is not simple or tidy – it is messy and complex, an ever-moving target.

Quality has a quicksilver nature, hard to grasp. Yes, it can be accurately reduced to a brief set of generic principles – and the international standard for quality, ISO 9001, does that admirably. At the same time, quality means a description-defying passion to excel. This passion drives some of its holders toward a widely-held vision so lofty it includes uplifting of – and poetic to – the human spirit!

These 'mountaintop' goals have to coexist along with such mundane chores as keeping out rainwater and durability to last half a century!

These (a brief set of generic principles, and over-arching, inspirational goals) are, respectively, the 'little q' and 'big Q' aspects of quality noted by Juran and Franklin[1]. How does one resolve the breadth – the pan-practice sweep – of such concepts?

The original vision for this handbook was much larger than the space available, and the result is better for it. When confronting severely right-brained readers – my primary market – with a pile of words, Mies' dictum is spot-on, and the arguments for Viagra don't apply.

The result is not intended as a one-stop shop for designing a QM system, although you could certainly use it for that. Rather, it is a network hub for information about quality in architecture.

It is also two books in one: a practical guide to theory and concepts, representing the 'Q' of QM; and a comic book story about a fictitious practice that closely mirrors the complex, untidy, messy, people side – the 'M' of QM – the reality that glides in and out of the main story.

Right to the very end, I was never sure that I could bring the two together. You won't be either. But it's not the end that matters: it is the journey, and the challenge.

Footnotes

1 Dr. J. M. Juran is one of the towering pioneers of quality. His work is of interest to design professionals, because he has focused on the design of planning for quality in services. In his 1992 work *Juran on Quality by Design: The New Steps for Planning Quality into Goods and Services,* he identifies a 'crisis' of quality, which he says has given rise to the 'big Q, little Q' terminology, where 'big Q' looks at the whole business, and 'little Q' equates quality with conformance to standards or specifications. Juran says 'Some companies have defined quality in terms such as conformance to specification, or conformance to standards. These are dangerous definitions when applied at managerial levels. At those levels what is essential is that the products respond to customer needs. Conformance to standards is only one of many means to that end.'

James Franklin's research on design quality has led to what he calls (after Juran) 'big Q, little Q' concepts of design quality. By 'big Q', Franklin means 'delighting the customers'. This he contrasts with 'plain old' quality, which he says '... gets measured in terms of how well the specified requirements were met with no quantifiable deficiencies or errors. It means being on time and in the budget with no discernible negligence – doing things the right way in sequential order.'

Foreword

Finally, a book on Quality in Architecture that is *not* mundane – a book that appeals to us right-brained individuals!

Straightforward and humorous, while rich in content, this book weaves together all of the elements for a successful quality-based practice of architecture, in one enjoyable read. With his choice of key resources, Nelson brings together and builds on the wisdom of the top thought leaders in the industry. Within these pages, you will find a comprehensive examination of what we, as practitioners, can do better in serving as the Creators of the Built Environment.

Using the art of storytelling, the book balances the serious issues of practice with a fun and creative approach that keeps your interest peaked as you gain a wealth of knowledge. In this approach, the elements of quality are applied to our daily practice in a holistic way.

The vignettes are unique graphic illustrations that reinforce the content, while greatly enhancing the effectiveness in understanding the information being shared. They will bring a smile to your face – as we are all able to see ourselves in the various situations cleverly portrayed.

As you read, you will be hearing yourself say 'I've seen that happen' or 'I've heard about that before' or even better yet 'Oh my goodness! I've been there!' Now you will recognize, and know how to overcome, the pitfalls of practice – by taking positive, quality-based initiatives.

This book is an all-encompassing guide to enhance our understanding of what we need to be doing everyday in our practices. Information is of no value until it is personally applied; until it is used to inform how one thinks and acts; by applying the gained information. Only then does the information become knowledge, for then it has relevance!

This book very cleverly provides the information for us to obtain the riches – the knowledge base – for an effective and successful design practice; and in so doing, increases our ability to enjoy what we do.

If knowledge is truly the 'currency for the 21st Century', this book provides the stepping stone to wisdom for all who read, share and apply the wealth of information contained in the following pages.

Eugene Hopkins, FAIA, SmithGroup

Introduction

Information is data endowed with relevance and purpose.

Peter F. Drucker

Data > Information > Knowledge > Wisdom

In 2001, The American Institute of Architects (AIA) embarked on what it called its 'Knowledge Agenda', in a historic, radical re-think and re-building of its member service activities. As a participant in several of the national 'Grassroots' meetings, where this agenda was vigorously debated and slowly hammered into shape, I and others came to appreciate the evolutionary path represented by Data > Information > Knowledge > Wisdom.

- *Data* is event-specific and factual. For example, a matrix of all of contractor requests for information (RFIs) and their causes, for a project, would be *data*.
- *Information* is a distillation and refinement of data; drawing valid conclusions from data. For example: the analysis of the matrices of RFIs for a number of projects, leading to conclusions that RFIs could reliably and predictably be sorted into causal categories, is *information*.
- *Knowledge* is a distillation and refinement of information. For example, knowing about the historical pattern of RFIs across many projects, designers can predict how much time they should allow for answering them, and how their responses should be varied according to the causes.
- *Wisdom* is a subjective distillation and refinement of knowledge. For example, a seasoned architect, armed with experience and knowledge about incidence patterns and causes of RFIs, will be able to spot a 'nuisance' or 'frivolous' RFI instantly, and will instinctively know how to best handle the situation to reduce or prevent its recurrence.

The Oxford Dictionary defines wisdom as 'possession of experience and knowledge together with the power of applying them critically or practically'.

Knowledge is the highest level of understanding that can be commonly held; *wisdom* exists only in the human brain, e.g. is personal and unique to the holder. When the holder of wisdom imparts it to others, it is received as knowledge.We do speak of 'collective wisdom'; I would argue that that idea refers to a group of wise people acting on a common issue.

This view of the relationship of information to knowledge is fundamental to the organization of this handbook and the documents that support it. The initial contributions of authorities in various aspects of managing quality, and case studies of practices, together with paths running out to an extensive collection of related, web-based resources, create a rich tapestry of relevant, valuable information.

This tapestry is rich in breadth – there are more than 30 professional disciplines involved in the management of quality in architecture; and rich in depth – a palimpsest of practice knowledge handed down through generations.

Too rich, in fact – no busy professional could afford the time to mine all that information.

'I know it's here somewhere'

We were promised the paperless office, only to find we have more paper than ever before. We live in the Information Age, and are, to some degree, lost in its vast dark forest.

Using the handbook web site

There are models for this dual approach. The PMBOK Guide (Project Management Book of Knowledge) is a concise 400-page guide to the collective knowledge of its membership. The other model is Wikipedia, a remarkable web-based, free-content encyclopedia, that anyone can edit, started only in 2001, that at this writing has over 1 million articles.

This handbook is also the gateway to that knowledge store, via the handbook's website, www.mqia.com. References to articles in **mqia** are listed at the end of each Part of this handbook, and referenced to the corresponding chapter number here.

That knowledge store will grow as there are more contributors, and evolve as contributors edit and update their input.

Contributors to this handbook are referred to as 'Key Resources' throughout.

Rather than rely on hard-wired URL links in the text (which can and will change), access is via a manual tabbing path, for example: [www.mqia.com > authors > Andrews, Ray]. This means that after going to the website, you click on the tabs or pages indicated after the '>' marks.

Voice & gender

Throughout this handbook I use the royal pronoun 'we'. Generally this means all of us as professionals in the design and construction industry.

Sometimes it means the key resources, those who provided case study information, and me as principal author. Hopefully the distinction will be evident by the context.

To avoid the awkward construction of dual pronouns (e.g. his/her), gender references in this handbook are masculine in the odd-numbered chapters and feminine in the even-numbered chapters.

Acronyms and definitions

Acronyms are identified at their first use, and are listed in Chapter 12.1, together with definitions of quality industry technical terms.

Leitmotif: Ackler Izmore + Shay Space Architects

This is a serious book, but offices that play together stay together, so we've introduced a little light relief, our leitmotif – the story of the office of Vern Ackler, Les Izmore and Clea Shay. Their story weaves in and out of the handbook, chronicling the course of a very important project for their firm.

This firm has recently completed a re-branding exercise to try to get away from being treated as a 'commodity' and to open up some new lines of business. They now call themselves AIS Space Architects (hoping to pick up some interior design commissions), and they've invested in a snazzy new website.

As their story opens, a wealthy Asian investor has seen their website (top of the Google list of returns) and has given them the job of designing the toilet block for his new space station. Be careful what you ask for! There is a catch, and that is that they have to produce a certifiable quality management plan by the end of the design phase.

Meet the folks at AIS. There is a rogue's gallery on the website. Any resemblance to people you know is purely intentional.

Acknowledgements

So many people have contributed to this project, over such a long period of time, that I can't possibly prepare an all-inclusive list.

This project could not have happened without the extensive knowledge and great generosity of the Key Resource people.

Key Resources Ava Abramowitz, Ray Andrews, Paul Hinkley, Bill Ronco, Frank Stasiowski and Françoise Szigeti have provided major support and advice, well beyond their roles as content providers. In addition to the Key Resources, others who have been especially helpful are:

Michael Lindell, for all the cartoons and for helping me keep the focus. Michael draws the characters, I fill in the bubbles. I've long wanted to write a cartoon strip, and Ackler Izmore + Shay provides the perfect excuse.

James Franklin, Tim Jefferies and David Stone, who prepared early drafts of material, and Erland Construction, Nihon Sekkei and Shooshanian Engineering, who prepared case study data, for inclusion that ultimately didn't survive the limitations of available space.

Julie Hlupar, for transcribing most of the quotations and finding lost connections, Peter Green, for conversion of the word processing versions to InDesign™, and Olivia Lennon for market research.

Max Rogalsky, for patient mentoring in the skills needed to create the www.mqia.com website.

Mark Kalin, Cliff Moser, Robert Smith, Grant Simpson, and Chris Straw, for advice, encouragement and support throughout.

Wendy Lochner, for early encouragement and advice, and Nancy Green, for incisive questioning and challenging of less-than-great ideas. Nancy's invisible fingerprints are all over this work.

Catharine Steers, for taking on this challenge, and Jodi Cusack, Laura Sacha, Jackie Holding, Chris Nolan, and the production team at Architectural Press, who made it all happen.

Eugene Hopkins, for inadvertently helping to inspire the approach with his driving energy on the AIA's Knowledge Agenda, and for contributing the Foreword.

My wife Jennifer Fall, for encouragement, proof-reading, and graciously and patiently putting up with my preoccupation with this project for so long.

And last but not least, somewhere up there, my father Ed Nelson, who taught me, many long years ago, to love the written word.

Key resources

In addition to the people noted on the previous page, I am deeply indebted to the following individuals, who prepared papers used in writing this handbook, who provided invaluable insights and advice, and to the practices listed below who shared their stories as case histories. The full text of most of these papers can be accessed on the website, www.mqia.com.

Ava Abramowitz, Esq., Hon. AIA
Lecturer, author and trainer, negotiation skills

Janet Allison
Janet Allison Consulting, Natick MA

Ray Andrews
Andrews Group, Melbourne VIC Australia

John Beveridge, AIA
John Beveridge Architect, Essex CT

Scott W. Braley, FAIA FRSA
Braley Consulting & Training, Atlanta GA

Dr. Penny Burns
AMQ International, Adelaide SA Australia

James Cramer, Hon. AIA
Greenway Consulting, Atlanta GA

Gerald Davis, AIA, CFM, IFMA Fellow, ASTM Fellow
International Centre for Facilities, Ottawa ON Canada

Ellen Flynn-Heapes
SPARKS: The Center for Strategic Planning, Alexandria VA

Paul Hinkley, BE AMAIPM CMC
Meta Consulting, Melbourne, VIC Australia

Gérald de Kerchove
PdK Consulting, San Raphael CA

Dr. Deborah King-Rowley
Burlington Consulting, Melbourne, VIC Australia

Hideki Kiyono
Mitsui Fudosan Company Ltd, Tokyo, Japan

Stanley Mehlhoff, AIA
PM/CM Japan KK, Tokyo, Japan

Jack Reigle
SPARKS: The Center for Strategic Planning, Alexandria VA

Dr. William C. Ronco
Gathering Pace, Inc., Bedford MA

David Standen, AM LFRAIA
Perth, WA Australia

Frank A. Stasiowski, FAIA
PSMJ Resources, Inc., Newton MA

David Sutherland
Fender Katsalidis Architects Pty Ltd, Melbourne, VIC Australia

Françoise Szigeti
International Centre for Facilities, Ottawa, ON Canada

Alan Travers
Civil Construction Products Pty Ltd, Melbourne, VIC Australia

Peter Whitelaw
Rational Management Pty Ltd, Melbourne, VIC Australia

Case studies

Anderson-Brulé Architects
San José CA

Add, Inc.
Cambridge MA

Geyer Pty Ltd
Melbourne, VIC Australia

Harley Ellis Devereaux
Southfield MI

RVK Architects
San Antonio, TX

1 Why Quality?

An important Ackler Izmore + Shay weekly staff meeting - democratic as always

1.1 Do I really need this?

The central issue for all *professionals is not how successful you are, but whether or not you are prepared to strive for* greater *success.*

David Maister

Perhaps longer versions of the chapter title question could be 'Will reading this book be worth my investment in time and money?' or 'Will the ideas in here actually improve my design practice, or is this just another management fad I should ignore?'

Five case studies describe how practices have applied principles of structured quality management to reduce errors and risk, increase client satisfaction, break into new areas of practice, increase profitability, improve staff retention, and – dare I say it – actually *change* the culture of their practices.

Twenty two key resources, each an authority on some aspect of design quality in his or her own right, join me in creating this 'one-stop shop' of practice knowledge. Their full contributions are on the handbook's web site. The handbook provides the links to more detail, as well as to the key resources' web sites and other resources, should you want more information on any topic.

Generic management books are generated by the ton each year. Generic quality management books are generated by the hundreds. But books on managing quality, specific to the design and construction industry, are generated very rarely.

Does one or more of the following situations describes your practice?

- Our services seem to be treated more and more as a price-based 'commodity'.
- Sometimes we lose the next project for a client, even when we've done a great job on the previous one.
- We probably do a lot more rework than we need to, but we don't know because we don't measure it.
- Our designers never know when to stop designing, and it impacts on the time to complete the project.
- Scope creep is a constant problem, and it's hard to get increased fees for it.
- We are expected to manage the rest of the project team, but find it difficult to get paid for doing so – and our people aren't very good at keeping the rest of the team on schedule.

These, and a lot of other situations that frustrate principals, are in fact ***quality*** problems in disguise.

The goal I share with my colleagues is to provide readers with useful ideas and examples from successful design firms around the world, presented in a no-nonsense, practical way. Based on my experience with other firms, I believe that using these ideas *will* improve design practice. More than 75 short chapters tackle these issues in a holistic, integrated way, using the principles underlying the international quality standard as a baseline for a practice-wide program for lifting performance.

So, do you *really* need this? If the bullet points above are irrelevant to your practice and your life, probably not!

1.2 What is 'quality'?

God is in the details.

Ludwig Mies van der Rohe

And, as every designer knows, so is the devil.[1] And so is quality. Indeed, the traditional (and prevalent) view of quality is that it is all about details: error-free documents, checking cross-references, interdisciplinary coordination, and so on. This view of quality is appropriate for a 'manufacturing' view of architecture, which sees the results of design as a 'product' – a building, a bridge, a park.

> ***Les Izmore was silent during Vern's announcement, reflecting on his idol's aphorism, the death of the astronauts in the Discovery shuttle disaster, Frank Lloyd Wright's remark about planting vines[2], and construction administration for the project. He thought 'There is no ivy in space, and the gods won't be very forgiving'.***

This handbook is about managing quality in architecture, in the traditional meaning of the word; design and managing the construction of the built environment – including buildings, engineering works, interiors and landscape architecture – and in the provision of all the services that these activities require.

The 'in the details' view of quality, however, is inappropriate, incorrect and inadequate for a perspective of architecture that is about *service*, and that sees products as *outputs* of service. If you are in the service business rather than the product business, then your perspective on quality will be fatally flawed if it is restricted to finding the devil in the details. A service perspective of design means that quality is a key component of all service functions, such as communication and client relationship management. This is the 'Big Q' view of quality[3], and it sweeps across every aspect of design practice.

What is quality? The official definition[4] is 'the degree to which a set of inherent characteristics fulfils requirements'. Requirement is defined as 'need or expectation that is stated, generally implied, or obligatory'. Put these together, and quality is 'the degree to which a set of inherent characteristics fulfils stated, implied or obligatory needs or expectations'. 'Obligatory' means compliance with all laws, statutes, codes, and regulations. 'Expectations' means that requirements are also defined by the 'customer', which in architecture means, besides the client, the end users and the public, and sometimes even financial institutions.

In short: there is very little, if anything, about design and construction industry output that doesn't come under the umbrella of 'quality'. All of this can be modified by adjectives, such as 'poor', 'good' or 'excellent' (the *degree* to which the *set of inherent characteristics* – read 'design' here – fulfils these diverse requirements).

Clearly, then, a program of 'quality' in architecture means *improving* the degree to which design fulfils needs and expectations.

Managing such a program involves three main activities at the project level:

- Quality ***planning***, which establishes quality processes appropriate for a particular project, determines resource requirements, and assesses project inputs.
- ***Continual improvement***, a process monitoring approach that seeks to identify potential quality problems and their causes, so as to prevent their occurrence.
- Quality ***reviews***, including quality *control* (QC), which seeks to identify and fix errors and omissions before release of documents. A QC example is pre-bid checking. Review techniques also include *design reviews*, design *verification*, design *validation*, *audits* and *feedback*.

Note that the above list does not include *quality assurance* (QA), which is defined as 'providing confidence' that quality requirements will be fulfilled. For example, the statement 'our goal is to meet and exceed client expectations' is quality assurance. The 2000 edition of ISO 9001 effectively dropped 'assurance' as key concept, replacing it with an emphasis on *customer satisfaction*. QA is best understood as express or implied promises to the client.

Taken together, these activities are called *quality management* (QM), and are focused on the linear progression inherent in every project: *inputs, processes* and *outputs*. I expand on these ideas in later chapters, particularly in Part 3.

This is a broad, and correct, view of 'quality'. However, this view is not widely understood in the design professions. Not a few people who are considered knowledgeable about quality processes often still talk of 'QA-QC initiatives' or other constructions that simply aren't accurate in the context of the international standard for quality, ISO 9001:2000.

Part of the confusion over meanings comes from the fact that the international quality movement is very young – about 60 years – and has evolved its international terminology over the past 15 of those years.

Design professionals, and master builders before them, have been dealing with what is now termed 'quality' for all of recorded history. Moreover, the idea of 'managing design' has been considered an oxymoron until only very recently: as little as a decade ago, the term was rarely used, and then regarded with great suspicion.

The prevailing view among designers was that tampering with this mystical, sacred process by 'managing' it would rob it of its vitality if not destroy it altogether. That view has not exactly disappeared, but forward-looking practices now do understand that the design process can – and should – be managed.

Hold on! Don't we *already* do this stuff?

This confusion of concepts, and the unfamiliarity of the terminology to design professionals, masks the fact that we all ***do*** a great deal of QM every day.

Sometimes well, and sometimes poorly. We just don't call it 'quality'.

James Franklin, FAIA, explores this phenomenon in his book *Architect's Professional Practice Manual* with a subchapter entitled *Don't Call It Quality Management.*

The TQM (total quality management) movement in architecture in the 1980's left those who tried it deeply disillusioned; the whole exercise gave 'quality' a bad name that persists today. The cultural 'leap' between the TQM of manufacturing and design practice was just too great.

Not wanting to discuss the concepts – not 'wanting to go there' – means that we have no objective methods for capturing and comparing information about how we did on previous projects, or benefiting from structured learning about the results. This approach puts us in the unfortunate position made famous by George Santayana: 'Those who cannot remember the past are condemned to repeat it'.

The goal, simply, is to do what we do better, and consistently. And for that, we need a common language. We need to 'go there' – talk about it – if improving the quality of our service to our clients is to be part of our agenda.

This argument does ***not*** mean that I am advocating a stampede toward the wholesale application of generic quality principles in everything we do. With extremely rare exceptions, practices that try that fail. To the contrary, the central thesis of this handbook is to start talking about the ideas, comparing what we *already* do to accepted principles of managing quality, and asking ourselves how we could improve on what we already do.

The above approach is highly pragmatic. The owners and key personnel of design practices have to really believe that change will benefit the firm, or a program of change will be ignored or undermined and sabotaged. Building this belief takes discussion, time, testing, evidence, and implementation planning.

Perceptions of quality in design

Setting aside discussing 'quality' and 'management' in the same phrase, perceptions about the meaning of 'design quality', vary predictably, with the 'eye of the beholder'. Two examples:

- Aaron Schwarz, AIA, writing in *Update 2004* to the AIA *The Architect's Handbook of Professional Practice* (hereinafter referred to as *AIA Handbook*) emphasizes the importance of *consistency* in design quality, and of the difficulty in achieving consistency in multi-office practices.
- James Atkins, FAIA, in the same volume, in a paper entitled 'Maintaining Design Quality', has an approach not unlike many clients; emphasizing the importance of budget management, value analysis, controlling substitutions, submittal review, controlling construction nonconformity, and design compromise.

Excellence vs. quality

We are what we repeatedly do. Excellence, then, is not an act, but a habit.
– Aristotle

The harsh reality of marketplaces is that it is very hard to develop a reputation for excellence for something that you do 'most of the time'. – David Maister

Stuart Rose, in his book *Achieving Excellence in Your Design Practice* says: *All excellent firms share one trait: an obsession with quality.* He goes on to note: *Quality, in fact, is almost synonymous with excellence in the eyes of most design professionals.*

In discussing this relationship of quality to excellence, Rose states ... *quality obsession is that last inch, that extra mile, those few extra steps that make the difference between a good job and a great job. A quality obsession also includes consistency. It involves a consistent commitment to go for the greatness, and to do what it takes to go from being good to being* excellent.

Design quality is often seen as more or less synonymous with 'design excellence'. The AIA has taken a leadership role in defining design excellence, and it is instructive to review briefly what the AIA learned in its 'Roundtable' discussions about excellence and how it is achieved.

In 1989 The AIA published *In Search of Design Excellence*, the results of what the then president Benjamin Brewer Jr., FAIA called in the Foreword 'an ambitious, careful, and serious investigation into the important subject of design excellence'. This compendium of 10 'excellent' papers on the subject included a 55 pp document by the then AIA Resident Architect James R. Franklin, FAIA, entitled *Keys to Design Excellence*. Franklin cites the 'Signature Firms roundtable' events as having produced the best answers to questions about design excellence. He defines design excellence as: 'the perceived quality of the experiences a building provides for three groups:

- The Profession – through design awards, publications, etc.,
- The Participants – client, architect, consultants, etc., and
- The Public – user groups, tenants, the community, through approval, support and enthusiastic use.'

Few would disagree with this somewhat complex definition, but its implications should not be ignored. By this definition, design excellence is achieved only when the *perceived* benefits are there for all three groups.

Norman Kaderlan, an astute observer of architectural practice, in his book *Designing Your Practice* observes: 'Expectations shape the relationship between designer and client. The client's expectations, however, are likely to be different from yours. ... The quality of service may be more important than the quality of work. Issues that are significant to you, such as design excellence, aesthetic impact, and making a design statement, may be less critical to the client.'

Here we see an important, perhaps fundamental, distinction, that of quality of *service* vs. quality of the *design* which results from that service. Frank Stasiowski, among others, has defined quality assurance as 'meeting and exceeding the client's expectations'.

Kaderlan notes: 'Expectations are like land mines. If you aren't clear about them, they can explode at the worst possible moment and destroy the trust you have worked so hard to develop'.

I return to these ideas later. Expectations of the client, and of other project 'users', are ***core*** to principles of managing quality processes in the design practice.

1.3 Can quality be managed?

Architectural practice has become one of the major design problems of our time. While addressing this problem will demand changes in how we practice, it must begin with a redefinition of design.

Thomas Fisher

The idea that design management is an oxymoron is sufficiently prevalent that the AIA Practice Management Knowledge Community Advisory Group (PM.KC.AG) has conducted sell-out pre-Convention workshops at AIA National Conventions in 2003, 2004 and 2005 with the title *Managing Design – an Oxymoron for the Ages?* – knowing the title would strike a chord with Convention attendees.

In the previous chapter, I noted that a lot of designers still consider the idea of 'design management' to be an oxymoron.

> ***Since accepting responsibility for chairing the Quality Committee, Clea was having trouble sleeping. It wasn't the idea of quality that was bothering her, it was her colleagues. As long as everybody stayed in their corners and did their jobs, things were OK. But she wasn't at all confident that 'pulling together' on a common project would go so smoothly.***

Managing quality and managing design are different things, but necessarily tightly related – because the design process is the essential deliverer of quality results. It follows that if the prevailing attitude in a design culture is that design management is an oxymoron, so is quality management. If one digs into this a bit, it turns out that the question translates to other questions, for example:

- Can people responsible for quality (or design) be managed?
- If so, what is the best way to manage them?
- Can people responsible for quality (or design) be trained to more effectively manage quality (or design) in their projects?

The answer to the first question is 'yes, most of them', even though the answer to the second might be the same as the answer to the lovely old question about how porcupines make love (very carefully). The answer to the third question has to be 'of, course, if they see the value in it'.

Practices don't manage quality; *people* in practices manage quality. If they are to do it well, however, people need:

- clarity about how 'quality' is defined, to the practice and to the client, on the project;
- knowledge of the processes that will produce the desired quality;
- appropriate tools and aids; and
- most important of all: a blame-free culture that supports learning from mistakes, rather than hiding them.

The widespread notion that being organized somehow stifles creativity is a myth or an excuse. Many creative people are surprisingly well organized. They have come to recognize that being organized helps to remove obstacles, giving them the space in which their creativity can grow and unfold. – Thorbjoern Mann

Having those basic requirements doesn't guarantee quality performance, however. Quality, however defined, demands a certain amount of discipline, and some people (including not a few designers) are not genetically disposed toward discipline. And some people are lazy, and really don't want to pay attention to detail.

I devote Part 5 of this handbook to a further exploration of this important topic. The point of introducing it here is to emphasize that everything covered in this volume has to be delivered by *people*. It doesn't happen automatically.

Firms spend huge amounts of time and money creating lovely quality systems that simply don't work, because they are not embraced by a critical mass within the practice. By 'critical mass', I mean enough senior people who understand, believe in, and consistently use the systems, that they virtually create a mandate for use throughout the practice.

And how does a practice leader motivate senior people to create that critical mass in his practice? The short answer: 'leadership'. See Chapter 4.1.

The Ackler Izmore + Shay Quality Committee meets for the first time, resolving nothing

1.4 What do clients *really* want?

My architect should understand what I need, not what I think I need.

Government client, *The Client Experience*

The most significant characteristic of the organizational clients is their disposition to view architectural production from a purely rational and instrumental perspective. This means that the organizational clients regard buildings as capital assets, which should be managed like every other source of productivity, income and profit. As a result, plans for new buildings and for the renovation of old buildings are judged in terms of their initial and maintenance costs, their resale value, their implications for corporate income, their usability as working environments and their possible effects on organizational efficiency and employee morale. All features of buildings come to be judged by these criteria, including the esthetic dimension, which traditionally was considered as outside the realm of this calculation. – Robert Gutman

There is a fair amount of thinking and research into the clients' view of the design process. Robert Gutman (see sidebar) identifies the client valuation of design as a 'bottom line' issue.

> ***Weldon disliked meetings and hated committees, but he was ready to get seriously involved, because in it he saw an opportunity to do something about what he considered to be the biggest roadblock to the firm's success – his colleague Hugh Brisse.***

Gutman's view is broadened by Kevin Green in the *AIA Handbook:* '... the vast majority of clients see the designed environment as a means to an end rather than an end in itself. Corporate ownership's threat to invest elsewhere always hangs overhead like a Damoclean sword, ready to fall for any decision that might diminish equity value'.

Ellen Flynn-Heapes agrees, noting 'Profit comes from customers. And one thing really matters to clients: they MUST reduce their risk and maximize their return. To the extent that they can, they'll hire the best in whatever it is that they perceive they need.'

Françoise Szigeti, Vice President of The International Centre for Facilities, disagrees, asking 'What is "best" for what purpose?' She notes that the above position is 'in contradiction with the concept of quality as fitness for purpose at a given cost. It implies that there is a "best", and that cost does not enter into the equation. Quality is relative, not absolute. It is (what is) most appropriate at a given cost.'

Frank Stasiowski FAIA has prepared a paper on this topic, available on the handbook website. He says:

> '21st century design firm clients want their designers to know them better than they know themselves. In fact, clients don't want just designers: ultimately, they want strategic advisors who understand the larger reasons why they want a building project and who can help them deal with those reasons. They want a designer who knows their industry ten times better than they know it – where the designer has a specialty in that industry and has a big picture of where it is going.
>
> 'But more, clients want someone willing to get in the trenches with them and know their specific business as though the client and designer had started the business together.
>
> They want someone who understands their larger dreams, their long-term vision, the reason they started the business in the first place.

It's not just 'listening' that clients want. Some 96 percent want a professional suited exactly to their problem area, whether technical, price, or process-oriented. – Ellen Flynn-Heapes

> They want someone who knows where they are going – and has already been there.'

Stasiowski says that this 'scenario' breaks down into three 'mutually nonexclusive components': **Communication**, **Setting Strategy** and **Delivering Value**.

In building his argument, Stasiowski quotes from a large number of sources and case studies. The gist of these points:

Communication: Learn to thoroughly understand your clients' businesses, and take every opportunity to show them that you do.

Setting Strategy: Look beyond 'the project'. Think as a business consultant, rather than as a designer. Set your business strategies to coincide with those of your clients.

Delivering Value: That is, value *as measured by the client*. Too often, as designers we attempt to impose our own values on the clients' projects. There is nothing wrong with expanding a client's awareness, but a basic conflict of project values will not lead to client satisfaction, referrals or repeat business.

Stasiowski concludes,

> 'The fact is that we add value by providing design solutions. That is our true product. The finest service we can offer – and the one the client wants (whether or not he or she knows it) is to find what the client needs to make his or her business thrive, then structure our service and price based on what the client wants to "buy". If we take ourselves out of the cost-driven commodity market, where price is all a client considers, we deliver the value the client really wants.'

The point here is that the *real* market for A/E services is changing, and practices that respond to these changes and stay at the front of the wave will prosper; those that don't will be washed away. In Part 11, I discuss these changes, the forces driving them, and some alternatives for meeting their challenges.

Can a profession adapt to a changing market?

Sometimes an entire profession can use an impending crisis to reposition itself to its advantage. The example I'm thinking of here is that of Australian quantity surveyors (QS). Begun by quantity surveyors brought out from the UK after WW II, the profession changed very little for nearly four decades. Then CAD systems started to replace manual methods. It didn't take too much thinking to figure out that, in due course, CAD would be able to do the lion's share of what a QS did.

I don't know if a conscious collective decision was ever made to change – but *change* the profession did – and in changing, its members moved themselves smartly up the food chain. Today, they sell 'cost planning' services to owners and developers, often before any architects or engineers are hired – and not infrequently they even advise their clients on the appointment of design consultants. Yes – they still do the old QS 'take-off' business – with modern, cost-effective tools – but that part of the business is largely commoditized, whereas the cost-planning business is not. And it won't be, because it operates at the 'trusted advisor' level.

To return to the question, What do clients *really* want?, think about the traditional strength of the A/E professions. We are, by training and inclination, first and foremost *problem solvers*. We are very good at it. But that skill presumes a problem has been identified – which is often not the case. Sometimes there is a stated or apparent problem, masking a deeper, more complex issue. Solving the surface problem is not really helping the client.

One practice that tackled this issue head-on is CRSS, which, under the leadership of William Peña, FAIA, developed a 'breakthrough' programming methodology called *problem seeking*, that has helped the practice to achieve the prominence it enjoys today.

Perhaps that sounds a little like 'looking for problems', which could have a negative connotation. Combining those ideas, I get *solution seekers,* which I believe is a much better description of what clients really want than 'problem solvers'.

Solution seeking

For two decades, I have read everything I could find on the topic of how practices successfully connect with their clients, searching for common denominators in their stories. From this, I conclude, with confidence, that the very best client relationships – where consultants enjoy a 'trusted advisor' status, where price is way down on the list of client priorities, and where clients keep returning, are those where:

'Business' is used here in the broadest sense – referring equally to institutional and residential clients as well as commercial clients.

- the relationship is focused on the client's business rather than the client's project;
- the client sees the consultant as expert in key aspects of her own business;
- consultants measure the value of their solutions by the effect they will have on the client's business.

All of which I sum up as 'solution seeking', a hallmark of the 'high-quality practice'.

1.5 How well do we manage our clients' perceptions?

If you're making progress on client satisfaction, skill building, productivity, and getting better business, you've got all the strategy you need. And if these ***aren't*** *your objectives – well, it's hard to imagine what you are up to.*

David Maister

To re-state the point made in Chapter 1.2, quality in architecture means *improving* the degree to which design fulfils needs and expectations. Expectations are forged in the broader arena of perceptions. Hence, our management of them is a quality issue.

There is only one way to exceed your clients' expectations: You must first lower them to some point below where you can deliver the project within the budget and schedule.

> ***Vern thought privately that the idea of producing a quality system was unnecessary, but if that's what the client wanted, he would make sure that his staff gave it priority, and keep his opinions to himself. Putting Hugh on the committee would ensure that the others didn't get too carried away.***

One of the consequences of architects' and engineers' brief flirtation with TQM (total quality management) in the mid-80's was the appearance of the motto 'we aim to meet and exceed our clients' expectations', on the backs of business cards and in firm vision statements. The idea acquired buzzword status, and although less common today, still hangs around in many practices, and in the minds of many design professionals.

Noble sentiment, dumb idea. Let's examine why.

It is generally accepted that a sizable segment of the population holds a curiously paradoxical view of design professionals, especially architects: They like the idea of being an architect and associate it with prestige – but at the same time consider architects to be impractical dreamers who have little grasp of pragmatic issues like time or money.

The latter is a poor perception that should be raised – right?

Possibly, to the extent that it isn't accurate (and, too often, it *is* accurate). But is promising to 'meet and exceed expectations' the way to raise it? A far better way is to actively demonstrate that your practice has an excellent grasp of practical matters like managing time and money.

If a client didn't expect you to meet his expectations, he wouldn't be talking to you, so proposing to meet them adds nothing to your value proposition. In the absence of knowing in detail your client's expectations, promising to exceed them is meaningless – and so, therefore, making general promises to exceed all clients' expectations is even more meaningless.

Professional society actions

My goal here is not a discussion of public perceptions about designers, but how to create the accurate perception that your practice stands out above the rest. 'Accurate' might be the tricky word in that thought.

The AIA, RIBA (Royal Institute of British Architects) and most other A/E (architecture/engineering) professional societies have ongoing programs designed to raise public awareness of the role of their members in society and to promote perceptions of value about the professions they represent.

No doubt these programs have a positive effect in the big picture. However successful they may be, however, they are best at positioning their membership relative to other professionals who are not members of their professional society. They can also be effective at alerting their membership to industry-wide attitudes and evolutionary change; the AIA's *The Client Experience, 2002* as a good example.

What these programs cannot do is improve the competitive position of a practice relative to its professional society competitors.

Shaping client perceptions

If meaningless promises about expectations aren't the answer, what is? There are several methods:

Referrals are one of the most powerful shapers of client perceptions. One kind word from a past client is more convincing than a whole brochure of words and pictures from you.

How can you get your happy customers to tell the world that you are the greatest?

Unsolicited testimonials happen, but rarely. Asking for feedback greatly improves the chances of getting feedback. You have a number of options:

- Discuss it at the outset of the project. Especially where the client has asked you for some concession (such as a fee reduction or accelerated schedule) that you'd be prepared to give anyway, getting agreement for a referral will cost the client nothing, and will be easily granted. You will probably have to remind them later!
- Whenever you get a verbal compliment, ask the client to put it in writing.
- At the conclusion of the project, set up a meeting specifically to discuss your performance, record the results, and request permission to use their comments.
- As part of your quality program: Explain, at the outset, that you have a program of continual improvement that relies on feedback from *every* client, and that you will want and expect it as part of the professional relationship. If the client is interested, you can also agree to provide them with feedback from your perspective.
- As a 'live' referral: Happy clients are usually only too glad to take an occasional phone call from another prospective client – especially when they know they will be forewarned.

Internet: Your website is an increasingly important perception-shaper that the best firms use extremely well. I cover this in Chapter 4.3.

Caring: Demonstrating an awareness of your client's business – and there are dozens of ways to do this – builds the perception that your practice is the right one to help solve issues it faces.

Data about the performance of your services *and* your projects: What measurable effect did a project have for a similar client's business? Listen to Sir Norman Foster talk about any of his projects, and you will hear about the way that his clients benefited from them, in very practical terms.

I'll return to the last two techniques in detail several times throughout this handbook, so will not elaborate here.

The AIS Quality Committee tables its first rough roadmap

1.6 Why do practices implement quality systems?

The obligation to the consumer never ceases.

Dr. W. Edwards Deming

The reasons many architectural, engineering, interior design and construction firms have chosen to implement a formal quality program can be adequately described under one or more of these categories:

- An external marketing imperative
- An internal marketing imperative
- A desire for improvement of some aspect of the firm's operations, such as greater efficiency, better productivity, better document control, etc.
- 'Total overhaul' – the decision to re-orient the firm's fundamental business approach

The external marketing imperative

The greatest value of a leader is in ensuring that a strategy is implemented. This is revealed by the very origin of the word 'manage' which derives from from Old French and, literally translated, means "the holder of the horses." The manager's key role is to ensure that all the horses are moving in the agreed-upon direction at approximately the same pace. – David Maister

By far, the largest number of firms first come to QM because external forces require them to. Sometimes it is government-imposed, as in the case of Australia and the UK, where certification is a requirement for many kinds of government projects.

Sometimes it is private enterprise, for example in the area around Southfield, Michigan, where the auto industries provide work for a number of architects and engineers. Some years ago, the auto manufacturers made it clear to these practices that they would need to embrace quality management if they wanted to continue to be employed. Many did, for obvious reasons.

The Standard states (Clause 7.4.2c) that one of the qualifications purchasers should consider in contracting with suppliers is the suppliers' quality systems. This, in turn, tends to give ISO-certified firms a distinct marketing edge with ISO-certified clients: All other things being equal, a certified firm will score more points in a comparative evaluation for appointment to a project team.

In Australia, some governmental agencies award extra 'points' in evaluation if the firm is certified.

The internal marketing imperative

The next largest group come to consider QM because they are aware that it may give them a marketing edge.

US firms seeking to expand their business off-shore know that ISO 9001 is increasingly a requirement around the world, and to either be certified, or on the way, increases the chances of success in the off-shore marketing exercise.

The AIA's 2000-2002 research on member firms working internationally showed that 35% of all firms of 50 or more in size where involved in international projects, and that an additional 6% of firms in the 50+ category were actively pursuing international projects.[5]

Improve the firm

Many firms rightly think that QM will improve their internal systems, sometimes as part of a response to external or internal marketing imperatives. For example, they think they will be better organized, find things faster, make fewer mistakes and do less re-drawing, give staff a clearer idea of responsibilities and more accountability for results, and help the firm do better than it is.

Of course, implementing a quality system will not, by itself, automatically lead to such improvements, but it will create a valuable context and monitoring system for making such improvements.

Re-orient the firm's whole approach to practice

Not a very high percentage of firms see the need to totally re-invent themselves – it is a fear-fraught undertaking, not for the faint-hearted. Sometimes, however, for some combination of reasons, otherwise good, solid practices have lost their way – usually by neglecting one or more key aspects of their business.

These firms face a slow, agonizing death without undergoing the business equivalent of a heart or lung transplant.

The inherent structure of ISO 9001 is one of the best tools available to act as a basis for managing a turnaround of a firm's declining fortunes, or pulling it back from the precipice. This structure, for example, can create a framework for implementing, monitoring and evaluation of the kinds of 'transformative' practices that James Franklin and Kyle Davy/Susan Harris have researched (see Chapter 8.3).

Not all firms wait until they are peering into the black, bottomless abyss. Some, aware of the ever-increasing rate of global change swirling about their practice, choose to develop the capabilities for re-invention while they are still doing perfectly well.

These firms often see ISO 9001 quality systems as at least one potential vehicle to guide them on their intended voyage through the uncharted waters of change, and – for these firms – the ISO 9001 methodology has great promise.

1.7 Which practices benefit from adopting QM?

I would guess that more than 90 percent of our lives are governed by established routines and patterns. Certainly 100 percent of our perceptions are.

Edward de Bono

Quality management is not for everyone, and firms should understand that the culture and 'personality' of the firm will substantially affect its ability to implement a QM system. This awareness, in turn, suggests the importance of profiling the 'QM-ready' practice. For firms whose culture/personality would make it problematic to stick to the task, this chapter includes suggestions for improving readiness.

Clea could see that this project was going to test her patience – she was not known for suffering fools. Provoking a fight with Hugh wouldn't help solve the problem – she'd have to figure out how to get him to buy into the project. 'Won't be easy', she mused.

The QM-ready practice

The table below will help you figure out if your firm will find it relatively easy or relatively difficult to successfully design, develop and implement a quality management program.

Table 1.7.1 *Ease or difficulty in implementing a QM program*

Easier	*More difficult*
Business is the primary focus	Design is the primary focus
Firm has a practice manual and expects everyone to adhere to it	Firm has no practice manual
Technical excellence is perceived as a high goal	Creative freedom is perceived as a high goal
Firm has a business plan	Firm has no business plan
Client signoff at milestones is sought and generally secured	Firm doesn't use milestones
Firm regularly prepares comprehensive project briefs before starting design	Firm has no clear procedure for project briefing
Principals are computer literate	Principals are not computer literate
Firm believes in and uses standard details	Firm does not use standard details
Firm has effective procedures for checking contract documents before bidding	Firm does not have effective procedures for checking contract documents before bidding
Firm has an effective POE (post-occupancy evaluation) program	Firm has no POE program

Consulting engineers, who typically more often use, and are more used to, a systems approach, usually find QM implementation easier than do architects.

The practices on the left side of Table 1.7.1 are more organized, more disciplined, and believe in a systems approach.

Firms described in the right hand column are not used to discipline, tend to be disorganized, and do not believe in a systems approach. For them, implementing a QM system would be like rebuilding a car engine, top to bottom.

Moreover, firms described in the left hand column are already well down the road to having a formal QM system in place – whether they realize it or not. It's mostly a case of filling in the gaps in their systems. For those firms, implementing a QM system will be like getting an engine tune-up.

The firms on the left will experience cultural *evolution*. Those on the right will experience cultural *revolution*; they will derive the greatest benefit from implementing a QM program, but it will NOT be easy, and it will not be speedy.

Getting ready

OK, you are a member of a firm that is more like the right column than the left – but you'd like to see the practice be more like the left column. What to do next – even if ISO 9001 certification is of no interest to you? You will need to achieve the following conditions, before your chances of success approach a respectable level of realism:

- Identify a clear set of goals to be achieved.
- Secure the honest support of all members of top management, even if some is only passive support.
- At least one member of top management is willing to act as 'champion' and really push for change.
- Somebody not in top management (maybe you) is willing to be the 'working champion' and do what Australians call the 'hard yards' of change[6].
- You can enlist one respected and dynamic leader in each department or major practice division who will work with you to effect change.
- Management agrees to a program of time release to work on the project, and the project is given project status.
- You assemble your team and prepare a costed 'quality project' plan and get it approved by top management.

That's just to get you on the starting blocks and into the race. Later chapters will take you through the next steps. By the way, the same steps apply to the left-column firm – but they'll be easy, a no-brainer.

OK, I can hear you asking: If we are already doing a lot of real quality management, why are these steps so important?

The answer, unfortunately, is what I call the 'auto-body' metaphor: like the fender on your car, which is formed by a huge press, once formed is difficult to reform without breaking it. The press that formed this fender of practice is the collective, inherent personality of the firm's first and (for larger firms) second tiers of management.

The fender really has to want to change *a lot* in order to reform itself.

Attempts to avoid these basic requirements mostly end in frustration and failure, and are ultimately counter-productive, because the failed attempt is perceived as the result of a flawed change methodology rather than a stiff fender.

AIS Space Architects Quality Committee circles around its mandate

Part 1: Sources, resources & notes

NOTE: *The Architect's Handbook of Professional Practice 13th Ed.,* Joseph A. Demkin, Exec. Ed., published by John Wiley & Sons, and its updates, is referred to below as *AIA Handbook.*

Sources

1.2 Atkins, James B. (2004) Maintaining Design Quality, *AIA Handbook, Update 2004*, Wiley, pp 101–114.

Franklin, James R. (2000) *Architect's Professional Practice Manual*, McGraw-Hill, pp 3.15–3.17.

Franklin, James R. (1989) *In Search of Design Excellence*, The American Institute of Architects, p 5.

Kaderlan, Norman (1991) *Designing Your Practice: A Principal's Guide to Creating and Managing a Design Practice*, McGraw-Hill, pp 99–100.

Maister, David H. (2001) *Practice What You Preach*, The Free Press, p 196.

Rose, Stuart W. (1987) *Achieving Excellence in Your Design Practice*, Whitney Library of Design, pp 7, 60, 62.

Schwarz, Aaron B. (2004) *AIA Handbook, Update 2004*, Wiley, p 88.

1.3 Mann, Thorbjoern (2004) *Time Management for Architects and Designers*, W. W. Norton & Co., p 35.

1.4 Flynn-Heapes, Ellen (2000) *Creating Wealth*, SPARKS: The Center for Strategic Planning, pp 45, 65.

Green, Kevin W. C. (2001) *AIA Handbook*, p 25.

Gutman, Robert (1988) *Architectural Practice: A Critical View*, Princeton Architectural Press, p 50.

Peña, William (1987) *Problem Seeking, An Architectural Programming Primer*, 3rd ed., AIA Press, Washington.

1.6 Maister, p 197.

Resources

www.mqia.com:

1.4a Stasiowski, Frank, *What do clients really want?*

Epigrams

1.1 Maister, David H. (1997) *True Professionalism,* The Free Press, p 40.

1.2 Mies van der Rohe, Ludwig, widely attributed.

1.3 Fisher, Thomas (2000) *In the Scheme of Things: Alternative Thinking on the Practice of Architecture*, University of Minnesota Press, p 92. Fisher is the Dean, College of Architecture and Landscape Architecture, University of Minnesota.

1.4 The American Institute of Architects (2002) *The Client Experience*, 2002, p 11.

1.5 Maister, David (1993) *Managing the Professional Service Firm*, The Free Press, pp 239-240.

1.6 Demings, Dr. W. Edward, widely attributed, a reference to Point 1 of Demings' 14 points of quality.

1.7 de Bono, Edward (1992) *Sur/Petition,* Fontana (HarperCollins), p 51.

Endnotes

1 For an interesting discourse on this idea, see http://c2.com/cgi/wiki?TheDevilIsInTheDetails.

2 'A doctor can bury his mistakes, but an architect can only advise his clients to plant vines'.

3 See footnote, page x.

4 From ISO 9000:2000. ISO definitions are available online at www.1stnclass.com/quality_glossary (hereinafter called the 'quality glossary').

5 These percentages are down from the previous survey, published in 1997, which showed that 53% of 50+ firms were working internationally, and 'across all firms, international billings accounted for almost 6% of the total net billings, and for those firms involved in international projects, international billings accounted for 20% of net billings.'

6 It is possible for the same person to be both the 'champion' in management and the 'working champion', but this becomes a major time commitment for that one person. Two, working closely together, are the best option in the mid- to large-sized practice.

2 Creating Efficient, Effective Quality Systems

Crunch time for the Quality Committee - and they're *not* ready

2.1 Evaluating your need for change

If you don't know where you are going, you'll probably end up somewhere else.

Yogi Berra

This chapter considers the evolutionary process toward development of an awareness about organizational cultural change, or what Jim Franklin calls *transformational* practice.

Vern was feeling very uncomfortable about the space station project. He needed this job badly, and couldn't afford to have it jeopardized. Clea had said she was frustrated, especially with Hugh, who seemed to be stone-walling. Clea wanted him to talk to Hugh about it.

Reality check...

I should point out that the concepts discussed in this section apply *only* to practices that want to be different, and better, than they now are. If you and your partners are perfectly content with the way your practice operates, and the staff and clients and projects you have – *read no further*. Give this book to someone less fortunate than yourself, and go and work on your golf handicap instead.

For the rest of you still with me, don't skim this lightly. Get a cup of tea (or something stronger) and read carefully.

One of the most important (but little appreciated) aspects of a formal quality management system is its ability to focus management attention on potential problem areas that would not otherwise be seen, and thus alert management to the need for resolution before it is confronted with a manifestation of the problem.

There is general agreement among those who study organizational change that effective change requires objective analysis of the present and a plan for the future. How can we get an objective analysis?

Can you see your reflection?

The problem with self-reflection as a self-improvement strategy is that most of us are too close to the problem to see it clearly. That's navel gazing. Looking in the mirror is a notoriously unreliable method of self-evaluation, as the image is distorted by all the biases (positive and negative) of the subject.

Problems facing practices are, for the most part, those of which the practice is unaware.

You don't have to agree with me on this point – most design professionals I know would say they are only too well aware of the problems they face.

Well, that is another way of saying that they don't know how to solve the problems they are aware of, because if they did, they wouldn't be problems any more.

The reason for my assertion is that we all value quality performance very highly, and as soon as a problem is manifested – or at least apparent to management – it tends to be addressed and resolved. Unfortunately this is knee-jerk management, and it can never structurally address the unknown problems. It is problem solution, not problem prevention.

Planning which is not based on present reality is doomed to failure. There is quite a body of literature available on this process, much of which would be relevant in varying degrees to design practice.

I have seen many well-meaning attempts at organizational change never get off the ground because the starting point – the launching pad – was vague and fuzzy. Management either didn't understand its firm very well, or was hanging on to unrealistic ideas about the capabilities of the organization.

One reason for this 'vague and fuzzy' corporate self-awareness probably springs from the idea of the design professional as a 'generalist' – a concept characteristic of architects, but usually not of engineers. The idea is 'We can do anything' and its corollary, 'Get the job first and figure out how to do it later'. As we will see in later chapters, this approach is not compatible with *any* concept of quality management.

For the present, we will consider some of the simpler methods of introducing objectivity into self-awareness.

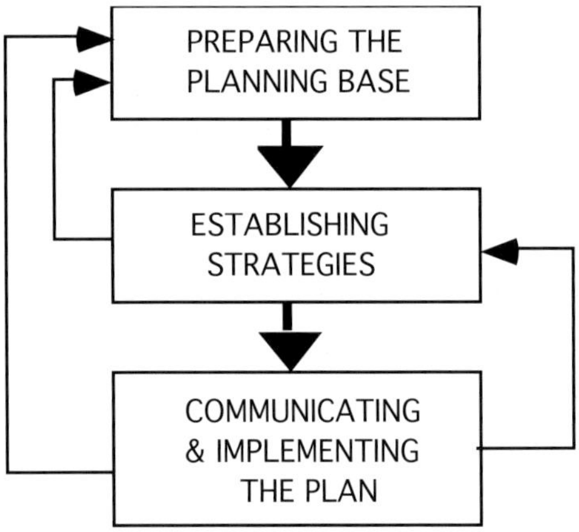

Fig. 2.1 *Smith's strategic planning model*

The process of getting from where you are to where you want to be is called *strategic planning*, which is the subject of Chapter 4.2.

One particularly useful, accessible and inexpensive source on this topic is Neville Smith's *Down-to-Earth Strategic Planning*. Smith sees strategic planning as an iterative, three-stage process, represented by the diagram at left.

In describing strategic planning, he borrows an idea invented by the science fiction writer Frank Herbert, called 'overstanding'. Smith defines over-standing as 'to overview the entire context' or 'seeing the big picture' and notes 'Overstanding is possibly the outstanding characteristic of strategic thinking'.

But how do we come to this point of 'overstanding', especially with respect to our current situation?

Management consultants have invented a number of ways of doing this. All of these techniques necessarily involve some method of introducing more objectivity into (and weeding subjectivity out of) our introspective processes.

SWOT analysis

One of the most common techniques is called the SWOT analysis. SWOT stands for **S**trengths and **W**eaknesses / **O**pportunities and **T**hreats. The strength/weakness evaluation is internal, about your firm; whereas the opportunities/threats evaluation is about factors external to your firm. Obviously the goal is to match up strengths with opportunities and to avoid competing where weaknesses correspond with threats.

The SWOT analysis should not be undertaken by management alone, as the biases in management's perception can get in the way of real understanding. Everyone in the practice should be involved. Some firms invite trusted colleagues and/or past clients to participate.

Some authorities disagree on the time frame. Key Resource Paul Hinkley suggests that SWOT analyses are best conducted either as 'snapshots' of the present, or forecasts of the future, and that mixing the two can lead to confusion.

Some sample categories for a SWOT analysis are shown overleaf (Fig. 2.2). These headings are very general, just to stir your imagination. The ones you develop should be as specific to your practice as possible.

The time frame is also important. The SWOT analysis should take as long a view of the situation as possible; two to five years.

Peer reviews

Peer reviews are acknowledged as one of the best ways for the owners of small professional firms to gain objectivity in understanding their practices' strengths and weaknesses.

Although there are endless variants on the concept, peer review techniques can broadly be categorized into two types, formal and informal. Taking the second first, an informal peer review system is one where you agree with another professional to be 'on call' and to give frank, honest and direct advice about those matters on which the other person seeks advice. The arrangement is reciprocal and there is no payment for the service either way.

One of the most productive peer review arrangements is to cross-share design reviews. That is, you have a principal from another practice come to all of your design reviews, and you go to all of his.

The 'fresh pair of eyes' from across town will see things that the design team could never have seen because they were too close to the problem. Of course, your peer review partner needs to be someone you can trust, and should not be chasing the same group of clients. This technique works for firms of any size, but is particularly useful for the very small practice.

Fig. 2.2 *Sample SWOT analysis matrix*

STRENGTHS	WEAKNESSES
Market position: • General reputation • Recognized market niche leader • Design awards **Resources:** • Stable, well qualified staff • Expert knowledge in specific building types / specialist skills • Experienced, self-starting support staff **Financial:** • Comfortable cash position • Predictable cash flow • Good receivables exceed debts • Good backlog of work • No claims of negligence	**Market position:** • Firm not well known • No track record in growth areas • No real differentiation from competitors **Resources:** • High staff turnover • Retirement/loss of principal • Support staff need constant direction **Financial:** • High overdraft /paying interest on operating capital • High receivables; some may be uncollectible • Low backlog of work • Subject to claims of negligence
OPPORTUNITIES	**THREATS**
Market: • Market growth in areas of firm's experience • Competitor has closed practice • Previous client has announced expansion plans **Economy:** • Improving business climate • Interest rates lowering **Government:** • Government spending on infrastructure to increase	**Market:** • High profile competing firm adding staff in our areas of expertise • Overbuilding to cause slowdown **Economy:** • Interest rates on rise **Government:** • Increased governmental requirements

Organizational peer review

Formal review is called 'Organizational Peer Review'. It was developed by the American Consulting Engineers Council (ACEC). The American Institute of Architects saw the positive effects of the ACEC's method, and rather than re-invent the wheel, it joined the ACEC system.

Here's how it works. If you are an AIA member, you request a peer review from ACEC. ACEC runs the AIA's Peer Review Program, but an AIA representative sits on the ACEC Steering Committee.

When you apply to ACEC, you get a list of qualified, trained peer reviewers, with information on each reviewer's experience, firm size, and other relevant data. You can choose anyone on the list.

What happens in the peer review? I quote from the AIA's document on the subject:

> At your request, one or more specially trained reviewers, who are practicing architects and engineers, will visit your firm to examine its overall business health. They'll talk with you and your employees and take a look at manuals, business plans, and other materials describing your firm's operation. They will evaluate the extent to which your firm is doing things the way you think they should be done. When they've finished their examination, they'll discuss their findings with you.
>
> The goal of the peer review is not to criticize, make comparisons, or cast judgment but to provide insights that will help you build a stronger, more productive, and more competitive firm. The primary topics reviewed are general management, human resources, financial management, professional development, business development, and project management.

Confidentiality is, obviously, crucial. Prior to the review, each reviewer signs a nondisclosure agreement. No written records are kept and any materials supplied to the review team are returned at the conclusion of the review.

Gap Analysis

As I work with professional design practices in Australia, Japan and the US, I increasingly find that gap analysis is a very effective and efficient tool to help organizations clearly see the space between their present reality and their preferred future.

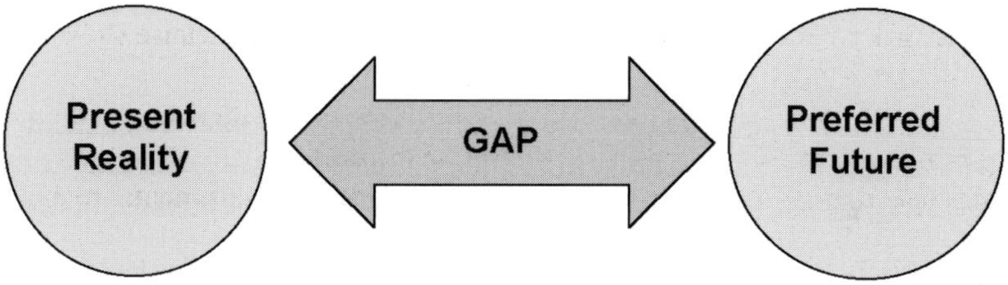

You can use an external facilitator to run a gap analysis exercise – or somebody who understands facilitation processes and has real objectivity about your practice can do it. It takes only an hour or two, to get a first cut on seeing what this gap is – and the result usually is a revelation to some people in the practice.

This gap exists for the vast majority of all businesses, including professional design practices – although this way of thinking about it is fairly uncommon. Sometimes the gap is small, indicating a firm operating very successfully and realistically; sometimes the gap is large, indicating a firm that is struggling with its identity, failing to understand its market, unrealistic about its abilities, or some combination of those.

Here are the basics of my method:

Get the key people together in some part of your firm; whether it is everybody in a small practice, or the key people in a division or section. It works best with no more than 10-12 people – but what is important is that ***all*** the key people representing the group must attend.

The ones hardest to get there are the ones that matter the most. Cell phones are shut off, and no calls get through.

First, ask every person in the group to describe what they think are the key elements of the firm's present reality.

Many people will name the same things, so 'not enough clients' or 'clients pay too slow' will get several ticks. Ensure that everybody contributes at least one item, even if only to clearly agree with a point already made.

Second, ask the group, by show of hands, to prioritize the list: 1 = most important factor in present reality, 2 = next most and so on.

Third, explain that for every element in the Present Reality list, there is a matching element in the Preferred Future list. This will be harder, but with a little prodding, you will get 'find more clients' or 'get clients to pay more promptly' responses.

The reason these answers come slowly is that participants are starting to think about process as they think about desired change; and the awareness starts to dawn that maybe the firm will have to do something different if desired change is to take place.

The Preferred Future list will be interesting, as it will invariably bring out things that have never been voiced before – especially when all participants have had a say. These new ideas will get debated, usually spontaneously.

There are three more steps to this process:

Fourth, get participants to identify some things the firm could or should do to get from its Present Reality to its Preferred Future, for each item (at least three things for each item; but not more than five).

Fifth, again test this list with participants, and make them prioritize the gap-closing actions.

Sixth, ask for volunteers to further research methods for each of the high priority actions, and agree a timetable for reporting back. Every participant **must** walk out of the meeting with an assignment (now do you see why all the key people have to be there?).

You see that what started out as an 'analysis' exercise has ended up as a 'do something' exercise. This is very important, because there is a tangible outcome, not just a gum-beating exercise.

Nobody can truthfully say it was a waste of time, because they each have to do something that will move the firm a little bit from its Present Reality to its Preferred Future.

Don't think for a minute that the process described above will actually get your business to the nirvana of your Preferred Future.

That wasn't its objective. The objective was to map the ground you and your colleagues want to traverse, and to start to rev up people for the challenge ahead. In the process, some new ideas will come to light, and some heads will peek out of the sand. That's a powerful outcome for 10-20 person-hour investment.

This topic is continued in the next chapter.

There are many mirrors

There are other evaluative methods for understanding your practice and the environment it operates in. There *are* other 'mirrors' available – such as environmental scanning, organizational analysis and portfolio analysis – outside the scope of this book, that you may come across.

Use any method that ensures objectivity and works best for you and your practice.

Moment of truth - show progress or lose the project

2.2 Mapping your preferred future

You must know where you are if you wish to go somewhere else!

Neville Smith

The purpose of this chapter is to emphasize the importance of understanding the role of business planning in quality service improvement.

Where are we, and where do we want to go? Where is our 'somewhere else'?

Regardless of one's orientation to quality management, it is impossible to structure an effective quality system without answering these fundamental questions – questions that many practitioners ask themselves frequently, but rarely answer.

Norman Kaderlan has researched the reasons why those questions do not get answered, and his findings are interesting. He says *fear of failure* is the most common reason why practitioners don't plan, *fear of success* is next, and third that they feel that *the planning process is unsuited to their temperament.*

Yet, we encourage our clients to overcome anxiety about new design, believe that our designs will contribute to their success, and sell planning as a service we are better at than anyone else!

Indeed, the process of establishing a quality management system often highlights the importance of a business plan, along with an analysis of the practice's skills base.

In this regard, one of the great benefits of a QM plan can be a systematic focusing on the firm's strong links and weak links (to use the old chain metaphor).

This process identifies the weak links and gives them the highest priority, such that, gradually, all of the things the firm does are as good as what it does best, but in a way which does not unreasonably strain its resources or induce culture shock.

Under an ISO 9001 system, the self-discovery process is called *internal auditing*, but this refers to the more formal process of assessing how the quality system is working. Auditing is covered in Chapter 2.10. Quality management relies on the establishment of business goals and objectives, which are part of the outcome of the process of business planning.

Without such goals and objectives, the audit function has no benchmark or standard against which operations can be compared.

Detail guidance of the business planning process is beyond the scope of this book. There are excellent resources available, for example, Frank Stasiowski's *Staying small Successfully* has a comprehensive chapter devoted to business planning for small design practices. Stasiowski defines six elements or steps to the development of a business plan:

- Mission and culture statements
- Marketing plan and direction
- Financial plan
- Organizational plan
- Human resources plan
- Leadership transition

Although the business plan itself is not part of a quality management system, there is a close relationship between the business planning process and quality management. For example, ISO 9001 requires that the firm have a *quality* mission statement (which might be part of a larger business mission, or identical to it). It also requires an organizational plan and, at the project level, human resource planning.

Another excellent source is Norman Kaderlan's text, noted earlier. Kaderlan devotes the first part of his book to describing the business planning process in detail.

On the specific subject of external forces acting on the practice – opportunities and threats – there is a whole chapter in Robert Gutman's book.

These ideas underscore the importance of determining your market position. The manufacturing industry does this by using the well-known product-price matrix that is used to define 'dogs, princesses, cash-cows and market failures'.

Another excellent approach to research in business planning is that of The Coxe Group, published as *Success Strategies for Design Professionals*. This text develops a concept the authors call 'SuperPositioning', which is a business/marketing 'game plan' based on the idea that all design firms can be organized according to a six-cell matrix, as shown below, and that a successful strategy can be developed if you know where you fit into this matrix.

The Coxe Group's book describes the characteristics of these six categories, and how firms in each can best 'position' themselves in the marketplace, depending on where they fit in the matrix.

This system is also a method for matching the firm profile to the client profile.

Design Technologies	Practice-Centered Business	Business-Centered Practice
Strong Delivery	A	B
Strong Service	C	D
Strong Idea	E	F

Organizational values

Figure 2.3 *SuperPositioning matrix*

The Coxe Group analysis questions whether or not the same rules that apply to businesses generally are applicable to design firms. Their conclusion is startling:

> For a decade, management 'authorities' have been writing article after article for both the professional and business press telling design professionals that they need to be more businesslike to survive in today's economy. Yet when professional service firms that have applied business principles to the fullest are examined, few cases that confirm the conventional premise of what being 'businesslike' implies can be found.
>
> In fact, for every engineering or architecture organization that is doing well under full application of business management, there are probably ten times as many firms doing as well or better by operating under a rather different set of rules – or no rules at all.

The Coxe Group, *Success Strategies for Design Professional: Super Positioning for Architecture & Engineering Firms*, 1987, McGraw-Hill. Reproduced with permission of The McGraw-Hill Companies.

It was this conclusion that motivated the The Coxe Group to develop their SuperPositioning theory.

It can fairly be said – as far as ISO 9001 QM issues are concerned – that the drive for a more businesslike approach comes from the business community that is involved in the development of QM methods; for example, the automotive industry. This community is, to a greater or lesser degree, your client group.

The fact that design firms can succeed without necessarily working to some recognized form of business planning may have something to do with size: over 80% of all practices are less than 10 persons, and nearly 60% are 1-4 persons in size. At this level, 'management' can function as the direct extension of the personality of the leadership of the practice. An organized person will, simply, *be* an organized practice.

If you accept the import of The Coxe Group's conclusion – and certainly many design professionals would agree – it follows that development of QM procedures directly relevant to the design disciplines is the best strategy to both effective quality and business management. That is the position this handbook takes.

2.3 Diagnostic audits

How will you contrive to make your subjective my objective? How will you shape up something tangible for me? How will I get a footing in this fog?

Louis Sullivan

The *diagnostic audit* is a term I use to describe an initial assessment of a company's readiness for quality system implementation. It is not a definition found in any of the quality standards.

> ***Les too felt a growing unease about the progress of the QM working group, from the vibes he was picking up. He suspected that there would be a major clash sooner or later between Hugh and Weldon, and that this project might be the thing that triggered it. He thought. 'I better talk to Vern about this – sooner rather than later'.***

This chapter outlines one method of achieving an objective view of your practice, as a helpful precondition to planning a quality management system.

There are some important differences between this concept of a diagnostic audit and quality audits, which are defined and discussed in Chapters 2.10 and 3.5. All quality audits are formal affairs, and must be conducted with objectivity and impartiality. There are three tests in the definition of a quality audit for '*quality activities and related results*': (a) compliance with planned arrangements, (b) implemented effectively, and (c) suitable to achieve objectives.

Prior to adoption of a quality management system, 'planned arrangements' and 'objectives' are not likely to be formalized, so it is not appropriate to use these measures as yard-sticks in a diagnostic audit.

By contrast, a diagnostic audit can be more informal and relaxed. The main purpose is not to test the practice in any way, but to help it to evaluate itself as a first step in embracing the introduction of new systems.

A secondary purpose is to inform the assessing consultant about the practice if that consultant is going to go on to help the practice develop its quality system.

A key observation from my work with professional design firms is that, because almost all firms value excellence, they focus attention on any perceived problem and fix it as soon as they can.

Objectivity and finding the 'weak links'

While the focus noted above tends to be a reactive approach that sometimes results in overlapping systems, these problem-fixing efforts are often successful, and in many practices serve to improve the firm's operations in terms of efficiency, reduction of risk and increased reputation.

A classic example from my experience was an otherwise superbly managed practice, with well-developed systems and a lot of pride in those systems – where the practice secretary had not backed up any computer files since her recruitment many months earlier.

The directors were completely unaware of this dangerous lapse of quality management and common sense.

If this firm had conducted its own diagnostic audit, it is likely it would have missed the potentially disastrous problem, because of their assumption that the secretary understood, and was following, good document management procedures.

This approach does not usually find the firm's 'weak links', however. Determining where the weak links are is an important purpose of the diagnostic audit. Doing this permits priorities to be established which result in the most dramatic improvement at the least cost and tends to build overall staff confidence in the implementation of quality management.

An outsider will ask the awkward and dumb questions that might not occur to the people within the practice. Thus the objectivity of the external auditor can be an important factor in discovering the firm's 'weak links'.

We can see from the above discussion that key objectives of the diagnostic audit are to identify the firm's strengths and weaknesses, and to thereby identify those areas that, if improved, will most benefit the firm. This simple 'cost-benefit analysis' has several goals:

- Identify and schedule for improvement those areas most likely to cause a firm to fail a formal system audit.
- Protect the firm from exposure to risk.
- Increase the firm's efficiency.
- Help to shape the firm's quality objectives.
- Help to create a framework for writing of quality procedures.

What does the diagnostic audit involve?

To complete a diagnostic audit for a typical small to medium sized practice, I find I need to spend two, or sometimes three, half-days in the firm, interviewing many of the employees and collecting information on the firm's systems. This is followed by a half to full day of evaluation and preparation of reports.

The kinds of things we look at in the firm are related to the informal quality management systems the firm has evolved in order to survive in business, such as:

- ✓ filing systems; file naming of correspondence and other documents
- ✓ general office organizational systems
- ✓ standard forms and how they are used
- ✓ organization of design briefs and client instructions
- ✓ design reviews
- ✓ staff role descriptions
- ✓ staffing assignments
- ✓ task scheduling
- ✓ specification data bases and updating
- ✓ checklist use
- ✓ standards and codes
- ✓ checking of contract documents
- ✓ tendering and contract administration procedures
- ✓ post-occupancy evaluation (POE)

From this assessment we normally produce two reports:

- One for general distribution to all members of the practice that highlights the positive results of the diagnostic and that responds to questions raised by those interviewed.

  This report has several purposes, but the most important is to assist management in selling the benefits of quality systems to a still-wary staff; in terms that are very practice-specific and that expose, in a non-threatening way, a few of the things everybody would like to see fixed anyway.

- A confidential report to senior management that is completely candid about specific problems as well as strengths. This report focuses on finding the best and most efficient way forward and includes specific recommendations for system design and implementation.

2.4 Building your quality system

Where do you want to go today?

Microsoft Corporation

Metaphor: Think of your practice as a locomotive, a powerful engine to take you where you want to go. Your locomotive is on the turntable, from which many tracks lead out. All have consequences. Make certain that you aim your engine down the track that will get you where you want to go. Hard to back up and start over.

The structuring decision is the most important one that you will make in the entire design of a QM system, so make it carefully, after considering all the viable options and discussing them with your partners and staff. You really must get this 'right first time'. Don't, and you'll do it all again.

Your whole practice should be solidly behind this decision, insofar as possible, which means it may take some time. Time well spent.

Before outlining your options, I'd like you to think about where your firm is now in relation to the discussion in Chapter 1.7. 'Where you are' is an important consideration in deciding where you want to go, and how you are going to get there.

Clea cornered Vern by the water-cooler when nobody else was around. 'Vern', she said, 'I need you to speak to Hugh. He's not cooperating.' Vern felt like he might be getting caught in his own trap, but he said 'I'll look into it'.

Five steps to creating a QM system

There are five steps to creating a design practice quality system:

- Establish your quality goals and objectives, then give them a 'reality check'.
- Select an appropriate structural approach.
- Find a 'champion'.
- Determine which processes should be documented.
- Create process statements (called 'procedures') to describe your quality system.

These steps are outlined below.

Step 1: Establishing quality goals and objectives

Many people, when starting out on this process, get confused over the difference between *goals* and *objectives*. Your goals are elements of your preferred future (See Chapter 2.1, third step under *Gap analysis*). Your objectives are the *means to the end*, the *methods for realizing your goals*.

Goals

Perhaps you think that your goals are self-evident. If they are to you, you are a rare design professional. If you didn't do the gap analysis process, and think they are, try writing them down.

Most of the design professionals I've worked with do a lot more work with the square end of the pencil (chewing, erasing) than they do with the pointy end, before they get to written goals they are satisfied with.

Most authorities stress the importance of keeping your goal statement concise, but you will find that this is *not* easy to do. Many practitioners start out by writing a page or two – a sort of stream of semi-consciousness about the zen of making a living through design.

If that works, put them aside for a few days, then see if you have changed your mind. If you haven't changed your mind by the end of a week, try them on your practice partners, your personal partner, your staff. Do they agree?

There is a lot of help available if you are still chewing your pencil instead of writing your goal statement. A list of good resources is included at the end of this Part.

Objectives

Objectives are the 'enablers' of your goals. There is general agreement in the quality industry about what makes a good objective; perhaps best summed up by Roy Fox: 'It is most important that objectives be definitive, quantifiable and measurable.'

If you write objectives that do not meet that simple test, they will be of negligible benefit to your quality system. It is the function of being able to measure change against your objectives that tells you whether or not your system is working. Some sample goals and corresponding objectives are shown in the table below.

Table 2.1 *Sample goals and objectives*

Goals	Corresponding objectives
Reduce rework to a minimum	Establish a process for recording and classifying rework, including timesheet tracking
	Hold office meetings semi-annually to encourage staff to accurately report rework and to understand that they won't be penalized for doing so
	Monitor rework, determine causes, and develop strategies to reduce rework
Reduce drawing and coordination errors to a minimum	Ensure that pre-bid drawing checking has a time allowance on every project schedule
	Record number of errors found in pre-bid checks and analyze quarterly
	Record RFIs on each project and compare them to pre-bid error history
	Establish an in-house training program for improved drawing checking and coordination checking

Is ISO 9001 certification a goal?

It doesn't have to be, but some practices set this as a goal because their clients expect it, and some set it because they believe it will add a dimension of discipline and rigor to their quality planning. If certification is a goal, you will need to relate your structure to it. If not, you can do whatever you want to improve your quality systems, and ignore the ISO 9001 structure.

Note the '**Best Buy**' recommendation in this reference.

If you decide that ISO certification is a near-term or ultimate goal, then you need to buy a copy[1] of ISO 9001:2000; study it, ask questions, and become familiar with it. Purchase information is included in Resources (3.1) at the end of Part 3: *Harnessing the Power of ISO 9001:2000.*

Reality check

When you are satisfied that you've got your goals and objectives pretty well right, compare them to other examples – ISO 9001 is a good, 50-point 'checklist', even if certification isn't a goal.

You *just* might, because of your focus, have forgotten something important. For example: if your focus was on improving end-of-service functions such as document quality and better contract administration, you may have missed the broader quality perspective, on things such as quality planning, leadership, client satisfaction or continual improvement.

Such a check might send you 'back to the drawing board' – or if not, at least confirm that your scope was right first time.

Step 2: Select an appropriate structural approach

You have three basic options: invent your own unique system, use a guide structure, or use an 'infill' approach – fit QM into your existing operations system.

Having seen the consequences of hundreds of practices going down these paths, my observations on their decisions are:

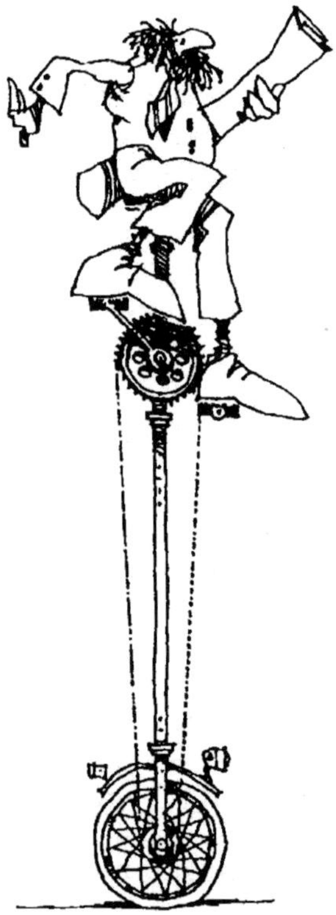

- Architects being architects (and the same is true for other design professionals), there is a strong tendency to think that our own practice is unique, and therefore our quality system needs to be unique. 95% of the time, this is a grand delusion, unsupported by reality. The strong odds are that our practice is a lot more like most other practices than we would like to admit, and the quality approach that works for them is probably going to work for us.
- Inventing a unique system costs a huge amount of money, involves a lot of tearing down and re-building, and takes a long time. When you finally get to a round wheel, it will look a lot like the other round wheels around.
- 'One size fits none' (see Chapter 3.4). Despite the points above, no standard approach will suit any practice 'out of the box' – some tweaking will always be required – because, in fact, each practice is *a little bit* different from every other practice.

Invent you own unique structure

The reason that inventing your own system costs so much and takes so long is that it is a 'greenfield site', without horizons.

Anything and everything is up for consideration, and everybody will have different priorities. Conversely, any standardized approach has relegated those battles to history, and draws fences around choices. In the trade-off, the fences win almost every time.

My recommendation – if you buy the above logic – is to use a guide structure and adapt it to your practice.

Use a guide structure

If you accept the logic, you need to decide on a guide approach. There are five possible options: ISO 9001, TQM, Six Sigma and the quality guidelines in the PMI PMBOK and Prince2 project management manuals.

> The American Society for Quality (ASQ) has published a guide for the interpretation of ISO 9001:2000 for the design and construction industry. See discussion in Chapter 3.4 and **Sources** at the end of Part 3 for details and order info.

My advice is that ISO 9001 is the only viable choice for design professionals. It is valuable as a guide whether or not certification is a goal.There are thousands of practices successfully operating ISO 9001-based QM systems. I know of only two practices that have successfully used TQM as the basis for their approach (one of those is described in Chapter 9.2). I have never heard of a design practice using Six Sigma as a basis.

> ISO 9001 is described in Chapter 3.2. If you want to know more about TQM and Six Sigma, you can get a quick overview of them on the handbook website (www.mqia.com).
>
> See Chapter 7.11 for a brief comparison of PMBOK and Prince2, and the QM requirements in each.

Both the PMBOK and Prince2 approaches are relevant to our industry, but both are only partial structures in that they address only project-related quality issues.

An infill approach

This is an attractive and reasonable choice if you already have (as most larger, successful practices do) a functional office management structure. That structure almost surely already includes guidelines for quality, either in a separate section, or dispersed among other policies and procedures.

If your practice fits this scenario, first identify those parts of your present system that relate to quality (wherever they reside) and prepare a list of them, grouped according to whether they are project-specific or practice-wide. This provides a baseline for what you want to add, delete, change, or improve.

> Another useful guide is the 'Ten Keys' structure described in the AIA Handbook, Thirteenth Edition, page 370. This model has more of a TQM orientation, but is still ISO 9001 compliant. It was developed when the 1994 version of AS 9001 was current; I've updated it to the 2000 version; you can find it on www.mqia.com.

The first consideration is whether to keep the 'quality bits' integrated throughout your system, or pull them out and treat it as a separate component. This is a complex question. Quality is, in reality, interlaced throughout every aspect of practice, so there are powerful reasons to keep it structured that way – provided that your overall system is really serving your practice well.

Alternatively, if your overall system isn't serving your practice well, and (you think) needs an overhaul, pulling out the quality initiatives will focus attention on them, and this can itself act as a catalyst for the improvement of the overall system.

> As one example of a QM system that is an integral part of a more comprehensive structure, look at www.practman.com. This approach positions QM as one of five interlocking and mutually inter-dependent project management disciplines.

Perhaps it is obvious here, but I'll state it anyway: If the above discussion resonates with you, you need a *custom* solution which is somewhere on a continuum between creating a unique structure and adapting a guide structure. Where you are on that continuum depends on the solidarity, completeness and efficaciousness of your existing systems.

What about 'model' systems?

Should you consider using a model system? I've had instructive (and humbling) experience here. In 1987, I developed a model QM system (called *ABC Architects*) based on ISO 9001:1987, upgraded it to ISO 9001: 1994. I sold this system in both versions to architects and engineers throughout Australia, and in the process helped about 200 design practices to gain ISO 9001 certification.

The *ABC Architects* system structure was developed as a practical interface between the way designers practice and the structure of ISO 9001:1994. As such, it may be useful as a guide in developing your own system. You can review and download this structure from www.mqia.com.

The first two versions of ISO 9001 were highly prescriptive. If a clause applied to your business, you had to document in your quality system. This suited the idea of a model system. The 2000 version of ISO 9001 changed all that sharply: out of a total of 50 clauses, only 6 are required to be documented by any business. The other 44 are required to be documented only if documentation is needed to ensure compliance.

Whether documentation of a particular procedure is required under ISO 9001 depends on a number of factors that will vary from practice to practice; for example the degree to which the kinds of projects the firm does are variable or consistent, the ratio of registered, senior staff to less experienced staff, and so on.

The firms that adopted the *ABC Architects* system without adapting it to their practice, in the main, failed to realize any lasting benefit from it. However, the firms that really did make the investment to adapt it to their practices are still using it, and are practicing better because of it.

Without getting into the details of this change here, the effect of the 2000 version was to all but destroy the viability of model systems. More on this in Part 3.

At present, I do not know of any model system applicable to our industry that adequately copes with the range of possibilities inherent in this change – and I haven't been game to try to build one myself! My advice on this: beware of generic ISO 9001:2000 model systems that are floating around in the QM marketplace.

Step 3: Find a 'champion'

What you need to do next depends on your resources. If you have a committed, skilled, QM-knowledgeable person on staff at Associate level or above, who is *passionate* about quality; give them authority and responsibility for firm-wide QM, and give them enough time (quarter to full time, depending on the size of your firm) to develop it. This person will be your 'champion'.

If you don't have such a person, bringing in the best specialist consultant you can find to help (see the discussion in Chapter 2.11). A key part of the consultant's role will be help create or find the champion to take over the responsibility, thus working themselves out of their role.

Step 4: Determine processes to be documented

The key point, which ISO has now built into the standard, is that documentation of processes that are fully embedded in the firm's culture, and work reliably, do not need words put around them to make them work better.

Except for just six processes that ISO requires to be documented in any ISO 9001-compliant system, the basic test (in my interpretation) is that you need to document only those processes that you need to ensure that your practice will do what you say it is going to do; will operate as planned.

If your goals include ISO 9001 certification, see Chapter 3.4 for a discussion of the processes required to be documented, and conditions relevant to the documentation decision.

In other words, write it only if you need it written. This is very practical thinking. So, how do you determine whether or not you need to document a process? Let's consider an example, say pre-bid checking of contract documents. Does it happen on all projects, or all projects where it was intended? If so, a written procedure is clearly unnecessary. If not (I hear you asking) how will writing it down make it happen any more often?

Of course, you can't change firm culture just by writing procedures! But it is a necessary starting point: a list of those actions the practice considers essential, against which change can be measured.

Here are guidelines that will help you decide whether or not to document processes, recognizing that it will often be a judgment call:

- The degree to which the process is critical to the firm's output (for example, design review procedures are always critical, and probably should be documented in most design practices).
- Firm size (larger firms are more likely to need documentation).
- Level of staff turnover (high turnover firms need more documentation of procedures).
- Experience level of staff (firms with predominantly senior professional staff need less documentation than firms with a lot of 'beginners').
- Project mix (firms with a wide variety of project types need more documentation than firms which specialize and know their project types very well).
- Whether or not you intend to audit performance of a process (you need a procedure to audit against).

In summary: whether or not you need a documented procedure depends on whether or not you can reliably produce an excellent result without one, considering all the factors that go into the achievement of excellence.

There is a corollary issue: whether or not people will actually use documented procedures where they are needed to reach that sought level of excellence. That is a culture and training issue. Clearly the whole matter of staff (and management) training is closely linked to the question of what is documented and what is not.

Step 5: Create process statements

Your quality procedures are everything you do. Simple things like updating trade literature catalogs improve the chances that you will specify products that are still available. These are quality procedures every bit as much as is design review.

Mies said, 'Less is more'. With respect to quality manuals, his advice is right. There is a powerful inverse correlation between the length of a written tool and the degree to which people will willingly use it.

Expect internal debate on this issue – remembering always that the real issue isn't whether or not you document a process – it is whether or not documenting it will improve the results.

This suggests that the *way* something is documented is all-important. Words may not be the answer, especially for architects. Pictures may be worth 1,000 words, or more.

You need to find ways to communicate what has to be done that are effective; that work. The best way to do that is, wherever possible, make process statements integral with the tools that go with them, as 'user instructions'. This ensures that they are seen on a regular basis. A good example is shown opposite.

This form, part of Thomson Adsett Architects' quality system, serves three purposes: a written procedure, a tool to carry out the procedure, and a checklist.

Some processes don't require forms. A good example of a brief set of procedures for management review, also by Thomson Adsett Architects, is shown on p 46.

Quality systems sometimes include *work instructions*, which add detail to the procedures, and are used as training guides for less experienced staff.

Putting it all together

The collected procedures form what is called a Procedures Manual, which is a confidential (non-public) document that governs how the practice operates. It may be a stand-alone document, or integrated into the firm's overall office manual (the latter is preferable).

The quality manual

The Procedures Manual is typically pared down to outline form that, together with the firm's goals and objectives and a description of the organization, is assembled into a separate document called a Quality Manual.

The Quality Manual is a public document, given to clients and prospective clients – and thus becomes part of the firm's marketing package. It is a *quality assurance* tool – providing assurance to clients about the firm's systems.

T A Quality Management **WORKING DRAWINGS CHECKLIST**
F9

Responsibility: Contract Documentation Staff under direction of the Project Architect.

Staff member: .... **Project Architect:** ....

Project: .... **No.:** ....

Use of this form. The intention is to record and communicate issues that affect the standard and content of the project drawings as well as facilitate checking processes. If in doubt, ASK!
Completion of a task shall be indicated by a tick "✓" in the check box. If a task / item is not applicable place a cross "**X**" in the check box. Whole sections not applicable to a project or to a particular staff member shall be crossed out & noted as N/A.
Note that any list is limited in it's extent and will not necessarily cover all issues.

INITIATION Issues to be advised by/discussed with the Project Architect.

Level of documentation: ....

Sheet title data: ....

....

Title block to be used: ❑ Standard ❑ Special

Drawing number structure to be: ....

....

❑ Orientation of plans on sheet is noted.

❑ Key diagrams/plans are required.

Window numbering to be: ....

Door numbering to be: ....

❑ RL **or** ❑ AHD for levels.

❑ Grid required & setout point noted.

Special points to note that are not on drawings to date:

Details: ....

Materials: ....

Legend: ....

Standard / modular fixtures: ....

Regulations / Acts / Codes relevant: ....

....

Other: ....

❑ Familiar with *W13 Graphic Standards*
❑ Familiar with *W16 CAD Drafting*
❑ Familiar with *W17 Drawing Office*
❑ Action / Query Sheets to be used by all staff

COORDINATION & CHECKING GENERALLY

❑ Additions/Refurb: Ensure limits of existing & new work are clearly shown.
❑ Structural: Check elements & dimensions with structural drawings.
❑ Compare elevations to floor plans.
❑ Compare sections to elevations & plans.
❑ Wall sections: Compare detail wall sections with building sections.
❑ References on drawings: Check that referenced details actually exist.
❑ Details: Check that they are referenced to plans, elevations & sections.
❑ Movement joints: Check locations & continuity in floor, wall & ceiling.
❑ Electrical/Fire: Check fixture layout with consultants plans & schedules.
❑ Mechanical: Check diffusers, grilles & registers with mechanical plans.
❑ Vents: Check locations with reflected ceiling plans & elevations.
❑ Room names: Check room names & numbers.
❑ Dimensions: Check dimension strings & totals.
❑ Dimensions: Check adequacy & accuracy.
❑ Finishes: Check data on room finish schedule against drawings.
❑ Plans: Check detail of plan enlargements against main floor plans.
❑ Multi storey: Check alignment from floor to floor. Perimeter shape, stairs, lifts, ducts.
❑ Grids: Check grids are consistent across sheets.
❑ If a floor plan is on more than one sheet check match/overlap of meeting lines.
❑ Eliminate references as "by others", determine & note responsible party.
❑ Check notes & details don't reference or repeat Spec issues/notes.
❑ Check for missing or incomplete drawing notes.
❑ Check references to consultants drawings are correct.

Management System Procedures **THOMSON ADSETT**

2 Management Review

2.1 At least annually, the Quality Manager shall convene a Management Review Meeting to consist of the Management Representative, the Quality Manager and at least one other Architectural Director from one of the local offices to review the system against the requirements of ISO 9001 and the Quality Policy and objectives.

2.2 The Quality Manager shall prepare an agenda and chair the meeting.

2.3 Input matters to be reviewed shall be itemised in an agenda and include:

- Follow-up actions from previous management reviews,
- Results of any quality audits conducted since last meeting,
- Quality system implementation on projects,
- Feedback, especially Client feedback,
- Status of any corrective or preventive action,
- Effectiveness in satisfying company quality policy,
- Changes that could affect the quality management system,
- Implementation and training,
- Recommendations for improvement, and
- Contract Managers' report/s.

2.4 Output matters to be reviewed shall include any decisions and actions related to:

- Improvement of the effectiveness of the quality management system and its processes,
- Improvement of the service from a Clients' perspective, and
- Resource needs.

2.5 The review shall be recorded including date, attendees' names, summary of discussion, reference to documents reviewed, data indicating the degree of compliance with ISO 9001, actions required, the persons responsible for actions and action completion dates.

2.6 The Quality Manager shall sign the minutes, circulate copies to attendees and store the original on the Management Review Meetings file. Resolutions made and actions required by individuals shall be communicated to all TA staff.

3 Supplementary Management Review

3.1 The Quality Manager and Management Representative shall normally meet every three months to supplement the Management Review. Issues covered shall reflect the Management Review Meeting.

3.2 The Quality Manager shall keep records of such meetings.

3.3 A Management Review Meeting may be conducted in lieu of a Supplementary Management Review.

4 Responsibility and authority generally

4.1 Personnel are assigned to positions as required. Individuals may be assigned to a number of project positions for any one project or hold a number of positions for a number of projects.

4.2 The person appointed to fulfil a function is authorised to take day-to-day decisions required by the procedure subject to any required confirmation by a more senior member of the Organization.

4.3 The person appointed to fulfil a particular function may appoint another team member to carry out the function but the original nominated person retains the responsibility for the function.

4.4 Where a team member is not available to fulfil a specified function, responsibility for the function reverts to the immediate senior staff member.

4.5 Personnel have authority and responsibility for the identification of opportunities for improvement to the quality management system and to services offered by the Organisation.

2.5 Planning your implementation

In changing the culture of an organisation to one of being quality driven it is necessary to creep up on the current management style rather than tackle it head on.

Roy Fox

What you are planning here is a culture change in your practice, large or small – and that will not go unnoticed! You need to have an approach to this change that is familiar and acceptable to the majority if you are to succeed. For design practices, there is only one viable option:

Treat QM as a project

This is the magic trick, the secret formula.

Do exactly with QM what you would do with any other project.

In my workshops, I take participants through the exercise of listing each thing they do when they get a new commission, then we apply those tasks to QM. The result: Suddenly the implementation of QM is easily understood.

Everything else flows from this simple rule, and can be readily understood by every practitioner. Understanding the process doesn't make it easy to implement, however. For some, this will be the hardest project the practice ever carried out.

Les and Vern met at their club for a drink. Les: 'I don't feel very good about this quality thing. I really believe we ought to do It – overdue, in fact – and now we have to do it, but I'm not sure we are getting anywhere.' Vern: 'What do you think the problem is?' Les: 'Well, there's been a little war brewing between Hugh and Weldon for some time – having them together on the task group seems to exacerbate that.'

Vern: 'Well, I've felt some tension there, but what could that possibly have to do with the new QM program?' Les: 'I think it has to do with change and their relative willingness to accept change. Weldon can't wait, but Hugh wants things to stay just as they are.' Vern: 'OK, I'll talk to Hugh.'

Anticipating culture change

The introduction of a formal quality system to a firm will mean some increased documentation of its quality procedures. If successful, in almost all cases such introduction will mean a certain amount of change in the way the firm operates.

This anticipation of change is one of the most important issues in contemplating adoption of quality management systems.

Just as the strengths of the people who make up the firm are reflected in its operating style, so are the weaknesses – biases, inefficiencies, lack of organization or chronic inattention to detail.

All corporate cultures are the way they are for very powerful reasons – reflecting the vision, energy, commitment and organizational style of the founders, current management and general staff.

Because of the durability of the forces that have shaped a firm's corporate culture, evolutionary change is possible, but wholesale, dramatic change is not, without severe disruption of the ability of the firm to operate.

What I have found is that all successful firms do most things right most of the time, but that the areas where firms could benefit by greater attention to procedure vary enormously.

To illustrate these differences, I use a little diagram, where each 'dot' represents some task the firm does.

Three hypothetical examples are shown following. Note that it would be very difficult to actually chart any firm this way; the figures are to illustrate the concept only, and to get you to think about how your practice compares to these structures.

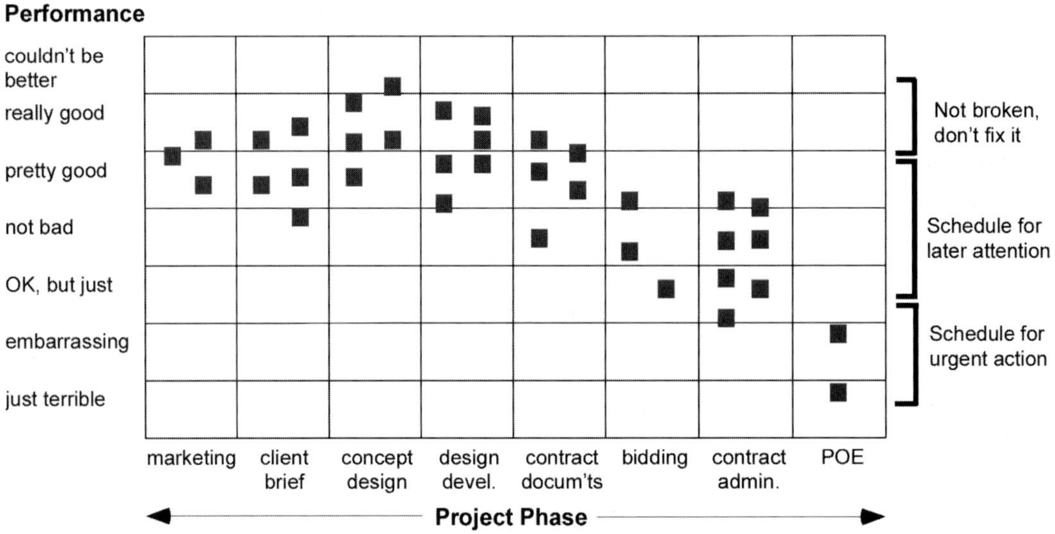

Fig. 2.5.1 *Profile of a strong design practice*

A firm with this profile tends to over-value some aspects of its performance at the expense of others. It will win many awards and attract more than its share of lawsuits. After an initial period of correcting a few glaring weak links, a long-term effort to improve documentation and contract administration skills to match the firm's design skills is recommended.

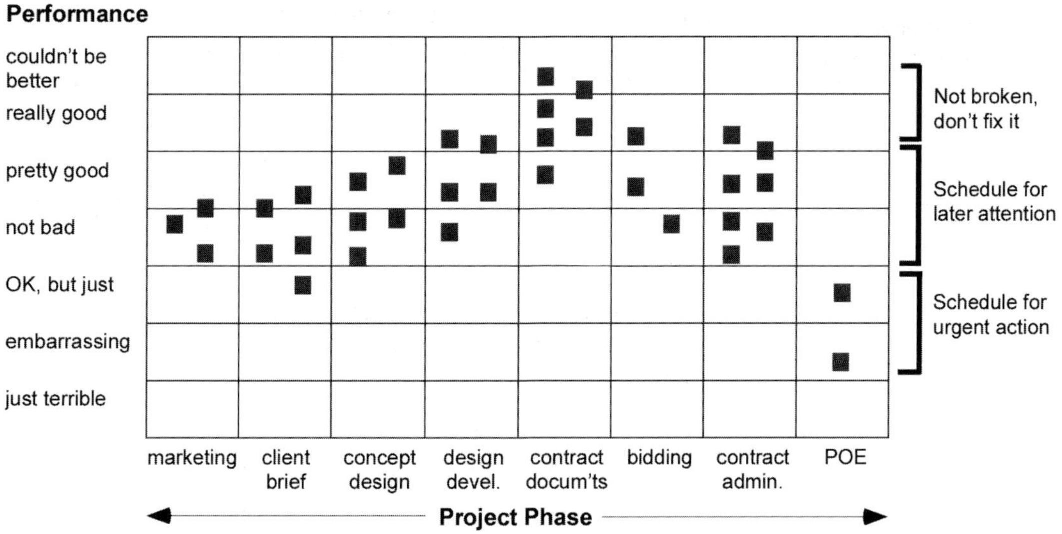

Fig. 2.5.2 *Profile of a strong technical practice*

This firm often finds it gets asked to do the documentation for the strong design firms. These firms are often reliable and efficient but their design skills may have declined after the founding director died a decade ago. Some new blood may be needed to improve the firm's design capacity.

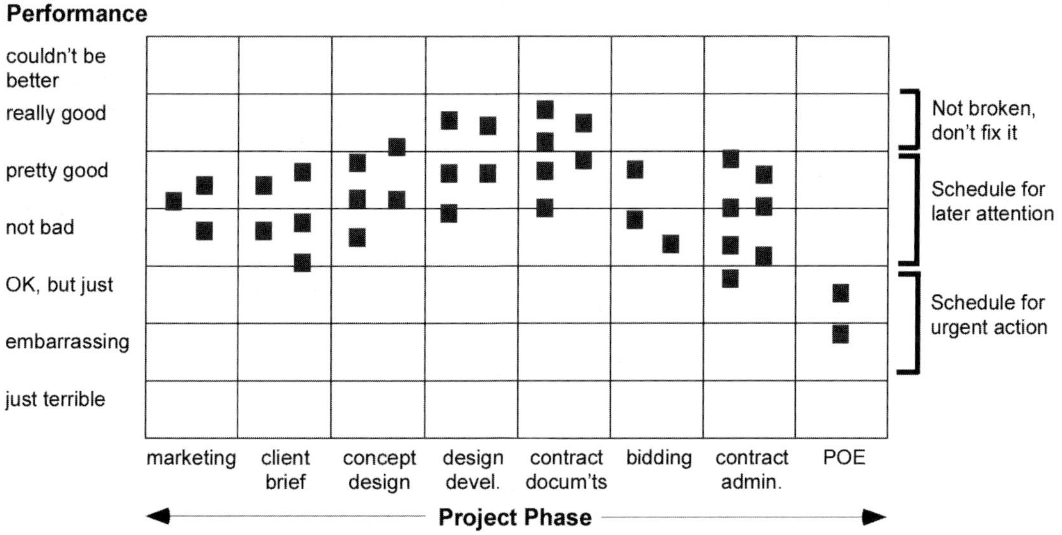

Fig. 2.5.3 *Profile of balanced practice*

The above firm is 'pretty good' at most things but rarely stars. Save for doing something right away about post-contract evaluation, the directors need to concentrate on a gradual lifting of performance across the organization, but probably in one area at a time.

In each of the above examples, what we see is that there are three general groupings of task performance: excellent, good, and needing improvement. This will be true for every firm. The point is to identify these groups for your firm; to know where to apply the focus for change. The analogy that seems most appropriate is that of the chain, with the chain being only as strong as its weakest link. The top group in each table contain the strongest links, the bottom group the weakest links.

Without regard to any other aspect of the firm's culture and performance, all firms have a common need to strengthen their weakest links, first to bring those to the level of the middle group and then to raise the middle group so the firm uniformly does its best in all ways.

As noted in Chapter 2.3, determining where the weak links are is an important purpose of the diagnostic audit. This permits priorities to be established which result in the most dramatic improvement at the least cost, which in turn tends to build overall staff confidence in the implementation of quality management.

Lastly, focusing on your weak links suggests a 'staged' implementation plan. This option is discussed in Chapter 2.6.

Returning to 'QM as a project'

A client comes to you and says:

'I have a project I want you to do. It is a hard project. It will take at least 10 percent of your time and of all senior people in your firm for at least 12 months, maybe up to 18 or 24 months, before you get enough of it done for me to pay you the first payment, which won't be set until we get to that point. Do you want to do the job?'

What is your response? Let's say that you really want to do this job. You know what your profit margin is, and it's not 10% percent, so to do this project, you – and your key staff – will have to make an investment of time, and some money. The payoff should be great, but much of it will be intangible, and hard to measure.

You know that if you don't give it adequate resources, a very careful schedule, and a realistic budget, you'll never get it done; never collect on the payoff. You also know, from long experience, that if you do plan it properly, give it resources and a budget, and stick to the plan, you will finish the job, just like any other job.

This project is quality management.

If any group of people ever had the training and experience to successfully carry out the implementation of a QM program, it would be design professionals. We do similar projects for our clients every day. It is our life.

There is one major flaw in the scenario posed above. Being aware of it is key to success in this project. Here is the flaw:

Much of the payoff will be intangible and hard to measure.

If your practice is like most, you will have assumed that the benefits will be intangible and hard to measure. That is because you have never measured the cost of quality in your practice. For example, there are very few design firms that log re-drawing on their time sheets. And re-drawing is only one of the many costs of quality that are hidden in design firms.

In fact, if you are a typical practitioner, you probably would argue that because design is iterative, re-drawing is not waste, it is part of the necessary process.

Maybe, but how much re-drawing? What sort of re-drawing? What is an acceptable level of re-drawing?

I will return to this question later. For now, assume that your acceptance of the idea that the benefits have to be intangible and hard to measure might be revised.

The practice as an auto body panel

In Chapter 1.7 I introduced the metaphor of 'practice as auto-body panel'. Even if it sounds silly, for a moment, think of your practice as an auto body panel, pressed into its smooth, unique shape by the force of hundreds of tons. Can you re-shape that panel? Not easily! What is the point? Your practice has been shaped by a force just as powerful, except that it happened over time.

That force is the complex interaction of the personalities of the founders and current management of the firm, creating the unique shape it now has (not necessarily smooth).

It doesn't really matter if you are a sole practitioner or the CEO of a 1,000 person multi-disciplinary international practice. If you want to implement quality management, you will have to go back and do some redesign on those presses. That is the fundamental message that I read, and hear, and see, over and over.

There is nothing in the literature of QM that I have read to suggest any other answer. That is not to say that you can't pick up some hot tips on how to run your practice more efficiently, or with less risk, or more profitably. You can, and you can find a lot of good ideas for doing that in the literature of QM.

The issue of process re-design sits at the very core of quality management philosophy. The 'presses' of our practice urge us very powerfully to find some way – any way – to put in place a QM system that stays well away from the forces that have shaped the practice.

Changing the culture of your practice

Somewhere early in the QM implementation process you, personally, must make a clear and unequivocal choice: *either you want QM for superficial reasons, or you want to change the culture of your practice.* This is a point where the road, your path, divides, and you must make your choice. The 'road less travelled' is the road of changing the culture of your practice.

There are a lot of perfectly valid reasons why you might not pick that more difficult road, for example:

- Your clients demand that you have 'QA'.
- You would just like to be 'more organized'.
- You would like to better control the risk of practice.
- You want to compete internationally.

There are plenty of examples of design practices that purport to have QM systems operating, but still manage to 'stuff up' the most routine operations as well as fail to provide an adequate level of professional service. When clients of those firms encounter failure to deliver, they become incensed; angrier about the poor performance than if the firm said it didn't believe in all this 'QM baloney'. The firms hurt themselves greatly by pretending to have something they really haven't got.

There is a central tenet in quality management: ***Never promise what you can't deliver.***

This is a good place to revisit, reiterate and reinforce the distinction between QA and QM.

QA is a promise, an *assurance*, to your client, and, by extension, to the public, that you have something special (quality) to offer them. QM is the combination of systems that ensure you can deliver on the QA promise. Thus, what is QA from the client's perspective is, from your perspective, QM.

The importance of QM training

Virtually every guide to QM stresses the importance of training. Dr. Juran says that 'planning by amateurs' is a major obstacle to good planning. For the design practitioner, your choices are to train yourself, or buy training from a consultant. The need for training is well documented elsewhere; I won't dwell on it here, other than to endorse this point completely.

If you have plenty of time, train yourself. If you are busy, it will be much more cost-effective to buy the training you will need. Make sure that the pace of the training is one you can keep up with.

You're on the diving board ...

Let's assume that you have decided to take on the QM project. This is a self-test. What are the key stages in your plan? Write them in the blanks below, in chronological order.

1 ______________________________

____

2 ______________________________

____

3 ______________________________

____

4 ______________________________

____

5 ______________________________

____

6 ______________________________

____

7 ______________________________

____

8 ______________________________

____

9 ______________________________

____

10 ______________________________

____

How does your list compare to my list? It's on the next page.

The aura of commitment

No other aspect of QM is so deeply thought-provoking as the issue of *commitment* to the process. Every book on quality contains anywhere from a few pages to whole chapters on the subject.

Few people want to say they are unwilling to make a commitment, fewer still want to really make that commitment to 'redesign the presses'.

The matter is complicated by the paradoxical nature of commitment. If you do decide on the 'road less travelled', no great bolts of lightning will illuminate your way. Nothing overtly obvious, in fact, will change. The people around you may not be conscious of the change, at least at first.

If you met someone at a party, would his commitment to QM be obvious? Could you tell? Probably not.

If he was noisy about it, you would doubt his commitment (who was he trying to convince?). The one thing I am confident of is that if a person's commitment to quality is real, *and* founded in reality, he will have an apparent, palpable aura of credibility. You will feel that you can trust him, and not be disappointed.

Clients can sense that, too. Here's my list....

Key Stages: Implementation of QM as a Project

1 Decide whether we want QM to seep into the bones of our practice, or stay on the skin.

2 Work out a rough timetable for the implementation, with some milestones.

3 Review our human and financial resources, and decide if we can commit the necessary resources for at least one year – assume 10% of all senior management time and 5% of all other staff time.

4 Work out the financial cost of item 3 and put it into our next yearly budget.

5 Call a meeting of the entire staff to discuss this project and its implications. Listen carefully to their comments.

6 Educate myself on the quality cost issues – I will need this to get through the next item.

7 Have a further meeting with my partners to decide if we are really going to do it, or not. Hear them out fully. Resolve the inevitable questions about who will pay for the time it will take, to our mutual satisfaction. This may take more than one meeting.

8 Revisit the implementation schedule with key staff. Agree to the milestones, in both time and substance.

9 Establish time-sheet codes for the project and set target time commitments to the project for all staff.

2.6 Implementing your plan

Almost invariably there is found to be a lack of consistency between what management believes it is concentrating on, what it has said it will be doing, and what is actually happening.

Roy Fox

Chapter 2.4 outlined a range of implementation options, depending on your starting point and where you wanted to go. Chapter 2.5 provided guidance in establishing an implementation plan. Regardless of which of the options selected, the purpose of this chapter is to highlight some aspects of implementation of your plan that could mean the difference between its success and failure.

Staged implementation

Guide manuals for previous versions of ISO 9001 have recognized that staged implementation is useful, even necessary, for many organizations, and have provided some guidelines for those versions of the standard.

The 'weak links' diagrams in Chapter 2.5 suggested the importance of staging implementation, working first on those areas of practice most needful of improvement.

Staging implementation makes good sense: it slows the change rate, which helps staff 'catch up' with changes, and lowers anxiety over change. It also commits less resources at any one time, easing the percentage of cash flow that funding the implementation takes.

Where there is staff resistance, staging implementation allows for some positive feedback from early improvements, thus reducing cynicism and creating positive expectations for further change.

In addition to using the 'weak links' analysis for setting up a staged implementation plan, the following matters should be considered:

- Any glaring inconsistencies discovered in a diagnostic audit.
- The degree to which the change activity will affect the overall quality of your output. For example, if bid document checking is sporadic and lax, there are potentially very damaging consequences for the practice – it should get high priority in staging.
- Customer complaints: If you've had negative feedback from clients on any issue (for example, authority of the project manager or communication), these items should be addressed in the first stage.
- If you are planning an ISO 9001-based system, the six sections where documentation is mandatory should be included in the first stage (see Part 3).

A staged implementation plan should clearly indicate which quality issues will be addressed in which stage, and what the beginning and completion dates are for each stage.

Champions and leadership

If you are serious about designing and implementing a QM program in your firm, you will need commitment for the following resources. Time requirements for these resources will vary with firm size, whether the firm is systems-oriented or systems-adverse, and other factors.

- Some 'quality time' from the senior management champion, to review progress, get involved, give pep talks, and have a quality management review meeting at least twice annually (especially in the first few years of the project).
- Significant release time for the 'working' champion, who will probably become the firm's quality manager.
- Release time for a quality planning committee (key people from each area of department) to meet, discuss, make recommendations, and deliver agreed changes, representing each major department or function in the firm.
- Release time for everybody whose input will take more than 5% of their time – this means adjusting their other project responsibilities.

Implementation actions

Chapter 2.5 introduced the idea of treating QM as a project, with the implication that you would need to create a resource plan for implementing it just as you would for any other project. The following actions will protect your resource plan and ensure that it works:

- Establish a timesheet code for your QM 'project'.
- Prepare simple, clear duty statements for each person with QM responsibilities (see *Staff buy-in* below), with deliverables identified.
- Balance commitments – consider and respect the firm's other obligations, without downgrading the importance of making time for the new obligation.
- Appoint a backup person for each person that has key implementation duties, so that in case of illness or other inability to carry out their duties, the process will keep on schedule.

Staff buy-in

> The ability to motivate people to welcome change and participate in it actively is not something any of us were taught in design school. Not many practitioners are skilled in this art.

The best way to achieve 'buy in', or taking ownership of the change process, by staff is to actively involve all staff in the decision-making process, at appropriate levels, and make all of them responsible for some part of the overall plan.

This means that they will have programmed time to work on their part of QM. Importantly, this includes all of senior management – no one should be seen to be 'above' the responsibility to make it work.

Getting people to take ownership of the process is not always so easy. Managers do not always know how to delegate authority, which is crucial to sharing ownership of change.

Sometimes staffing adjustments are required. On one recent project I was involved in, where the firm already had an established quality control department, the head of that department was giving lip service to the proposed restructuring – but was in fact behind the scenes doing everything possible to sow discord and sandbag the changes. After months of trying to get him to buy in to the new program, in the end senior management had to solve the problem, and they did it by giving him a 'promotion' – to a different job in a remote outpost of the company.

The idea that staff will acquire some ownership of change often sounds like they will have more responsibility and have to do more work, without being paid for any more hours. This is partly reality, and partly fear of being exploited.

It is also of the utmost importance to make it clear that the system to be developed will not be 'cast in concrete', but is fully intended to be improved over time.

Without the support of the whole practice, the process of evolution really will not ever happen.

Because the way the entire program is presented and managed is so crucial to its acceptance by staff, if the principals of the practice do not have these skills, either they should get some training in them, or get the help of a consultant who has them.

One of the stand-out lessons from David Maister's research on profitability (see Chapter 5.2 for related discussion) is that in the excellent companies, people who couldn't fit in to the culture were asked to leave, no matter what their strengths were – this point came up in interview after interview.

Monitoring progress

Prepare a QM project schedule, with milestones, and post it prominently. Update if/as required, and mark progress on it – with actual as well as target dates.

If progress is lagging, find out why. Maybe some people simply aren't pulling their oars, and they need to discuss their work plan with their supervisors. Maybe they really have too heavy a workload, in which case, their workload needs to be reallocated, so that either they are freed up to do what they have to, or their QM implementation responsibilities are assigned to someone else.

Only if the firm, overall, is experiencing a temporary, very heavy workload, such that there really is no more capacity, should the implementation schedule be changed.

And it is dangerous to do this more than once – that is a signal to staff that management really isn't very serious about improving its quality management. In effect, it means that you really aren't treating it the same as you would any other project – and that breaks the cardinal rule for successful implementation.

2.7 Measuring change

Measure what you value because you will become what you measure.

James P Cramer / Scott Simpson

Probably because of our collective reluctance to embrace the idea of measuring change, there is precious little written on the subject in our industry. The only comprehensive study I know of is Chuck Thomsen's *Managing Brainpower, Book Two: Measuring*, which is still available and well worth reading.

Thomsen's main focus is on compensation, managing firm ownership and financial performance.

We architects are not, by nature, measurers, and we are deeply suspicious of anybody wanting to measure what we do. This creates a serious problem for any practice trying to get from its present reality to its preferred future, because – without some measuring – we don't know where we are on the journey.

Cramer and Simpson's epigram message is accurate, because measuring is a focusing of energy, that conversely *places* value on the measured attributes, causing the person or practice to move in that direction – becoming a self-fulfilling prophecy.

This idea segues into the three key points about measuring change:

- Again, less is more: measure *only* what you value. A few key measures, consistently applied, are far more valuable than a complex system no one has time or motivation to carry out or review. You can always add more later.
- Measuring can't be a separate thing from the rest of practice – it has to be completely integrated into the functions it measures.
- Quality measuring can't be separated from other measuring, such as financial performance. Develop a single, coordinated approach to collecting and analysing the data you need to improve the way your practices operates.

Change you might want to measure

Cramer and Simpson say *Good leadership sets clear expectations for measurable results.*

There are five main categories of change that you could consider measuring:

- Money and time.
- Risk.
- Client satisfaction.
- Staff satisfaction.
- Contractor relationships.

Taken in order:

Money and time

These are always in lockstep: change that saves time (without compromising quality) increases profitability. Time is money. More commonly used measures include:

- Profitability – overall, by client, by project type, by office location, by project director, by project manager and by project.

A thorny problem for most design practices is the way that uncompensated hours are tracked. Some practices treat them as part of the staff's overall contribution – their salary buys an unspecified quantity of time. These firms tend not to log hours over the 'standard' work week, which means that records of how long something took to complete are always low and wrong, creating future fee assessment inaccuracies.

Other firms, whether or not they provide 'time in lieu' for these hours, log them as a way of keeping accurate project histories. This approach has advantages and disadvantages.

- Work in progress (WIP), measured in average days from time logged on timesheets to date of invoicing; overall and by project. WIP is important because of its effect on cash management requirements and as a barometer of project scope control.
- Accounts receivable (AR), measured in average days from date of invoicing to receipt of payment; overall and by project. AR is important because of its effect on cash management requirements and as a barometer of client satisfaction (the first indication of client unhappiness may be a slowdown of payment).
- Utilization, measured as the ratio of billable time to total staff hours. Some practices exclude administrative staff time from the denominator; the effect is to make utilization look better than it really is.
- Write-offs (uncollectible invoices) and write-downs (project work never invoiced). Both are important as a gauge of how well the practice manages project scope and client relationships.
- Labor multiplier (actual vs. target), measured as total income divided by gross salaries. Important as a gauge of overheads management.
- Average hours per drawing, measured by project type and by client. Important as a measure of production efficiency and for improving accuracy of fee proposals.

Risk

Chapter 8.2 discusses the quality-risk relationship. Measures some practices find useful include:

- Long-term claims history, including size and frequency of claims, insurance excess payments, informal claims settlements, and write-offs/write-downs.
- Legal costs and staff time spent dealing with claims and potential claims, by client, project type and contractor.

Client satisfaction

Most students of CRM (client relationship management) say that unhappy clients tell others about their experience far more often than do happy clients; some quote ratios as high as 9:1. Measures for client satisfaction include:

Why not make client evaluation contractual? Explain to *all* clients that your firm seeks to constantly improve its services, and therefore wants and expects performance evaluations at key points. Identify those points in your fee agreement.

- Repeat work, included sole-source (no competition) projects.
- Unsolicited thankyou letters.
- Regular paper surveys: commonly used, but of low-to-negligible value, especially when number scoring is used.
- Paper evaluations at key points, such as project completion or major milestones: better than regular paper surveys, especially if structured for open-ended answers.
- Talk to them, face to face, and ask the questions you might not want to hear the answers to: they will tell you!

Market research firms use structured surveys that provide a baseline response, but they will tell you that the most important results always come from the open-ended questions, such as 'Is there anything else you would like to add?' or 'How could we have improved our level of service?'

Staff satisfaction

Most personnel evaluation forms are worthless. They address mundane issues. They use criteria such as 'responds to directions cheerfully', 'dresses well', and 'does neat work', but never cover such relevant points as 'tells the boss when the boss is wrong', 'listens and responds to clients', 'leads criticism of poor corporate procedures'.
– Chuck Thomsen

Common sense tells us that happy staff are more efficient, more productive, and more likely to produce quality outcomes. David Maister's research (Chapter 8.3) proves a powerful connection between staff satisfaction and profitability.

How do we find out whether or not our staff are happy campers? Chuck Thomsen takes a dim view of survey format evaluations (see sidebar). The following measures work for many firms:

- Performance reviews, including '360' reviews (some observers have doubts and cautions about '360' reviews.[2]
- Exit interviews (for everybody who leaves).

Don't get hung up here on hard, numerical ideas of evaluation. The most important kinds of information you will ever collect about people won't be reducible to a number, but can still be 'measured'. You need trends, not facts.

Contractor relationships

Should you care about what these people think? Well, they are in a position to directly and indirectly influence your clients' opinions. They have a full arsenal of tools to make your life miserable. They can chew up all your profits at the end of an otherwise good project. And there is a lot to learn from them. Useful measures include:

- Patterns of RFIs (requests for information), by project type, size and contractor. Paul Tilley's research (Chapter 7.9) suggests a connection between document adequacy and RFI incidence.
- Change order history, by reason for the change order, project type, contractor and client. It is important here to honestly record the causes, including those resulting from designer error.
- As with clients: talk to them, face to face, and ask the questions you might not want to hear the answers to: they will tell you!

Besides keeping a tight rein on contract administration, the data these measures provide is used by some practices as a powerful marketing tool – clients' comfort levels are increased significantly when they see that the designer has good cost and time management tracking tools in place.

Quotation from Chuck Thomsen reproduced with permission of The American Institute of Architects, 1735 New York Avenue, NW. , Washington, D.C, 20006

2.8 Capturing & holding corporate memory

Specifiers will agree to become 'keepers of the system' and become expert at office information systems.

Mark Kalin

Boston-based specifier Mark Kalin made that prediction back in 1990. Whether it is the specifier or somebody else, *somebody* has to be keeper of the system, and that keeper is almost certainly going to be a highly systems-oriented person. Machines are getting better all the time, but they'll never know which information should be kept.

The most valuable information accessible to the practice quietly and surely slips through the fingers of those who guide the firm, and is lost forever. Hence, this chapter on 'corporate memory'. It's all too often more of a 'memory' than 'corporate'.

Corporate memory, like personal memory, is what the corporation remembers from its past experiences. How clever the corporation is depends on how much it can remember. Architectural practices, for the most part, remember precious little considering the richness of their past experiences. WHY?

Because, in all but the smallest and most stable practices, most of the firm's prior experiences happened to employees who moved on and took the corporate memory – which was paid for by the firm – with them, nearly intact. Think of that memory as a library of original manuscripts, of which no copies exist.

If the person leaving took with them a stack of those manuscripts, the directors would get very excited. But that is what usually happens when a person leaves your employ. It's just that the manuscripts were never written down, and you don't see them marching out the door.

But, you say, 'That is the way it has always been; why is it an issue? Besides, the younger architects are really only learning what the senior architects know, and it is part of our professional ethic to educate them.' Quite so, but our profession is evolving at a faster rate than ever before. Today it is more likely that the senior members of the firm do not understand what the younger members are doing, especially if they work at a keyboard.

Multi-skilling & specialization

You might disagree, but I suggest that it is becoming increasingly impossible for directors to understand exactly what their best employees are doing, and when they leave, what they did while with the firm.

Architecture is very rapidly breaking into specialties, whether the generalists like it or not, and to the extent that architects become more multi-skilled; move out into new areas of expertise; the more this specialization will characterize our practices.

New employees, arriving at a firm with an empty corporate memory library, will re-invent their piece of the corporate wheel-rim from their background experience, which at best will mesh with what was done before, and at worst will reverse it (assuming that what came before was good stuff).

The best firms will begin to find efficient ways to capture that corporate memory as it is experienced, sift it, store it, and have it available as an accessible resource, rather like collecting, sorting, processing and warehousing the by-products of manufacturing.

What does corporate memory look like?

How will I know it when I see it? The forms corporate memory can take are as varied as the people in the firm. Some examples:

- ✓ Standard details
- ✓ Standard proformas, such as room data sheets, schedules
- ✓ Information about products, especially new products, which isn't in the catalogues
- ✓ Information on reliability and maintainability of products
- ✓ Research methods; setting up cost-effective, reliable procedures
- ✓ Better specification clauses
- ✓ Design information on specialized building types, such as hospitals or golf courses
- ✓ Access to media contacts
- ✓ Design information on system assemblies, especially high-tech mechanical and electrical systems, and their architectural requirements
- ✓ Computer routines, especially mini-programs and algorithms that improve standard applications
- ✓ Knowledge about clients' needs, preferences and attitudes
- ✓ Knowledge of techniques outside 'normal' practice, such as the ability to set up financial proformas, life-cycle cost studies, cost-benefit analyses, etc

Benefits

The benefits to capturing more of corporate memory are many, but would include the following:

- ♦ Everybody in the firm will spend less time hunting for extant pieces of corporate memory.
- ♦ If the process IS efficient, the time savings will outweigh the cost of organizing it.
- ♦ The firm will be able to respond to new challenges more quickly and be less dependent on the time commitments of its 'experts'.
- ♦ People will become less indispensable, but at the same time, more highly valued for their contribution.
- ♦ The departure of a key person is less likely to handicap the firm.
- ♦ Errors will decrease because of less wheel re-invention. Documentation costs will drop, and contract documents will be more reliable.
- ♦ Some of the time spent re-inventing new methods of production will be replaced by more time spent on design and original work.
- ♦ The directors will have a greater understanding of and appreciation for what their employees are up to.

- The 'lone wolf' types will find the new environment uncomfortable and will quietly wander off.

More on feedback

In QM-speak, this process is called feedback: having a formalized method of learning from everything you do, such that the ways of doing it are continually undergoing evaluation and change to become better. Every firm does that to some degree – usually in a vague, erratic and random way. If you want to have a QM plan that respects ISO 9001 principles, the method will have to be formalized and operate predictably.

What could you do to begin to capture that elusive corporate memory? Here are some ideas:

- Make corporate memory a priority. Talk about it. Get your staff to talk about it. Focus on the experience your firm has lost in the past, and should have retained.
- Make someone responsible for corporate memory (your 'keeper of the system') and ensure that she dedicates some time to it each week. Request that she prepare a summary monthly report.
- Get rid of scraps of paper. Buy everybody in the office a cheap, bound notebook, which they are to use as a diary, writing everything in it: phone numbers, details of calls, meetings, anything which falls outside the firm's formalized project reporting procedures. When these notebooks get full, they can be turned into the 'memory minder', where they will form a chronological record of experience of every person in the firm.

  The notebooks' creators will want to photocopy parts of it, copy forward some information, etc. That is fine. But the original goes into the firm's corporate memory.

  Some people will resist this idea enormously, or will agree to it but never enter anything. Maybe they don't belong in the firm. Maybe they need to understand that one of the reasons they get a paycheck is to create such a record of their work in the firm.

> One well respected interior design practice in Australia, Geyer Pty. Ltd. (Melbourne Brisbane and Sydney), has used this system for a long time with great success. Members of the firm are expected to show up for meetings with their corporate memory notebooks, and they do. The firm regards the record of this collected memory as one of its most important assets. See Chapter 9.2 for a profile of Geyer.

- Institute a *regular* office procedure of cleaning out the piles on and under desks, returning not only information borrowed from the library, but new information that belongs in the library.
- Establish a regular system of filing information at the close of any project, where someone who is ***not*** part of the project reviews the entire file and sifts out collected data that has a general firm value. If such data is important to the permanent project record, make copies for the file or make references in the permanent project record as to where the removed items can be found.
- Develop resource profiles on every staff member and circulate them, so that everyone in the firm will know who is specially skilled at what, and can go to them for advice.

- Have regular meetings of staff that focus on areas where the firm needs more knowledge to do its job better. Assign investigation and reporting duties to persons who are interested in following up these ideas. Set time limits and parameters.
- Reward people who internalize the corporate memory capture process, support it, and creatively support it. In a medium to large firm, this could be dinner for two at a nice restaurant, awarded monthly; or perhaps quarterly in a small firm. Or perhaps a Friday off with pay, or a fine book or set of CD records of the employee's favorite music. Whatever the reward, it should also benefit the employee's spouse/partner.

- Believe in it yourself, and set the standard. People will do *amazing* things when someone they respect puts high value on something and creates an atmosphere of acceptant expectation.

This list could go on for many more pages, but you will have the idea. The point is to tailor a program to ***your*** practice!

2.9 How much will it cost?

Cost-effective quality management systems mean improved performance, greater client satisfaction, lower PI premiums, and professional peace of mind.

Ron Baden Hellard

There is disagreement at the guru level as to the value or necessity of measuring the cost of quality programs. Most agree that it is important to try to determine value, but the question is: How far should one go? Where is the point of diminishing returns, where more information costs more than it is worth?

It is clear that quality costs something, particularly when implementing a new program. It is easier to measure direct quality costs than indirect costs. As I noted earlier, very few architects track re-drawing costs, or the value of discarded, half-finished contract documents. It is also not easy to measure quality profits, in large part because of the 'one-off' nature of design projects. The cost-benefit analysis itself also comes at a cost, and this cost must be appropriate for the value of the information received from doing it.

Vern was feeling grumpy. Very grumpy. 'This is a slippery slope', he thought. 'Why couldn't they just whip up a nice little QM plan, show it to the client so he's happy, and get back to work? Why does it have to be such a big deal?'

It is helpful to consider the standard models of quality costs that the manufacturing industry has worked out over many years, because they provide some insight into the issue, and help us to translate these concepts into our own industry. There are two such models, widely used. The first, the *Quality cost model* is shown below. This model requires a little explanation.

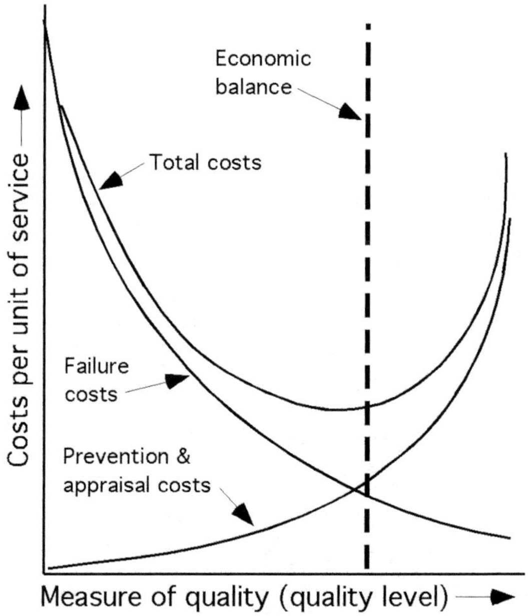

Fig. 2.9.1 *Quality cost model*

What this diagram shows is that small increases in spending on prevention and appraisal yield huge dividends at first, but as there are fewer and fewer mistakes to find or prevent, the cost of finding and preventing them starts to get higher and higher per unit of work.

The total quality cost is the sum of the failure cost and the prevention and appraisal cost. You can see that the total cost reaches a low point and then starts to climb. In most cases, there is a point where failure costs equal prevention and appraisal costs, usually at a slightly higher quality level than the low point of total costs.

Authorities suggest the optimum economic balance is somewhere between these two points: increased quality is available at a very low increase in overall quality cost.

The second model, below, describes what happens to the various elements of quality costs as the quality system 'matures'. This is called *Distribution of quality costs*.

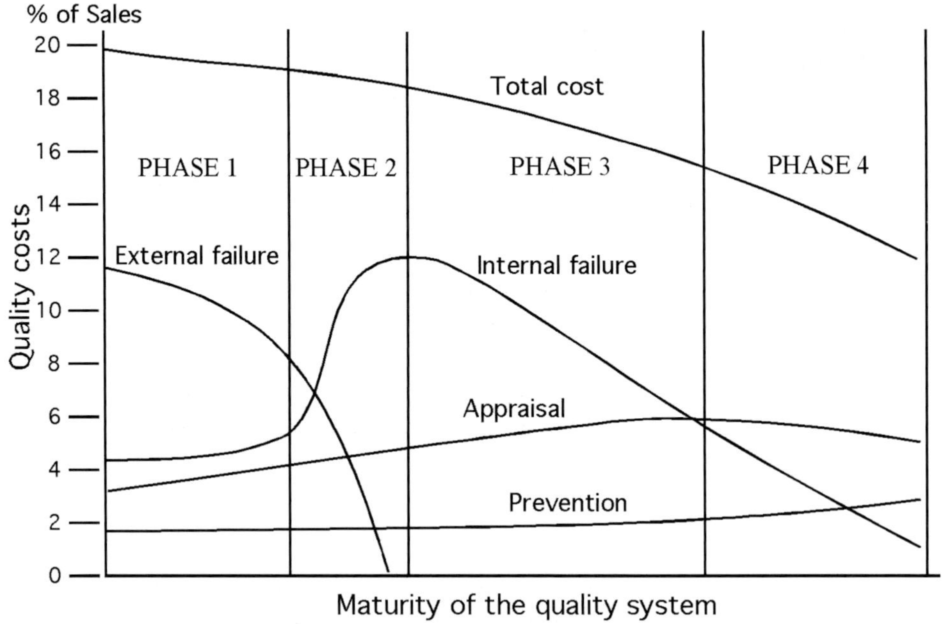

Fig. 2.9.2 *Distribution of quality costs*

This diagram shows a number of interesting things:

- In most industries, total quality costs are about 20% of gross output at the start of a quality program. This cost is made up of about 12% 'external' failure e.g. customer dissatisfaction, returns, defective goods; upwards of 4% 'internal' failure (detected before shipping); upwards of 3% appraisal costs; and about 2% prevention costs.
- Phase 1: After introduction of QM: As we saw in the previous graph, very small increases in spending tend to reduce the external failure rate dramatically, but at first there is not that much of an increase in 'internal' rejections. The defective products are discovered in final checking, not on the 'assembly line'.
- Phase 2: As the system matures a bit more, the internal processes start taking hold, and manufacturing finished quality starts to improve dramatically – huge gains are made, but there is a high cost, because semi-completed products are still being scrapped or reworked.
- Phase 3: As the assembly line processes begin to operate better, mistakes made and discovered have peaked and begin to drop slowly.

  The combination of prevention and appraisal costs continues to rise slowly. The rate of external failure has virtually gone to zero.

- Phase 4: The total cost of quality drops slowly but surely.

Can we meaningfully translate these ideas into our own industry? Let's consider them in turn.

External failure

In the building design industry, external failure includes:

- Interpretative design failure: misinterpreting the client's needs and requirements.
- Endangering the public, through bad structural design or selection of materials that could cause injury, such as using smooth tiles in sloped exterior walks.
- Mistakes in contract documents: dimensions that don't add up, calling up a product as one thing one place, something else in another.
- Discrepancies and ambiguities between the drawings and the specification that could cause confusion and result in claims for extras.
- Failure to coordinate the work of different design disciplines, causing any of the above.

It is important here to understand the difference between external failure and the *cost* of external failure. In our industry, the *cost of external failure* includes:

- Professional liability insurance premiums.
- Deductibles paid when there is a claim.
- Loss of senior professional time spent defending the firm when there is a claim.
- Loss of senior professional time spent resolving problems to prevent claims from being made.
- Re-drawing to instruct contractor to correct error.
- Loss of income through client's refusal to pay.
- Loss of future profits if a repeat client goes away.

We can see quickly that the first item would not change much if external failures decreased substantially, and the second and third items would be reduced but not eliminated (because of 'shotgun' claims), but the cost of remaining items are closely linked to the level of external failure.

Internal failure

In design, internal failure almost always consists of re-drawing time when an error or coordination failure is discovered.

Depending on when the problem is discovered, it can also include things like reprinting and re-sending of documents.

The cost of internal failure, then, includes:

- Re-design and/or re-documentation.
- Re-checking (appraisal) of the revised work.
- Communicating of revisions to others in the team, and possibly to client and/or contractor, including printing, binding, shipping.

There often are flow-on effects caused by internal failure, such as when the necessary revisions imperil the schedules for other work, or the client or contractor claims delay costs due to time slippage of the delivery of the documents.

Appraisal costs

Appraisal costs include labor to perform:

- Design reviews.
- Internal checking (of your own work).
- External checking (coordination with work of others).

Prevention costs

Prevention costs include:

- Personal time of management required to instill a greater quality consciousness and build motivation.
- Time required to establish and maintain the quality system.
- Training.
- Employing more experienced people.
- Project quality audits.
- Team reviews at project completion.
- Post-occupancy evaluations.

> Roy Fox has stated that, in his view, all inspection activities should be classified as quality failure cost. He says this means our quality improvement activities should be aimed at eliminating inspection activities as well as the failures they are used to detect. Even more profoundly, he emphasizes, we should consider inspection as the technique of last resort when developing new quality assurance processes.

It is interesting that quality management authorities peg the costs of prevention at a constant 2% of turnover, as shown on the *Distribution of quality costs* diagram above. So far, there is not sufficient evidence to know if that figure would be appropriate for the design industry. I have heard reports of firms spending up to 5% of gross on prevention, but I suspect that would include the start-up, one-time costs of initially developing and implementing the quality system.

One of the things that typically happens when a firm puts a QM system in place is that a number of other functions get updated, and these costs are seen as being caused by introduction of the quality system. An example is that piles of obsolete forms get thrown out and replaced, which should have happened anyway.

Can we get a handle on these costs?

If your practice is typical, you could implement a quality system and never know whether it was costing or saving you money. Why? Because, if you are like the vast majority of design professionals, you have *no idea* what you now spend on quality.

Do you track the cost of re-drawing? Of course, all re-drawing is not 'doing things wrong', or even avoidable. But much of it is. If we never begin to measure how much re-drawing we do, we will never get to the question of how much of it is avoidable, or how to avoid it. Do you track the amount of time you spend resolving discrepancies during construction? Not likely!

But *how much* will it cost me?

The most expensive implementation program I've heard of – $2.25 million – comes from Albert Kahn Associates (AKA), an international practice headquartered in Detroit. I also know of a number of well-organized, systems-thinking small practices that successfully implemented model programs for as little as $3,000 – $5,000.

> In the 1980's, US auto manufacturers faced the reality that they would either learn to work like their Japanese competitors or face extinction. Led by Ford, they all adopted QM approaches. As they saw the benefits, they also started to require that their suppliers (including their architects) embrace QM.
>
> Albert Kahn Associates was one of those firms. QM provided a gateway to becoming a totally different kind of firm, just as it was for the auto companies. The $2.25 million AKA spent was not just to design and implement QM – it was spent on the cultural transformation that followed from it.

How much it would cost in your practice depends on a lot of factors: firm size, the 'readiness' factors discussed in Chapter 1.7, and many others. Your practice will be *somewhere* between those extremes!

However, simply looking at expenditure is to miss the point altogether: one must consider the complete picture of the costs of *not* implementing quality improvement. Hear what Gordon Holness, Chairman and CEO of Albert Kahn Associates, Inc., has to say:

> Albert Kahn Associates started its Total Quality Service (TQS) Program six years ago at a time when we were successful and content with the quality and content of our product. With the help of a consultant, we spent considerable effort in internal training, the development of our staff, and in understanding TQS philosophies and culture. Probable cost was in excess of $1.25 million over a period of three years.
>
> Along the way, we became far more customer-focused, developed better client relations and services, established a wide range of benchmarking tools such as issuing client surveys on every project and conducting internal client surveys with our staff. We were the first A/E worldwide to achieve Ford Motor Company's Q1 Certification in 1995, but not before our first audit showed that we had no idea of the realities of establishing a quality system.
>
> As a result of the TQS program we changed our entire organizational structure. With it, we moved away from a technical department-driven, internally-focused operation to an externally-driven market focus group operation with studio teams and team centers. We revised our operations by eliminating top down-driven corporate board committees and going to a cross-sectional TQS Steering Committee with process improvement teams to drive change.

> We moved on toward QSA-S/QS 9000 as a common standard for automotive OEMs.
>
> We have now completed the final lap of obtaining ISO 9001 Certification in November 1998, learning from each step in the process as we progressed through our gap analysis, pre-assessment audit, preliminary audit, and initial audit. Is that the end? No, it's just the beginning and we have a long way to go with our continuous improvement program.
>
> Our internal auditors are identifying necessary corrective action items that we need to address and we will shortly be going through our next external audit to review our progress and assure compliance.
>
> Current expenditures between TQS and ISO are probably in the order of $2.25 million in personnel time and training. That's a huge investment for a company of our size. Has this expenditure been worthwhile? I personally believe so. Our corporate profitability has steadily and significantly improved (by more than 20%) over the past five years.

I strongly recommend reading the rest of Gordon Holness's article – see Part 2 Sources for the URL.

If Kahn's experience scares you, consider this idea. What is your excess (deductible) on your professional liability policy? Let's say it is $100,000 – not an uncommon number these days for a mid-sized practice. If the implementation of a quality program saved you *just one claim* where you had to pay out the excess – and did nothing else – would it be worth spending $100,000 on?

Quality cost systems for designers

A quality cost system won't prevent mistakes, but it will help you understand where the problems are, and where you need to focus your attention in order to prevent them.

If we don't start analyzing the coordination errors found before and after issuing documents for construction, we will never find out which ones could have been prevented. Here are my recommendations for finding out what your quality costs are now:

- *Everybody* fills in a time sheet. No exceptions.
- Add two new categories to your time sheets: Re-work due to internal error, and Re-work due to consultant coordination.
- Explain the importance of tracking re-work to your staff; monitor the change and spot-check results.
- Estimate, as well as you can, the past average annual cost of preventing and defending claims.
- Profile your quality costs *now*, before you implement a quality system, so you will be able to evaluate the benefits later.

2.10 Internal quality system audits

It is relatively easy to identify what is wrong with an organisation. It is a completely different thing to put it right.

Roy Fox

Does this QM jargon need paraphrasing? I'll try: It's a careful look in the company mirror, to find out if you are really doing what you say you are doing. What you say you are doing is the audit criteria. The evidence is not hearsay, it exists, it is recorded. The objective is to compare the two, and find out how well your acts fit your intentions.

ISO 9000:2000 *Quality management systems – Fundamentals and vocabulary* defines an audit as a 'systematic, independent and documented process for obtaining audit evidence and evaluating it objectively to determine the extent to which audit criteria are fulfilled'.

'Audit evidence' is defined as 'records, statements of fact or other information, which are relevant to the audit criteria and verifiable'. 'Audit criteria' is defined as a 'set of policies, procedures or requirements used as a reference'.

ISO 9000 notes that internal audits are 'conducted by, or on behalf of, the organization itself for internal purposes and can form the basis for an organization's self-declaration of conformity'.

Audit types

There are three types of audit, called first party, second party and third party. Internal audits are first party, often called self-audits. Second party audits are carried out by one organization on another, for example between a contractor and a subcontractor. Third party audits are carried out by independent, certified auditors. These last two types (both external audits) are discussed in Section 3.5.

The internal audit

In Chapter 2.3 I discussed the *diagnostic audit* as a preliminary evaluative tool, noting that the diagnostic audit could be fairly informal.

The self-audit process is the most important of all audits, providing management with information on whether or not its policies are being met, if the system is as efficient and as effective as it should be, and whether changes are needed.

ISO 9001-based audits, by contrast, are formal affairs. This audit process is a powerful QM system improvement tool, equally applicable to non-ISO 9001 systems and ISO 9001 systems, which is why it is included here.

Internal audits may be undertaken by trained members of an organization's own staff or by hired, professional auditors. There are advantages in both options; the main consideration is which approach provides the most cost-effective information.

It is usual for internal audits to be performed by the firm's Quality Manager, who may be any senior member of the practice, with delegated responsibility for maintenance of the quality system.

Typically, an audit either covers general administrative functions or specific projects.

A question often asked is whether specialist knowledge of the area or activity to be audited is required. In theory the answer is 'no' because the auditor should be looking for objective evidence based on the requirements of the standard and provided by the documented system and conformity to it.

In practice some general knowledge is probably preferable to assist in the analysis of the acquired data and in the formation of a judgment. However, the auditor must be independent and not have *direct* responsibility in the area of any audit undertaken.

'System' vs. 'compliance' audits

Another distinction: There are two sequential stages to an external audit program, which need to be discussed here to avoid confusion:

- 'System' or 'desktop' audits, where the QM system is compared to the standard.
- 'Compliance' audits, where the actions of the organization are compared to its QM system.

> To avoid confusion, I use the term 'desktop audit' to mean an external audit comparing your system to the standard. Just be aware that an external auditor is likely to use the term 'system audit' here. See also Chapter 3.5.

Except where an organization is in process of building an ISO 9001-compliant system, all internal audits are compliance audits.

Because design is so heavily project-based, it is useful to restrict an internal audit to either the practice-wide parts of the QM system, or to a specific project. In this handbook, the word 'system audit' is used in this context, to mean an internal audit of non-project systems.

What does the internal audit involve?

The process of internal audits begins along with the implementation of a quality management system. It has three main functions:

- To find out how well implementation of the quality system is progressing.
- To see if implemented systems are being maintained.
- To find out if the firm is ready for an external certification audit (ISO 9001 systems only).

> To audit all elements across the practice would be like a stock-taking in a department store; you would have to shut down the practice for a few days!

To reinforce the point made above, it usually works best to either audit a few elements of the quality system across the whole office (system audit) or to audit all relevant quality systems for a single project (project audit). The use of standard forms simplifies and greatly speeds up the audit process, as well as ensuring consistency.

It is customary to use rating scales in setting up audit forms, where a numerical value can be entered to show the relative degree of compliance – this makes it easy chart overall progress of the firm through successive audits, and helps to highlight problem areas.

The whole issue of assessment ratings is, however, still being debated by standards associations and client groups. Most consultants have developed standard audit forms, and will provide you with examples for internal use if you retain them for external auditing.

Audit planning

System audits should focus on specific system elements, for example to look at the way design verification is working across a number of projects. Project audits should consider all system functions for a single project or phase of a project.

ISO 10011: *Guidelines for auditing quality systems* recommends the following checklist for inclusion in an audit plan:

- ✓ Audit objectives and scope.
- ✓ Identification of individuals having direct responsibilities regarding the objectives and scope.
- ✓ Identification of applicable reference documents.
- ✓ Identification of audit team members.
- ✓ Date and place of audit.
- ✓ Identification of aspects of the practice to be audited.
- ✓ Expected time and duration of audit.
- ✓ The schedule of meetings to be held with the auditee (in this case, others in the firm who have to participate in the audit).
- ✓ Confidentiality requirements.
- ✓ Audit report distribution and expected date of report.

As you can see, not all of these items are needed for an internal audit in a small firm. It is important, however, that your audit plan describe briefly those items from this list that are applicable.

You can expect that your audit plans will be examined as part of an external audit of your firm, should you be seeking ISO 9001 certification.

How often should you audit?

There are no fixed rules, but the basic idea is that you audit often enough to be sure that your systems are working as you intended. For system audits, each documented function should be audited at least once a year, and probably twice a year in the first two years of implementation.

For project audits, it depends on the type and complexity of projects that you do. Most practices with QM systems would audit every large, complex project at least once, and carry out a second audit if the first audit showed significant nonconformities.

For firms that do a lot of similar, repetitive type projects, auditing every third or fourth project once is adequate. For firms that do a lot of small, short projects, such as residential remodelling, auditing one in ten or more projects is probably adequate. In the early days of implementing a new system (say the first two years), more frequent project audits are recommended.

If audits show that systems are really working as intended, audit frequency can be lowered; conversely, if audits show a serious level of nonconformities, frequency should be increased.

Nonconformities: major or minor?

A convention has grown up in the audit industry that assigns a 'major' or 'minor' status to nonconformities; the former obviously being more important than the latter.

The idea generally is that major nonconformities prevent certification and minor ones, referred to as 'discrepancies' are noted for follow-up but do not prevent certification. Several international certifying groups use this terminology.

Some auditors do not use the term 'discrepancy', referring instead to all inconsistencies as nonconformities. There is no requirement to use these designations; indeed they are not even mentioned in ISO 10011, the Standard governing audits. For purposes of internal audits (especially in small practices), the distinction is not considered essential.

Discrepancies vs. nonconformities

The audit process results in a list of discrepancies. Depending on the nature of the discrepancy, it may be cause for raising a notice of nonconformity (a nonconformity is defined as 'nonfulfillment of a requirement'). It depends on the seriousness of the matter, and the consequences of not correcting the discrepancy. In practical terms, if you would insist that something is serious enough to require action, you are, in effect, 'raising a notice of nonconformity'.

Requirements are both internal (the firm's quality procedures) and external (the project brief, codes, standards and other regulations).

Audit results and follow-up

All audits require that the results are discussed with the auditees, and that agreement is reached with them as to the nature of any corrective action required, and the timetable for doing it. The audit cannot be 'closed' until these actions are completed and verified.

The audit process doesn't end with the audit report: Management must act on the findings of the audit, and this action will be considered in an external audit. Therefore management's follow-up actions must be documented. The results of audits must be considered in management's review of the quality system, and should be an agenda item for those review meetings.

What does all this mean?

No doubt you are thinking that this is all a huge amount of work, for dubious benefit. Yes, my description may make it sound that way. However, well-designed audit forms used by experienced people can make the process highly efficient and effective in terms of finding out how well the practice is *really* doing – and that is the whole point.

Even on a major project, it might take one person-day to complete an audit, which will provide management with a 'snapshot' of that project's quality level – a tiny price to pay, considering the downside consequences of undiscovered problems.

With the right tools, a system or small project audit can be completed in a couple of hours by one person, which will highlight any potential problems before they rear their ugly heads.

Project audits can have very powerful returns – it's like shining a searchlight into the dark corners of the practice.

In fact, just knowing that there will be an audit sometime in the future tends to keep project teams on their toes, and can sharply reduce sloppy record keeping practices.

Improving your auditing

Getting the help of a trained auditor to get started will get you on the right path more quickly. However you set up your audit program and audit forms, you can be certain that there is a better way to do it – this an important arena for continual improvement. Refine your audit approach through trial and error, always seeking a better, more efficient and more productive way to audit your firm's systems and projects.

Simplify forms as much as possible, using checklists rather than written descriptions.

2.11 Using expert help

X *is an unknown quantity and* spurt *is a drip under pressure.*

A temp we once hired

This chapter describes the kind of specialist assistance available in setting up quality management systems, and offers advice on how to effectively use such help.

With every perceived shift in the relationship between a services industry and the public, another new industry of helpful entrepreneurs springs up overnight. Some professions (notably accountancy) see themselves as men and women for all seasons, and add every new fillip to the range of consulting provided. This situation sometimes creates confusion for users of these services.

Busy professionals who recognize they need assistance in coping with the relationship shift have to assess widely varying claims about how much, and what kind of, help is appropriate, and what it should cost. There is almost nothing written about finding the right help.

When Clea briefed Anne, the consultant doing the diagnostic audit, she alluded to some serious differences of opinion, without naming anybody. She asked that Anne question all senior staff closely on their attitudes toward quality.

Key questions

There are a number of questions to be resolved in engaging quality management consultants:

- Is it better to do everything ourselves, rather than rely on consultants?
- If we use consultants, will there be a problem of 'ownership' of the resultant system?
- How important is it that a quality system be unique to our practice?
- If we decide to employ a consultant, how should the brief be structured?
- What should we watch for in interviewing prospective consultants?
- Are there any key points to be included in a contract for consultant services?

There are other related questions that are of concern to some practices, but if you can get satisfactory answers to the above six points, your chances of a good consultant relationship will be greatly improved. Let’s take the questions in order.

Q1: Is it better to do it ourselves?

There are two main determiners as to whether or not you should engage consultant help in designing and/or setting up a QM system:

- Firm size: Small firms rarely can afford the down time of a senior person to become educated about QM, design a system, and structure its implementation; whereas larger practices can.

- Time: The more in a hurry you are to get results, the more important it is get someone on board who knows what he is doing. It usually takes 12 to 24 months to get from start to a fully operational QM system, and can take a lot longer when the people planning it are also starting from point zero.

There are other issues related to this question, pro and con:

Advantages:

- If the consultant is any good, he will bring to the firm the best ideas of dozens or hundreds of other firms, and your practice will be enriched in the process.
- The outsider will always have an objectivity; a perspective; that is extremely difficult for management to gain.

Disadvantages:

- There is an 'ownership' issue (see next question).
- If you make a mistake in picking the consultant, it will cost you a lot of time and money to get back to the point of re-starting.

Q2: Is 'ownership' of the system an issue?

The answer is, *it depends*. It depends on how fully the consultant appreciates the ownership question, and guides the entire process so that the system really belongs to the practice every step of the way.

I have heard it said that if a consultant really does his job well, the clients will believe all the ideas were their own. I believe this, and think it particularly apt in this situation. Unfortunately, I have seen some quality consultants push (in the name of quality management) their own concepts of how firms ought to practice. The result is that they create systems in their own likeness, not that of their client.

There always comes a 'handover' time in a client-management consultant relationship where the client should be taking over from the consultant; transferring the responsibility in-house. The actions and meetings leading up to that point are crucial to the successful transfer of ownership, and demand a certain amount of skill on the part of the consultant.

Q3: Do we need a system unique to our practice?

This question is closely linked to the previous one. I've seen a tremendous range in the desire for unique system design. Certainly this interest isn't a function of firm size – some tiny firms believe everything they do must be unique, as do some very large offices.

Nor does this interest appear to be particularly related to the firm's design ethic, e.g. the 'uniqueness' with which it approaches design problems. It appears that design firms are more similar (at least compared to other professions) than most design professionals think is the case.

We design professionals have a mobile work force. Designers and draftspersons float from office to office, and in most cases 'slot in' to the new environment very quickly. They *know* what to do when they get there. Why? Because the way design firms work is so similar, not only across the country, but around the world.

As a QM consultant working with the earlier, more prescriptive versions of ISO 9001, I responded to this differing need by supplying a 'model' system to those with a low index of need for uniqueness, and advising them on how to adapt it to their practice, while helping those with a greater need for uniqueness to develop 'one-off' systems.

What was interesting is that almost always, the system design and development process saw those with a greater 'need' for uniqueness lose some of that 'need' – it rarely stands up to scrutiny; it was just an idea they had.

Similarly, many of those who started out working with a model system (so they could save money) ended up modifying it extensively to suit their practice. In other words, they had a fairly individualized practice, but never saw it that way until they started to compare their way of working to standardized procedures.

Q4: How should we brief a quality consultant?

Most design consultants have relatively little experience with management consultants – for many practices, their attorney and accountant are the only model, and not one that is all that useful.

Let's say that you have decided to seek some help in improving your quality systems, and you want to write some kind of program or specification of the service, so you can 'compare apples to apples'.

A good way to get at the issues here is to look at them from the perspective of *your* clients. If you are an architect, you know from experience that most clients of architects either don't really understand what architects do, or have significant, erroneous ideas about what to expect from an architect.

You know that you have to educate the client, and that it is wise to do so before entering into a contract. *You are in the same situation as your client.*

So, get yourself some free advice before you prepare that brief. Talk to several consultants and compare notes, and *don't* let yourself be talked into a deal before you are ready.

Of course, you can get by without the helper, but it is likely to take longer and cost more, provided that you find a compatible helper. Many firms believe that a quality system should be, philosophically, 'home-grown', without reliance on external resources. The rationale is that the changes are more likely to 'stick', than if outside help was used.

There is a reasonable logic to this approach, but in some cases where I've seen it happen, one strong-willed individual tends to hijack the development process and create a system without adequate team consultation. As a result, others' noses get out of joint, and the project fails. Obviously, selecting your internal champion requires careful attention to personalities and firm dynamics.

Here are some issues to consider when talking to the pros, and when writing your 'request for proposal':

- Do you want a generalist or a specialist? In this case, a generalist knows a lot about QM but not much about design practice. A specialist knows a lot about design practice and enough about QM. (My bias is showing here.)
- How deeply do you want QM to seep into the bones of your practice? This is a crucial question, discussed in Chapter 2.4. The answer may determine the generalist/specialist question.
- Do you prefer fixed fees with fixed scopes of work, hourly fees with estimates, or what? Design professionals deal with this question every day, from the other side – the issues are similar.
- How willing are you to let a consultant inside your practice? Do you have a fear about privity? Do you think you have advantages that you want to keep from competitors?

  This cuts both ways. If you want a consultant to bring you the best ideas of all those other firms she has helped, then you have to be willing to share yours. If you want the confidentiality of a lawyer-client relationship, make that clear. But don't expect to have it both ways.
- How much of the needed resources can you bring to the equation? You will find that some tasks are best done by a consultant, some best done by your practice, and there are a number where it doesn't matter. But it will cost you one way or the other to get them done. If you elect to do them in-house, you must be prepared to allocate budget and time to see that they get done.

Q5: Interviewing issues

These comments apply both to informal discussions while you are educating yourself on the consultant's marketing nickel as well as to interviews of short-listed contenders.

- Is the consultant a *good* listener? Does he ask more questions, or offer more opinions? Do you feel as if he cares more about your practice, or about his credentials?
- Is he a generalist or specialist? If a generalist, what is his awareness of your particular specialty? If a specialist, test his awareness of broad QM knowledge.
- Raise the 'ownership' issue and pay particular attention to the responses. How does he manage ownership transfer?
- Talk through the resources question. What are his strengths, his weaknesses? Does he admit to any of the latter? What does he expect from you in the equation?
- Get a list of references, and talk to all of them. Raise the points made above.

Q6: Key points in a contract for QM consultant services

If you put yourself in *your* client's position, you will be more likely to get this right. However, there are some very important differences.

The most important product that the QM consultant produces is not pieces of paper with words on them, or flowcharts and graphs, but rather is a very intangible commodity: a truly workable awareness of the benefits of improving the quality of *your* services. And not just to you, the manager, but right throughout your practice.

The operative word here is *workable*. Do you feel it is workable? Do your staff? You can see that this is not so easy to measure, because you *yourself* are the greatest contributor to, or obstacle in the way of, the consultant's success.

Aha! You are in a partnership with the consultant. *You both win, or you both lose.*

Do not engage a quality management consultant you wouldn't be comfortable with as a business partner.

For, in truth, for the duration of his employ, he will be – to some degree – your business partner.

System design and certification specialists

There are two kinds of specialists in the quality world: those that assist with system design and implementation, and those that perform compliance audit services. To do both for the same customer is unethical, and a conflict of interest.

Some organizations (including some international players) get around this little problem by having two companies, both owned by the same parent. All they are doing is obeying the letter of the rule and flaunting the spirit.

A quality system design specialist should be able to recommend independent quality audit firms, and assist its clients in obtaining the right one for them. Stay well away from anybody that offers a package of both services.

At its best, the systems design specialist becomes functionally integral to the practice for a period of time, much as a lawyer or accountant would – knowing the firm thoroughly, and helping it to craft solutions that are right for it. The auditor, on the other hand, *must* keep an arms-length relationship.

2.12 Continual improvement

Institute Never-ending Improvement.

Roy Fox

Continual improvement is a requirement of QM theories. More importantly, it is the central ingredient in lifting productivity and in differentiating the practice in the competitive marketplace. Yet, continual improvement in most design firms is, at best, sporadic, unplanned, undisciplined and rarely monitored.

Anne spent an entire day talking with AIS staff, one on one, and another half day going over all the records for three projects. She promised a report to Clea within two weeks. Clea asked her not to 'pull any punches', and to be clear and direct with any recommendations.

How is 'continual improvement' different from what we now do?

Most, if not all, architects believe they practice some sort of continual improvement: learning new technologies, striving to create better design, improving efficiency and profitability. What is the difference between this belief and the meaning of 'continual improvement' as used in QM systems?

One way to answer this is to compare it with the AIA's decision to make professional development (PD) mandatory. That debate took a long, long time; but in the end the leaders of our profession decided that 'voluntary' improvement just wasn't good enough for the times we are in.

Although we all value excellence very highly, we tend to have a 'problem-solving' rather than a 'problem-prevention' approach to excellence (especially technical excellence). We ratchet forward in knee-jerk fashion, fixing whatever goes wrong.

So, whether you like it or not, PD is no longer an option (in the U.S.). Under any QM structure, the same is true: continual improvement is not an option. It is central to the system.

In Chapter 2.5, we looked at some simple diagrams of profiling aspects of the practice, to see what needed to be fixed *before* it went wrong. Continual improvement is a formalization of that process – a structured program where management collects information about the firm, reviews it to a plan, and makes decisions about the future.

Continual improvement in TQM

This handbook is not about TQM, but with respect to this particular topic, it is instructive to look at the TQM experience.

In TQM parlance, continual improvement is omnipresent and never-ceasing, as the term suggests. In discussing this point, Roy Fox notes (writing in 1991) that it is only the Japanese who then had 20 or 25 years of TQM experience.

Observing that there were very few U.S. companies that had more than ten years of TQM experience, he says 'Reality is that we have to take the virtues of never-ending improvement very much on trust, with only the Japanese and a few others around the world to act as models.'

An important factor in planning for continual improvement is the resistance of any culture to change. The technique often used to work on this change is called the Santayana review, after the Spanish-born U.S. philosopher George Santayana, who observed, as noted in Chapter 1.2: *Those who cannot remember the past are condemned to repeat it.*

Fox also notes that in many American companies, the experience is that four or five years of effort produce relatively low changes in the corporate culture, and that the response is often to cut out the training and other key parts of the quality system, thus ensuring its demise. He sums up the problem thus:

> Maintaining commitment to a long-term strategy where the pay-off can often only be measured ten years down the track in terms of prosperity and status in the marketplace is undoubtedly difficult when maintaining cashflow is a daily problem.

This prospect may not sound very encouraging to you. It is one of the reasons why all members of the firm's management must have 100% commitment to the concept of continual improvement if QM is to succeed. Anything less will crumble when the going gets tough.

You cannot expect immediate benefits to a continual improvement program – they will take time to show their value. The design & construction industries have almost no long-term experience in the benefits of continual improvement – there is no alternative to taking it on faith.

Continual improvement in ISO 9001

In ISO 9001, continual improvement is a more finite process, which takes place to a pre-planned schedule, with specific inputs and outputs. The concept of continual improvement under ISO 9001 (compared to TQM) is easier to grasp and implement. You will know if you have done what you were supposed to do.

ISO 9001 implements continual improvement through management review of audit results, corrective and preventative actions, and other quality functions.

Continual improvement in action

In this context, consider the diagrams on pp 48-49, which suggest, by contrast, that you needn't fix things that 'aren't broke'. This doesn't mean, however, that they can't be improved!

The old adage about a thing being 'never so good it can't be improved' is apt when extending the concept of continual improvement back into system design. However, the QM system has to be there to support the practice and help it become more efficient.

How much time and energy should be spent on this activity? Experts do not agree; some insist that improvement must be happening every day in every sphere of activity; others hew to 'if it ain't broke, don't fix it' pragmatism.

My experience is that the natural inventiveness of most creative people, if outlets are provided, leads to a natural, evolutionary system refinement. However, for various reasons, some system elements seem to get 'locked in', frozen in time, and are hard to dislodge even when it is clear they need fixing. These need a structured review approach.

Both the PMI *PMBOK* (Project Management Body of Knowledge) and the British *Prince2* project management systems emphasize the importance of Lessons Learned[3]. It is one thing to collect lessons learned from project experience; it is another to translate that learning into continual improvement of the practice, and for that you need the disciplined involvement of senior management. That is mandated in an ISO 9001 QM system, but you don't need to have an ISO 9001 system to turn lessons learned into practice improvement.

The tribal imperative

I have emphasized earlier that the culture of a practice is the way it is for very powerful reasons – all 'people' reasons. But it is not just the founders and directors who shape the practice, it is everybody in it, through an exceedingly complex web of personal interactions.

Because we value the contribution of each member of the practice, we keep some kind of truce with each of them, easy or uneasy. We live with their demons, and they with ours; so it has been from the dawn of time. Those who don't fit in wander off or are ejected. The office is a little tribe, with tribal customs; part of the bigger tribe of related design professionals (within which there is considerable mobility).

In this context, change – any change – is guaranteed to threaten someone's sense of place and order in the tribe, and a lot of activities follow: digging in of heels, maneuvering for position, demanding assurances of stability, etc.

The bedrock reason why the cultural change inherent in all types of continual improvement is so difficult is because it can potentially 'mess up' the tribal balance in the practice, and every member of the tribe can smell it coming a mile away. Even those who want it, and asked for it, can fear it.

It is for this reason that I like the ISO 9001 approach to evolutionary change. Because it is prescriptive, it is also relatively non-threatening, even to the more vulnerable of our colleagues.

Copyright rules prevent me from quoting the guidelines, but sub-system element 8.5.3 requires you to take *preventative action,* which is defined[??] as 'action that will eliminate causes of potential nonconformities in order to prevent their occurrence' with respect to activities related to the quality of the service you provide.

The operative word here is 'potential'. This is not knee-jerk response to problems; it is preventing the problems from occurring in the first place. It is also not an activity seriously practiced in most design firms.

Developing an action plan

Here is my list of steps in a continual improvement action plan:

- Conduct a mandatory process evaluation, on every project, at two points: When the project is out for bids, and the team still together, and at the end of construction. Keep records of these reviews.
- Put in place a post-occupancy evaluation (POE) program – for every project – where you visit the project about a year after it is completed, and talk to the people who use it and maintain it – to find out how you could have made it better, from their point of view. They'll know, and they'll tell you if you ask them. Keep records. You might want to tape record these meetings. See Chapter 8.1 for more information on POE.
- Set up a suggestion box for ideas on practice improvement, and give a substantial monthly prize (like dinner for two at a good restaurant) for the best suggestion. This will involve everybody in the practice in the program. And implement the good suggestions!
- Look at new ways to measure performance improvement; for example the number of requests for clarification of contract documents, and the number and cause of change orders.
- If you're not already doing it, ensure that performance reviews are conducts with every employee at least annually (twice a year is better). Note that 'performance' here means performance of management as well as performance of staff. Top management gets reviewed by staff, and should expect to present their professional goals and how they are doing at meeting them.
- Conduct an exit interview with every person who leaves the practice. Try to learn how the person sees their experience, and how they think the firm could improve. Record results.
- Hold a top management meeting at least twice a year (three times is better) to review the results of the above steps. Look for patterns of repeat failures and try to discover their root causes (which may well be management issues). Publicize the results, and take concrete steps to implement the outcomes.

Management review

Further to the last step above:

Once we have got a handle on these potential problems, then what? The leaders of the practice are obliged to consider them on a planned, regular basis and ask themselves whether the findings are conducive to furthering the goals of the practice. If not, they are to make appropriate adjustments. This presumes that they have established those goals, of course.

This process is simple, clear, *relatively* non-threatening, and doesn't even have to take a lot of time. Nevertheless, it can be demanding of the practice. It 'regularizes' activities that should, but rarely do, happen in every practice.

Scheduling change

Each practice can schedule its detection, analysis and elimination of potential problems in any way it wishes. Common sense tells us, of course, that unless this process is enough of a part of the regular business of the practice to be continuously felt, it will have little meaning.

Under ISO 9001, we are at liberty to focus on any quality processes that we wish, in any order. This allows the practice to schedule its continual improvement activities in a way that is compatible with its workload. However, the imposed regularity of self-audits and management reviews ensures that the workload does not permanently eclipse the improvement program.

Part 2: Sources, resources & notes

Sources

2.1 Franklin, James R. (2000) *Architect's Professional Practice Manual,* McGraw-Hill Professional Publishing.

Practice Management Professional Interest Area (1993) *Organizational Peer Review,* (Quoted by Nelson, TQM and ISO 9000 for Architects and Designers, 1996, McGraw-Hill) American Institute of Architects.

Smith, Neville I. (1994) *Down-to-Earth Strategic Planning,* Prentice-Hall.

2.2 Coxe, Weld et al (1987) *Success Strategies for Design Professionals: SuperPositioning for Architecture & Engineering Firms*, McGraw-Hill, p 22.

Gutman, Robert (1988) *Architectural Practice: A Critical View*, Princeton Architectural Press, pp 22; 97-111.

Kaderlan, Norman (1991) *Designing Your Practice: A Principal's Guide to Creating and Managing a Design Practice*, McGraw-Hill, p 12; pp 9-50.

Stasiowski, Frank (1991) *Staying small Successfully: A Guide for Architects, Engineers & Design Professionals*, John Wiley & Sons, p 13.

2.4 Fox, Roy (1991) *Making Quality Happen: Six Steps to Total Quality Management,* McGraw-Hill (Sydney) p 77.

2.5 Juran J. M. (1992) *Juran on Quality by Design: The New Steps for Planning Quality into Goods and Services*, The Free Press, p 3.

2.7 Thomsen, Chuck (1989) *Managing Brainpower: Organizing, Measuring Performance, and Selling in Architecture, Engineering and Construction Management Companies; Book Two: Measuring*, AIA Press, p 22.

2.9 Holness, Gordon, from an article on the Internet entitled QFD/TQM/ISO Fads, Fancy or Factual Benefit?, URL: http://www.albertkahn.com/news_art_full.cfm?artid=3.

2.12 Fox, Roy, pp 196, 198.

Resources

2.4 For ISO 9001 requirements on documentation of procedures: *ISO 9001:2000*, clause 4.2.1(d), p 2.

For help with mission and vision statements, goals and objectives (in this order):

Stasiowski, Frank A. (1991) *Staying Small Successfully: A Guide for Architects, Engineers, & Design Professionals,* John Wiley & Sons, pp 6-23.

Fox, Roy, pp 72-93.

Kaderlan, Norman, pp 9-31.

Rose, Stuart W. (1987) *Achieving Excellence in Your Design Practice*, Whitney Library of Design, Chapter 6.

2.6 For help with staff buy-in, I suggest:

Fox, Roy, pp 83-7.

Patching, Alan (1994) *Partnering and Personal Skills for Project Management Mastery,* Chapters VI: *Belief Systems*, VII: *The Process of Change,* and VIII: *Personality Types,* publ. by Alan Patching & Associates, Double Bay, NSW Australia, offer an excellent description, written for design professionals, of the psychology of change and how that process is affected by personality.

Peters, Thomas & Robert Waterman (1982) *In Search of Excellence*, Harper & Row, Chapter 8.

Rose, Stuart W., Chapter 5.

Stebbing, Lionel (1990) *Quality Management in the Service Industry*, Ellis Horwood, pp 52-4.

Thomsen, Chuck. All three of the small books in this set are worth your serious study, but on this topic, note especially Chapters 1 and 2 in *Book One: Organizing.*

2.9 For useful information on the cost of quality (in this order):

Stebbing, Lionel, Chapters 2 and 3.

Stasiowski, Frank A. and David Burstein (1994) *Total Quality Project Management for the Design Firm,* John Wiley & Sons, Inc., pp 265-71.

Crosby, Philip B. (1979) *Quality is Free,* McGraw-Hill, pp 101-7.

www.mqia.com

2.4a Nelson, Charles, *TQM / Six Sigma Overview.*

2.4b Nelson, Charles, *Ten Keys 2000.*

2.4c Building Technology Pty. Ltd., *ABC Architects model system structure.*

Epigrams

2.1 Attributed to Berra by Norman Kaderlan (and others). See *Designing Your Practice: A Principal's Guide to Creating and Managing a Design Practice*, p 9. Some sources attribute the quote to Casey Stengel.

2.2 Smith, Neville I., p 24.

2.3 Sullivan, Louis H. (1918) *Kindergarten Chats*, published 1947, Wittenborn, Shultz, Inc., republished unabridged, Dover Publications (1979) p 33.

2.4 From Microsoft's software advertisements.

2.5 Fox, Roy, p 105.

2.6 ibid. p 119.

2.7 Cramer, James P., and Scott Simpson (2002) *How Firms Succeed: A Field Guide to Design Management*, Ostberg, p 224.

2.8 Kalin, Mark (January 1986) Automation and the specifier, *The Construction Specifier,* Construction Specifications Institute, p 82.

2.9 Hellard is former Chairman of the RIBA Management Committee.

2.10 Fox, Roy, p 70.

2.12 Fox, Roy, p 195; step 6 of Fox's six-step program.

Endnotes

1 Copyright law prohibits the inclusion of ISO 9001 in this handbook, without royalty payments that would increase the handbook cost. ISO definitions are available online at www.1stnclass.com/quality_glossary.

2 A 360 review involves getting feedback about an employee from a wide variety of sources in addition to his or her manager. For a brief discussion of the method, see www.michaelhsmithphd.com/newsperfreview.

3 For information on PMBOK and Prince2, see Chapter 7.11.

AIS: The story so far....

It was a glorious, crystal-clear winter Sunday morning. Clea was up early, taking her wolfhound Rapper for a long walk on the beach, and trying to get her mind around the space project and its difficult sister, the quality program.

Clea felt the 'ground was shifting' at AIS, but she didn't feel she quite had the measure of the shift, or whether it was good or bad. She decided to think through the project progress first, as it seemed like the easier of the two.

Once again, they had ignored their rules, and started the project without a signed contract. Now they had a contract, which included some clauses she thought might come back to haunt them, but Vern didn't seem to want to discuss it with the client. The client did pay their first invoice promptly, so that was good. And he'd shown flexibility about submitting the quality plan.

Mauri was full time on the project, thorough and careful – early stages were going well. Les was tracking a lot of old projects, but was keeping a close eye on design. Weldon had taken the responsibility for research, and was learning everything he could about design issues in space station construction.

Clea felt she would soon have to get involved in the day-to-day project management, but right now it seemed OK, and she could let it go along as is.

As she turned her mind to the quality project, she was struck by the way different people were reacting to the ideas coming out of the discussions. She felt that it was getting very complex – too complex – and that there was a lot of wheel-spinning with little forward motion. And time was getting tight, even with the extension.

(continued on page 90)

3 Harnessing the Power of ISO 9001

3.1 The ISO 9000 family of standards

3.2 ISO 9001:2000 > architecture

3.3 Myths, half-truths and truths about ISO 9001

3.4 'One size fits none' – Fitting the standard to design practice

3.5 External audits & certification

We get to meet the client!

AIS: The story so far (cont.)

Some changes were totally unexpected. Candy had long viewed the library responsibility as a boring chore – she was a 'people person' and thought the library was a stuffy place. But she had somehow become very energized by the QM idea, had whipped library into shape in three weeks, and was now a tiger about getting people to keep their filing up to date.

All this had raised Candy's self-confidence and self-esteem, and she had started dressing 'up' a bit, with some new low-cut blouses. The drafting room boys took to calling her 'Eye Candy', which she pretended to be annoyed by. Clea grinned wryly to herself, 'I guess quality is what you think it is!'

Candy had also ordered five copies of ISO 9001, one for each of the task group members, and one for the library. If Hugh had opened his, he wouldn't admit it. But Weldon's copy was already dog-eared and filled with notes to himself.

Clea was puzzled by Vern's position. She thought, 'He's talking the talk, but not walking the walk'. She'd found out from his wife that he'd been in for a prostate check, and there was a possibility that he could have a tumour. Maybe this was on his mind, but she was worried that he wasn't taking more interest in something so important for this big project.

Clea thought about Les. Design was his thing, and he always deferred to Vern on business matters. If Vern got sick, she realized she would have to get more involved in practice operations, even though she was the junior partner.

Hugh had fastened onto his old checklists as the heart of whatever QM plan they would produce, and had actually got them updated and was requiring his drafters to use them.

She knew Hugh was otherwise useless, but she'd have to put up with him on the group – but she could count on Les, Weldon and Mauri for support. She could see that she really had to take command, rather than trying to facilitate a group result, or they would never make the new deadline.

With a feeling of resolve, but not really happy about it, Clea pushed all these thoughts away and spent an hour throwing sticks for Rapper to retrieve.

3.1 The ISO 9000 'family' of standards

ISO 9000:2000 lists four standards in the 'ISO 9000 family of standards': ISO 9000, ISO 9001, ISO 9005 and ISO 19011. At this writing, there are 29 ISO QM standards. Those of relevance to design and construction are briefly described below.

ISO 9000: 2000

Quality management systems – Fundamentals and vocabulary.

Establishes a starting point for understanding the quality standards; defines terms and definitions in quality standards, and is useful in avoiding confusion and misinterpretation of terms.

ISO 9001: 2000

Quality management systems – Requirements.

This is the core quality document. See Chapter 3.2.

ISO 9004: 2000

Quality management systems – Guidelines for performance improvements.

Organized to match the structure of ISO 9001: 2000, it includes the entire 'requirements' text of ISO 9001:2000, and extends that text with substantial guidelines for implementation, particular with regard to continual improvement programs. It includes extensive examples, and although general in nature, is a useful summary guide for ISO 9001 implementation.

ISO 10005: 2005

Quality management systems – Guidelines for quality plans.

Guidelines to assist in the preparation, review, acceptance and revision of quality plans.

ISO 10006: 2003

Quality management systems – Guidelines for quality management in projects.

Guidelines to help users ensure the quality of project processes and products, although written to match the structure of ISO 9001:1994.

ISO 10007: 2003

Quality management systems – Guidelines for configuration management.

Helps users ensure that a complex product continues to function when components are changed individually – applicable to major construction projects.

ISO 19019:2005

Guidelines for the selection of quality management system consultants and use of their services.

Guidance in selection of QM system consultants and evaluating the competence of a quality management system consultant.

ISO 19011:2002

Guidelines for quality and/or environmental management systems auditing.

Guidance on the principles of auditing, managing audit programmes, conducting QM system audits and environmental management system audits, and guidance on the competence of quality and environmental management system auditors.

Guiding principles of quality

The standards listed above are united by a set of eight principles that help practices improve performance. These are (my interpretation of the language of the Standard):

- Focus on client relationships.
- Leading the practice.
- A 'systems' approach.
- A process-based methodology.
- Teamwork / participation of people.
- Continual improvement, through feedback mechanisms.
- Logical, criteria-based decision making.
- Positive subconsultant relationships.

3.2 ISO 9001:2000 > architecture

A quality management system demands only enough *paper to demonstrate what the requirements are and that they have been met.*

Tim Cornick

The ISO 9001:2000 makes clear that the decision to implement a QM system should be strategic (e.g. be part of a strategic plan), and also makes clear that its design and implementation will vary according to many factors. ISO 9001 emphasizes that there is no intent to require uniformity of systems.

Structure of the Standard

Copyright law prevents the inclusion of the text of the standard. If you intend to build a QM system that complies with the standard, you will need to purchase a copy – see purchasing information at the end of this Part 3.

ISO 9001:2000 has the following high-level structure:

1 **Scope**

2 **Normative reference**

3 **Terms and definitions**

4 **Quality management system**

5 **Management responsibility**

6 **Resource management**

7 **Product realization**

8 **Measurement, analysis and improvement**

The first three headings cover scope, references to other standards and supply basic definitions. Sections 4 to 8 are the parts that become active in a compliant system.

Approaches to QM system design

It is now internationally well accepted that the structure of a quality management system should follow the structures familiar within an industry.

Basically, there are two ways to approach the design of a quality management system: follow the structure of the standard; or adapt the structure of the standard to one's own industry.

The structure of the standard works reasonably well for some industries, and not well at all for others. Industrial processes (including construction) are not all that dissimilar to the structure of the standard.

Design practice, however, is structured somewhat differently, and does not 'flow' in the same way as the standard. For this reason, the second option is the only one that makes any sense in the design industry. In project management and construction, the decision isn't quite as clear-cut, but I would still recommend the second option.

The only people this choice affects are the external auditors – but if you provide a good 'roadmap' to your system, they will have no trouble working to it.

Minimizing terminology confusion

As you review generic quality documents (including the below-referenced www.mqia.com matrix), keep in mind that 'services' are the same as 'products' in quality lingo – so in place of 'product', read 'service' and the outline will seem more relevant. In the reductionist language of the quality standard, there are *processes*, that result in *products*.

> According to the quality glossary, ISO 9000: 2000 defines 'process' as 'a set of interrelated or interacting activities which transform inputs into outputs', and 'product' as the 'result of a process'.
>
> There are four 'generic' product categories: services, software, hardware and processed materials.

This distinction can be confusing to design professionals, because we generally do not see any difference between the idea of *process* and *service* – they are really the same thing in the way we approach our business. We think of 'products' as physical, tangible – like a set of plans or a design report – but see them only as a 'by-product' of our more important activity, the processes we call service.

This view is not always appreciated by clients, however; a majority of whom discount the process aspect and measure the product aspect of what we do. This difference in perceptual values can be the cause of a breakdown in client communications.

In this sense, the disparity between the terminology of the standard and the internal perceptions in the design industry only highlights the differences that exist between the design professionals and their clients. Grappling with this issue conceptually helps designers to better communicate with their clients, for the benefit of both.

There is a second, related terminology issue: The standard identifies a generic flow of inputs > processes > outputs. This model is closer to the design and construction industry perception of how it all works. One could perhaps equate 'outputs' with 'product' here, but that is too simplistic. A product is the integrated sum of a number of 'outputs' (my definition).

Do not let these terminology issues bother you – just be aware of them when you read the standard, and think about which aspects of your practice relate to the standard's clauses.

'Applicability' issues

A possibly confusing aspect of ISO 9001 is the degree to which it is 'applicable' to an organization. Clause 1.2 says the standard is applicable to all organizations. This clause also provides for exclusions to such generic application, but provides that such exclusions are limited to those within clause 7 *and* which do not limit the firm's ability to satisfy client and other requirements (such as regulatory requirements).

Claiming any other exclusions voids claims of conformity to the standard. As a practical matter, there aren't many exclusions available for design firms, because clause 7 covers design! For more on this, see Chapter 3.4 (Step 1: Exclusions).

Relating ISO 9001 to design practice

Here you need to turn on your computer, and go to www.mqia.com > Standards > 3.2a *ISO 9001 in Architecture*, which is a detailed, 5 page analysis of each clause in the standard, and how it relates to the practice of architecture. Download the document. You'll need it to relate to references to the standard throughout this Part 3. And, as noted earlier, you'll also need a copy of the standard itself.

You may find the ASQ document *ISO 9001:2000 Interpretative Guide for the Design and Construction Project Team* useful. See Resources at the end of this Part 3 for details.

The left column reviews the standard according to its structure, so that you become familiar with that structure, and can come back to it with confidence. As you work your way through this matrix, refer to the corresponding clauses in your copy of the standard, if you have one. At first reading, this comparison seems daunting. Is it really the 'vast quantities of paperwork' mentioned in the epigram to (the next) Chapter 3.3? Let's analyze it. The 51 sections (excluding headings) of the standard can be grouped as follows:

Table 3.2 *Documentation of standards clauses*

Need for documentation	Total no.	ISO 9001 clause numbers
Mandatory	6	4.2.3, 4.2.4, 8.2.2, 8.3, 8.5.2, 8.5.3
Probably required for most A|E|C firms	23	4.2.1, 5.1, 5.2, 5.3, 5.4.1, 5.5.2, 5.5.3, 7.1, 7.2.1, 7.3.1, 7.3.2, 7.3.3, 7.3.4, 7.3.5, 7.3.6, 7.3.7, 7.4.1, 7.4.2, 8.1, 8.2.1, 8.2.3, 8.4, 8.5.1
May be required for typical A|E|C firms	8	5.4.2, 5.6.2, 6.1, 6.2.1, 6.2.2, 7.2.2, 7.2.3, 7.5.4
Probably not required for most A|E|C firms	14	4.1, 4.2.2, 5.5.1, 5.6.1, 5.6.3, 6.3, 6.4, 7.4.3, 7.5.1, 7.5.2, 7.5.3, 7.5.5, 7.6, 8.2.4
Total	51	

Documentation, then, is required for somewhere between 29 and 37 standards, for a typical firm. Some can easily be combined, for example, the three under 7.4 would likely be grouped as a single procedure.

How big is a procedure? If carefully written, one page suffices for all but a very few. Counting those that can be grouped, an average of a page per procedure is adequate. Oftentimes one sees much bigger quality manuals – but on a closer look they will contain a lot of standard forms, checklists, guide notes and other information that aren't actually part of the procedures.

Comparison with your office manual

If your firm is like the typical, reasonably well-organized A|E|C organization, the following will very likely be true:

- You will have an office manual *much* thicker than 29-37 pages.
- This office manual will include many of the topics covered by ISO 9001 (although it won't typically be compliant).

- This office manual won't be up to date throughout, and parts of it may be redundant.
- Its use will be occasional rather than regular.
- Some people in your firm won't know what's in it, or even where to find a copy.
- When there are problems on a project, it is often because the manual wasn't followed.
- There will be regular firm resolves to get the manual up to date and ensure that everybody uses it, but there isn't ever enough time to do the update or enforce use.

If the bullet points above sound just a little familiar, your practice is one that will truly benefit from adopting an ISO 9001 approach.

Just one more point before moving on: If you are a project manager or construction manager, the above matrix will still be more or less appropriate, except that you won't need procedures for the 7.3 series – you won't have responsibility for project design. If you are an interior design firm, it is likely that that you will need a procedure for 7.5.4.

This brings us to the conclusion of this overview look at ISO 9001, ready to consider, in Chapter 3.4, how the structure of ISO 9001 can be adapted to fit into a format more like that of your office manual; like the way you instinctively run your business. First, however, something on 'myths, half-truths and truths'....

3.3 Myths, half-truths and truths about ISO 9001

QA – something that involves vast quantities of paperwork.

Carol Nader

This chapter reflects the author's personal views about the role of QM in professional practice, based on working on the implementation of quality systems with over 200 design practices over more than fifteen years. The concepts expressed here do not always accord with conclusions put forward by other authorities.

If you look up 'quality' in Wikipedia (www.wikipedia.com), you'll find an article about perceived deficiencies in implementing quality systems.

Draw your own conclusions!

The concept of QM comes with considerable 'baggage' in some circles – popular ideas about what it is, and what it is for, and what it involves. All of these ideas have elements of truth, but sometimes they are distorted, inaccurate, and misleading.

We need to get these concepts in perspective, in order to have a useful discussion about the potential role of quality management in a professional practice.

One of the reasons for this baggage may be the zealous, 'all or nothing' exhortations of the great gurus of total quality management (TQM) that, at least in the US and Japan, preceded introduction of the international ISO 9000 family of standards.

Without making any judgment one way or the other on TQM, readers should be aware that ISO 9001, by contrast with TQM, is ***not*** 'total' in its approach. Rather, it is designed for incremental implementation, it applies to a business only to the extent that it does apply, and its foundation is one of logic, rather than emotional commitment.

These are important distinctions. Despite the varying (but generally common) philosophical ground between leading TQM theories and ISO 9001, the approach to implementation is fundamentally different, and this difference makes for a very different implementation experience. What are some of the myths, half-truths and truths about ISO 9001?

'QM is another layer of controls – nice, but not necessary.'

The idea that QM is something that you can 'add to' a practice comes from people who really don't understand QM at all (and this includes a few who have tried to implement a concept they didn't understand, and as a result experienced a failure of implementation).

Every single element of quality management already exists, to a greater or lesser degree, in every business, including professional design practices. Many of these elements may be operating at an unconscious, or semi-conscious level, but they still exist.

What the ISO standard does is to identify these elements, provide a structure for organizing them, and establish some parameters for documenting their existence.

In the process, the quality system increases significantly the emphasis the firm places on these elements, by way of using them to drive improvement in the firm's overall output.

'QM involves a lot of unnecessary record-keeping.'

At the risk of annoying some readers, I would suggest that many of the people who believe this may be running businesses that fail to keep necessary records, and don't want to change.

ISO 9001 requires only that sufficient records be kept to demonstrate that the business has actually done what it had set out to do, with the standard of care being that an independent observer would agree.

QM may well increase record-keeping for some practices, but if applied appropriately, will not create *unnecessary* record-keeping.

'QM costs a lot of money, with uncertain returns.'

This myth/half-truth flows on from the previous one, sometimes as a way of clinching the first argument. It does cost something to run a well-organized business, and to generate records that can verify that this is happening. What is missing from this half-truth is that there are also – for most businesses – considerable (but often hidden) costs in *failing* to maintain reasonable records.

There is an element of truth in this assertion, however. Building and implementing a QM system has a real cost, and the returns are, indeed, uncertain. It is a business investment.

Proponents of this myth ignore the boy scout motto 'be prepared'. Being prepared does have a price, but it also has paybacks in both 'downside' practice issues (risk reduction) and 'upside' practice issues (marketing edge).

At the very heart of QM theory is the concept of being able to demonstrate that you are what you say you are. The practice that has honestly implemented a QM program will have conclusively underpinned its claims in both marketing and risk management.

'QM requires that we write up a lot of procedures for things we already know how to do.'

This one is a half-truth, in part fostered by legions of certifiers who were keen to see documentation of activities so that they would have something to inspect.

In the 1994 edition of ISO 9001, documentation requirements were not completely clear. Even though there was a significant authority of judgment available to the effect that the documentation should fit the need for it, some certifying agencies were clearly expecting more, and many firms seeking certification were 'going overboard' in generating superfluous documentation.

The 2000 version of ISO 9001 resolves this problem. As noted in Chapter 2.4, out of 51 possible procedures, only six are required to be documented by any ISO 9001-compliant organization. This setting of the 'lowest common denominator' is a welcome and useful revision.

What the new version does, however, is put the responsibility for deciding what other procedures require documentation squarely back on the business, as discussed on page 94.

In making these evaluations, the firm can take into account its size, the complexity and interaction of its processes, and the competence of its personnel, a reasonable approach.

The net result of these changes is that the new version is much less prescriptive, and vastly more flexible, than the 1994 version.

3.4 'One size fits none' – Fitting the standard to design practice

The biggest single mistake design practices make when addressing ISO 9001 is to think that they have to change the way they work to suit the requirements of the standard. All built-environment practices, all over the world, share a common approach to problem-solving, vastly more similar than most would expect, recognise or perhaps even admit to.

Because ISO 9001 operates primarily at the approach-to-problem-solving level noted in the sidebar at left, it can (and does) effectively work as a global standard. This does ***not*** mean, however, that each practice should interpret it, and implement it, the same way. Quite the contrary: the key to successful implementation is in recognising similarities ***and*** differences.

To the extent that practices are similar, common systems can be usefully employed to lend coherence and order to repetitive functions, as in the case of design layering guidelines. These common systems sharply improve the ability of practices to work together harmoniously and to reduce the learning curve for new staff – without losing their competitive edge.

As similar as our practices might be in the basic methodology of practice, none are exactly the same either, and any description of practice process should reflect these differences.

ISO 9001 represents the lowest common denominator of such coherent systems. For example, it describes the kind of information that a practice should retain in its quality records, but not the basis for organizing or storing such information. In this case, the requirements for information retention as suggested by PI (professional indemnity) insurers for good risk management would exceed the minimum recommended by ISO 9001.

Observations about similarity of design practice aside, there is truth to the idea that 'one size fits none'.

What needs including in a QM system?

What aspects of practice should a quality system describe? This is relevant to any discussion of developing a system based on ISO 9001:2000, because the standard permits considerable latitude in what should be described in writing (*documented*, in the language of the standard).

There is another potential determiner of whether or not a process benefits the firm by documenting it. Assuming that the practice has goals that are not quite within its grasp, writing down procedures that will help the practice to achieve those goals is an important reason to do so – that is the first step in realizing them.

The answer (noted in Chapter 1.4) is that documentation is required if such documentation is 'needed by the organization to ensure the effective planning, operation and control of its processes'. As you can see, here the need for documentation will vary widely practice to practice, depending on how well its standard procedures are understood and ingrained in its culture.

This change (from the previous version of the standard) puts greater authority in the hands of the quality manager, in designing and implementing a system, but it also requires more thought and care.

Most quality managers will find the distinction between procedures that require documentation, and those that don't, to be confusing and the line between them sometimes difficult to draw.

Explaining this distinction to external auditors presents another layer of uncertainty.

I am not, at this writing, aware of any published guidelines that address this aspect of quality system design in the design and construction industry (although there may be some in preparation). Table 3.4.1, next page, is a first attempt to bring some clarity to the matter, in a way that will stand up to external audit.

Two approaches...

There are two ways to approach the material in this section, summarized in the boxes below. This chapter takes the left-hand approach.

Swallow whole and digest slowly	Bite off a piece at a time
Get the big picture first, then work out the details.	Begin with the details, build up to the big picture.
Advantages: Faster overall, and product consistency will be higher.	**Advantages:** Suits the comfort zone of more people, less daunting.
Disadvantages: Tough work. Some people choke on it and decide it is all just too hard.	**Disadvantages:** Takes longer, and some earlier developed procedures will probably need re-writing.

At the end of this chapter, there is an outline of the steps in the right-hand approach.

Here are the four steps to adapting ISO 9001:2000 to your practice, 'swallow whole' approach.

Step 1 - Exclusions

Do all of the standard's clauses apply to your business? Exclusions are permissible (but only from the Section 7 group) and the reasons for exclusion require documentation.

Project managers and construction managers generally do not need the 7.3 group, and professionals who never have custody of the customer's property don't need 7.5.4. Virtually all contractors will need a procedure for 7.6, but most design professionals won't.

Prepare a list of exclusions, and the reasons why they can be excluded – one well-written sentence each is enough.

Step 2 - Determining if documentation is required

The first step in analyzing the standard's requirements with respect to whether documentation is or isn't needed is to consider the kinds of factors that would make a difference.

The key point is whether or not documenting the procedure will improve the firm's ability to ensure effective operation and control of its processes. The table below outlines key factors.

Table 3.4.1 *Key factors in determining if documentation is required*

Firm size	The larger the firm, the less likely it is that all staff will be fully informed about policies and procedures that would affect quality of output, and therefore the greater the need for documentation.
Turnover	High turnover equals less knowledge about policies and procedures that would affect quality of output.
Qualifications of staff	A firm that has a high percentage of permanent, qualified architects, compared to numbers of drafters and contract personnel, will have less need for documented procedures to ensure the 'effective operation and control of its processes'.
Complexity and diversity of projects	A firm that sticks to a limited product range will have a high level in built-in expertise about the quality issues in that product type, and less need for documentation.
Sensitivity of projects to quality variability	This factor is about system redundancy: Quality is simply more important in some project types than others eg if your business is designing clean rooms or sophisticated medical environments or other 'high risk' projects, your need for documented procedures will be much greater than for a firm specializing in residential developments, spec office projects or industrial buildings.
Training and communication	An active training and information-sharing program will keep staff current with quality requirements, and reduce the need for documenting them. An ongoing mentoring program, participation in risk management training programs, professional training in quality management, and/or peer review programs also reduce the need for documentation.
A high degree of customer satisfaction	A demonstrated high level of customer satisfaction, such as the lack of customer complaints, high incidence of repeat customers, lack of claims alleging negligence, letters of appreciation, and awards for projects (especially by customer industry groups) all indicate that procedure documentation is not needed to ensure quality performance.
Use of common standards	Where the firm uses industry-wide, proven standards, such as AIA contracts or CAD layering guidelines, the processes of working with them has little need of documentation.

What is or isn't documented, according to ISO 9001, depends on several factors; for example, staff ability and training, the nature of the business and its services or products, and how complex its processes are.

We can see from this, for two otherwise comparable firms, but which rate differently to the above criteria, one could require significantly more documentation of procedures than the other.

Step 3 - Setting the level of documentation required

Provide only as much detail as your people need to 'get it right first time'. If they really understand what's required, then very brief 'reminders' are adequate. My advice: Start lean and add detail when and where it is clear that you need it.

The examples from Thomsen Adsett Architects at the end of Chapter 2.4 are very good examples of an approach that really works.

Step 4 – Explaining why you aren't documenting

Having decided what you want to document, and what not, you need to explain why you aren't documenting some procedures. I suggest that you might introduce your quality system by profiling the 'culture quality' that already exists in your practice, as a general way of deciding on the appropriate level of quality system documentation, as well as to cite specific reasons for documenting or not documenting procedures for particular requirements.

> The point of this discussion is not to duck out from under the need to document procedures – rather, it is to save you from documenting procedures unnecessarily.

Your quality system should include a simple matrix diagram that covers every clause of the Standard, identifies your firm response to that item, and either refers the reader to the corresponding procedure, or justifies why one isn't needed. Referring back to the 'key factors' table, the following conditions would suggest the need to document, or not document procedures. These are examples of how you might describe your practice profile.

Table 3.4.2 *Documentation of standards clauses*

Reasons to document	Reasons not to document
Ours is a large practice, with several branch offices. We require that quality procedures are understood across the practice	Ours is a small office, where we work closely together and have a shared understanding of quality management principles
Our firm has grown rapidly, and includes a number of people who have not had the time to learn our culture	We have a high staff retention rate, with the average duration of employment of xx years
We are a 'teaching' firm, and believe in selecting talented young designers and 'growing' them into firm leadership	We have a high percentage of licensed professionals: xx % of our technical work force
Our firm undertakes a wide range of projects, of varying complexity	Our firm is well known as having expertise in the areas of xxx and xxx, and we generally do not take projects outside these areas
Our firm is a leader in highly technical projects, demanding high and consistent quality control procedures	Our firm specializes in traditionally low-risk areas of design, where our well-understood quality culture achieves results expected by our clients
Our firm is in the process of developing an overall professional development program (weak, but if that is the reality, it is part of your profile)	Our firm has an ongoing, intensive approach to training, averaging xx hours per year per technical employee Our firm has an active knowledge management program to ensure that all staff have access to the information they need Key staff members have undertaken intensive training in quality (and/or risk) management We have a undertaken formal peer review process
Our firm continually strives to meet and exceed our clients' expectations	Our firm is proud of the way it consistently meets our clients' expectations, as evidenced by our high rate of repeat clients (xx %), our very low claims history (xx claims per 100 projects), and the many letters of appreciation received from clients
Our firm is a leader in developing new methods of project delivery, and in creating new and better ways of addressing industry issues	We use only industry-standard agreements and contracts, as well as standard guides such as the AIA CAD Layering Guidelines

How many of those descriptions fit your firm?

Three points stand out here: First, either side of the pairs of reasons are equally valid and positive. Second, wherever possible, quantify your profile, where you choose not to document. Third, there are very good reasons why some firms need a more comprehensively documented quality system than others.

You may wonder why I've dwelt on this so extensively. The reason is that, as you think about each of the standard's requirements, I want you to be thinking about the degree to which each of those requirements affects the way you practice, and whether or not your firm would benefit by having it documented.

How to do it 'a piece at a time' successfully

I close this chapter with an outline for the alternative approach, preferred by most firms, especially where they are trying to develop a QM system without the help of an outside specialist consultant.

Step 1: Check your current information structure / project filing code, or whatever organizational system you use. Look at the examples on the handbook website. Ask yourself if your system is optimized for your practice, check it with others in your firm that have an interest in these issues.

If it is working well for you – great – don't fiddle with round wheels. But if it needs updating, do that before attempting to connect it to ISO 9001.

Step 2: Break your current information structure into a series of logical groups – at least six, not more than 12 – by major headings. Rate each of these groups according to their importance in terms of overall quality output of the firm.

Architects almost always put the design process at the top of this list; contractors will put project quality control and subcontractor management near the top.

Step 3: Set up a time schedule to run 24 months, and program these groups for action according to their order on the list – each will be allowed 2 to 4 months to get right. Fix 'start' and 'complete' dates for each group.

Step 4: Identify the person in the firm whose responsibilities are most closely associated with each of the groups. That person will have to be responsible for that part of the overall program. Ensure that they accept that responsibility; if not, resolve it with senior management.

Step 5: Identify the clauses in the Standard that relate to the items in each of your groups. Buy the Standard, if you haven't got a copy.

Step 6: Get going on the first group, monitoring progress toward the deadline. Start implementing that part of the system when it is complete, concurrent with starting development of the next group, and so on, until all are done.

Step 7: Gradually build your quality manual from the output of these elements.

The above program is manageable, it has worked for hundreds of practices, and it will get you there if you keep on top of it.

3.5 External audits & certification

Chapter 2.10 *Internal quality system audits* overviews the audit process. If you skipped that before, read it before continuing with this chapter – most of the information there also applies to external audits.

There are two types of external audits, called 'second-party' and 'third-party' audits.

Second-party audits

The 1994 version of ISO 9001 required the evaluation and selection of subconsultants on their ability to meet subcontract requirements, including their quality system, and to define control over subconsultants based in part on quality audit reports and quality records. As a result, it was common in many industries for organizations to audit their subcontractors, or at the very least to require them to supply information about their QM systems.

The 2000 version of ISO 9001 is less specific in this regard, requiring only that the firm establish criteria for subconsultant selection and evaluation. Thus, it is up to the organization to determine whether or not it will have specific QM system requirements for its subconsultants.

Second-party audits are carried out by one organization on another, for example between a contractor and a subcontractor, or between a client and a consultant.

Architecture/engineering (A|E) practices generally do not audit subconsultants, preferring to rely on supplied evidence of the functioning of the subconsultants' QM systems (including the results of self-audits) where they put a value on this kind of information.

However, we often see cases where general contractors will audit some subcontractors, and in the case of design-build projects, will audit their A|E team. Owners who are QM system-oriented sometimes will audit their A|E teams, most commonly using project managers to carry out the audits.

Many A|Es dislike the idea of being audited by a client or design-build team member. If you have no formal QM system, there is nothing to audit (no basis for comparing what you say you do with what you do). If you are required by a contractor in a design-build arrangement, or by a client, to show evidence of a QM system, it is an indication that they may plan second-party audits.

In this situation, it is a good idea to inquire about their audit policies, so you will know what to expect. Of course, going through an audit and looking good increases your reputation with that project partner or client.

Should you decide to carry out second-party audits on your subconsultants, the guidelines in Chapter 2.10 will apply.

Third-party audits

The third-party audit is an independent certification of your quality system and your compliance to it by an organization accredited by the International Standards Association (ISO), or by a national standards body accredited by it.

Third-party certification is accepted internationally as evidence of a complying quality system. Certification is usually for a period of three years, after which it must be renewed through re-audit.

Keep in mind that you are are paying for the audit process! Don't pay more for an audit and certification than necessary. Firms performing this service are commercial; their prices and their terms vary. It is best to obtain and compare fee schedules for a number of audit firms before selecting one.

However, during this period, periodic reviews are required (usually half-yearly or quarterly), and a charge is made for this review.

There is no point bringing in the outside auditors until your own internal audit program shows that you are ready for them, and should pass such an audit.

Appoint an auditor that you feel comfortable with, and that has experience in auditing firms in your industry.

After narrowing the choices to two or three, interview them, just as you would if you were appointing an attorney or financial consultant.

The audit process

There are five steps to the external audit process:

The 'desktop' (system) audit, normally conducted at the auditor's premises, where the auditor compares your QM manual to ISO 9001, and checks it for compliance. The auditor will be particularly interested in any parts of the standard that you have excluded from your system, and will look carefully at your reasons for doing so.

He will also pay particular attention to any parts of the standard that you have chosen not to document, and your reasons for not documenting. Unless your reasons are clearly stated and logical, these two points are likely to result in questions. It stands to reason that a discussion about exclusions and non-documentation should be part of the interview with your preferred auditor before appointing the firm.

If the auditor finds that your system is essentially compliant, you will proceed to the next step. If not, your QM manual will be returned with a list of non-compliant items for you to work on prior to the next step. In this case, the system audit will have to be repeated.

Entrance meeting: At the beginning of the compliance audit, the auditor will ask to meet with a number of people in your firm, to explain the audit process and answer any questions. The list of items in Chapter 2.10 under *Audit planning* will form the agenda for this meeting.

The compliance audit: Over a day or two (possibly longer in large firms), the audit team will 'fan out' and do a thorough 'quality health check' of your systems, with the goal of finding out if your actions follow your QM manual or not. If random checks for any aspect of your system show compliance, they will move on to other areas. If random checks show non-compliance, they will dig deeper to see if the non-compliance is occasional or systemic. They will keep notes on findings.

Exit meeting: Auditors will compare notes, reach conclusions, and ask to re-assemble the people attending the first meeting, perhaps including others in areas where nonconformities were found. The lead auditor will present the audit report verbally, highlighting the findings, and answer questions about the process and results. After this meeting, auditors will prepare a written report for the firm. If you passed the audit, a certificate will be issued.

Audit follow-up: Your firm must act on the results of the audit, following up and correcting any nonconformities, within a time frame agreed with the auditors during the exit meeting. When your corrective actions are completed, the auditors will return and recheck those issues only – leading to certification if successful, or a further list of nonconformities for action if not.

Finding an auditor or registrar

Unfortunately, the new listing service described at right does not have a category for construction, as did the previous, now discontinued, register. There is a 'Scope' category, but it is accessible only under a personal file, and in the US, most of those registered do not list their scope of qualification.

A good way to locate a registrar (a company accredited to certify organizations to ISO 9001) is to go to the website of the ANSI-ASQ National Accreditation Board, http://www.anab.org/.

One way to locate an auditor (a qualified individual) – besides looking in Yellow Pages – is to go to the website of RABSQA International, http://www.rabqsa.com. Go to the Directory & Registers menu, then select either Accredited Quality Auditor or QMS Auditor.

Auditors registered under the old experience-based scheme are listed as QMS Auditors. They all have until the end of 2006 to upgrade their qualifications to Accredited Quality Auditor under a new competency-based process. You can learn more about this on the RABSQA website.

Part 3: Sources, resources & notes

Resources

3.1 For info on **guiding principles** of quality: ISO 9000:2000 *Quality management systems – Fundamentals and vocabulary.*

For **info on design and implementation of quality programs** generally: The best and most complete source for QM references is Quality Press, the publishing arm of the American Society for Quality – see http://qualitypress.asq.org. A copy of their publications catalogue is available free of charge, and they have a 'look before you buy' policy that lets you read a sample chapter online of their more popular titles.

For **purchase of quality standards:** ISO quality standards (and information about them) are available from the following sources (check for currency – URLs can change):

- Techstreet, http://www.techstreet.com/cgi-bin/publishers. Techstreet is a central point for accessing almost every technical standard in print.
- ISO Online, http://www.iso.ch/iso/en/ISOOnline.openerpage.
- The national standards organization in your country (which may be is less expensive than buying through ISO). You can find contact details for your national standards body through the ISONET directory, on http://www.wssn.net/WSSN/index.html.
- ***Best buy:*** *ISO 9001:2000 Interpretative Guide for the Design and Construction Project Team,* ASQ Design and Construction Division, John R. Broomfield, Editor. This 125 pp guide includes the complete text of the operative clauses in the standard, as well as ASQ's guidelines for interpretation – and at USD $40.00, it is about one third the price of purchasing the standard from ISO Online. It includes a sample 5-page quality manual and a sample 20-page QMS Specification for a metropolitan transport authority. You can order it online as a download, and you can download an executive summary, free. The URL is http://qualitypress.asq.org/perl/catalog.cgi?item=E1204.

www.mqia.com:

3.2a Nelson, Charles, *ISO 9001 in Architecture.*

Epigrams

3.2 Cornick, Tim (1991) *Quality Management for Building Design*, Butterworth Architecture, p 8.

3.3 Nader, Carol (18 February 2002) in an article on business jargon in *The Age* newspaper, Melbourne, Australia.

4 Vision, Leadership, Planning & Brand

4.1 Quality, leadership & responsibility

The trouble with most professional-firm planning is that it is full of visions, goals, missions, and ambitions – in other words, what we want to have happen – and completely lacking in how we are going to make it happen.

David Maister

Possibly many of them (us) secretly yearn for the old Beaux Arts-inspired atelier model, where one learned architecture by sharpening pencils for the master and paying close attention to what he did.

A classmate of mine at the University of Minnesota went off for two years to study at Taliesin under the great master. When he got back, I asked him what he had learned. He looked at me for a long time and finally replied, 'I learned how to shovel cow manure and how to look at the sun.' Vern, if you are out there somewhere reading this, send me an email – that was 48 years ago, and I'd like to re-ask the question.

A Hedgehog Concept is not a goal to be the best, a strategy to be the best, an intention to be the best, a plan to be the best. It is an understanding of what you can be the best at. The distinction is absolutely crucial. – Jim Collins, *Good to Great*

There are hundreds, if not thousands, of in-print books on leadership, many of them excellent. Most design professionals (at least those I talk to) haven't read any of them; indicating they don't see the relevance of others' experience to their practice leadership; they don't see leadership as a practice issue; or both.

> ***Vern was having a sleepless night, and not very happy. Had he accidentally opened Pandora's box with this project? Not that he could see any alternative – they badly needed this job, and – given the nature of it – he thought Tung had a right to demand high quality, and proof of it. Nevertheless, what he considered 'normal' tensions between young and old in a design practice felt like they were spiralling out of control. He decided that he had to be more decisive, and finally went to sleep wondering how he'd do that.***

Leadership *is* a practice quality issue. Every observer of professional design practice worth reading has something to say on the topic, almost all of it worth thinking about. If you are one of those design professionals who has never quite got around to it, Resources at the end of this Part 4 has specific references to what I consider some of the best thinking on leadership, by both our fellow design professionals and others, eminently worth reading.

Key Resource Frank Stasiowski has written extensively on leadership, including a thorough and thoughtful paper entitled *Firm Leadership and Quality Management*, written for this handbook. You can download it in its entirety from www.mqia.com – see the reference under Resources, at the end of this Part 4 .

Key resource Ray Andrews has also written an article on leadership for this handbook, *Practice Leadership and Managing Quality*, also available for download on the handbook website. I won't attempt to apply the *Reader's Digest* technique to these already succinct thoughts on leading your team, just encourage you to sample from them.

ISO 9001 and leadership

Leadership is deemed a quality issue in ISO 9001, where leaders are referred to as 'top management'. Leaders are asked to show commitment to, and 'continually improve' QM – through five kinds of action: communicating, setting quality policies and objectives, holding reviews of management and providing adequate staff and other resources.

Each of these actions is developed in brief but specific statements – refer Clauses 5.2, 5.3, 5.4, 5.5, 5.6 and 6.1 (if you have a copy of the Standard).

If you look past the generic language of the Standard, and mentally translate the concepts into the language of architecture, these 'requirements' will make perfectly good sense – exactly the sort of activity that we call 'best practice'.

Leadership's responsibilities

Most of the great gurus of quality are unified in their views that quality of leadership is squarely on the path toward service and product quality. Dr. Deming, in particular, lays responsibility for low productivity and low product quality squarely at the feet of management.

It is the responsibility of management to discover the barriers that prevent workers from taking pride in what they do. – Mary Walton, in *The Deming Management Method*

Think about the truly great practices that you know, and what makes them different from the rest. We tend to worship the 'star designers' and try to be like them, but the great success stories in architecture have leaders who know how to inspire and motivate their people, and how to bring out the very best in them.

To use my metaphor of the auto-body fender, these practices are the opposite of rigid: however sleek the lines of the practice image, the 'fender' is infinitely malleable, able to evolve, change, grow, and constantly reform itself as its people, its clients, and its business environment changes.

Useful management theories

The leader of a large, successful Sydney practice has no office. His desk is out in the open, same as everyone else's. There are a couple of glass-walled meeting rooms nearby in case a conversation needs privacy – but there are no offices in that practice. It feels good. I observe that, increasingly, the best practices are doing away with private offices for management.

I know a very good architect who somewhat sheepishly admits that his preferred management method is MBHIMO – 'management by hiding in my office'.

There are almost as many theories of management as there are writers on the subject, and every year a few new ones emerge to 'move your cheese', or whatever. My favourites, however, are MBAQ and MBWA. If you don't know what those acronyms mean, you should – they will never go out of fashion, or diminish in usefulness. They are defined in Chapter 12.1.

Is leadership lonely?

Ray Andrews writes about 'loneliness at the top' in his paper – the feeling that there isn't anybody in the practice with whom you can share your fears – and consequently, your joys. I'm not sure if many architects experience this, but if you do, think about razing your office and moving out onto the shop floor of your practice. You'll have other issues – but one of them won't be loneliness!

4.2 Quality in strategic planning

Creating a great firm, one that fulfills a dream of any choosing, is well within the reach of every practice owner. What separates success from failure, however, is whether the firm's leaders are willing to design the company – or not. To be the executive designers of the firm *is indeed a high calling and a lifetime career challenge.*

Ellen Flynn-Heapes

Planning is the topic of Clause 5.4, ISO 9001:2000, and is emphasized by the great majority of quality experts. For a select list of recommended reading, see Resources at the end of this Part 4.

Design professionals do three principal kinds of planning:

- Planning as a service to clients.
- Project planning.
- Strategic planning.

The second and third of these are important practice quality issues. I discuss the second in Chapter 7.3.

Strategic planning is the tool that charts the course for the practice. Firms that do it well and regularly are almost always on a clear course somewhere between their present reality and their preferred future. Firms that don't are typically drifting, using a scattergun approach to marketing (if it moves, shoot at it).

If you can't measure a goal, it isn't worthy of being in the strategic plan. – Scott Braley

Key resource **Ellen Flynn-Heapes**, founder and past president of SPARKS: The Center for Strategic Planning, and a pioneer in the development of planning models for design professionals, prepared a 30-page chapter on the subject for this handbook. Into which, unfortunately, it will not fit. You can download it in entirety from the website. Jack Reigle, the new President of SPARKS, has contributed to this summary.

Achieving a Strategic *Strategic Plan,* by Ellen Flynn-Heapes and Jack Reigle

Strategic plans map the future. The map, however, isn't the same as the territory. It's your unique interpretation of where you're going, neither a road atlas that details everything nor a broad-brush conceptual overview.

Most of us fail in planning when we look only at the firm's projected revenues and expenses for the coming year. Others fail by studding the plan with generic platitudes about quality and growth. Almost everyone trips when planning to diversify, especially through mergers and acquisitions.

Most firms have one overarching objective for their planning: to create more value for themselves, their staff, and their clients. *The key in answering this question is to figure out how the firm can be really special – not just bigger.*

Strategic planning methodology and ISO 9001 share one common, important issue: the capability of a firm to undertake projects under consideration. Moreover, strategic planning maps the future, and aims the practice. ISO 9001 requires that planned growth, or change, is matched by resources, and provides the method for monitoring development of these resources.

Our own benchmark of a successful firm is whether the client respects you enough to happily accept your (audacious) schedule and fee, and walk away feeling lucky!

Elements of this objective, creating more value, include the following:

- focus the firm's resources on the most strategically important elements of the enterprise,
- build a distinctive leadership position in the marketplace,
- align actual practice with vision and strategy,
- enhance financial performance and rewards, and
- innovate something.

What's the recipe for a high quality, potent strategic plan? We can unequivocally identify five central decisions every effective firm must make. These decisions represent levels of logic in the design of your company. They work in concert to identify where the passion is, what you can ultimately do with that passion, and how *specifically* to organize your firm to realize your dream. We call this framework *The Sparks Playbook.*

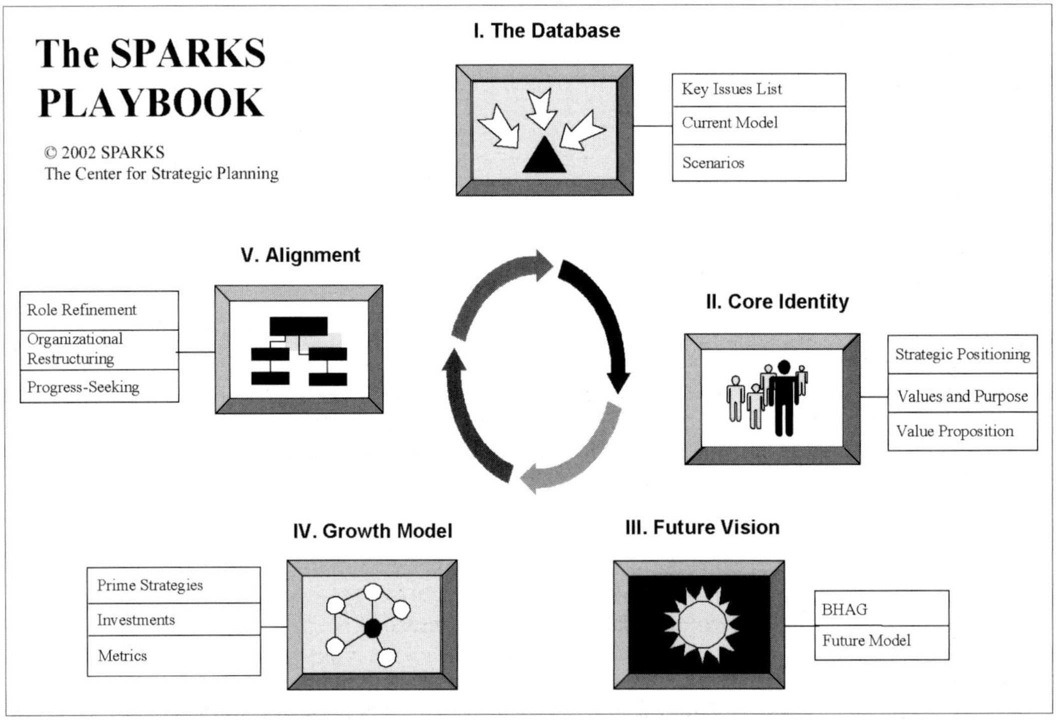

Fig. 4.2 *The SPARKS Playbook*

The Sparks Playbook identifies five essential decisions required for quality strategic planning, along with elements of each.

The beauty of strategic planning is its elegant framework for helping people to think through a worthwhile company direction, and then to purposefully make it real. Although good strategic planning can be a very sophisticated process, this summary highlights five core decisions for design firms. Each decision represents a level of logic in the ongoing process of company design. Since these decisions are such strong catalysts to resounding effectiveness, we call them ***Catalytic Decisions***.

Catalytic Decision 1: The Why

Decision One kindles the fire, pinpointing the knowledge and motivation needed for decision-making. Through the Issues Summary, Current Model, and potential Scenarios List, decision one forms a program for meaningful, focused discussion.

Catalytic Decision 2: The Who

Decision Two identifies who we are and what we stand for. It coalesces the firm's Identity, in contrast with other similar firms. It establishes common ground with a Purpose for the firm and shared Values. And it makes explicit the kind of culture the firm wants to create and the contribution it wants to make to the world.

Catalytic Decision 3: The Where

The 'big, hairy, audacious goal' or *BHAG* is a dramatic goal for the future, set in deliverable terms, and with a long time horizon. It's the 'end state' that galvanizes every current action and puts each investment into perspective. The end state is painted in a Future Model, which visually depicts how the firm works when the BHAG is achieved.

Catalytic Decision 4: The What

Comparing its images of success with its current model, the planning team sees the gap and devises the best strategies and tasks to close the gap. This culmination of the previous decisions is the Growth Model, a graphic depiction of the firm's future vision linked to action. The Growth Model includes only the highest-leverage strategies and tasks that will achieve the firm's future.

Catalytic Decision 5: The How

Decision Five is about aligning the firm's resources, specifically people and money. Roles must be refined and skills added, budgets allocated and progress defined and supported.

***These five Decisions are covered in detail in the full version of this paper on the handbook website,* www.mqia.com.**

Success stories: What strategic planning can do:

Creating a Design Identity:

A West Coast architectural firm, known for its 'vanilla' work and aggressive marketing, aspired to be a fine design firm. Through strategic planning, they reinvented the firm with aggressive pursuit of design competitions, hiring design-oriented graduate architects, and an office re-design. As of today, the firm has won ten international design competitions, including a new airport in the Far East.

The Entrepreneurial Culture:

A Midwestern engineering firm had lapsed into a tired bureaucratic culture through its practice of hiring former state agency staffers. To infuse entrepreneurial spirit, the strategic plan called for a visionary principal in the president's role, an aggressive hiring initiative, a targeted acquisitions program, and a new compensation structure. Today they are a national player in program management.

Ownership Transition:

An East Coast urban design firm saw trouble when the CEO announced his future retirement plans. Of the eight second-tier managers, none was prepared for the top role. Through strategic planning, the firm created a set of 'mini-firm' studio teams with assigned principals, performance goals, incentive compensation programs, and training for those leaders. Two excellent candidates for president emerged. One was selected for the top strategic-external job, and the other for a well-defined internal-operations co-leader job.

Carving a Niche:

A Southeast interior design firm competed poorly as a local, generalist practice. With good planning, the firm chose to focus on one clear niche that they loved: resorts. By hiring strategically, including economic and operations experts, and launching a creative positioning campaign, they now enjoy a thriving niche practice with clients around the country.

Many firms neglect the first law of integrity: Knowing one's identity and what's most important to accomplish. Many firms chase whatever opportunities arise, slavishly service clients, and find themselves in a never-ending rat race. To create respectful partnerships with clients, firms must be worthy partners – strong players who know their stuff. The best clients respect firms that will listen, of course, but will then *lead them* to their desired outcome.

To reach this position, firm leaders must compose their organization with care – and continue to nurture it – so as to attract the right clients and staff, and to offer distinctive value to their chosen clients. Strategic planning is the way to focus on this composition. It is the path to making careers meaningful, worthwhile, and rewarding.

4.3 Brand, presence & quality

Branding is about naming something with the intent to 'own' it in the marketplace.

Ellen Flynn-Heapes

I recall being somewhat anxious at the start of my consulting career about my ignorance of the art of brand management. I still know very little – but am now reassured that nobody else knows much, either.
– Paul Dickinson

My earliest primer on brand was the Sears Roebuck catalog, which I studied intently. From it, I learned the almost all manufactured goods came in three grades: good, better and best; and that 'best' had more features, was more durable and cost more than 'good'.

FLLW

As a young tadpole in the early 60's, I worked for a time for Minneapolis architect Harry Eldon Gerrish, who went through 'phases' rather like Picasso went through color periods. When I was there, he was in his 'copper' phase, and every project got a copper roof whether the client wanted it or not. Brand – yes – but perhaps not the best!

Branding is a ***critically important quality element*** of design practice. Why? Because – after direct written and verbal promises made to prospective clients – it is your most significant vehicle for creating client expectations. Your brand is your silent quality assurance program.

If your brand does not differentiate your services offer from your competitors, those services will be treated as commodities, to be bought primarily on price.

Now, unless you stopped to think about that, go back and read it again. And then think about where you fit in that formula – even if you disagree with the premise.

Branding with a hot iron was the standard method of knowing which horses and cattle belonged to which rancher in the American old west, before there were fences.

The idea is an ancient one; no different than ring seals impressed in wax on letters, maker's marks on jewellery, marks pressed into wet clay pots before firing, or the personal stamps still widely used in Japan and China as signatures. They all say the same thing: this is mine, or this is of me; from me.

From this concept comes the idea of brand as a logo or symbol, such as the Nike 'swoosh' or the emblems that adorn the front of every automobile. Brand, however, can be much more diffuse, and powerful. Think about Frank Lloyd Wright's prairie houses or H. H. Richardson's Romanesque output – we think of them as 'styles', but they were also powerful brands.

Think about Australian architect Glen Murcutt, and you think curved corrugated wrought iron – and vice versa – even though most of his designs use straight corrugated iron.

Design style as brand creates an expectation of the 'look' one will receive if that designer is appointed. One of Boston's most successful architects of the first half of the twentieth century, Royal Barry Wills, mastered, perpetuated and in fact helped to create a New England vernacular style, even though he was looked down on by many of his peers because he chose not to embrace the 'modern' movement. But his clients knew what they would be getting, they wanted it, and they kept him very busy.

Brand is also about reputation. Engineers, in particular, have many opportunities to develop special design expertise.

Such expertise can make them the first choice of architects, owners and project managers, without price being a consideration. Sometimes, practices can 'corner the market' with talent, and take a commanding lead in a marketplace because of it. One engineering group's Sydney office is a current example; their reputation for bridge design gives them the lion's share of that kind of work in NSW; a vast market.

Electronic age branding

Twenty years ago, becoming 'computerized' was a sign that a practice was 'with it'. Not a few practices bought computers just to impress clients with their modernity, but didn't actually use them for CAD – they were just for show. Today, tee-squares are a rarity, and computers no longer have that caché. Today, it is your web site that counts.

The easiest, fastest way for a prospective client to learn about your firm, and to compare it with others, is to look at the websites of firms it is considering. Unless the prospective client has some other, powerful connection to your services, they will in the first instance assume that you will have a website, and if you don't you are probably too small, can't afford one, or just not bothering to play by the present 'rules'.

According to the AIA's research, in 2002, firms that had a website or were planning to build one that year were 84% for practices of 5-9, and 95% for practices of 10-19 (see sidebar).

These figures indicate that out of ten readers of this book, about nine will have websites. How good is your website? Does it really convey your strengths, and how your firm's offerings are special? Does it offer something of real value to browsers, such that they will bookmark it and return to it – or is it just another architect's advertisement?

Let's look at a few websites that (I believe) meet the above test of a good one. For this, you'll need to get online.

Foster and Partners (www.fosterandpartners.com)

If you are not familiar with Foster's website, take a little time to browse around in it, getting a feel for its ease of access, information presented, and user-friendliness. Personally, I think it is one of the best, if not the best, architect's website on the Internet. Note: it is designed and maintained by the firm.

Gensler (www.gensler.com)

Again, spend a little time in this site, getting a feel for it, and comparing it to the Foster site. It is also extremely good, but very different from the Foster approach. Find the 'brand strategy' page, and browse through the 'offices' pages.

Gray Puksand Architects (www.graypuksand.com.au)

Gray Puksand has built up a niche business in renovating and refurbishing past-their-prime office buildings in Melbourne. They do a lot of other work as well, but they are particularly well known in this specialty. What makes their services package interesting is that they include property business management and retail/corporate strategy help *as an architectural service*.

AIA firms in 2002 that had a website or were planning to build one that year were as follows, by firm size:

1	64%
2-4	73%
5-9	84%
10-19	95%
20-49	99%
50-99	98%
100+	100%

(AIA 2003 Firm Survey p 59)

Fanning/Howey Associates (www.fhai.com)

Fanning Howey has a nicely designed, uncomplicated site – not earth-shattering at first glance – but take look at what's available from their research page. They have provided their clients and future clients with a wealth of free, downloadable, useful information.

Foxhollow Goodson Group (www.foxhollowgoodson.com)

Akers and Associates (www.akerscbs.com)

Lastly, take a look at two sites whose firms offer church-building services, and notice how they target their value propositions to the mindsets of their intended clients. Notice Akers' two 'guarantees'. These guarantees are not really very different from what any respectable practice would do, but pitching them the way they have clearly sets them apart from firms that make no guarantees.

Next steps

I encourage you to explore more sites, especially of those whom you consider to be your competitors, to see what their value propositions are, and how they are to similar or different from your own.

See Resources, at the end of this Part, for references.

Keep in mind the thought with which I open this chapter: Your brand is your most significant vehicle for creating client expectations. And, your website is the 21st century place to 'hang out your shingle'. To make people keep returning to it, you have to put really useful stuff in it that they can take away.

4.4 Commitment to change

Resisting change is as futile as resisting weather, and change is our weather now. It is that constant and that predictable.

Warren Bennis

This is a very short chapter, but Bennis's point needs emphasis.

In previous chapters, I posit that there are powerful forces that resist change in the way firms practice. No firm is immune. Whether or not change happens in a harmonious way, or a dislocated, chaotic way, depends almost entirely on how committed the firm's top leaders are to a willingness to change, starting with themselves. *Lead, and they will follow.* That works, and nothing else will.

ISO 9001:2000 demands little from top management, but what it demands is mission-critical, and its structure makes it easier for busy leaders to manage the commitment – mainly through scheduled reviews of quality performance.

Cramer and Simpson call the requisite approach 'fire in the belly', noting 'If your firm tolerates less than full commitment by its principals, everyone gets sold short.'

J. L. Ashford says that quality systems can be implemented only from the top down. He notes that long-established customs should be examined – and perhaps abandoned:

> Skeletons have to be brought out of cupboards and vested interests have to be challenged. Inevitably many people will find this process disturbing and uncomfortable. When the going gets rough, as it will, management must maintain the momentum.

Part 4: Sources, resources & notes

Sources

4.1 ISO 9001:2000 *Quality management systems – Requirements.*

The reference to 'moving cheese' is to Spencer Johnson's bestseller *Who Moved My Cheese?*

4.2 Braley, Scott (2004) in an address to the Practice Management Knowledge Community Breakfast, AIA National Convention.

4.3 Dickinson, Paul (2001) *It's Not About Size – Bigger Brands for Smaller Businesses,* Virgin Publishing Ltd, p 76.

4.4 Ashford, J. L. (1989) *The Management of Quality in Construction*, E. & F.N. Spon, p 181.

Cramer, James P. and Scott Simpson (2002) *How Firms Succeed: A Field Guide to Design Management*, Ostberg, pp 256, 259.

Resources

4.1 Bennis, Warren (1989) *On Becoming a Leader,* Perseus Books. If you can afford the time to read only one short book on leadership, you cannot do better than this one.

Goleman, Daniel (1998) *Working with Emotional Intelligence*, Bloomsbury. If you can take the time to read only three books on leadership, this should be one of them.

Kaderlan, Norman (1991) *Designing Your Practice,* McGraw-Hill, pp 32-48.

McKenna, Patrick J. and David H. Maister (2002) *First Among Equals*, The Free Press. This is the third book I'd recommend on leadership generally.

4.2 Cramer, James P. and Scott Simpson, pp 50-3.

Kaderlan, Norman (1991) *Designing Your Practice,* McGraw-Hill, pp 9-30.

Maister, David H. (1993) *Managing the Professional Service Firm,* Free Press Paperbacks, pp 223-43.

4.3 Cohen, Jonathan (2000) *Communication and Design with the Internet,* W. W. Norton & Co., Chapters 4 and 7 (pp 52-95; 148-77). Cohen is a practicing architect, and his text is particularly relevant to architectural practice.

Flynn-Heapes, Ellen (2000) *Creating Wealth*, SPARKS: The Center for Strategic Planning, p 113-29. Ellen Flynn-Heapes, is past president of SPARKS: The Center for Strategic Planning, a company design lab for building great organizations. Ellen has written or contributed to seven books and over 100 articles on company growth and transition in the design professions. SPARKS partners consult with firms, agencies, and owners dedicated to the built environment.

SPARKS can be reached at (703) 838-8080 or at www.ForSparks.com.

4.4 Ashford, J. L., pp 181-2.

Cramer, James P. & Scott Simpson, pp 256-9.

www.mqia.com:

4.1a Stasiowski, Frank, *Firm Leadership and Quality Management.*

4.1b Andrews, Ray, *Practice Leadership and Managing Quality.*

4.2a Flynn-Heapes, Ellen, *Achieving a* **Strategic** *Strategic Plan*.

Epigrams

4.1 Maister, David H. (1997) *True Professionalism,* The Free Press, p 158.

4.2 Flynn-Heapes, Ellen (2004) *Achieving a* **strategic** *strategic plan,* www.mqia.com.

4.3 Flynn-Heapes, Ellen (2000) *Creating Wealth*, p 113.

4.4 Bennis, Warren, p 172.

5 People

Party time at AIS - last Friday of the month

We have a happy QM Task Group, at least for the moment ...

All about Alice...

Your penalty for skipping the serious stuff is a lunchtime assignment: mosey on down to your nearest bookstore that stocks business titles, find David Maister's *Practice What You Preach,* turn to pages 113-120 and read 'All about Alice'. If you don't buy the book, I owe you a drink.

If you've just been reading the cartoons and skipping the serious stuff, you've come to the right place.

You've come to the **right** ***place, because here is where the cartoons – the 'present reality' – intersect with the principles and theories of the text – the 'preferred future'. Here they cross paths on the journey.***

It's not the QM system that is hard to design or implement – what takes time, in huge slabs, is the culture change that gets in the way. Our friends at AIS Space Design aren't struggling with the wording of their quality statements; they are struggling with human nature, and the challenges that brings to any small but fundamental change in most organizations.

The agendas of the 'dynamos' tend to upset the agendas of the 'cruisers', and threatens the security of the 'losers', both of whom hunker down and resist whatever is about to happen, or even might possibly happen. As a result, we get a lot of hidden agendas, which become major, time-devouring roadblocks to evolution and growth of the practice.

Dr. Deming's point is well made: 'Remove barriers to pride of workmanship' – but what happens when the practice owners are the barriers? Savvy practice owners recognize the potential for being unconsciously obstructive, and brave up to '360 degree' performance reviews.

5.1 Client relationship management

To stay competitive and therefore valuable, throw out all your old assumptions about how you 'should' do business. Think unexpected, contrary and outrageous thoughts. Align your organization with your clients' interests first, forming a kind of 'virtual partnership' that can accomplish amazing things by breaking down traditional client/ architect barriers.

James Cramer & Scott Simpson

Michael Lindell, our intrepid cartoonist, received a letter from *Fortune* magazine, saying that they had been learning about him, and they knew ten things about him, which they listed. He says they were 'spot on' with eight, and the other two were arguable. He was so impressed that he bought a subscription. *Fortune's* data mining was, in his case, a total success. Can you translate this idea to your own marketing program?

CRM is a recently coined business acronym; short for 'customer relationship management'. In some circles, it has a meaning that designers would find alien: to mass marketers it means collecting vast amounts of data by using customer incentive programs and other sources (fair means and foul) to learn the details of certain markets, 'mine' that data to profile buying habits, and then target prospective customers with tailored 'buy this product' strategies.

To architects and other built environment professionals, it means something more like 'quality care' of the clients we've got, so they pay their invoices promptly, overlook any reasons to sue us, say nice things to their friends about us, and come back when they need another project. I'll use CRM in this sense.

We tend not to associate CRM with marketing or market positioning However, I suggest to you that we *should* more closely associate marketing and CRM, and that we can learn something valuable from the mass marketers.

In case the above two arguments haven't jumped off the page at you, I'll spell them out: (a) Should not our total approach to finding, and working with, clients be identical – all part of a single plan and implementation? and (b) As part of such a plan, should we not find out as much as possible about our prospective clients before creating that plan?

Few organizations in the real estate game understand CRM better than Mitsui Fudosan Co., the largest real estate developer and second-largest housing developer in Japan. Key Resource Hideki Kiyono, MFC Customer Satisfaction Manager, whose role is to translate Mitsui's CRM knowledge into guidance of Mitsui's architects, has this advice, prepared for this handbook:

An owner's perspective by Hideki Kiyono

Owners develop and manage condominiums or commercial buildings as their business. Keys for success in business are customer satisfaction, speed, and ambitions (goals). Customer satisfaction is the most comprehensive and important factor. Owners are customers for architects but customers to owners are users, which means users are the *real* customers for any project.

When we think of condominiums, users choose only one among a lot of condominiums, and their measurement is how they will be satisfied with the condominium. Consequently, architects should consider how users would make a 'good living' in the condominium and evaluate that in their design considerations. Users don't buy a unit by itself – but a *life* there.

First Impressions

When people are going to buy something, how long do they think before their decision? It might depend on the commodity, such as chocolate, shampoo, TV, car, or condominium. However, according to a survey, there seems to be little difference in time in choosing between shampoo and a condominium! The *difference* is whether customers would feel uneasy or not after their decision.

Customers who buy condominiums have uneasy days, thinking whether it was a good choice or not. The process of buying a condominium takes some days, of course, but most people have almost decided when they have good, strong impressions at the first glance of excellent model rooms (display suites) or a beautiful exterior. Mitsui Fudosan expects these impressions to be carefully planned, designed and directed by its architects. This is the beginning of winning customer satisfaction.

Total Quality

The first impression (of a new project) is the 'Wow! factor', which touches the customer's heart in looking at the building or being inside it. A 'touching space' contributes to customers' experiential satisfaction, and we call it EQ, for experiential quality. EQ comes from creativity in the design approach. Mitsui Fudosan also defines two more qualities, LQ and OQ. LQ, latent quality is the opposite of latent defects, which might cause loss to customers in the future. As LQ will be hidden after completion, we are very careful in construction process. OQ, object quality, is the obvious finish or surface.

These three kinds of quality put together are the *total quality*. The architect should understand the required standards of the three kinds of quality in the project, to accomplish total quality. Total quality is evaluated by prospective purchasers and finally valued by owners. Customers are not professionals regarding quality, but they actually evaluate and pass judgment on the condominium. Architects are expected to express the feeling of total quality in the project by realizing the three kinds of design quality.

The Chinese characters that form the Japanese word for quality, hing-shitzu, translate as 'object quality', and this is mirrored in the Japanese approach to quality, which insists on perfection in project finishes.

My work with Mitsui in 2001-2003 involved helping them to reposition their overall approach to expand their customers' appreciation of a more comprehensive idea of quality. Specifically this meant introducing the ideas of unseen or 'hidden' quality – latent quality (the opposite of latent defects); and the kind of quality you could feel, but not see – which we called 'experiential' quality.

This 'quality triumverate' adds depth to Mitsui's marketing program, creating an unassailable marketing differentiator, as well as 'raising the bar' for their architects (with EQ) and contractors (with LQ). As a result, 'EQ-LQ-OQ' has become a new part of their language, a way of talking about specific aspects of a project that all within the organization – as well as their customers – understand. - Ed.

More info...

There is lot written on CRM specific to our industry as well as to professional services consulting generally. I've noted some of the better examples under *Resources* at the end of Part 5.

5.2 QM in human resources

Many of the changes that a firm makes to adapt to outside conditions affect staff more than anticipated and often in unexpected ways.

Cynthia A. Woodward

The concept of 'human resources' strikes many as being somewhat impersonal and even debasing. Its use is so widespread, however, that we'll use it here – even though 'HR' is just a fancy term for 'people'.

Ms. Woodward continues:

> To some degree, careful planning can minimize the impact of change. Unanticipated reactions can be addressed as they occur. Be prepared for signs of unrest by realizing that they may appear.
>
> In the uncertain environment in which design firms work, change is perceived to be caused by a downturn in work that may necessitate a reduction in staff. Even potentially positive changes, like the addition of a new partner, introduction of a CADD system, sudden growth, new project types, or internal reorganization, require a period of adaptation.
>
> Preparation for change must work from the top down. When managers of a firm accept that change is going to occur, they should educate themselves about it and then develop strategic plans for smooth implementation.

Candy approached Clea, asking if there was something more she could do to help, now that the library was up-to-date and people's filing trays were not overflowing. Clea suggested that she organize up-to-date **resumés** ***for everybody in the practice, including updating their training records. 'Good as done', she said – perhaps a little overly confidently....***

For an amusing (and true) account of what can happen when a manager refuses to delegate, read Ray Andrews *'The Story of Uncle Victor'* on the handbook website: www.mqia.com > People > 5.1a.

HR is a quality matter. ISO 9001 requires management to provide personnel who are competent, trained, skilled and experienced, and to provide training and maintain training records (clause 6.2), as well as to provide appropriate work environments (clause 6.4).

These requirements are expanded in the guide document ISO 9004, with useful recommendations on how to involve people in the improvement of the effectiveness and efficiency of the organization, guidelines for assessing competence, planning for education and training, and considerations of work environments.

Design practices seem to have a curious ambivalence about HR. In my time on the AIA Practice Management PIA Advisory Group (later Practice Management Knowledge Community), we surveyed AIA members to determine their practice priorities, in terms of what their 'hot button' issues were.

Over two surveys, one in a 'hot' market, and another where there was a turndown in work, HR and HR management came as the top priority both times – roughly 40 percent of all respondents said it was one of three key issues in their practice.

Quotations from Cynthia Woodward reproduced with permission of The American Institute of Architects, 1735 New York Avenue, NW. , Washington, D.C, 20006

On that basis, we built the 2003 Practice Management Fall Conference around this theme, with a stellar faculty, very well promoted. Guess what? Hardly anybody came! Conclusion: AIA members see HR as very important, but won't pay to learn more about how to improve their HR programs! Go figure.

On that basis, should I devote a long chapter to it here? Is anybody still reading?

What I can tell you is that the majority of authorities in practice management consider this to be a very important topic. If you *do* want to know more about how to get the best out of your people, how to keep your best people from wandering off, how to find and attract the best people, those who have the answers have written about it – extensively and well. I've identified some of the best of these under ***Resources*** at the end of Part 5.

One of the biggest challenges when hiring smart people is controlling your ego. – Frank Stasiowski

What I can also tell you, from observing what I would call the 'emotional climate' in a huge number of design practices, is that practice managers who really know how to motivate and excite the staff they are responsible for are fairly rare. Not that they don't want to – they don't really understand how to, and are almost never coached in the art.

I have observed that in those practices where the managers are 'enlightened', and have these skills, productivity and efficiency simply are not issues.

David Maister's research is *most* interesting here, and should be a clanging wake-up bell to every practice leader. You have to read his book to get the full picture, but what Maister discovered was that employee satisfaction is an incredible lever of profitability.

On the basis of results from these four indexes of employee satisfaction, a one-point jump in ratings (say from 4 to 5) – a 10 to 15 percent improvement in satisfaction – *caused a 42 percent improvement* in financial performance, including both profitability and growth. Here are the questions:

- I am highly satisfied with my job.
- I get a great sense of accomplishment from my work.
- The overwhelming majority of the work I'm given is challenging rather than repetitive.
- I am committed to this firm as a career opportunity.

Now, before you start administering these questions, digest the rest of his research. If, as a practice boss, you would like to increase the profitability of your practice, here is an opportunity! However, to take it, you will need to figure out how to raise the overall satisfaction of your staff. Think about that in terms of my experience in running the 2003 AIA conference on HR.

5.3 Quality in design management

Forget about getting it right first time – the goal is to get it right last time.

David Sutherland

Managing design processes is central to QM thinking: ISO 9001, clause 7.3, requires that the organization plan and control design and development, with specific requirements for design inputs, design outputs, and design reviews.

'Development' in ISO 9001 language is best understood in the design firm as being equal to 'documentation'.

What Sutherland, Director of Planning at Fender Katsalidis Architects, Melbourne, refers to here is the process of iteration that marks virtually every design effort. Because of the complexity of most design problems, and the nearly infinite number of possible solutions, good design goes through a series of iterative 'what if?' loops that create and reality-test increasingly detailed solutions. He comments that the 'right' design solution is often defined by a point where the designer has run out of time, money or patience – that is, has explored as far as *practically* possible all the possibilities to improve the design.

The concept of 'right first time' is incremental, working to get each step of the iterative process as 'right' as possible, in the context of the full complexity of the whole design. Thus, quality is continuously 'managed' within the design team at the micro level, as well as by practice leaders at the whole practice level.

Scott Braley's contact details are listed in section 5.3 under *Resources* at the end of Part 5.

Key Resource **Scott Braley** prepared a 9-page chapter for this handbook on this essential topic. I've edited his paper down to fit the space available here, but you can download his unabridged chapter from *www.mqia.com > People > 5.3 Quality in design management.*

Quality in design management by Scott Braley

Design is the defining core competency of design professionals, and it is a highly regarded skill among building professionals as well. Moreover, notwithstanding the sometimes flip and incendiary comments of some, clients *do* care about design and they do care about quality. In fact, everybody cares about design, and everybody wants design quality managed. That interest and concern is pervasive; it is expansive and it is essential.

A sure sign of naiveté – and typically a premonition of trouble ahead – is a statement along the lines of 'I'm going to manage the design on this project.' On the other hand, wise leaders and design professionals consistently say 'we're going to manage the design process' or 'we're going to manage the design quality.' Important and telling distinctions indeed!

My experience has been that it is both frustrating and ill-advised to attempt to limit or define the boundaries of design in the overall project development process. That experience is shared by design managers around the globe. *As much as some might like, you cannot simply draw a ring around 'design' and then 'manage' design.* That is the first lesson we must learn, and it is a constant thought we must maintain as we address quality in design management.

Any designer worth his salt will tell you that design is a disciplined endeavor. The problem is, we just don't know when the 'Ah-ha!' is going to come! Worse, neither we, nor the builders and clients, know when they'll reach *their* personal 'Ah-Ha'.

Design professionals and design managers alike continue to express a valid concern that we find it hard to know when 'enough is enough'. Not because we lack skill, discipline or commitment. Rather, because we simply cannot read the client's mind, or the builder's mind – or even our fellow designer's mind – regarding quality.

Virtually every participant in the design and construction process will admit that design is important. It is more difficult to reach consensus on just how to manage design.

Managing quality in design is a big part of how this handbook came about, and the primary focus of this chapter in particular.

When combined with the suggestions included in the other chapters, you need look no further to answer 'how to manage quality in design.'

Similarly, most will tell you that it's an ongoing struggle to know how much to document, how much to dictate, how much leave open to interpretation. I refer to this as *'bridging the abyss of trust in managing design quality.'*

While it is not possible to manage 'design' per se, it is possible to manage design quality by focusing on both process and standards. In this chapter we'll discuss just how to do that – with an approach that I have found works for all types of projects (architectural, engineering, process, information technology) and all types of clients (private, public).

Moreover, this approach can be applied in market sectors throughout the world with a minimum amount of refinement based on cultural and regional preferences.

Who manages quality in design?

Although it is widely bantered about, and sounds delightful on the surface, what does *not* work is to say that 'managing quality in design is everyone's responsibility.' When it becomes 'everyone's' responsibility, no one is responsible!

Some one person must accept responsibility for and successfully complete those three essential tasks. *There must be a single design manager on every project.*

While there are many participants, and clearly each has a say, the fundamental responsibility for managing quality in design belongs squarely to and with the design manager. *The design manager is the individual project team member designated to be responsible to: (a) define project-specific design quality, (b) implement a plan of action to foster design quality, and (c) ensure that appropriate design results are achieved.*

Some will say this working definition sounds a lot like the role of 'project manager'. Others will say the role is clearly that of the designer. Still others will say it's the construction manager, the owner, or the client representative. Experience indicates that virtually any of those position titles will work, so long as the role and responsibility is discussed and agreed among all team members. Regardless of title, the role is the same.

Defining and managing quality is both an illusive and critically important endeavor. To make the job easier, begin by defining quality in terms of expectation/agreement, requirements, standards, process and result.

Manage expectations, reach agreement

Quality is defined by expectation. Let's look at the process of managing expectations vis-à-vis design. Begin with a clear understanding that *expectations are not agreements.* Expectations involve only one person, agreements engage two or more people. You cannot manage quality in design based on expectations – you must have clearly understood agreements.

At best, it is difficult to obtain clear agreement. At worst, design activities begin with the gossamer hope that we'll reach agreement or consensus as we go forward (look out!).

We are talking about two or more people having the same idea and understanding of what is achievable, what is going to happen, what can be expected and what is promised in terms of end result. It is imperative that the design manager facilitates a process that moves all parties away from the isolation of expectation to the collaboration of agreement.

Consider the influencing constituents and stakeholders, including the client, end user, design firm leaders, builders, the public and the 'design professionals' themselves. We list the design team last not because they are least important – rather, because a wise designer / design manager knows that genuinely listening to the constituents, and interpreting their thoughts into the language of design, is the quintessential role of the designer. That is not to say that the designer is reduced to a highly skilled stenographer or interpreter. Rather, in this respect the designer is more than a listener and cataloger – *the designer is a sensor and a creator.*

There are a variety of forums to 'listen' to constituents, manage expectations and reach design quality agreements. The optimum forum is face-to-face. You may wish to use historical references, previous personal experiences, contemporary undertakings, even tours of existing facilities – or a combination of these. A 'neutral' facilitator can help. The agenda for these discussions is similar and straightforward. As a design manager and as a facilitator, I have found it best to begin with, and stick to, six basic questions. They pack quite a punch and in answering them you'll get all you need to manage expectations and reach agreement on design quality. They are:

While some argue that this conversation needs to take place only once, we have found that truly successful design managers repeat and refine the expectations/agreements balance by having design dialogue sessions before project work begins, and at key strategic points throughout the overall design process.

- What do we, together, hope we can achieve?
- What must we achieve at a minimum?
- What is the horizon of possibility?
- What are the boundary limits of 'difficult,' 'improbable' and 'impossible'?
- What is most, to least, important among all the variables?
- What really gets us excited – in both a positive and negative connotation?

We have found that these discussions are best conducted in informal to semi-formal work sessions. They are most productive when the client is allowed and required to begin the dialogue.

Document design requirements

Regardless of how you choose to manage expectations, *formal documentation of design requirements is an essential component of design agreement.* In fact, many have found that the process of documenting design requirements in and of itself does much to identify and manage expectations.

You can use a variety of techniques, including but certainly not limited to, traditional briefing or programming processes, extended needs assessments, comparative modeling or simply cataloging project assumptions and understandings.

Every client – public or private, profit or non-profit, experienced or new to the game – has some form of quality goals and objectives in its working vocabulary. Forget the jargon of the design and construction industry (or at least 'translate'). Use a language that will resonate with your client. As we help design teams 'speak' in the client's vocabulary, we have often created bi-directional translation guides.

A technique we have used with great success is based on developing and using a design vocabulary that is patterned after the client's business or functional vocabulary.

Design requirements should be documented in categories such as image, form, function, technical performance and constructability. While those were not listed in order of importance, we have found them a good place to start. We find it best to document these in a draft format and literally review them line-by-line with the client.

No client can – or should be expected to – understand and agree with design requirements that cannot be documented succinctly in written form. We believe the design manager should be the author. This documentation process should proceed through a disciplined and logically progressive sequence of listening, preparing draft(s), refining, reaching agreement and approving via 'sign-off' (by both the client and the design team).

We find it best to review, confirm and refine design requirements at three key intervals – these are: at every project phase change (e.g., when moving from concept to detailed design), at every major phase change (e.g., any single or multiple changes which represent an aggregate of 10% of project cost), and at pre-determined calendar milestones (e.g., every month).

I have not met a good designer who opposes documenting design requirements. Virtually every designer with whom I have worked told of the difficulties of working as members of teams that have no clear understanding of design goals and requirements.

In addition to the documentation efforts, the design manager should ensure that all members of the project team (including client and builder) agree upon a process for evolving, refining and testing the design requirements as the project goes forward.

A final, and crucial, technique is to establish a 'design precedence' and 'design hierarchy'. Design precedence refers to the agreed understanding that design will progress through various stages, and design quality will be evolved. As such, as the design progresses, previous design quality is superseded. For example, a conceptual or schematic design solution supersedes the tabulated program or briefing requirements, and so forth in all subsequent phases of development.

Design hierarchy on the other hand refers to the agreed upon level of importance and relative ranking of various types or areas of quality that comprise a project's overall design. For example, one team may agree that functional design quality ranks higher in importance that technical quality.

To illustrate – as a manager of the design team for a collegiate library project, my fellow team members and I decided that the benefits of occupant comfort and the psychological influences of darkness ranked relatively higher than exterior image and form.

We therefore eliminated multi-floor vision glazing in favor of a more traditional and user-friendly form of fenestration in the lounge/reading room. In a high-rise office building project, we made a conscious design quality decision that the level of design detailing should be greater in the public lobby than in the individual floor lobbies of a major anchor tenant's space.

Similarly, in a solar collector field project we agreed that steam generation capability and consistency would outrank solar conversion efficiency in determining collector design.

While these types of decisions may seem basic and even intuitive to some, the design manager must address them in a generic manner. That is how design quality requirements are defined and managed.

Establish design quality standards

A design standard in this context is nothing more than a predetermined and agreed-upon level of performance.

This definition applies to four cardinal areas of design – image and form, documentation and constructability, functional operation (by the end user) and the design process itself.

The responsibility of the design manager, and the design team, is to determine which standards should/must be considered, develop standards as appropriate, and determine how the standards will be applied. Some standards exist and are readily known – building codes, ordinances, professional regulations.

As design professionals, we must identify, research and bring these standards to the process. Other standards exist but are not so readily known – client standards and procedures, commercial requirements (e.g., insurance and risk underwriters).

The design manager can express project-specific design standards from three distinct perspectives:

Absolute design quality

Comparable design quality

Relative design quality

These 'perspectives' are explained in detail in the unabridged version of this chapter on the website.

As design professionals we must request, and require, that the client identify, research and bring these standards to the process. Still other standards do not exist or are not so readily known. These are custom-designed standards, and it is the design manager's responsibility to craft these as part of the standards process.

As these three categories of standards are blended, it is important to craft and document a project-specific standard for design quality. We have found it best to express these project-specific standards in absolute, comparative or relative terms.

Absolute standards stand alone and establish minimum levels of acceptable design quality. Comparative standards are based on a benchmark. Relative standards are linked to a similar project or design component that helps define design quality in terms of 'better than', 'same as' or 'not as stringent as'.

Craft the design process

The next step in the collaborative process of managing design quality is to focus on the design process itself. *It is important to define and map the design process at the earliest stages of project activity.* On my projects, we craft design process either before work begins, or concurrent with the first five percent of project design activity. Crafting the process is an essential element of developing the project approach and project work plan.

The best technique for crafting the process is to progress through a series of logically linked questions. We suggest you assemble the key team participants and address the following questions. While order of questions is not rigid, it is important to establish a 'process logic' that is both comfortable and appropriate for your specific design team. The questions we use to conceive and map the 'design process' are:

How will we define the design problem?

How will we conceive design ideas, concepts?

How will we probe design solutions?

How will we test alternative solutions?

How will we make the initial and 'big' decisions regarding design direction?

How will we document and communicate the design ideas and progression of thought?

How will we critique design?

How flexible will we be throughout the process?

How will we make the final decision on design?

We have found it best to address these questions in a two-phase approach. I counsel design managers to meet first with the design team and develop a set of 'draft' answers and craft an outline design process. This 'draft' is then reviewed and fully developed with the client and builder members of the design team. A key consideration is the avoidance of 'pride of authorship' in the processing efforts. In particular, we as design professionals must accept our role as design leaders with a balanced demeanor.

I have experienced great success among design teams who act as stewards of the design process, while those who dictate process are doomed to ultimate failure. Be mindful that we must be firm and committed as we guide the team in defining process, but not so strong in our direction that we lose commitment and 'buy in'. *With too little direction the designer or design manager may be seen as lacking in expertise. With too much or too forceful direction the perception will quickly shift to cries of 'design arrogance'.*

We have found this approach to be a formidable challenge for those design professionals and design managers we have helped through the years. Most firms who use this approach find that using a facilitator is essential. Either a designated member of the design team or an outside facilitator can fill the role. Impartiality and dispassionate leadership are essential requirements of this individual, and design team members may find it quite challenging to subdue their personal opinions and motivations.

Finally, as the team creates the design process, it is important for all parties to address a multivariate overlay of considerations regarding influence and timing. The 'influence' guidelines define who will have input, influence, control, review and/or approval authority. The 'timing' guidelines pertain to the point in the design process at which an individual will have that influence – before, during or after the design decisions is made.

Ensure acceptable results

If you are unsure of the differences between 'assure', 'ensure' and 'insure', the website version of this chapter covers these ideas – important distinctions in design quality.

Once these actions are taken, and process is defined, the final step in managing design quality is to focus on results.

It is at this juncture that managing design quality blends with and is inextricably linked to the other chapters of the handbook. *Results, final outcomes and ultimate satisfaction in quality are the product of all of the recommendations and observations made in the handbook.* Let's take a look at the part we play during the 'design' phases.

First, let's get on the same page regarding definition. When we speak of ensuring we mean just that – ensure. Some debate the meaning of the word, and others have watered down the intent by saying that 'insure' and 'ensure' are just different spellings of the same word. It has been my consistent experience that this is a fundamentally and critically important vocabulary and glossary lesson to learn. Moreover, in today's changing economic and risk marketplace the pressure on the design is increasing.

As design professionals we are charged with the responsibility and right to ensure that design quality is managed and achieved. We are responsible and should be empowered to ensure (take appropriate action, have appropriate authority) that design quality is achieved. We are not responsible to carte blanche insure (be financially responsible for) the quality of all that is designed.

The full version of this chapter also contains examples of varied and refined design quality standards.

And we certainly are not responsible to insure (pay for) every lapse in design quality or failure to meet design expectations. This is among the most volatile issues in today's design and construction industry, and participants around the world struggle with issues of financial responsibility, errors/omissions, failure to meet expectations and bruised egos.

*The point for design professionals and design managers alike is know and define their responsibilities, and take the appropriate actions to **ensure** results.*

Within the purview of 'ensuring' design results, we as design professionals and design managers should begin with 'result' assurance. In my experience, design quality 'assurance' should at a minimum address the following key questions:

- Are roles and responsibilities clearly understood and being fulfilled?

- Is there a plan and process to achieve the goal(s)?
- Is the plan understood by and being followed by all participants?

Let's look also at ensuring our design goal or goals:

- Are there design goals?
- Are the goals truly aggressive and achievable?
- Are the goals linked to our standards?
- Are we fulfilling our expectation and achieving our goals?

Finally, let's examine the concept of ensuring appropriate 'control' with regard to design. We have found it best to focus on three design perspectives: concept, filters and execution.

- Is the fundamental design concept sound – does it 'work', is it appropriate, is the design going in the right direction?
- Are our design filters working well – are we catching mistakes early in the process, are we making mid-course corrections?
- Are we executing as planned and intended – are others interpreting our design documents and intent appropriately, are we supporting the other members of the team as needed, are we/they achieving the levels of quality we intended?

In summary, design is what we do – it is our core competency. Managing the quality in design is the nucleus of that competency. In my work with design professionals, builders and clients I have consistently found that too little is failure just as sure as too much is failure. Recalling the wisdom of Irish lore – when it comes to quality in design management 'enough is a feast'.

Hugh experiences an unpremeditated buy-in, for the wrong reason

5.4 Team-building and coaching

Coaching ... lies at the heart of developing others. Excellence in this competence is emerging as second only to team leadership among superior managers.

Daniel Goleman

As business changes, so do the traits needed to excel. Data tracking the talents of star performers over several decades reveal that two abilities that mattered relatively little for success in the 1970s have become crucially important in the 1990s: team building and adapting to change. And entirely new capabilities have begun to appear as traits of star performers, notably change catalyst and leveraging diversity. New challenges demand new talents. – Daniel Goleman

Is team-building a quality issue? Yes, it is: Just think about what it takes to get a project designed and constructed today. Success – as measured by the quality of both processes and results – is almost entirely dependent on team dynamics. Yet, only very rarely do any of the people responsible for creating and managing those teams have any training in the delicate art of team-building.

Team building *is* an art, not a science – and one that must be learned if those doing it are to build great teams. Goleman, whose ground-breaking study of emotional intelligence found that the 'crucial' need for these skills is a fairly recent phenomenon (see sidebar). Team-building skills are best learned through coaching – another relatively rare skill in design and construction circles.

Most team dynamics in the design and construction industry are more dysfunctional than not, incredibly inefficient and time-consuming. Not that there aren't brilliant examples, but – in my experience – they are fairly rare.

You can learn something about coaching from reading books, but reading won't make you a coach. It's something one learns first-hand in a coaching environment: observing a master at work, seeing how people (including one's own self) respond and change and grow with a talented coach.

Team management is required as a function of ISO 9001. Clause 7.3.1 requires firms to manage what it calls 'interfaces' between members of design and development teams, such that proper communication is ensured and responsibilities are clear (my interpretation).

The best team-building coaches I've had the pleasure of working with are Key Resources William Ronco (See 6.8, his chapter on partnering) and Scott Braley – see 5.3.)

Ronco, writing in the *AIA Handbook, Update 2005*, notes that teams often have advantages in synergism, idea generation, motivation and organizational linkages. He also cautions that teams typically face problems with performance slippage, individual negativity and passivity, members keeping an individual focus, 'groupthink' that fosters responsibility avoidance, questionable ethics, and ineffective leadership.

He notes that 'the challenge for team building is to tap into the strengths teams offer while reducing or eliminating potential problems.' Ronco says there is no 'team-building process', noting 'Each firm must develop an effort tailored to its personality and the personalities of the individuals in it. Team building is generally developed as a series of activities intended to improve a group's communication and ability to interact.'

Team building often takes place as a 'retreat' away from the office. Ronco cautions that effective team-building is an on-going process; that 'it is preferable to spread team-building exercises over several months, with clear assignments and pilot action steps between sessions.' Ronco's practical advice in the *AIA Handbook 2005 Update* covers the following steps to designing team-building activities for architects:

- Assessing team performance.
- Using personality profiles to build mutual understanding and trust.
- Clarifying team goals.
- Strengthening regular group meetings.
- Facilitating meeting participation by all team members.
- Clarifying individual roles and responsibilities and identifying mutual information needs.
- Engaging in group decision-making exercises.

Norman Kaderlan's chapter *Working with Groups* (see Resources) is an excellent description of group dynamics that provides good background understanding if you are thinking about team-building. He notes 'The *way* you do things affects how well you do them'.

I noted above that the way to learn coaching was by being coached, not by reading about it. However, if you want to sneak up on the topic, and are a little nervous that your well-concealed weaknesses might be exposed to the light of day in a coaching environment, there is no better place to start than by reading McKenna and Maister's *Part Three: Coaching the Team* from *First Among Equals*. Here are the titles of the chapters in their analysis, to whet your appetite:

11 Clarifying group goals: *Does your group have specific, clearly articulated, shared objectives?*

12 Develop your group's rules of membership: *What do members of your group owe to each other?*

13 Build team trust: *What gets group members to trust each other?*

14 Throw down a challenge: *Has your group selected an exciting challenge?*

15 Energize your meetings: *What are good meeting disciplines?*

16 Give recognition: *How do you acknowledge accomplishments?*

17 Resolve interpersonal conflicts: *What do you do when team members fall out?*

18 Deal with your crises: *How do you respond to dramatic events?*

If you've read these two pages, and thought you were now going to know how to be a team-builder or coach – and didn't get there – remember that my goal is to provide an information hub to what you need to know – to save you hours and hours of searching to get to the right place, first time.

5.5 QM & improving performance & productivity

Any set of criteria for excellence should include the ability to adapt.

Geary Rummler and Alan Brache

Geary Rummler and Alan Brache state that organizational systems adapt or die. They say the success of the survivors depends on the effectiveness and speed with which they adapt to changes in the external environment – such as client's needs, competition or economic change – and in their internal operations – such as rising costs, inefficiencies or new service opportunities.

Few topics in design management raise designers' hackles as quickly as a discussion about improving productivity or measuring performance – the very idea is heard as code for driving people harder and harder. The idea of 'work smarter, not harder' is an old cliché; meaningless.

Dr. Stephen Covey, guru of *7 Habits of Highly Successful People*, uses the metaphor of the woodsman cutting down a tree. A passerby asks him why he doesn't sharpen his saw, and he replies that he is too busy cutting down the tree to stop and sharpen the saw.

I live in a country where there still are butcher shops, where the meat does *not* only come shrink-wrapped. I've observed that the first thing the butcher does when I ask for a piece of steak or whatever, is to wack his already razor-sharp knife across the whetstone a few swipes. No matter how sharp the tool, or how small the project, each project deserves tool-sharpening. *If only we could start to think that way!* As long as we have a strong negative reaction to productivity improvement, we won't 'get it'.

Productivity improvements are not about grinding endlessly away at the tree trunk, they are about *sharpening the tools* at every available opportunity. Tools, here, means *processes*, not pencils! And 'sharpening' means *adapting*, as emphasized by Rummler and Brache.

I first met Dr. Debby King-Rowley at a Melbourne conference on trans-national education, where we were on a speaker panel together. Debby was part of the Motorola team that developed Motorola's successful bid to win the first Malcolm Baldridge Award for Quality. That winning program became Six Sigma, and Debby became part of the Motorola University faculty, who travelled the world, training others in the Motorola methodology.

Debby now heads up Burlington Consulting in Melbourne, and her clients are still world-class companies.

Key Resource **Debby King-Rowley** comes from the world of big-company corporate training. Her clients include some of the largest companies in the world; an environment almost diametrically opposite to your typical design practice. I was interested to see that, when asked to write something about performance improvements in architecture, she zeroed in on exactly those things that we struggle with, such as reducing re-work and finding simple ways to 'sharpen our tools' through process standardization and other strategies.

Here is Debby's chapter, edited to fit the space available. Her unabridged paper is on the website: www.mqia.com > People > 5.5a *QM & Productivity.*

QM and Productivity by Deborah King-Rowley

This chapter looks at the relationship between QM and the productivity of design firms. The question may readily be asked, is that relationship positive, negative or inverse?

If you take the currently most popularly held view, you might quickly respond that it is a negative relationship.

Your argument might be that since you are spending more time on writing and referring to documentation, you have less time to do your 'real work', and therefore you are less productive. You may be a little less cynical and respond that it is at least a positive relationship, and that the effort you expend on QM is matched by an increase in the productive output of you and your firm. The desirable relationship is, of course, that of an inverse relationship between the two concepts. That is, over time the amount of effort that has to be expended on QM decreases while the productive output of your firm, as a result of implementing QM, increases.

These three possibilities can be shown as graphs:

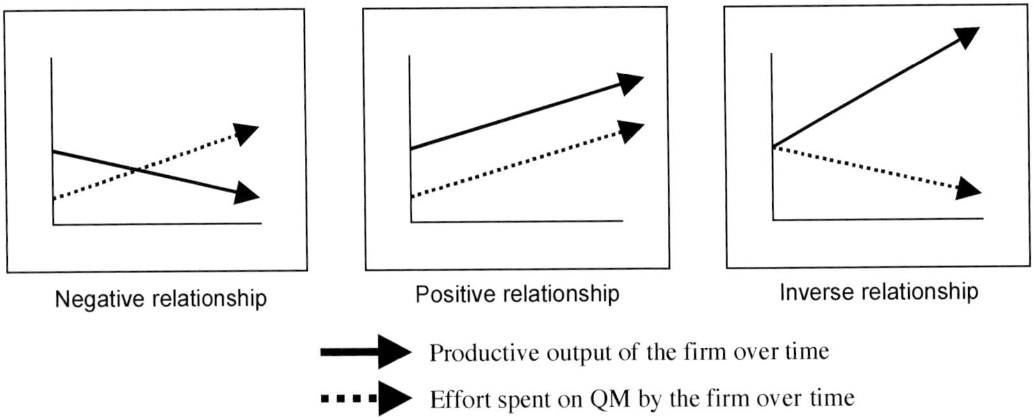

Figure 5.5.1 *Productive output vs. QM effort*

Key questions ...

What do we mean by productivity? At what period of time during the QM implementation schedule are you taking the snapshot?

According to the *Concise Oxford Dictionary*, one meaning of productivity is 'the effectiveness of productive effort'. Anytime the word 'effectiveness' shows up in a definition, I think it is important to bring up the word 'efficiency' as well since the two can work well in tandem.

In this context, what do we mean by each? In leadership and management lingo, effectiveness means 'doing the right thing' while efficiency means 'doing things right'. What if we combine these two concepts and look at the phrase 'doing the right things right'? Wouldn't this equate to organising our work to meet and exceed the expectations of our clients with no rework needed? This sounds very much like QM and a sound goal that would please clients and create opportunities for the firm, that is, opportunities for increased creativity and productivity.

Increasing creative opportunities

For architects, the more time and opportunity for creativity, the better. But how does QM provide increased opportunity for creativity and productive output?

To answer this, let's take a look at artists at work. Regardless of the medium in which they work, there are some aspects of their work that artists perform routinely once they have built up their experience and have had ample practice. After a lot of experience, their approach to some aspects of their work becomes standardised. As an example, some phases of an artist's commission could be shown as a workflow, below.

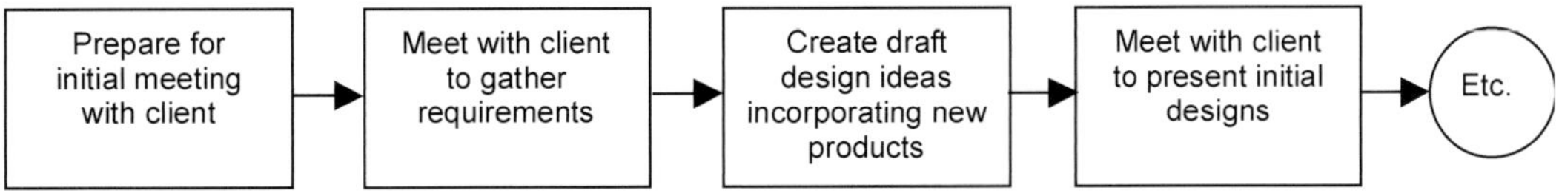

Figure 5.5.2 *Workflow for an artist's commission*

Architects' work effort and creativity need not be expended on determining how to conduct some of the work in many of the phases. Some of this work can and should be standardised, and as this work is standardised, it frees up architects to use their creative energy for design.

For example, determining a set of questions to be used in the initial meeting with the client would reduce the amount of effort and time used in any future initial client meetings. Architects would likely be the more experienced party in the meeting as this would be a routine part of their work while it is possibly the first or second exposure to the experience for the client.

Benefits

What are the benefits of having this part of architects' work standardised? At a minimum, architects have the opportunity to bring additional value to the meeting, bringing up items that might well be overlooked by the more novice clients. The architects' reputation is enhanced as being 'easy to do work with'.

Often the benefits are more tangible than this. There are three specific benefits that are directly related to creativity and productivity. Let's examine these.

Rework: By asking specific, pre-determined probe questions, architects will often uncover expectations earlier that otherwise might erupt later in the process either jeopardising the design completely or causing rework. ***Rework is the prime enemy to creativity and productivity.*** Doing the same work twice eats up design time, creative energy and profit for the architects and induces frustration for the clients. This can generally be avoided by clarifying requirements upfront.

Increased reliability: When architects are on their own to determine the intent of client meetings, the questions to ask in leading the meetings, and the means of documenting the inputs from the clients, you would expect significant variation in the results of the meetings.

We can see from just looking at the example of standardising the approach to the initial client meeting that significant opportunities exist to increase the productivity within design firms.

As opportunities exist in the subsequent work undertaken by architects, another prime opportunity for increased productivity is that of building in standardized client checkpoints, aligned with key project milestones.

Some may go well and required information collected. In others, patchy information may be gathered, requiring follow-up calls, contacts and meetings. All of these add up to more time and expended energy. The pre-determined questions can help ensure with greater reliability the results of the client meetings.

Reduced preparation effort: Use of the pre-determined probe questions reduces the amount of effort that architects will need to spend in preparing for their initial meeting. Often the work required to prepare for meetings is seen as a distraction from the creative work of designing. If this is the case, then having some of the work required for the meetings prepared in standardised formats and fully adopted by the firm as 'how we routinely conduct our client meetings' frees architects to expend most of their energy on a creative design.

Learning curves in design

Experienced architects internalize phases of their work, along with specific questions, techniques and templates to aid them in the various steps. The amount of time it takes these masters to accomplish their expert levels varies from one to the next. It takes numerous projects and accompanying errors, lessons learned and 'do-differentlies.' We all know this as the 'learning curve'.

The shapes of individuals' learning curves are established by their own unique learning pattern. For some, working their way through a project is just that, moving from one task on to the next with the end in mind, and all energy focused on achieving that target. When they finish the project, they have achieved that success and may have attained a little wisdom that they can apply to the next project. For others, each project provides an opportunity to learn. At each phase, they are exploring options, considering alternatives, weighing up potential decisions, noting outcomes and growing professionally.

How can a firm benefit from the learning curve of the latter person? Are they lessons learned only for the individual, or can they be shared across the practice to the benefit of others and future clients? How can new designers learn from others' experiences to become more productive *earlier* in their careers?

Some may answer that you simply team up the novice with a more experienced architect. While this helps, it does not ensure success.

It exposes the new designer to the lessons of one master, *only* if that master thinks out loud as he proceeds through the phases of the project.

A better answer for bringing new designers up their learning curves more rapidly is to implement QM in the firm.

The underlying assumption of learning curves is that as we experience events we learn from these interactions at an *incidental level,* and that we unconsciously store these lessons away in our memory for retrieval and use in the future. With repeated exposure and involvement in events, we continually grow our repertoire of knowledge to aid us in the future.

By standardising and documenting some aspects of architects' work, new architects can learn at an *intentional level*. The lessons to be learned are not left to chance, but are channelled by the knowledge that has been systematically collected across the entire firm's experiences and built into standardised processes. The new entrants will be able to manoeuvre their way through standard processes much more effectively and efficiently from the very first project to which they are assigned. This will give them the opportunity, along with the other architects, to spend their creative effort on the design itself.

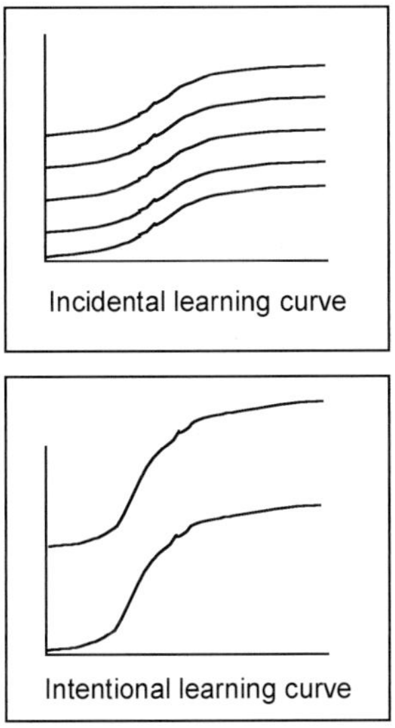

Figure 5.5.3 *Learning curves*

As illustrated here, with the implementation of QM, new architects can potentially achieve much higher levels of productivity with involvement in fewer projects, than when they are dependent on their own incidental learning. Thus the firm is able to reap productivity and profitability in the early days of hiring new architects.

Implementation issues

As with the implementation of any new concept or system, it takes concerted effort in the early days to learn what is to be done differently and concerted effort to implement the new behaviours.

Over time, the new behaviours become old hat and don't require effort, although they may still require some time to perform. For this reason, you would expect to see a sharp increase in the front end of a curve tracking effort being spent on implementing QM. Over time, the curve line would be expected to decrease significantly and level off to a minimum amount of effort.

Perhaps it would be helpful to keep in mind the Pareto Principle; that is, you want to get 80% of the result with 20% of the effort. No one would expect architects to spend more time on managing their work to meet their clients' requirements than working on their designs for their clients.

While it might seem like they are doing just that in the early days of implementation, in short time, they should be able to get 80% of the benefit of QM with no more than 20% of their total effort going into QM.

5.6 Teamwork in a matrix-style practice

Team management is a – perhaps the *– key to project success.*

Frank Stasiowski

Key Resource Paul Hinkley has prepared an extensive paper on this topic for this handbook; too comprehensive to be included in the space available. This chapter outlines his conclusions. You can download his paper from the website: www.mqia.com > People > 5.6a: *Quality Teamwork & Leadership.*

Quality teamwork & leadership by Paul Hinkley

Paul Hinkley, BE, CMC, AMAIPM is a Melbourne-based engineer, planner and software innovator with decades of team management experience worldwide.

This chapter outlines some practical guidelines for effective organization, teamwork and leadership for dynamic architectural firms focused on quality with responsiveness and flexibility, at the same time as keeping staff committed, satisfied, creative and productive.

For many years, staff in design offices and architectural firms worked for one boss. With the advent of greater demands being made on architects over the last two decades, and the greater emphasis on project teams, employees have found themselves working for two or more bosses.

Such organizations are more dynamic and flexible but more complicated and potentially chaotic. For many staff this is challenging and stimulating; for others it is confusing and often stressful. This challenge has been recognized by many companies as the 'matrix problem' and there are many vexed opinions about the effectiveness of various 'structures' or 'solutions'.

Unfortunately, many fail to see that the problem does not have solutions or structures: it is not a really a 'problem', but a fact of modern business and management. The need for responsiveness and flexibility in project and quality management is not going to go away, especially while turbulent business conditions prevail through the global economy (and may indefinitely into the future).

Over the last century there have been three types of organizations in both commercial and public environments, including design firms, by either intent or default: traditional hierarchical, laissez-faire and matrix-style. They compare as follows:

Factor	Traditional hierarchical	Laissez-faire	Matrix-style
Client and Quality focus	Internally focused, until client pressures prevail	Individually focused	Natural balance between client and quality focus and commercial imperatives
Responsiveness and flexibility	Slow to respond and resistant to change	Flexible but reactive to change	Fast to respond and flexible in approach, depending on leadership
Objectives and responsibilities	Simply defined vertically, and structured by policy and procedures	Typically unclear and chaotic	Negotiated vertically and horizontally by the leaders
Efficient coordination	Efficiently controlled by bureaucracy	Haphazard, ad hoc	Efficiently planned and coordinated by leaders
Sharing of expertise	Minimal sharing of resources	Ad hoc sharing of resources	Planned and continuous

The reality of the modern business environment is that all organizations have to cope with the problem of sharing scarce or costly resources between projects – in our case, skilled designers, architects, engineers or other specialists. For the last two decades, it has been simply impossible, or too costly, to allocate these people to a particular single project, one at a time.

The traditional and laissez-faire organizations have the distinct advantage of simplicity, but are less responsive to continual improvement and change.

The old cliché that 'no one can serve two masters' has been overturned by the dictum that 'all staff must be prepared to serve more than one master'. Today, every person in the team has to enjoy, tolerate or cope with the reality that one boss is not enough and two might be too many. My observation over more than two decades is that most people thrive in these conditions because of the stimulation and opportunities, but a minority find it quite difficult and personally threatening. This is a *leadership* issue.

The success of matrix-style organizations is relatively more dependent on effective leadership (than the other types). Examples of matrix-style organizations are shown in the website version of this paper. Managing and leading a modern matrix-style organization requires some discipline, commitment and commonsense, but it is not rocket-science. Exactly how you do this will depend on your particular firm, the business environment you operate in, and your broad quality objectives, but some basic practical guidelines are as follows (for details of these, see the website paper):

- ***Be clear about your principles:*** As are the manager or leader, be clear with yourself and with others about the general principles of your organization in terms of the five dimensions, or 'factors', in the diagram above, and the relative priorities of each.
- ***Minimize complexity:*** Poor management increases complexity and inevitably causes difficulties in monitoring and controlling projects; in the flow of information between team members; in delays in decision making because of the negotiation required and the possibility of conflicting instructions and guidance.
- ***Set project objectives:*** Provide clear project objectives in terms of quality, cost and time and functional technical objectives, so that all team members are working to common goals.
- ***Work to deliverables:*** Clarify and agree on exactly what your project or design deliverables are, on a daily or weekly basis. Ensure there is agreement within the project team who is responsible for each of the deliverables.
- ***Support those who follow:*** Ensure that responsibility for deliverables extends to working and coordinating with those to whom documents are 'handed over', such as engineering subconsultants.

In summary: The matrix-style practice is not so much an organizational structure as a set of principles and guidelines. These must be appropriate to practice objectives, the project objectives, the team leader and the team.

5.7 Dealing with independent project managers

If you don't like being managed, develop your management skills.

Is dealing with project managers a 'quality' issue?

Yes: The PM is the agent of the client, responsible for ensuring that project requirements are achieved, and often for interpreting them. The main purpose of QM is to ensure that project requirements are met. Therefore the PM interface becomes a quality issue.

Project management (PM) is the world's fastest-growing profession, and arguably the youngest[1]. Contrary to the opinion of some architects I know, it's providers are *not* similar to those of the world's oldest profession. Perhaps because it is a young and evolving profession, the level of professionalism one encounters varies greatly. At the top end of the scale, practitioners bring great benefits to projects: they understand thoroughly and respect the perspectives and needs of the consultant team as well as other project stakeholders, they bring superb management skills, and they add value at every step of the process.

At the other end of the scale are the practitioners who appear to have emerged from under rocks, who win work by promising to carve their fees from the consultants' fees, who have little understanding of that which they purport to manage, who do not add value, and who appear to see themselves as mule-train drivers, whose main tool is a coiled whip. We've all encountered these pseudo-PMs.

Most independent project managers in the design and construction industry are somewhere in between these extremes.

Certainly the Project Management Institute (PMI) is working globally to increase the professionalism of project managers.

Making the project manager 'look good'

When thinking about this topic, I am reminded of a terrific talk I heard many years ago, about 1987. I was a founding member of the then recently-formed Project Management Forum, the forerunner to the Australian Institute of Project Management (AIPM). The Forum had asked Daryl Jackson, a prominent Melbourne architect, to address their meeting. His reputation drew an SRO crowd.

His opener was that he had learned that the most important role of the architect was to make project managers look good, and that he would tell us about twelve ways he had learned to do that – which he did for over an hour. It was a hilarious, brilliant 'send-up' of the profession and the people in the room – story after story about how the PM had stuffed something up and how he had to sort it out and then praise the PM for a great job. They loved every second of it, 'rolling in the aisles' with laughter.

He closed by saying that the reason he did his best to make project managers look good was because then they would recommend him for their next project.

That closing brought a sober quiet to the room, as they realized the powerful home truth of his point, and their complicity in it.

Dealing with reality

Most architects and designers I know have had experiences with PMs who are less than great, and prefer projects where there isn't an independent PM on the team. At the same time, they realize that as the world of design and construction evolved, a need was created that their professions did not recognize or fill – and that a new profession emerged to fill it. Our reality is that project management is here to stay, and on the increase worldwide.

What are the strategies for ensuring the best quality of that relationship? There are four basic strategies:

1 When the PM is at the low end of the professional scale

Unless the project is one you absolutely must have, walk away. The project will run into problems, and you'll be blamed for them. Let your competitors take the lashings and stumble in the mire.

2 When the PM is at the high end of the professional scale

Watch closely and learn everything you can. These are skills and knowledge you *really* need.

3 When the PM is somewhere in the middle of the scale

First, reduce your need to be managed. The more, and better, project management you do, the more you will be left alone to do it. Forget about the fact that somebody else is being paid for it; you are working toward the fourth – and best – strategy.

Second, follow Jackson's advice when and as needed. Make the project manager look good. It will bring you more work.

4 When you can, pre-empt the role

As soon as you have the skills and knowledge, move up the food chain, and offer professional project management as a core service, competing directly with the independents. Start small, with loyal clients, and go as quickly as realistically possible to the high end of the professional PM scale.

For more information about the role of quality in project management, see Chapters 7.10 and 7.11.

Part 5: Sources, resources & notes

NOTE: *The Architect's Handbook of Professional Practice 13th Ed.,* Joseph A. Demkin, Exec. Ed., published by John Wiley & Sons, is referred to below as '*AIA Handbook*'.

Sources

5.2 Maister, David H. (2001) *Practice What You Preach,* The Free Press, p 81.

Stasiowski, Frank (1991) *Staying Small Successfully,* John Wiley & Sons, p 139.

Woodward, Cynthia A. (1990) *Human Resources Management for Design Professionals,* The American Institute of Architects Press, p 84.

5.4 Goleman, Daniel (1998) *Working with Emotional Intelligence*, Bloomsbury, pp 9-10.

Kaderlan, Norman (1991) *Designing Your Practice*, McGraw-Hill, p 108.

McKenna, Patrick J. and David H. Maister (2002) *First Among Equals,* The Free Press, Part 3 – Chapters 11-18.

Ronco, William C. (2005) Team Building for Architects, *AIA Handbook, 2005 Update,* pp 69-79.

5.5 Rummler, Geary A. and Alan P. Brache (1995) *Improving Performance: How to Manage the White Space on the Organization Chart,* Jossey-Bass, p 12.

Resources

5.2 Dawson, Ross (2000) *Developing Knowledge-Based Client Relationships: The Future of Professional Services,* Butterworth Heinemann. Dawson focuses on adding value to relationships at every level of practice, using knowledge transfer as the medium. Written to generic professional consulting, it is an excellent guide to understanding the processes that underlie this important topic, but 'nuts and bolts' types will find it theoretical.

Demkin, Joseph, Ed. (2001) *AIA Handbook*, John Wiley & Sons, Part 1: Chapters 1-5: pp 1-68, various authors.

Greusel, David (2003) Communicating with Clients, *AIA Handbook 2003 Update*, pp 57-67.

Kaderlan, pp 94-106.

Lawless, Peggy and Wendy Pound (2004) Researching Client Needs, *AIA Handbook 2004 Update*, pp 57-70.

Maister, David H. (1993) *Managing the Professional Service Firm*, Free Press Paperbacks, pp 53-120.

Maister, David H. (1997) *True Professionalism,* The Free Press, pp 171-7, 195-202.

Rose, Stuart W. (1987) *Achieving Excellence in Your Design Practice,* Whitney Library of Design, pp 48-69.

Stasiowski, Frank and David Burstein (1994) *Total Project Quality Management*, John Wiley & Sons, pp 7-13, 235-63.

Stasiowski, Frank, pp 103-111.

5.2 Cramer, James P. and Scott Simpson (2002) *How Firms Succeed: A Field Guide to Design Management*, Ostberg Library of Design Management, pp 192-6.

Kaderlan, pp 74-92.

Lewis, Celesta (2004) Keeping Key Staff, *AIA Handbook 2004 Update,* pp 91-100.

Maister, David H., *Managing the Professional Service Firm*, pp 143-205.

Maister, David H., *True Professionalism,* pp 56-74, 105-14.

Maurel, Kathleen C. et al, *AIA Handbook,* Chapter 9: 221-54.

Stasiowski, Frank, Chapters 4 & 5: pp 137-76.

Stitt, Fred, Ed. (1992) *Design Office Management Handbook*, Arts & Architecture Press, pp 39-41, 277-308.

Woodward, Cynthia A. A superb, across-the-board, single-source, must-read for big-firm HR managers (but its advice is appropriate for firms of any size).

5.3 Allinson, Kenneth (1997) *Getting There by Design,* Architectural Press. The only book I know of on design management for architects. Well-written, thorough; its British style might seem a bit theoretical to US architects. Recommended reading for design managers.

Atkins, James B. (2004) Maintaining Design Quality, *AIA Handbook 2004 Update*, pp 101-14.

Scott Braley, FAIA, FRSA, is President of Braley Consulting and Training, Atlanta, GA. He can be reached on 404-252-9840 or scott@braleyconsulting.com.

Stasiowski, Frank and David Burstein, pp 47-75.

Stitt, Fred, Ed., pp 54-8.

5.4 Kaderlan, pp 109-28.

Lencioni, Patrick (2002) *The Five Dysfunctions of a Team,* Jossey-Bass. A quick-read, novel-form allegory on team behavior. Worth reading if team-building is part of your role.

5.5 Cramer, James P. and Scott Simpson, pp 103-5.

Maister, David H. (2001) *Practice What You Preach,* The Free Press. However often you read this book, you'll learn something new and useful about performance and productivity.

McKenna, Patrick J. and David H. Maister, Chapter 22: pp 241-57.

Rummler, Geary A. and Alan P. Brache. The classic work on the topic, extremely readable, filled with valuable insights. If your passion is process, this is for you.

5.6 Eisenstadt, Kathleen and Donald Sull (January 2001) Strategy as Simple Rules, *Harvard Business Review.*

Kotter, John, (December 2001) What Leaders Do. Breakthrough Leadership, *Harvard Business Review.*

Rosenbach, W.E. and R. L. Taylor (1989) *Contemporary Issues in Leadership,* 2nd Edition, Westview Press.

www.mqia.com:

5.1a Andrews, Ray, *The Story of Uncle Victor: The consequences of not delegating quality.*

5.3a Braley, Scott, *Quality in Design Management.*

5.5a King-Rowley, Debby, *QM and Productivity.*

5.6a Hinkley, Paul, *Quality Teamwork & Leadership.*

Epigrams

5.1 Cramer, James and Scott Simpson, p 118.

5.2 Woodward, Cynthia, p 84.

5.3 Sutherland, David, in conversation with the author (2005).

5.4 Goleman, Daniel, p 147.

5.5 Rummler, Geary and Alan Brach, p 12.

5.6 Stasiowski, Frank, *AIA Handbook,* p 443.

5.7 Nelson, Charles.

Endnotes

1 PMI was formed in 1969, just 36 years ago at this writing. PMI has more than 160,000 members in 146 countries. Over 90% of that growth has occurred within the past ten years; annual membership growth exceeds 20%.

6 Business, Connectivity & Marketing

6.1 Improving the business practice model

David Maister argues that a good way to profile your firm is to look at the kind of services your clients expect. He divides these into three groups: those who require Expertise, Experience and Efficiency.

He calls the firms that provide these services, respectively, Brains, Grey Hair and Procedure. He notes: 'Increasingly, firms will have to decide which type of client need they are attempting to serve, and organize their affairs appropriately'.

There have been architects for five thousand years, yet the heritage of their accumulated experience does not spell the answer to success in the world of today. Why? Because the practice of architecture has been forced to take a course in business and to accept efficient, aggressive organization in business as the price of survival.

Royal Barry Wills

Wills, a prominent Boston architect in the 30's and 40's, wrote that in 1941. Since then, nothing – and everything – has changed!

This handbook considers the way we work, in light of the changes in our business environment. This chapter looks at ways we could improve our existing model (which has been around since the days of our forebears). Chapter 8.3 looks at alternatives to our existing model – a somewhat more radical approach.

Three very significant changes have been eroding the shores and undermining the foundations of traditional design practice over the last couple of decades:

- The commoditization of professional services.
- The growth of design-build.
- The rise of the independent project manager.

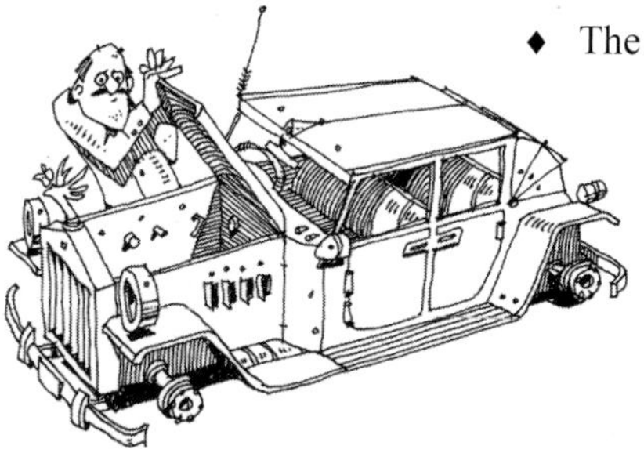

The reasons why this is happening have been debated by experts; they are complex, and the evidence is circumstantial. I won't regurgitate their conclusions here, except to say that I agree with those who say we've largely brought these consequences on ourselves by our failure to seize opportunities that opened as our business climate evolved. We didn't hear Wills.

These changes are powerful forces, and they are *not* going to go away. If you want to be successful in the future, you *will* figure out ways to improve your business model such that you can live gracefully and profitably with these evolutionary changes.

And what (you might ask) has this to do with quality? Read Wills' epigram again. Design may be the body of practice, but business is the engine, gear train and wheels. Unless you are independently wealthy, your ability to provide excellence in design is inseparable from your business skills. Indeed, the better your business skills, the more time you will have to devote to design.

I have a prescription for the first of these changes, which I'll get to in a moment. The second is covered in Chapter 6.9, courtesy of John Beveridge, and the third is covered in Chapter 5.6.

First, to 'tune up' your practice model, you need to have a clear idea of where you are starting from. In Chapter 2.2, I noted the The Coxe Group's 'SuperPositioning' model, which identifies all practices as being either 'practice-centered businesses' or 'business-centered practices', and in each case being one of three types: 'strong delivery', 'strong service' or 'strong idea'.

Practice-centered practice	Practice-centered business
Business-centered practice	Business-centered business

Figure 6.1 *Stasiowski's businesss model*

Key Resource Frank Stasiowski has developed a variant of this model, (shown left) which looks first at the basic driver for a firm, which can be summed up as 'making money' (business) or 'creating design' (practice). Over this basic driver is the 'centering' that further defines how the firm sees opportunities – leaning either toward money or design. Stasiowski says that there are very few firms in either the upper left or lower right – that the majority are in the other two quadrants. In both cases, firms value both design and money – but one will come first.

Norman Kaderlan (after The Coxe Group's model), divides design practices into three groups: those designed for Efficiency (strong delivery), for Service (strong service) and for Innovation (strong idea).

There are other models for developing a sense of what drives your practice; see references under Resources at the end of this Part 6. The key point is that it is common for the various leaders in a practice to give these drivers different priorities, and their priorities come into play as soon as you attempt to reposition the firm's business approach – often leading to dissension and disagreement. These issues become roadblocks in the path from your present reality to your preferred future, discussed in Chapters 2.1 and 2.2.

Backing out of the commodity trap

I suggest to you that all the services we provide can be sorted into two piles: those that can be commoditized, and those that can't. Most projects involve a mix of these two – and sometimes it is hard to distinguish which is which.

Clients are increasingly seeking to 'level the playing field' so they can reliably obtain the best value, which means a pre-determined level of service for the lowest price. There is nothing inherently wrong with this approach, of course – except that when applied to a service industry, there will always be somebody prepared to offer what *appears* to be an equal service at an unsustainable price.

My perspective is strongly and clearly that any effort to improve a practice business model must be in a direction away from commoditization. All other answers lead straight to the lowest common denominator of practice, and you don't want to go there.

Before you get too precious about the inseparable value of your design services, think a bit about out-sourcing. These days, a lot of reputable firms outsource documentation, onshore or offshore. That's a commodity. Specs have been outsourced to specialists for decades. There are plenty of construction managers around who know how to do contract administration. These are commodities, even though some of them require a high degree of knowledge.

Alternatively, almost all of that we do that is hard to commoditize is the front-end part – conceptualising, planning, scoping, designing, problem seeking, problem solving.

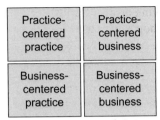

Hocking the crown jewels

We have a remarkable track record of giving away – for little or nothing – our most valuable services, in hopes of getting back a fat drafting job that can just as well be done by somebody else somewhere else – and that is exactly what fuels commoditization.

I think of these precious services, which really cannot be commoditized, as our 'crown jewels', pawned as a sort of security in a bid for a piece of the action in the bazaar.

Of course, smart clients (especially the 'spec' developers, who have mastered the black art of gambling with other people's money and talents) expect us to do that, and an amazing number of our colleagues still fall for it. I see it all the time.

What am I talking about here? Those of you who appropriately value your various service groups know, and don't spend much time building kites for others to fly. Here's the idea:

Project viability services vs. project delivery services

The services we offer (and this applies to all the players on the professional team) that cannot be commoditized are those it takes to take a project to the point where we *really* know whether or not it is viable. By viable, I mean that we will know:

- What the project will look like.
- That it will serve its functional purposes (and we know what those are).
- How much it will cost, and what its return on investment will be.
- The impact it will have on its environment.
- Its infrastructure requirements and operating costs.
- Risks are identified and quantified within reason.
- That there is a very high probability that all permits required to construct it can be obtained, including overcoming any objections to it.
- Options for delivery, assessed and prioritised.

In this model, the object is to do whatever it takes to get to this point of knowing as soon as possible, and not to do *anything* else. Once at this point, you have a package of great value to the client, that simply cannot be obtained piecemeal in anything resembling an efficient way. In terms of traditional practice, this is probably about halfway through design development, but it clearly includes some services that we rarely do at this point in traditional practice.

Your fee for this service package should reflect its value, not its cost. Not one speck of this package should be given free, or underpriced, in hopes of 'getting the project'.

Because, once you are at this point, the rest of what has to be done is the part that can be done many ways, by many parties – and is therefore a commodity, which can be bought from the lowest bidder.

Project delivery

Now, when you are at this point, both you and the client have a lot of choices. If the client is sufficiently impressed with what you have done, he may well want you to continue on and provide the rest of the traditional package, and that might suit you. Or he might want to use other resources; other methods.

A recent trend in some progressive practices is the growing of skills in infrastructure planning and design. A good example is the Brisbane, Australia office of Hassell, which has built these skills and is very successfully creating projects to utilize them.

However, it might also suit you to turn over the heavy lifting to somebody else, staying on in an advisory or 'bridging' role[1], and using these special skills to prepare project viability services for other clients. If you are shaking your head on that, reflect on the risk that goes with the project delivery part of the package.

To be able to utilize this idea, you will either have to learn some new skills, or align yourself closely with people who've got them. Review again my list of what project viability includes: I'm referring to construction cost, infrastructure requirements, risk management and the like.

Value pricing

At the heart of the idea above is *value pricing* – a business technique that Frank Stasiowski has championed for many years. I won't attempt to detail it here; if you want to end-run the commodity trap, I suggest that you read his book on the topic. See Resources at the end of this Part 6.

6.2 The role of QM in improving communication

When people feel that they understand one another perfectly, they are often actually operating by what psychologists call 'pseudo-communication'; that is, they think they have reached a common understanding when, in reality, they have not.

DPIC Companies

Communication is a quality topic – not only because common sense says it must be – but because ISO 9001 requires it both internally and externally (clauses 5.5.3 and 7.2.3).

A failure to communicate sufficiently applies both for our internal communication, within the practice; and with clients, other consultants, and others outside the practice.

In the small design office, communication is taken for granted; it happens naturally. This is often the case, and it probably is true that architects are relatively egalitarian in the dealings with staff. Yet some practices have (to an outsider's eyes) almost unbelievable internal communication problems, and claims histories show that many practitioners have trouble communicating with their clients.

Many experts who do team-building consultation put much of this inability to communicate to personality differences; they use Myers Briggs *Type Indicator* testing to help people understand where each other is 'coming from'.

Typical small-practice architects are not likely to engage professionals to help them learn to communicate better, even though they would accept that whatever communicating skills they now have, probably could be improved.

Listening

Listening is a special communication skill, and often, even people who understand how important it is aren't very good at it (my wife agrees here). Norman Kaderlan says 'Perhaps the most critical communication skill you can develop is listening', and offers good advice on this skill, summarized below. I've only given you the outline of his points; they are well worth reading in full.

- ❑ When someone is talking, first focus on what is said and then on what you think is really meant.
- ❑ When you are talking, watch the listener.
- ❑ Relax and clear your mind.
- ❑ Listen to everything the person says.
- ❑ Don't pre-judge the person or the message.
- ❑ You can listen much faster than a person can talk. Try to listen without analyzing, without interrupting.
- ❑ Take accurate notes to have an accurate memory of what was said.
- ❑ Listen for intent as well as content. If unsure of what was meant, ask for clarification.

Do we take communication for granted?

My experience is that a central problem in communication improvement is in taking that capacity for granted. As a result, the busy firm owner never does get sufficient time to either instruct or listen to his staff.

My own experience is that women are more sensitive to this need and more likely to make the time.

If you are too busy to properly instruct or listen to your staff, the only solution is to *change your calendar,* to use Tom Peters' concept. This means, simply, for the person in charge to move communication improvement from the back of her mind to the front, and to keep it there, doing everything which can be done to make it work better. Of course this has to be balanced with all of the other things the practice leader has to do, but just an awareness and a commitment can make a tremendous difference in the outcome.

After this 'attitude change' at the top, there are a number of specific actions the practice can take which will significantly improve its communicating capability. Here is my list.

I am sure that you could create your own list, from your own experience. The hard part is to remember to follow your own advice.

- ***Always remember that those around you have different priorities; different pressures, different agendas.*** They may not believe in working a 14-hour day, even though they accept that you do. A lot of miscommunication results from 'the boss' thinking that all staff see the world the way she does.
- ***Most people are reluctant to challenge their leader.*** Even if you would prefer that they did sometimes. People survive peacefully by subordinating their own views. You might well have to stop and probe around a bit to get that great idea out of a key staffer.
- ***Ask questions.*** Followed by more questions. When you know the answers to your own questions, bite your tongue.
- ***Give people time to formulate answers.*** Nobody wants to look foolish. Advance notice allows a person to think through an issue; do a bit of research. Asking people under a lot of pressure to contribute meaningfully to a debate isn't doing them any favor, it is putting them in an impossible situation.
- ***Having asked the question, don't demean the answer.*** The best solutions have their negative aspects. They will become apparent in due course. What is your goal – better communication, or right answers? In the words of that old pop song, 'accentuate the positive'.
- ***If an idea is full of problems, don't kill it yourself.*** Ask someone else (a temperate person) what she thinks. If the idea gets a bucket of cold water, ask for another opinion from someone who will support anyone. What is your goal – better communication, or right answers? The person who missed it today may solve it tomorrow – the last thing you need to do is gag her by criticism.
- ***Reward good ideas.*** Everybody secretly wants to be a hero. Appreciation is empowerment.
- Lastly: ***DON'T ANSWER YOUR OWN QUESTIONS.*** Unless the only reason for asking was to hear yourself talk.

Can you hear your clients?

The sum of my research indicates that, for our industry, no single element of quality improvement is so important or so much needed as improving communication at all levels of the organization: with your staff, other consultants, and your clients.

> It is crucial ... for you to manage the client's expectations so they are consistent with yours, and with your ability to perform. That involves three steps. The first is consciously creating an accurate image in the client's mind of what your practice is and what it can do. The second is understanding the client's expectations. The final step is negotiating any differences to reach a mutually acceptable agreement. – *Norman Kaderlan*

> Norman Kaderlan, *Designing Your Practice*, 1991, McGraw-Hill. Reproduced with permission of The McGraw-Hill Companies.

Designers have a particular problem with respect to client values. It is brought on in part by the educational process, which powerfully reinforces the importance of *design*. We get out of school knowing how to 'design', but not how to do much else. We want to 'get some clients', so we can design something for them.

Every graduate, having put in the minimum time required to become registered, has a basic decision to make: To either continue to gain more education by working for others, or to gain more education at the expense of her clients. The more impatient take the latter course, but they immediately run into the classic problem that all young practices face: their clients want to see *experience*. (The clients aren't dumb.)

How do you get that experience, that first chance to prove that you really *can* design that child-care center, school extension, what have you? The obvious thing to do is 'puff up' whatever experience you have, as much as you can, to give your prospective client confidence enough to give you your chance.

BAD START! Let's consider Kaderlan's first point from the sidebar: ***Create an accurate image in the client's mind of what your practice is and what it can do.*** If you do not do this – if you stretch the reality – you will confirm, or raise, the client's expectations to a level that you will be struggling to meet every step of the way. You will have fashioned your own noose.

What is the answer, then, to 'breaking into' a new line of service? To answer, I'll tell you about a project I heard of, from a person who was on the selection committee to design a new child-care center. The committee had decided to put only firms with demonstrated experience in similar projects on the short-list. Its advertisement for a registration of interest drew over 60 applications, including over a dozen with suitable experience.

The committee put five of the most promising contenders on a short-list, and then decided to add a sixth, a firm that had the most interesting proposal out of this huge group. This firm said that they had no prior experience in child-care centers, and for that reason they would give it their best effort.

The committee members were so impressed with the proposal, including the firm's candor and honesty, that they decided to interview the firm, but agreed they wouldn't offer them the job.

Result: the firm was just as impressive in the interview, and it won over the committee, and won the job.

Now we will turn to Kaderlan's second point, ***understanding the client's expectations***. I noted earlier that clients' expectations are rising, and that clients expect their consultants to have a *client-centered* approach.

Understanding the client's expectations

What is a client-centered approach? It means, simply, that you have to think about the project from the client's point of view, rather than from yours. Some of our more illustrious architects of the past have been openly contemptuous of the clients' ideas; the architect 'knew best' and that was that. Those days are history, and just as well.

> Sometimes you will have to be creative in finding ways to communicate adequately with your client. I am reminded of one Boston client who simply could not visualize anything – floor plans, sketches, perspectives just didn't do it. The project was a large, new kitchen. In the end, we mocked up the whole kitchen, full size, in cardboard, in her garage. She walked in, and her face lit up. Suddenly, she understood the whole design – and approved it.

The only way to understand the client's expectations is to ask a lot of questions. And more questions. And listen carefully to the answers.

How can you tell if the client understands you? Several authorities, including Kaderlan, recommend asking the clients to tell back to you, in their own words, what they understood from your explanation. Listen carefully to that telling: if it is different from *what you meant*, then you're still not communicating adequately.

Too many design professionals are uncomfortable with any differences between their clients and themselves, so they try to ignore these differences in the hope that they will go away. Some make the really stupid assumption that when the clients see the design, they will immediately understand the importance of good design, and forget all objections.

What is more likely to happen is that after seeing the design, the client will be calling her lawyer.

In selling, the process of resolving all impediments to the sale is called 'reaching closure', and it is a specialty in the marketing game. Essentially, reaching closure is pure negotiation. As I note elsewhere, you should improve your negotiation skills. If this advice is not pertinent, then you are a rare designer indeed.

We have come to the third of Kaderlan's points: ***Negotiate any differences to reach a mutually acceptable agreement.***

Here I would like to emphasize the word *mutually*. If the best that you can negotiate is not really acceptable to you, then think very hard about whether you really need that project. You are capable of true negotiation only when you have the ability, both financial and mental, to walk away from the deal.

There are only so many hours in the day, and in your professional life. You owe it to yourself to use them the best way you can, and – except in the rarest of circumstances – you should *not* use them up on projects that will be a burden to you.

6.3 Quality in market positioning

Not until you have positioned your firm can you set your price. Price is secondary – positioning comes first. Value is created when your clients don't ask the price.

Frank Stasiowski

Scott Braley's contact details are listed in section 5.3 under *Resources* at the end of Part 5.

This chapter draws on the extensive knowledge and experience of Key Resource Scott Braley, who has prepared an extensive paper on the topic for this handbook. This chapter is a brief summary of his paper. You can download the complete version from the website: www.mqia.com > 6.3a *Quality in Market Positioning.*

Market positioning, by Scott Braley

Design professionals who seek success may initially see 'quality' as a 'given' in the marketplace, and as a fundamental interest of potential clients. Unfortunately, these assumptions do not do justice to the intricacies of determining 'position' in the market.

Market 'position' can have many different meanings in the A|E|C industry. In this intentionally brief summary, we'll focus on market 'position', market 'positioning' and key methods and actions that can be used to identify and achieve desired market position and necessary positioning actions.

Position is a noun, positioning is a verb. While that may seem a bit basic to you, *making and understanding this distinction is as important as anything you will do* to further your cause in establishing your position in the market.

Both 'position' and 'positioning' are relative terms. Each term, and all the associated actions and reactions, requires a benchmark or reference of some kind. While the specifics vary depending on which dictionary you consult, *'position' is fundamentally your place, your situation, your desirability or your esteem related to something or someone else in the marketplace.* It follows logically that *'positioning' is that set of actions that enhance or achieve your desired place, situation or esteem.*

Position is relative in three dimensions

In our consulting and training work – which is focused on the A|E|C industry – we position in three dimensions – process, product and perception. As noted in Chapter 1.2, quality is defined as 'the degree to which a set of inherent characteristics fulfils requirements'. How – and how well – a design firm does this determines its market position.

If you read Chapter 2.1, you will recognize Braley's point as a restatement of the Gap Analysis model. Although presented there as a strategic planning tool, the effect of closing the gap between present reality and preferred future has the added benefit of *positioning* the practice in its preferred market(s). – Ed.

To be successful, design professionals must consider quality position in terms of how you provide quality (i.e., process), what level of quality you delivery (i.e., product), and how your clients and others view your quality performance (i.e., perception). The three key questions you must ask are: where we are (i.e., current position), where do we want or need to be (i.e., desired position), and what do we need to do to get there (i.e., positioning).

In our work with both design professionals and with client entities, we use the same three working definitions:

- ***Process*** pertains to design and service activities. Process positioning includes how design is conceived, how projects are delivered, client relations, the manner in which a client is served (not to be confused with types of services that are provided) and the overall workings of design from beginning to end.
- ***Product*** pertains to results. Product positioning includes the physical results of the design process (e.g., a building, a piece of equipment, a systems installation), the interim deliverables and instruments of service (e.g., models, drawings, CADD files, images, contracts), the design project goals (e.g., functional performance, budget and schedule achievements, aesthetic image) and the overall 'finished project' itself.
- ***Perception*** pertains to feelings and impressions. Perception positioning encompasses the awareness, observations, sensations, feelings and mental image of the design professional – in terms of both process and product.

Process vs. product orientation

Both design professionals and clients assert that process and product go hand in hand. While this makes sense on the surface, wise design professionals know that there is always a more/less important relationship between process and product. We have found that either hierarchy is appropriate, and either will produce the perception of 'good' or 'high' quality.

> This process vs process agreement is so important that we have found it helpful to force a distinction by suggesting that the two cannot be considered of equal importance.

It is crucial for the design professional and the client to agree upon which is more important – process or product. This agreement is best when reached early in the life of the project, and tested frequently throughout the term of project work.

It is incumbent on the design professional to address and establish the 'process vs. product' relationship with the client. This is a fundamentally important strategic relationship because *design professionals cannot define desired market position until they determine their own view of process vs. product. Moreover, design professionals cannot achieve desired market position until they consider and determine the client's view.*

Design professionals and clients view position differently

It is enlightening and amusing to observe how differently design professionals and clients approach the issues of quality in market position – yet, how consistently they arrive at common ground viewpoints. *Each begins from a seemingly 'totally different' point of departure – yet both end up at the same position!*

Most design professionals move through a labyrinth of progressive steps along a common logic path based on the premise 'if we have a good process then we will produce a good product which will then put us in a desirable market position.'

Some modify the progression to follow a logic map of 'good products and good processes produce desirable positions in the market; therefore, we should do our best to integrate process and product.' Either approach has the potential to produce the design professional's desired quality position in the market.

As we work with clients, we see a fundamentally different dynamic at work. Their approach to a quality-based market position is more varied and unpredictable. Some clients are distinctly focused on process while others are demonstrably more interested in product. These tend to adopt a logic that says 'it really doesn't matter how you get there, just produce a great project result.' Still other clients rely primarily on their trust-based perception. That is, they form an opinion – a perception – of the design professional's quality position, and rely on the assumption that this perception will become reality in both process and product.

Savvy design professionals who are aware of these differences are well ahead of the curve in achieving their desired 'quality position' in the market.

Exclusive positions are not always good/bad

For many design professionals and clients, emphasis on 'high' or 'low' quality is a form of relative exclusivity. That is, the logic implies, so a design professional can achieve a clearly differentiated and exclusive position in the market by producing or providing 'high quality'. end results or interim services. Few however seek the exclusivity of being a design professional associated with 'low quality'. *The often overlooked fact is that an emphasis on 'high quality' is not always beneficial, and an emphasis on 'low quality' is not always detrimental.*

> The key point: Any exclusive market position – whether based on process, product or perception – must be tailored to and weighed in comparison to the client's view of that market position.

Experience indicates that most design professionals will attempt to set themselves apart from others by emphasizing 'high' quality in process, product and/or perception. In many cases the design professional's vocabulary of quality related to market position highlights words such as 'high', 'rich', 'robust' and 'optimum'. It is my personal experience, and consistent advice to design professionals, that a more successful approach is embodied and implied by such words as 'tailored', 'market responsive' and 'client-specific'.

Quality position is time-dependent

Market position is significantly influenced by the time-dependent nature of quality. While the various combinations are seemingly endless, consider three axioms regarding this time-dependency:

- *Process quality axiom* – Design phase processes are relatively more influential than construction phase processes in determining market position. Moreover, process quality is most influential on market position before and during the design phases of a project.

- *Product quality axiom* – Final project results are more important than interim project results. Moreover, product quality has increasingly greater influence on market position after the project is complete and as subsequent similar projects are completed.
- *Perception quality axiom* – Current perception is more important to clients, while long-term perception is more important to design professionals. Moreover, perceptions, regardless of their origin or factual basis, will weigh more heavily than logical or objective arguments in determining market position.

Independent and linked quality positions

A 'linked' quality position can also be achieved by referencing well-known standards or guidelines (e.g., LEED, ISO 9001).

An independent market position is one that is established and maintained solely, or in great measure, by the positioning actions of the design profession. A linked market position is one that is established and maintained by the design professional either through associating with or identifying with a group of similar or related professionals.

A design professional can create an independent market position by asserting and proving that its process, product or perception is unique when compared to other design professionals. Conversely, a design professional may wish to create a 'linked' market position by showing how its process or work is similar to that of other great design professionals.

Defining and positioning methodology

In our quality-related work with design professionals as well as clients we use the following step-by-step methodology:

- Identify the market sectors or marketplaces.
- Determine the position, or positions, to which you aspire.
- Concurrently, identify the positions to which you may be assigned by clients.
- Divide these various positions into two categories – 'attractive' and 'unattractive'.
- Use 'process', 'product' and 'perception' to determine how you would describe your firm's current condition as well as where you wish to be in the future (i.e., 'target' position).
- Analyze this list considering: Client's view, timing, cost to change position, and return on investment if the target position is achieved.
- Create and implement an action plan to achieve your 'target' position.

We have found that these considerations, combined with this methodology, produce a genuinely worthwhile and effective approach for the design professionals seeking to employ quality as a driving factor in defining and achieving market position.

6.4 Quality in business development

The ideal condition is to own a position in the client's mind.

Ellen Flynn-Heapes

> We tend to confuse these three terms, and not infrequently (and incorrectly) use them interchangeably.

Definitions first. Business development is composed of two sequential stages: marketing and sales.

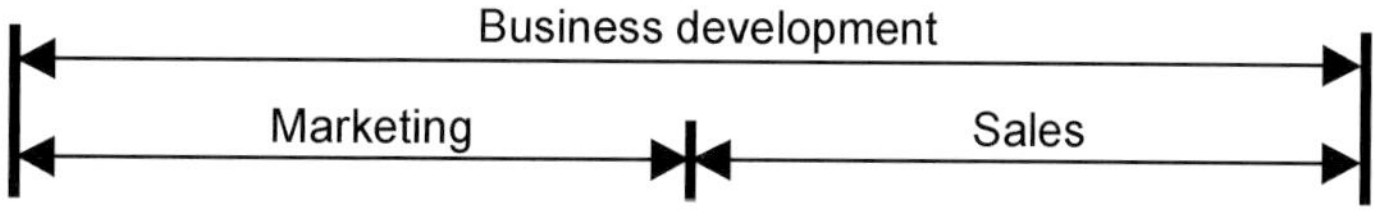

The simple difference: marketing is about clients; sales is about projects. Marketing goes from client identification up to the point where a specific project is identified. Sales goes from that point until you have a contract.

In the previous chapter, we looked at how a practice establishes (positions) itself in the marketplace. There are lots of excellent words written about professional services marketing; I won't try to reinvent them. See *Resources* at the end of Part 6. What I do want to do is consider how QM intersects with the marketing process.

There are three key quality issues in business development: *Client/ project selection, Value alignment* and *Honesty.*

Client/project selection

Often, architects (especially young ones, starting out) say to me, 'We'll take any project we can get'. This is called the *shotgun approach* (shoot at anything that moves). Think about that a bit. What that really says is, 'We won't worry about whether or not we can actually do this project; get it first and figure it out later'.

This is *not* – repeat ***not*** – a quality business development approach.

Poor client/project selection is a significant cause of lawsuits against design professionals. Why? First, there is no matching of skills and experience to client requirements. Second, this designer is likely to get the clients and/or projects other more experienced designers avoid. Third, the approach creates a negotiating climate wherein the designer is more likely to accept fees that are too low and contract conditions that are onerous.

Quality designer professionals select quality clients with quality projects, and carefully match their expertise and resources to client requirements and expectations.

Value alignment

In every instance, project success depends on an appropriate alignment between the client's project goals and objectives with the design firm's goals and objectives.

The difficulty we have with this idea is that our self-perceived goals and objectives are (or should be) constant; whereas the project goals and objects will be different for every project. So, alignment seems difficult and/or impractical, and is not often considered as a valid driver in creating and maintaining the client relationship.

Moreover, there is frequently a lack of alignment of values within the practice itself. There are three primary value areas in the practice; which, together with the client's requirements and reasons to appoint, make five sets of values the practice can choose to either bring toward alignment; or choose to ignore. They are shown in the top row of table below. In the second row are some of the more common values that populate these areas.

Table 6.4 *Value alignment areas*

Client's requirements	Appointment reasons	Marketing approach	Practice culture	Project objectives
Make statement/ firm image Short-term ROI Long-term ROI House operations Streamline business/cut operating costs Decrease operating costs	Trust & direct experience Reputation Cheapest price Fastest draw in town Building type experience Saw a great example of design expertise Drop-dead interview	Past projects (experience) Excellence (won awards) Exceed expectations Talent Sustainability, green design Understand client's business Tailor services to client's needs	Win awards Make firm statement Keep enough work coming in Happy campers General pride & satisfaction Make money Better communities Green design	Award winner Make personal statement Raise profile Make money Reward staff Just like designing Decrease operating Costs Improve client's business

The values in these areas will vary greatly from practice to practice and from client to client; even from project to project. For example, under *Practice Culture*, 'Make money' or 'Green design' might be at the head of the list rather than 'Win awards'.

The key points this table demonstrates are:

- Client's requirements and the reasons they appoint are not always in alignment; in fact they are typically *not* aligned.
- Every practice has a culture, stated or unstated. If unstated, there is almost surely to be a lack of alignment between that culture and both the way the practice markets it services, and the values that the project team bring to a particular project – and even if stated, discrepancies often exist.
- There is often a correlation between marketing approach and reasons to appoint, but this correlation tends to be a surface correlation rather than operating at the level of values.

Take your mind back to the discussion of present reality vs. preferred future in Chapters 2.1-2.2. In that context, when a practice is unclear about its values, and how these values are expressed in the ways they do things (for example, marketing or planning projects), the gap between its present reality and its preferred future will be large.

Alternatively, those practices that have debated and agreed these values, understand them, and consciously extend them throughout their practices will not only have a narrower gap between present reality and preferred future, they will be working toward the latter.

To bring the discussion back to quality in business development: the best practices align their values such that the marketing people *know* that the value proposition they pitch is really the same one that the design team will deliver. 'What you see is what you get.'

In addition, these marketers work hard to identify and resolve discrepancies between the prospective client's project requirements and the reasons the client would make the appointment. They do this through research, questioning, and testing of variations on their value proposition.

Honesty

When we are pitching for a project, of course we want to put our best foot forward, which means putting our past experience in the best possible light, to create reasons why the client should appoint our practice to the project. There is sometimes a very fine line between dressing the truth in an elegant gown, and padding up the gown here and there for greater effect.

In Chapter 6.2, I told the story of a firm that wanted a child-care facility project but had no experience in that project type. Their approach was utterly honest – 'we've never done one' – and their honesty probably was a critical factor in their success.

Being truthful goes beyond citing past experience, it includes promises to the client about the future (QA – quality assurance). For example, it is not truthful to say that a principal will maintain continuous oversight of the project unless that is really the case.

If there is anything clients hate, it is the 'key person switcheroo', where the firm shows up at the interview with their most impressive and qualified project manager – and implies (by her presence) that she will be running the project. Then, job won, a less skilled person gets put in charge. *This is not truth in advertising!*

This has happened so often that many experienced clients now demand that the people who will do the job are the ones who are sent to the interview. Clients should not have to demand that; they have a right to expect it.

6.5 Quality in managing client financial arrangements

Show me the money!

TV series title

This chapter draws on the extensive knowledge and experience of Key Resource Janet Allison, who has prepared a paper on the topic for this handbook. This chapter is a summary of her paper.

Janet Allison on *Managing receivables*

Never argue with anyone who owes you money or has a loaded gun. This is a very important concept to understand. Ultimately a firm's success is based on quality management of both projects and finances. Cash flow is the lifeblood of any business, and far too many firms operate in financial crisis. Damage control and 'dialing for dollars' keeps project managers and project executives from being billable. Communication and well-defined credit and collection guidelines contribute to positive cash flow.

By treating each project as a 'first date', you will not get sloppy and skip the all-too-important steps it takes to ensure quality management of your income.

Quality management of income starts with each new project, whether this is an existing client or one new to your firm.

The ground rules

Communication with clients not only tells you what they want from your firm, but what your firm needs from them. Having very defined credit and collection guidelines removes the grey areas and misunderstandings that arise so easily around money. These guidelines need not be very elaborate, but with these in place your firm has removed the possibility for misunderstanding and frequently costly discord that leads to uncollectible receivables (or worse, litigation).

Many people are not comfortable discussing money matters with their clients. Clients really like this!

With credit and collection guidelines in place, the project manager and the project executive are not the 'heavies'. The guidelines are from the firm's management committee and are not negotiable. If the client knows what the rules are it is easier for him to understand the process. If your firm is billing in a timely fashion, there is ample time for the client to discuss what he perceives as a problem.

Credit checks

Many firms are now routinely performing credit checks, not only for new clients, but also annually for existing clients – as a way to check their financial health. With new clients, you can see who controls the money, how the company is run, and what payment history they have with other venders.

Existing clients, with whom you have a history, may have gone through a restructuring or have been acquired by another firm or one of the many other changes that impact credit. An annual credit check will let you know how to proceed with work for the client. This is another tool to help ensure quality management of income. No surprises!

Project startup

When a new project is starting, assign one person in your accounting department to be the contact for your client. Your accounting person then becomes responsible to the client to handle any problems that arise through the process to help ensure prompt payment. By including this as one of your services you are not taking your project managers away from billable time. We forget that we are in a service industry!

All too frequently, when an error occurs in billing, turnaround for the corrected invoice is very slow and you then wind up in the next billing period and the whole receivable starts to be skewed, negatively impacting cash flow.

Frequently the only things that separate you from your competition are your client relationships and good service. Building relationships with your clients' accounting departments is a must. To know the flow of payables from the client side is very important – especially when, if you are a subconsultant, your invoicing needs to be to your client before a cut-off date, to insure subconsultant invoices are included in the normal billing cycles.

Your accounting department contact should call your client seven to ten days after your invoices have been sent out to see if they have received the invoice and is it correct.

At this point, if there is a billing problem, you can request that the client mark up the invoice with what they feel is incorrect and fax it back to your accounting department. This eliminates the 'fax me a copy' when you call in thirty days looking for payment. Your accounting staff is responsible; now, to see to it that if a problem has occurred that your firm makes the correction promptly. Remember: *Service, Service & Service.*

Contracts

Remember that receivables begin during the contract negotiations. If your client has a specific billing format that they need, make sure that you understand what it is and follow their request. Have your accounting contact get a copy of what the invoice needs to look like. Clients are usually quite clear as to what degree of backup they require.

Sensitivity to client billing requirement can avoid having hundreds of thousands of dollars held up and ultimately negatively impacting cash flow.

Sending a complete bill in the correct format and all backup attached will help shorten the turnaround time of your receivables. Inability to bill properly erodes client confidence and just makes the client scrutinize your bill more and more carefully.

Starting work without a signed contract is very foolish. Litigation with public clients has clearly established that no fees are owed without a contract. If the contract is actively being negotiated, at the very least, a letter to proceed, signed by the client, is necessary.

Additional services are one of the largest causes of uncollectible receivables. All to0 often, project managers and project executives find the client asking for additional services. There is nothing wrong with that – as long as work is not started until the client signs the request form. Forms for additional services can be very straight-forward. If your firm has these terms and conditions printed on the back of the Request for Additional Services, the request then goes straight to the contract.

Lack of signatures on contracts, change orders and other additional services cause unnecessary losses to firms and are a sign of poor quality management.

Emotion

Money has no emotion. People become emotional when discussing money. Always remember; if you have done what the client has requested and in a timely fashion, then you are entitled to be paid for your services. Collect what is yours.

Contacts that the accounting department develops are frequently different from those that are made by project manager or project executives. When the whole picture is put together you have one solid relationship built on communication. ***This is quality management!***

Experience has shown that taking project managers and project executives off being billable can negatively impact cash flow. Keeping on top of receivables is a job in itself and should not be left to a slow day or Fridays at 3:00 pm (as is so often done).

Collecting receivables should never alienate your client. If you ascertain that all billing to your client is correct and you are doing your work, it is fair to explain that you have been instructed not to deliver documents until the account is brought current.

This needs to be said in a tactful manner, as it is not your job to become a bully. Remember, at this point the client still has your money. In business, from time to time your client can experience cash flow problems, as all firms at some time are a little strapped for cash. If your client is in this situation, you can, if you have in the past developed a solid relationship with him, work out payment terms. This gets you at least a partial payment and the rest to come in following payments.

It is hard for someone to say that they cannot pay a bill. Listening is an important part of any relationship. Sometimes, what the client does not say is more important than what he does say. If you can help your client out, in a tactful way, and he then pays your firm in full, that is one more way to build the ever-important relationship.

6.6 The quality consequences of fee cutting

By reducing design fees to minimise costs, clients and developers were, by their own actions, contributing to the problems which lead to inefficiencies in the construction process and increases in overall project costs.

Paul Tilley

CSIRO is the Commonwealth Scientific and Industrial Researtch Organisation, the peak Australian government research organization.

Very little research has been done anywhere on the important relationship between design fees and document quality. One notable exception is CSIRO. Paul Tilley and Stephen McFallan of CSIRO conducted a survey program in the late 1990's, on behalf of a broadly-based coalition of Australian construction industry sponsors, that sought to quantify these relationships and their consequences. Their research was presented at a CIB[2] conference in Capetown, September 1999, and published in May 2000.

Research methodology

The analysis of the results of the research total some 300 pages in three reports; we have room here only to touch on some of the more interesting outcomes. The **Resources** section at the end of Part 6 provides links for information about these reports.

The author thanks CSIRO for permission to publish these extracts.

CSIRO surveyed clients, contractors, designers, other consultants and legal advisors by several means, receiving a total of 134 responses. The study was designed to investigate changes in design and documentation quality over the previous fifteen years and to determine whether there is a causal relationship between reduced design fees and increased project costs due to a reduction in design quality, causing excessive problems downstream in the construction process.

To ensure that the survey addressed only pertinent issues, two industry workshops – one for contractors and one for design professionals – were undertaken as part of the background investigation stage of the study. The workshops identified a number of design and documentation attributes as having a direct impact on the quality of design and documentation achieved, as follows (in order of importance):

Table 6.6.1 *Design/document quality attributes*

Design quality attributes		Documentation quality attributes	
1 Functionality	7 Material selection	1 Accuracy	7 Conformity
2 Relevancy	8 Aesthetics	2 Clarity	8 Certainty
3 Proper examination of design proposals	9 Material efficiency	3 Final checking	9 Relevance
4 Constructability	10 Ecological sustainability	4 Coordination	10 Standardisation
5 Site compatibility	11 Life-cycle costs	5 Completeness	
6 Economy	12 Innovation	6 Timeliness	
	13 Expressiveness		

The results of the survey showed that both designers and contractors felt that the degree of incorporation of the design quality attributes had improved marginally over the previous 12-15 years, with some exceptions:

- Contractors thought that (3) *Proper examination of design proposals* had dropped significantly; and that (4) *Constructibility* had declined.
- Both contractors and designers felt that that (10) *Ecological sustainability* had improved significantly.

By contrast, there was significant disagreement between designers and contractors over the quality of documentation. The latter felt that there was serious decline in all areas except (10) *Standardisation*. Overall, 52% of designers and 69% of contractors felt that design quality had declined, and 68% of designers and 88% of contractors felt that documentation quality had declined. Both groups also agreed that the decline in documentation quality had been greater than that of design.

Design fee levels

Getting It Right The First Time!: As I was in the final moments of proofreading corrections, I learned of a great project carried out by the Queensland Division of Engineers Australia: A 68-page research paper on the topics covered in this chapter, including reference to much of the work of Paul Tilley.

This valuable resource is available free of charge, and can be downloaded from the Internet: Go to http://qld.ieaust.org.au. On the home page, under the heading *What's New*, click on 'more...' at the bottom of the section; you will get a complete list of articles; it is in there.

Included is a useful and extensive bibliography. Don't miss this! My thanks to Chris Chetham, of Fairweather Proberts, for alerting me to it.

To examine changes in design fee levels, designers were asked to indicate the project fee percentage required to provide a proper service, produce quality design and documentation and make a reasonable profit for projects of differing sizes/price ranges and complexity over the specified time periods.

The graph below shows that, according to designers, the level of design fees required to provide a proper service has only declined marginally over the previous 12 to 15 years, with the required level of fees for simple projects declining the most at just under 5%. These decreases in the required fee levels are most likely due to improved information technologies, which allow for improved efficiencies within the design processes.

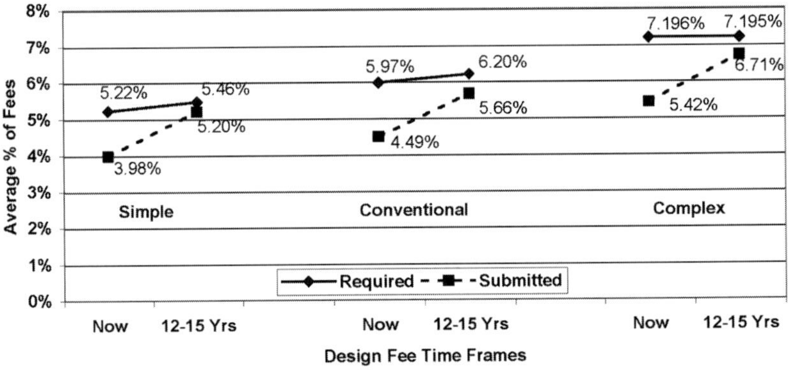

Figure 6.6 *Change in design fees over time*

When designers were asked to indicate the fee levels needed to be submitted to actually win the work, the responses revealed an average decline of approximately 21% for all three project complexity levels over the previous 12 to 15 years.

Comparing the difference between the fee levels submitted now to the fee levels required now, responses revealed that the disparity between the two fee levels represented an average decline in real designer fee income of approximately 24% for all three project complexity levels. It appears that the levels of fees being obtained are well below those required to provide quality design and documentation services.

Impact of reduced fees on design and documentation

Designers confirmed that the reduction in fees over the previous 12 to 15 years has directly impacted the quality of design and documentation. The responses indicate that lower design fees have had a highly detrimental effect on most design attributes, with the two attributes affected most being *proper examination of design proposals* and *innovation*.

Designers indicated that the reduced fees levels have detrimentally affected documentation *completeness, certainty, coordination* and *final checking*. These results correspond directly with the design and documentation quality attributes considered by designers to have declined most in the level of incorporation. Other significant impacts of reduced design fees include:

- a reduction in the quality of the service being provided;
- insufficient personnel to carry out the work, causing an overload on those available;
- a greater use of junior and inexperienced staff; and
- a lack of profit, leading directly to a reduction in the levels of in-house training and research and development.

Impact of design and documentation deficiencies

Construction process efficiency is affected by the occurrence of non-desirable elements of construction, such as rework, variations (change orders), cost overruns, extensions of time, program delays, contractual disputes and requests for information. To determine the impact that design and documentation quality has on these elements, contractors were asked to indicate what proportion were considered to be directly attributable to design and documentation deficiencies. The results:

Table 6.6.2 *Proportion of non-desirable construction elements due to design/documentation deficiencies*

Requests for Information (RFIs)	58.0%	Program delays	38.1%
Variations (change orders)	51.6%	Extensions of time	38.0%
Contract disputes	50.3%	Rework	37.6%
Cost overruns	45.6%		

Contractors were also asked whether the level of design and documentation quality directly influenced project cost and time at tender stage. In response, 93% indicated that design and documentation quality did influence the price submitted for a tender, while 75% indicated that it also had an influence on the time allowed for a project.

To determine the extent to which design and documentation quality influences project cost and time at tender stage, contractors were asked to indicate what allowance – either negative or positive – would generally be incorporated within their tenders, based on differing quality levels. The results:

	Standard of design and documentation				
	Excellent	Good	Average	Poor	Very poor
Time	–1.2%	0.2%	2.4%	7.1%	11.3%
Cost	–1.3%	0.3%	2.5%	7.2%	11.4%

Table 6.6.3 *Contractors' allowances for variances in design/documentation quality*

As can be seen above, when design and documentation quality is considered to be very poor an average of just over 11% was added to both the estimated project cost and time allowance. Even when the standard of quality is considered normal, an additional allowance of approximately 2.5%, on average, is included. However, at the other end of the scale an average reduction of over 1% in the tender allowances is given when design and documentation is considered to be of an excellent standard.

Researchers' conclusions (in brief)

The survey results indicate that all sections of the industry agree that there are major problems with the design and documentation process in the Australian construction industry, and that these problems are leading to construction inefficiencies and increased project costs. From a contractor's perspective, the deficiencies occurring in design and documentation were steadily increasing over the previous 12-15 years, and are causing corresponding increases in inefficiency in the construction process, resulting in decreases in project quality and increases in overall project costs.

Designers, while also acknowledging this reduction in design and documentation quality and services, consider the primary causes to be reducing design fees, decreasing project design and delivery times, and an increasing number of clients with unrealistic expectations and an inability to properly define project objectives and requirements. Both contractors and designers noted the increasing use of junior and inexperienced staff to carry out design functions. Designers suggested that this was a direct result of reduced fees and inadequate design time, limiting the type of staff available and the extent of supervision and in-house training provided.

By reducing design fees to minimise costs, clients and developers were, by their own actions, contributing to the problems that lead to inefficiencies in the construction process and increases in overall project costs. The results of the surveys clearly show a need for clients and developers to allocate adequate funds and time to the planning and design phases of a project, in order to maximise construction process efficiency and minimise overall project costs.

Editor's comments

First: CSIRO and the organizations that sponsored this research deserve a round of applause from both designers and contractors. They have validated what we know anecdotally. It is unfortunate that other professional organizations have not tackled this issue.

Second: The conclusions here are inescapable: Shaving design fees simply doesn't make any economic sense. Yes, one could argue that these results are based on perceptions rather than 'facts' – but the evidence is that contractors *price the projects according to the quality of the documentation.*

Let's take, for example, conventional construction. The consensus is that (on average) fees of about 6% are needed to carry out an adequate design and documentation, but designers can only get, on average, 4.5%. In simple terms, they can only do about 3/4 of a complete set of documents. One could reasonably conclude that this would result in either a 'poor' or 'very poor' result from the contractor's perspective – which according to them, would raise their costs and their prices by about 7 to 11% – and take a similar longer period to complete. This for a saving of 1.5% in fees!

Similarly, paying the designer enough to get an 'excellent' set of documents (and giving them enough time to do so) will return both cost and time savings about equal to the difference in fees.

What can you do with this information?

You can give your clients a copy of this chapter – it is on the mqia website. You can also download the complete paper this chapter is based on – see Resources at the end of Part 6.

You can use this information to have a discussion with some (but not all) clients about the benefits of providing adequate funds and time to prepare adequate documentation, and not to believe competitors who promise the impossible. You can keep accurate records of the real costs to prepare quality designs and documentation, and build a file of this information to support your negotiations.

Finally, you can – especially in a seller's market – simply turn down opportunities where you cannot create a quality result without losing money. Never enter a fee negotiation without knowing your 'walk away' point!

6.7 Quality in strategic alliances

Groups don't cooperate, people do.

David Maister

Reasons for forming strategic alliances are many, including seeking to gain experience in new building types, moving into new geographic markets, competing for projects beyond the size the firm can handle alone, reducing risk exposure on complex projects, and 'growing' the practice without hiring more staff.

Strategic alliances are joint ventures intended to be long-term and/or apply to multiple projects. The other key difference is that joint ventures tend to be transactional in nature (with economic issues prevailing), whereas successful strategic alliances are built on common or synergistic visions and longer-range objectives, as expressed in shared values.

On that basis, what establishes *quality* in a strategic alliance?

Let's return to the definition of quality: 'the degree to which a set of inherent characteristics fulfils requirements'. Here, the 'requirements' are the alliance partners' goals. Alliance characteristics that help achieve these goals create quality alliances.

Shared values

The first and most important of these characteristics – as noted above – is a set of *shared values*. Do not mistake this as a 'motherhood' statement – it is mission-critical. It means two things:

- Both alliance partners are internally clear and unified as to what their own practice values are – they have been through formal strategic planning processes and are working toward a preferred future.
- These values are discussed, and form the basis for entering the alliance.

I said that these visions and objectives could be common or synergistic. The latter means mutually complementary, but not necessarily the same. For example, it is not uncommon for *strong idea* firms to team up with *strong delivery* firms (see Chapter 6.1); the former taking responsibility for design and the latter for documentation.

Pitfalls to avoid

The strong idea / strong delivery alliance can run into problems where the strong idea firm thinks that it is more than 50% responsible for project success, and starts to treat the strong delivery firm as a drafting service. Practices that work successfully together recognize this danger, and take care to ensure that design responsibility is shared and credit rewarded equally.

Another common pitfall is inherent in alliances between firms that differ on the practice/business matrix described in Chapter 6.1.

For example: Suppose the practice instincts of one partner dictate that they should keep designing after the design budget has been used up, and the business instincts of the other say 'Stop designing!' Here is the potential for misunderstanding and disagreement over several key factors, not the least of which is the relative value of hours expended to reach a design solution.

Strategically aligned people

As the epigram notes, it is people, not groups, that cooperate. It follows that selection of key people to represent each side of the alliance is critical to success: they are the 'carriers' or 'enablers' of the value-sharing process. The further apart the cultures of the alliance organizations, the more important it is that these 'pairs' of people can relate and work well together. Here are two techniques used by practices that have mastered the art of alliances:

- Each provides a key person in the other firm's office. This person acts as the conduit through which all alliance communication flows, and thus provides an accessible, on-site 'interpreter' of the content.
- The idea of pairing is extended through the hierarchy in both alliance partners, as shown in the diagram below.

Table 6.7 *Pairing hierarchies in strategic alliances*

Alliance Partner A	Alliance Partner B
Principal	Principal
Project Director	Project Director
Project Manager	Project Manager

This model is especially useful in international alliances, and is used to escalate issues that aren't speedily resolved at any level. For example, if an issue can't be resolved within 24 hours at the project manager level, it is automatically escalated to the project director level, and so on. As you would expect, this highly motivates prompt issue resolution!

Finding and choosing the *right* alliance partners

If your practice has been in a couple of strategic alliances, you will *know* what the key issues are. For those that haven't, here is my prescription for creating a good alliance the first time.[3]

- ***Set objectives:*** Be absolutely clear why you want or need to be in a strategic alliance. These reasons must accord with, and grow from, your overall strategic plan (see Chapter 4.2).
- ***Map your needs:*** Based on the objectives, decide what you can provide, and what you need your alliance partner to provide.
- ***Develop selection criteria***: Create a profile of the ideal partner.
- ***Develop a search strategy:*** Check out the best choices carefully.
- ***Negotiate*** a comprehensive alliance agreement.

Selection criteria may include, as appropriate:

Communication and language compatibility Experience in similar building types Firm size and structure Similar design approach and philosophy	Technical resources Geographic proximity to project(s) Personality/professionalism of people to be assigned to project(s) Relative cost of services to be provided CAD systems compatibility

There are four search strategy options:

- Pick firms from *Reed Design Registry*[4] (if you are searching in the US), contact them, develop a shortlist, and interview them in their offices.
- Contact friends in the geographic area and ask for suggestions.
- Contact professional society in geographic area; ask for recommendations.
- Use a professional service with local knowledge to find and search candidates.

Prospective partner checkout

Here is a quick checklist for checking out your top candidates:

- Talk to objective referees, including clients and previous alliance partners, if any.
- Look at sample documents they produce. Are they up to your standards?
- Look at their records management systems. Are they compatible with yours?
- Eyeball nominated key alliance contacts. Are they the kind of people you want to work with? Would you hire them?
- Check with the local chapter of their professional association. Have any actions of unprofessionalism been brought against them?

And – above all – welcome the same rigor back. You want them to be as careful as you are!

For more info ...

For an expansion and extension of the ideas in this chapter, including advantages and disadvantages of the four search strategies, critical success factors for alliance success, and how to structure a good alliance agreement, see my paper on the website at www.mqia.com > 6.7a.

6.8 QM improves partnering; Partnering improves QM

Our distant forebears moved slowly from trial by battle and other barbaric means of resolving conflicts and disputes, and we must move away from total reliance on the adversary contest for resolving all disputes. For some disputes, trials by the adversarial contest must, in time, go the way of ancient trial by battle and blood. Our system is too costly, too painful, too destructive, too inefficient for a truly diversified people. To rely on the adversarial process as the principal means of resolving conflicting claims is a mistake that must be corrected.

Warren E. Burger

This chapter was prepared by partnering expert and handbook Key Resource Dr. William C. Ronco – Ed.

QM & partnering by William Ronco

Construction partnering has a two-way relationship with QM: QM improves partnering, and partnering improves QM. In fact, the potential partnering has to improve QM is so strong that it is important to consider including partnering in any QM program.

What is *partnering*? Partnering has been around for nearly thirty years, but many architects and engineers still do not know what it is. Worse, many *think* they know what partnering is. They say, 'we've always partnered with our clients', but register surprise when they learn the more specific definition of partnering.

Construction partnering is a highly structured form of team-building, initiated by the US Army Corps of Engineers. Partnering workshops involving key members of the project team (architects, engineers, owners, contractors, sub-contractors, etc.) to plan and manage project coordination and communications, anticipate and address problems and conflicts before they become serious.

Originally resisted by many in the industry, partnering has come to be embraced by contractors and owners, because it offers effective conflict resolution and communications management. Many government and corporate projects require partnering in their original bid documents. Some project insurers also require partnering. The Associated General Contractors sponsors awards for partnering efforts and provides extensive, excellent materials to enable contractors to develop and participate effectively in partnering efforts.

Architects and partnering

The AIA encourages partnering and provides excellent materials on partnering for architects. Partnering potentially offers architects the same benefits for effective project management that it offers contractors and owners.

However, many of the architects we have worked with in the 100+ partnering efforts we have led have been less than enthusiastic about it.

Some have been cool to the partnering process; others have expressed outright disdain. One 'signature' architect explained, 'What's all the fuss about communications? If partnering doesn't protect the integrity of my design concept, why should I care?' More recently, however, we have encountered a growing number of architects who support partnering. Often, we find that architects who are interested in QM also support partnering.

How partnering addresses QM issues

Partnering workshops usually include work in four different topic areas. QM issues surface in all four areas:

- ***Taking stock:*** Workshops begin with an open, facilitated discussion of project issues, concerns, roadblocks and opportunities. Quality issues surface here as project team members discuss their concerns about how the project will get built, what threatens the success of the project, why it will be important to address key items.
- ***Building mutual understanding and trust:*** Working with the Myers-Briggs Type Indicator or other similar tools helps surface how different project team members are likely to approach project issues differently. These tools open up discussion about how different types are likely to define quality differently, use different standards for quality, value different aspects of quality.
- ***Goals statement or partnering charter:*** Writing and signing a detailed project goals statement or partnering charter engages the group in useful discussion to agree on major project issues including expectations for quality, fit and finish, accuracy of drawings, coordination, accessibility, budget, etc.
- ***Refining key processes and procedures:*** Participants work on refining key project processes that impact quality including RFI management, turnaround, usage, tracking; change order management, tracking, etc.; substitutions uses, preferences; priority of schedule, cost or quality issues; regular project meeting agendas; processes for anticipating and managing differences of opinion when they occur.

> One factor that makes partnering effective in producing lasting results is that the workshops evenly balance focus in all four of these areas.

Quality management improves partnering

Architects who are involved with QM both perform more effectively in partnering and get more out of partnering. Partnering often involves extensive work on aspects of project management that are likely to be addressed in any QM program:

- Quality and accuracy of working drawings.
- Development of processes and procedures.
- Specifics of translating a design into a completed building.
- Clarifying expectations about quality.

- Establishing the understanding that quality and attention to detail are important.

Architects who have already begun to address such factors are likely to perform more effectively in partnering. Conversely, architects who are more 'design-centric', and who may have neglected QM are likely to find partnering to be a painful experience. Some would allege that it is a good thing that partnering often forces architects to address quality issues they have been neglecting. However, it is difficult for people to embrace new thinking if it is forced on them.

Partnering improves quality management

While it may be obvious that QM improves partnering, it is not necessarily so clear that partnering improves quality management. Many architects have QM programs that appear to be very effective yet they have never been involved with partnering. We believe such architects are missing out on two important benefits that partnering produces for quality management.

First, including partnering in QM helps QM to connect to the external world outside the firm: to projects, contractors, clients, engineers. This external link is important because too often, QM programs can develop a focus that is overly internal. They monitor and track drawings in the firm, study processes in the firm, involve staff in the firm. At its worst extreme, this kind of QM program can evolve into a kind of arrogance and blindness to real issues that occur on projects.

Linking QM with partnering breaks up any kind of internal focus for quality with more of a concern for life outside the doors of the organization. Moreover, other professionals and disciplines on a project are likely to have perspective and insight that provide real value for any QM program.

William C. Ronco, Ph.D., is President, Gathering Pace Consulting, Bedford, Massachusetts. Together with Jean S. Ronco, he is the author of *The Partnering Manual for Design and Construction* and *The Partnering Solution*.

You can obtain more information, and contact details, for Mr. Ronco on the handbook website: www.mqia.com > authors > Ronco.

Second, including partnering in QM makes it more likely that QM will include processes for communications as well as for assessment and measurement. The focus of many QM programs – creating lasting processes and procedures – may be anathema to more creative, free-spirit designers who prefer less structure and consistency in general. However, processes do help produce higher levels of quality.

Partnering almost always includes developing communications processes and procedures, e.g. for handling RFIs, tracking changes, monitoring client input. Such processes are a useful supplement for any QM program because they help translate quality standards and values into everyday project practices.

6.9 Quality in design-build

Teamwork is important. Providers who can demonstrate established communication channels and relationships among team members should have an advantage in the fast-paced design-build process.

Hanscomb Means Report

Key Resource John Beveridge reaches back to ancient Roman times – the architect Vitruveus – to argue for *quality* in architect-lead design-build. Citing Vitruvius' *firmness, commodity and delight* maxims, Beveridge's paper on the subject is summarized below. You can download Beveridge's unabridged version from the handbook website: www.mqia.com > 6.9a *Commodity, firmness & delight in design-build.*

Commodity, firmness & delight in design-build by John P. Beveridge

Each team member should (and usually does) care for each of the three components. But – and this is an important 'but' – each member invariably brings to the table individual definitions, priorities, and agendas. The success of the project, and therefore its quality, is directly linked to the *mutual* understanding and respect for team members' *different* goals and aspirations for the *same* project.

For each member of the design-build (DB) team (owner, builder, and architect) these three key components are obviously important. Each must be present to the degree required by the needs of the occupants, the economic circumstances, and society. However, I submit that each component generally gravitates to being the purview of one particular member of the team. Each has its own special interest in the project.

The owner may be more apt to define quality in terms of commodity: 'How well does this structure satisfy my needs in terms of why it was built in the first place?' The builder may be more prone to define quality in terms of firmness: 'How well have I built this structure? Will it stand up over time? Am I proud of my workmanship?'

The architect, as may be expected, while certainly cognizant and respectful of the other two criteria, will want to also assure the delight: 'Is this a handsome structure? Does it contribute positively to the environment? Has the building accomplished as much as it can architecturally, given the programmatic and financial dictates placed on the design?'

QM in design-build

The key elements for a successful DB project are essentially the same as any other project delivery method, namely:

- mutual understanding of the project's overall goals, the program of needs, the budget and the schedule;
- mutual buy-in of each team members' definition of quality as well as the value that each team member brings to the project; and
- mutual trust and respect for each party and confidence that each member will do his/her part honestly and with the utmost professionalism.

Although it may appear to be an oxymoron, the greatest DB project success is often achieved if the project is conducted in a 'traditional' (i.e. design-bid-build) manner. The owner needs to feel confidant that he is not pitted against a 'two-headed monster'; that the architect and builder are not in alliance, gleefully plotting against his interests.

The last item speaks to the big difference between DB and traditional design-bid-build delivery. Mutual trust, respect, and confidence are critical for the success of any DB project. Checks and balances associated with traditional delivery systems are, on the surface, absent.

The architect and builder are a single contractual entity, not two as is the norm where each independently contracts with the owner. In perception (and sometimes reality) there can be understandable prejudice against the 'fox watching the hens' syndrome. If, for no other reason – and there are others – QM procedures must be firmly in place for DB project delivery.

To build trust and confidence, the following QM issues should be in place prior to initiating any work (Note: the website version of this chapter expands on these points):

- A team approach to the project must be established. The owner, builder, and architect should play important, visible roles in the process. Both architect and builder need direct access to the owner, be in attendance at meetings, and have access to all project information, The owner needs direct access to subconsultants and subcontractors.
- Roles and responsibilities must be clearly defined. Who is responsible to whom, and for what? A good way to communicate roles and responsibilities is a simple matrix of assignments, perhaps broken down into primary and secondary levels of involvement.
- Lines of communication must be clearly established. The best document for this is a simple team organization chart.

What about design-led design-build?

There are compelling reasons for the design professional to lead the DB team:

- This methodology allows the designer to return to the role of 'master builder'. The designer maintains overriding control of the project, and therefore, the *quality* of the result.
- The architect usually has a closer relationship to the client than the contractor, particularly in understanding the process of programming and development of design. Both issues are absolutely essential and germane to QM.
- Throughout, decisions must be made that affect the aesthetics, functions, and budget of a project. The architect is in the best position to understand the global implications of these decisions.

Implementing QM in DB

DB success depends on implementing QM procedures at each stage of project realization, as follows (the website version of this chapter expands on these points):

Points of contention:

Materials: Unless the owner has a very clear RFP (Request for Proposal) he must be prepared to accept materials and systems as dictated by the design-builder. This is potentially one of the most contentious areas of any DB project. The tighter the quality is defined in the program, the more assurance that the owner will get what he asked for.

Schedule: The design, the materials, and the systems selected during the design phase dictate the schedule outcome. Complex assemblies, long-lead items, and weather-sensitive construction should be avoided, or, at the very least, factored in.

Project definition: Basic project parameters (program, budget and schedule) may be established by one of three methods:

- The owner establishes a comprehensive Program of Needs and Performance Criteria, and issues an RFP to DB firms; typically for a guaranteed maximum price (GMP) contract.
- The owner issues an RFP containing the requirements. The DB firm proposes a program based on these requirements.
- The owner retains the design team and develops a bridging delivery model.[1]

Regardless of the method, a firmly established (and understood) program of needs, budget, and schedule is absolutely essential at the outset of the project.

Design: Translate the program into a design that reflects the owner's requirements, consistent with the budget. Critical issues are: (a) all parties are involved and visible throughout the process, (b) deliverables are set at the beginning of design, and (c) a design and scope contingency must be incorporated into the budget.

Documentation: In addition to those above, critical issues are: (a) it is paramount that the owner approves, in writing, the design and budget prior to starting documentation; (b) the design team members have worked together and know each other well; and (c) they produce full documentation – it is required both for QC and budget control.

John Beveridge, AIA, recently retired as Principal with The S/L/A/M Collaborative and President of The S/L/A/M Construction Services Division, a CM organization established to serve the firm's architectural clients. – Ed.

Construction: The more the DB project is managed in a traditional project delivery manner, the more that quality will be maintained. Key issues:

- Hold weekly job meetings with the owner, contractor, and consultants participating. Keep and distribute minutes.
- Tour the project on a regular basis, with the owner and contractor.
- Maintain an open book policy regarding payments to subcontractors. The architect should be required to perform in the traditional manner in terms of reviewing and signing off on monthly requisitions.
- Avoid the temptation to short-circuit or eliminate paperwork. Maintain the standard stream of shop drawings, RFIs, SIs (Site Instructions), etc. It protects everyone in the long run.
- Close out the project in standard fashion: prepare a punch list with owner's participation; hold a post-construction critique; be assured that client is satisfied with the project. Experience indicates that this method is utilized most often by clients with ongoing construction programs.

Experience says this project completion method is the best marketing possible for getting the next job.

Part 6: Sources, resources & notes

NOTE: *The Architect's Handbook of Professional Practice 13th Ed.*, Joseph A. Demkin, Exec. Ed., published by John Wiley & Sons, is referred to as '*AIA Handbook*'.

Sources

6.1 Kaderlan, Norman (1991) *Designing Your Practice,* McGraw-Hill, p 55.

Maister, David H. (1993) *Managing the Professional Service Firm,* Free Press Paperbacks, pp 21-30.

6.2 Kaderlan, pp 98-9, 100. Kaderlan's Chapter 6 is an excellent summary of verbal and non-verbal communication, well worth reading.

Peters, Tom (1987) *Thriving on Chaos: Handbook for a Management Revolution,* Pan Books, pp 412-14.

6.6 Tilley, Paul A. et al (September 1999) *Design and Documentation Quality and its Impact on the Construction Process*, an address to the CIB W55 & W65 Joint Triennial Symposium, Capetown (Document CIB_99). See also the sidebar notes on p 174.

Resources

6.1 Cramer, James P. and Scott Simpson (2002) *How Firms Succeed: A Field Guide to Design Management*, Ostberg Library of Design Management, pp 54-97.

Kaderlan, pp 53-73, 153-63.

Stasiowski, Frank (1993) *Value Pricing for the Design Firm*, John Wiley & Sons.

6.2 Abramowitz, Ava J. (2002) *Architect's Essentials of Contract Negotiation*, John Wiley & Sons, 162-8, 178.

Cramer, James P. and Scott Simpson, pp 63-8, 106-8.

Myers, Isabel Briggs and Peter B. Myers (reprinted 1993) *Gifts Differing: Understanding Personality Type*, CPP Books. Excellent source for information on Myers Briggs.

6.3 Cramer, James P. and Scott Simpson, pp 16-20.

Maister, David H. (1993) *Managing the Professional Service Firm,* pp 121-42.

Maister, David H. (1997) *True Professionalism*, The Free Press, pp 167-70.

6.4 Cramer, James P. and Scott Simpson, pp 22-38.

Rackham, Neil, and John R. DeVincentis (1998) *Rethinking the Sales Force: Redefining Selling to Create, and Capture Customer Value*, McGraw-Hill. The whole book!

Thomsen, Chuck (1989) *Managing Brainpower, Book 3: Selling,* The AIA Press.

6.5 Cramer, James P. and Scott Simpson, pp 150-78.

Kaderlan, pp 99-106.

6.6 Tilley, Paul A. and Stephen L. McFallan (2000) *Design and Documentation Quality Survey: A Survey Investigating Changes in Design and Documentation within the Australian Construction Industry and its Effect on Construction Process Efficiency* (three papers: BCE Doc. 00-113 *Designer's Perspective*, BCE Doc. 00-114 *Contractor's Perspective,* and BCE Doc. 00-115 *Comparison of Designers' and Contractors' Perspectives*), CSIRO.

6.7 Maister, David H., *Managing the Professional Service Firm,* pp 329-44.

6.8 Ronco, William C., and Jean S. Ronco (1996) *Partnering Manual for Design and Construction*, McGraw-Hill. This is the best source available on partnering.

6.9 Flynn, Larry (February 2002) Return of the Master Builder, *Building Design & Construction.* Recommended reading on designer-led DB.

Gupta, Ron, and Paul Doherty, *AIA Handbook*, Chapter 18.10, pp 612-5.

Moreno, Elena Marcheso, *AIA Handbook Update 2003*, pp, 31-9.

www.mqia.com:

6.3a Scott Braley, *Quality in Market Positioning.*

6.6a *The quality consequences of fee cutting*, a downloadable copy of this chapter.

6.6b Tilley, Paul A., et al, (September 1999), *Design and Documentation Quality and its Impact on the Construction Process.*

6.9a Beveridge, John P., *Commodity, firmness & delight in design-build.*

Epigrams

6.1 Wills, Royal Barry (1941) *This Business of Architecture*, Reinhold Publishing Corp., Foreword.

6.2 Maister, David H., *True Professionalism*, p 160.

6.3 Stasiowski, Frank, *Value Pricing,* p 18.

6.4 Flynn-Heapes, Ellen (2000) *Creating Wealth*, SPARKS: The Centre for Strategic Planning, p 50.

6.5 TV series produced by Independent Pictures.

6.6 Tilley, Paul, November (2000) *Cost-cutting Leads to Poor Value,* Address to the Hong Kong Institute of Value Management International Conference, p 4.

6.7 Maister, David H., *Managing the Professional Services Firm*, p 335.

6.8 Burger, Warren E., Chief Justice of the United States, in 1984.

6.9 Hanscomb Means Report (January-February 2004) *Design-build becoming a revolution,* Vol 16 No. 6.

Endnotes

1 The bridging concept is the brain-child of Chuck Thomsen, Chairman of Houston-based 3D International, and George Heery, formerly head of Atlanta-based Heery International. Bridging is similar to the novation model (where the client assigns – 'novates' – the partially-completed design contract to a general contractor), except that the original design team stays on, in the employ of the client, to ensure that the design is executed faithfully. The project is bid at the end of the design phase, and the builder takes over the responsibility for documentation, employing its own design completion and documentation team. The stunning elegance of the bridging model is that it preserves the accountability of the design team, it avoids any conflict of interest, it preserves the vital feedback connection, and it still has all the cost/time-control benefits of the design > document/build model.

2 International Council for Research and Innovation in Building and Construction. CIB's website is www.cibworld.nl.

3 These notes are adapted from a presentation I gave in December 2000, in Atlanta, at the PSMJ Strategic Alliance Conference.

4 The *Reed Design Registry* replaces the *Profile* that was published by Construction Market Data prior to 2005. See http://www.reedregistry.com.

7 Project Quality: Techniques that Deliver Results

7.1 QM tools for the built environment practice

7.2 The project brief

7.3 Project quality plans

7.4 Design reviews

7.5 Project quality audits

7.6 Checking & checklists

7.7 Document management

7.8 QM & performance specifications

7.9 Measuring documentation quality

7.10 Quality in project management

7.11 Quality in project management: Prince2 vs PMBOK

7.12 Value management for designers

7.13 Quality issues in international materials procurement & logistics

7.14 Design quality issues in construction management

Just when you think you've got it all together, a new stakeholder pops up!

7.1 QM tools for the built environment practice

When selecting a QI tool, select the tool that will make your point at a glance.

Peter Mears

'QI' in Mears' epigram stands for 'Quality Improvement' – Ed.

This ***very*** brief chapter is a doorway to information on the tools of quality relevant to the practice of architecture. My previous book *TQM and ISO 9000 for Architects and Designers* contained an extensive chapter describing 90 quality tools, techniques and systems, drawn from a number of sources, with examples of how they are used in design practice. That list and the examples provided are still relevant. Even in a chaotic world, some things don't change.

Rather than repeat or try to condense that information here, I have put the complete chapter on the handbook website. You can download it in .pdf format from www.mqia.com > Projects > 7.1a *The Designer's TQM Toolkit.*

Some frequently-used QM tools are described in other chapters of this handbook; for example:

3.5 External audits

5.4 Team-building

6.8 Partnering

7.3 Project quality plans

7.4 Design reviews

7.6 Checklists

For readers who think that anything labeled 'TQM' has nothing to do with their practices, I suggest that you are *already* using many of these tools. For example, the descriptions and examples include such tools as flowcharts, checklists, pie charts, bar charts, brainstorming, focus groups, benchmarking, team building, design review, partnering, peer reviews, pre-bid checking, constructability reviews and record drawings – all 'stock-in-trade' for many design practices.

Every design practice I have ever seen employs a variety of quality tools and techniques; they just don't think of them in those terms.

7.2 The project brief

What are called in the U.S. 'program' and 'schedule' are in Commonwealth countries called 'project brief' and 'program' or 'programme' respectively.

In this chapter I will use the Commonwealth countries' terms – just a slight cultural shift for US readers!

A brief is everything an architect needs to know about the building a client needs. The client's yearnings, ideas and vision should be clearly expressed in it, together with every activity and important piece of equipment or treasured possession to be accommodated.

Frank Salisbury

If the purpose of a QM program is to 'get it right the first time', agreement on what the job is about is undeniably a crucial issue.

However, with all but the most experienced clients, the process of brief creation goes on well into schematic design and design development, and is usually more the responsibility of the architect than the client. This situation is well known and accepted. What is not so well known or accepted is that this process creates some of the particular problems that cause risk for the architect. If the architect, in helping the client develop the brief, gets the brief wrong, the design will also be wrong.

When you are working on what issues the project brief and the briefing process need to address, do not forget the people who will be responsible for it after you are all done. Read Chapters 8.5 *QM in Facilities Management* and 8.6 *QM in Asset Management.*

If the project is a people workplace, consider Chapters 8.7 and 8.8.

Failure to get the client to formally accept (sign off on) the brief is endemic among architects, a failure that ultimately imperils them.

For architects, one of the most powerful benefits of an ISO 9001 QM system is the ***requirement*** to ensure that the brief is agreed between the parties. This forces a necessity to clarify contractual terms both between architect and client and between architect and subconsultants.

It forces the client to come to terms with suggestions put forward by the architect, rather than to tacitly permit them but criticize them later. The necessity for resolution of the brief also can act to force the architect's attention on the details of the project, and chase away woolly thinking and possibly inappropriate dreams of making the project an 'award-winner'.

The brief as 'driver' of the design review process

The thoughts of the client tend to come in over the course of the project, sometimes by telephone and sometimes in scribbled notes or more formal correspondence. These 'instructions' from the client all form part of the brief. The project brief is an important document against which the design must be tested in design review. The reviewer must refer to the project brief in order to review the design.

Practically speaking, the only way the design review can function so as to meet the intent of ISO 9001 is to have access to a concise and complete project brief. Hence all communications from the client regarding the design must be collected together and readily accessible.

One of my past clients, a high-profile practice in Western Australia, developed a way of preserving briefing data that is a quality auditor's dream. For selected projects (most large ones), on all design documents up through the completion of design development, they put the entire project brief right on the design drawings, in a space reserved on the right-hand fourth or third of the drawings.

What happens more often is that this information is scattered throughout the project files; virtually irretrievable as a unified document. Therefore we need a regularized way of channeling this data into such a unified document.

A simple way to accomplish this is to have the project brief as a heading in your project filing system. Then all documents forming part of the client's instructions, or copies of them, are filed there, and that file comprises the complete project brief.

Another good way to help to properly develop the brief is to begin the data collection in a formalized way. An example is the *Project Data Record*, shown on the next page. Many firms have developed and use forms such as this example – they all have the benefit of beginning to organize information about the project.

This particular example picks up some other requirements of ISO 9001, such as the assignment of project responsibilities, defining whether preparation of the project brief is the client's or the consultant's responsibility or both, defining quality management parameters for the project, and setting up the distribution schedule for controlled project documents.

Building Technology
puts your name, address, contact numbers & ACN here. This is the standard style and font. Special layouts are available.

Project Form **PF01**

Project Data Record

Project	Approved by:
No.	Date:

PROJECT DATA

Complete project title: Location/ address:

CLIENT DATA

Name:
Address:

Tele: ______ Fax: ______
Contact: ______ Mobile: ______

BUILDER DATA

Name:
Address:

Tele: ______ Fax: ______
Contact: ______ Mobile: ______

OWNER DATA (if different from client)

Name:
Address:

Contact: ______ Mobile: ______
Tele: ______ Fax: ______

CONSULTANT TEAM

INSTRUCTIONS:
Identify all project consultants in the matrix below. Enter an 'x' if they are subconsultants or separate consultants in the left two columns; enter an 'x' opposite their project responsibilities in the remaining columns. Up to 5 disciplines can be entered for the first subconsultant; 2 each for the second and third, and 1 each for the other four. Use a second page if there are more than 7 consultants or 13 disciplines.

Subcontract	Separate contract	Project manager	Civil engineer	Structural engineer	Landscape architect	Hydraulics	Mechanical services	Electrical services	Fire services	Lifts & escalators	Acoustical consultants	Geotechnical	Cost planner / QS	Other:	Details
															Firm: / Proj. Dir. Address: / Tele: Fax: Proj. Eng. Mobile: Tele: Proj. Eng. Mobile: Tele: Proj. Eng. Mobile: Tele: Proj. Eng. Mobile: Tele: Proj. Eng. Mobile: Tele:
															Firm: / Proj. Dir. Address: / Tele: Fax: Proj. Eng. Mobile: Tele: Proj. Eng. Mobile: Tele:
															Firm: / Proj. Dir. Address: / Tele: Fax: Proj. Eng. Mobile: Tele: Proj. Eng. Mobile: Tele:
															Firm: / Proj. Dir. Address: / Mobile: Proj. Eng. Tele: Fax: Mobile:
															Firm: / Proj. Dir. Address: / Mobile: Proj. Eng. Tele: Fax: Mobile:
															Firm: / Proj. Dir. Address: / Mobile: Proj. Eng. Tele: Fax: Mobile:
															Firm: / Proj. Dir. Address: / Mobile: Proj. Eng. Tele: Fax: Mobile:

Date Printed 5/12/2005

7.3 Project quality plans

Planning is the activity of (a) establishing goals, and (b) establishing the means required to meet those goals.

Dr. J. M. Juran

By whatever name it goes under, the outcome of the quality planning process is a *plan*, which I'll call by its common acronym, PQP. In every version of quality systems, this plan is what drives the 'excellence factor' in the design output. In simple terms, the PQP establishes the results that design is to achieve.

PQPs can be very simple tools – one page – for simple projects, and a small book for major projects. They can be stand-alone documents or combined with other project planning documents, such as the project brief, design management plans, communication plans, risk plans, etc.

Thomson Adsett's *Design Road Map*

Let me describe a first-class example of a PQP that *really* works for the practice that uses it. Thomson Adsett Architects (TAA) is an Australian design firm with offices up and down the East coast and in a number of SE Asian cities. They have been certified to ISO 9001 for many years.

TAA has two key QM planning documents:

- Design Road Map: A 6-page, pink-paper, short-form PQP that captures key project data in a series of checklists covering:
  - design inputs;
  - design outputs;
  - work plans and methods;
  - engagement (contract details);
  - schematic design;
  - documentation;
  - building approval documentation and contract documentation;
  - construction – Contract administration; and
  - post-occupancy / service phase.
- Job Book: A 25-page guide to using the Design Road Map, with instructions and guide notes to everything in it. This is the 'user manual'.

These two documents are bound together and set up for *each* project, regardless of size, at project initiation. Experienced staff are completely familiar with the Job Book, so they really refer to it when mentoring new employees. For new employees, it is their 'bible' to success in the practice. Every section must be checked and signed off by the project architect when its work is complete.

At project completion, the project architect completes the back section of the Job Book, which includes:

- A design validation report to the Quality Manager, covering:
  - a confidential post-engagement report;
  - a client feedback survey;
  - a post-occupancy evaluation (POE) (if scheduled); and
  - a feedback evaluation.
- A building cost analysis
- Archival records and instructions
- The post-engagement report, providing for identification of a wide range of problems found in doing the project
- A review of built environment (if a POE was scheduled)
- A brief lessons learned report

If this discussion appeals to you, and you have a similar in-house checklist system or other tool that you would like evaluated for its compliance with QM standards, I will be happy to do that for a modest fee. Just contact me on info@buildingtech.com.

And here's a challenge: If you don't mind that I talk and write about your great tools, as I have in this example (and without using your name), I'll even give you a ***free*** evaluation.

Can you find a better deal than that?

TAA has refined this simple tool over nearly two decades; the Job Book is now in its 13th version. It is both remarkably thorough and extremely efficient. The four pages of checklists – just two pieces of paper – include more than 150 tasks that can be used to tailor the firm's management of the project to specific conditions.

Of course, there are thousands of possible tasks that *might* apply to any project – but this small, manageable group contain the Pareto Principle *critical few* that apply to most of this firm's aged care projects; their main niche market.

TAA is building its retail sector clientele, and is creating a special version of the Design Road Map for retail projects; again, to identify the efficient subset of tasks that apply to that market niche. They say that the differences have more to do with different client expectations than with building type differences.

The Design Road Map is started at the beginning of a project, and progressively completed as the project moves through its stages.

No – this system doesn't prevent 100% of errors and omissions – but it gets most of them, most of the time. And that's about as good as it gets for any quality tool in an industry where every project is a 'one-off'.

TAA staff understand the value of this simple tool, and they use it. No, they probably wouldn't give you a copy; it is part of what makes their practice unique; a service quality differentiator. You can, however, see two sample pages of the TAA Job Book in Chapter 2.4 to get an idea of the structure.

However, even if they did give you a copy, your practice wouldn't know how or why to use it. These things really must be developed over time to suit the unique character of the practice and the projects the practice takes.

7.4 Design reviews

Design review is the most critical aspect of a quality management system for a building design practice.

Tim Cornick

All architects and other designers do design review: usually informally, as a 'desktop crit', and usually without keeping any records of the review. These reviews typically look only at the design itself, at its internal cohesion; rather than focusing on whether the design is actually complying with its requirements.

The 'desktop crit' vs. ISO 9001 design review

Design review is a requirement of ISO 9001, which mandates it (clause 7.3.4):

- Reviews are performed according to plan
- Ability of design/documentation to meet requirements is evaluated
- Problems are identified and solutions proposed
- Participants in the review include representatives of functions concerned with the review stage
- Records of the review are kept

A design review checklist is an excellent prompt for the review process, which can also serve as the planning and recording tool. An example is shown on the next page.

ISO 9001 also requires design and development *verification* and *validation* (clauses 7.3.5 and 7.3.6)

Verification means that the design is checked to ensure that design/development output meets design and development input requirements.

Validation means that design and development is checked to ensure that the resulting product (or service) meets requirements for specified application or intended use.

(My interpretation. The ISO 9000 definitions for these terms are simiolar but different.)

Verification

There are several acceptable methods of design verification, but the one most applicable to architecture is design review. Thus, the design review will satisfy the verification requirement. For engineers, the most applicable method is usually performing alternate calculations.

Validation

The chief requirement of design validation is to determine whether or not the design satisfies the client's requirements. If the client's requirements, expressed as the project brief, are made part of the design input requirements at each stage, then a design review can satisfy all three of these requirements.

If a well-designed form is used to plan, prompt and record the design review, the cost of this formal review process would be no greater than an informal review. The benefits of this formal review, however, could be very significant. One of the problems with the traditional review is that it is 'ad hoc': It happens when there is time for it to happen, and when everyone gets busy, the reviews either don't happen, or they are not thorough enough.

The planning and reporting requirements of the ISO 9001 design review process force the practice to think ahead, schedule reviews at the right time, make sure that everybody is in attendance who should be there, and ensure that the design is checked against all of the relevant criteria.

Building Technology puts your name, address, contact numbers & ACN here. This is the standard style and font. Special layouts are available.	**Project Form**	**PF07**
		Design Review Checklist

Project	Prepared by:
No.	Date:

Type of review:

- [] Internal
- [] Client
- [] Consultant audit

INPUTS to be considered (Check appropriate boxes):

- [] Quality Manual
- [] Project Quality Plan
- [] Project brief
- [] Codes/regulations
- [] Approved schematic design
- [] Approved design development

Other (list):

- [] _____
- [] _____
- [] _____

MATTERS FOR REVIEW (Check appropriate boxes):

1 ☐ Design inputs
2 ☐ Project brief
3 ☐ List of significant restraints
4 ☐ Acceptance criteria
5 ☐ Design changes
6 ☐ Schematic design output
7 ☐ Design development output

8 ☐ Contract documentation
9 ☐ Subconsultant coordination
10 ☐ Consultant coordination
11 ☐ Specifications
12 ☐ Design calculations
13 ☐ Marketing/tenanting
14 ☐ Environmental impact

15 ☐ Site data
16 ☐ Initial cost
17 ☐ Life cycle cost
18 ☐ Value engineering
19 ☐ Buildability
20 ☐ Safety
21 ☐ Performance

Other (list):

22 ☐ _____
23 ☐ _____
24 ☐ _____
25 ☐ _____
26 ☐ _____
27 ☐ _____
28 ☐ _____

ATTENDEES
Enter names & firms. Enter project role under "Code".

DR = Director
PD = Project director
PA = Project architect

QM = Quality manager
RE = Design reviewer
PS = Project staff

SC = Subconsultant
OT = Other

CL = Client
CO = Consultant
PM = Project manager

NAME	FIRM	CODE

RESULTS of design review: Identify by number in front of matters reviewed, as above. Use reverse side if extra room is needed.

REVIEW STAGE:
- [] Schematic Design
- [] Design Development
- [] Contract Documents

Completed by: _____
Date: _____

▌ABCsp PF07	▌Ver. 3.1h	▌Date: 1.4.19:	▌Page	1/ 1

7.5 Project quality audits

A quality audit is an independent review of quality performance

Dr. J. M. Juran

The basic idea of an 'audit' is that you compare actual performance to planned and required performance. Essentially: 'How well did we do this time?' Perhaps it is obvious, but you can't do an audit – can't find out 'how well we did' – unless there is a project plan that establishes the intended performance. Accept that idea, and it follows that the audit will always be couched in terms of these comparisons – which may be against external requirements (set by the client) or by internal requirements, e.g. our own QA – our promises to our clients about our performance.

Are audits worth doing?

The answer to this question depends on whether or not you want to know how well your projects perform compared to either your own goals, or the client's requirements, or both. If you are not interested in that information, skip the rest of this chapter.

Most design practices make assumptions about how well they are doing on a project basis, but rarely ask the tough questions that will give them a second opinion. Those that do are often surprised by the results. Example: The local office of a top international engineering firm hired a new Business Development Manager. He discovered that there was no record of client feedback other than quarterly surveys, which didn't really contain much useful information. So he went out and interviewed all of the firm's clients over the previous three years, and prepared a report on his findings.

This report identified an extraordinary opportunity: Clients said, across the board, that all the firms they dealt with were lacking in 'client care' – the touchy-feely stuff. These clients made it clear that resolving this issue would give the firm that worked that out a huge marketing advantage – and their future business.

Was the Business Development Manager rewarded for this news? No – he nearly 'got the sack' because senior engineers in the firm resented the finding, and were ready to shoot the messenger! *They didn't want to know!* The good news is that he is still there, and this particular office is now one of the most profitable offices in the entire practice, which spans over two dozen offices in a dozen countries.

The value of information

Some years ago I was facilitating a quality workshop at the AIA National Convention. When we got to the discussion on change order management, a participant stood up and told us the following story:

> Ten years ago, we decided to do something about change order requests. They were taking up too much time and energy, and eroding our profitability during contract administration. We wanted to know the cause of all these requests. So we started keeping track of them, on every project.
>
> We've done that now for ten years. We know exactly, for any kind of project we do, the number of change requests we can expect, and we know what percentage of those will be created by clients changing their minds, what percentage by the contractor wanting the change, what percentage caused by mistakes we made, or any other reason. We also know how long these change orders prolong the project.
>
> What we didn't realize when we started this was how valuable that information really was. Sure, we now manage them better. But this information has become our most powerful marketing tool. When we talk to potential clients about how we manage change requests, and show them our records, they get very excited.
>
> Their reaction: 'Here is an architect that understands how to manage time and money!' This record, and the knowledge, gives us a huge advantage over our competitors, who have no such records, and really don't know'.

The audit process

That firm was auditing just one small aspect of project performance, change orders. The Business Development Manager of the engineering firm was auditing client satisfaction. An audit simply captures and records key project information. It can be as simple or as extensive as you like. Perhaps it is obvious, but still worth saying: a simple audit takes almost no time at all. The most time-consuming part might be a visit with the client to find out how well the client liked the services you provided. Not the *project* – but the *services*. A great award-winning result, badly delivered, won't get you a repeat client!

ISO 9001:2000 requires (clause 8.2.1) that internal audits are planned and carried out, especially regarding client perceptions about whether or not you have satisfied their requirements.

Here I want to return to the story of the engineering firm. They are an ISO-certified practice. ISO 9001:2000 (clause 8.2.2) allows you decide how to set up audit processes. This firm satisfied the ISO 9001 requirement by sending out a quarterly survey to active clients, asking for responses on customer satisfaction. Efficient? Of course. Useful? No – a waste of paper and clients' time, at least in my opinion.

Nothing beats a face-to-face meeting, with a question something like, 'Henry, how did we really do on this project, from where *you* sit. Give it to me straight.' Henry will tell you, if your tone and body language tells him that you really do care, and are listening.

You might not be ready for this, but you can learn a lot about your practice by asking similar questions of the contractors that build your projects.

Capturing vital information from clients, contractors, building users, or the public is an audit *external* to the project. Don't confuse this with an *external firm audit*, however, as described in Chapter 3.5. A project audit normally also includes capturing vital internal information. The table below is a good guide to the kinds of information you *might* want to collect about a project:

Table 7.5 *Audit checklist*

External to the project	Internal to the project
♦ Client satisfaction • Planned cost vs. actual • Planned completion vs. actual • Quality of client relationship ♦ User satisfaction • Post occupancy evaluation (See Chapter 8.1) • Building management satisfaction (Operability) ♦ Contractor relationship • Buildability feedback • Change order history • RFI history	♦ Planned profit vs. actual profit ♦ Met schedule deadlines ♦ Rework ♦ Achieved planned QC measures, e.g. checking ♦ Project feedback as planned (See Chapter 2.8)

Who does the audit?

Answer: Anybody but the leaders of thc project team. Reason: They can never be impartial, and if they missed something doing the project, they would be the people least likely to discover it later. It is for this reason that ISO 9001 does not permit auditors to audit their own work.

After the audit

What happens after the audit? ISO 9001:2000 (clause 8.2.2) covers this by charging management with responsibility for ensuring that prompt action is taken to deal with both the problems found and their causes. This is good advice. Why bother finding out how well your project was handled if you don't intend to fix any problems you learned from doing it?

7.6 Checking & checklists

Many architects and engineers do not devote enough time to a final coordination review. Those who know how to coordinate documents tend to be very experienced. Ironically, those experienced in the process are often thought to be too valuable for such work. Result: the least experienced person in an office frequently makes the final coordination review. Sometimes designers wait until the last minute to consolidate drawings for other disciplines. Result: no coordination review at all.

DPIC Companies

Checking of design output is the lowest common denominator of design quality control, and as DPIC has noted, one where all too often we fail. Checking seeks to find mistakes, not prevent them; much less eradicate cultures that tolerate mistakes. Checking initiatives succeed or fail based on some simple guidelines:

Table 7.6.1 *Checking success vs. failure*

Checking success	Checking failure
Checking is planned and scheduled	Checking is not planned or not scheduled
Checking takes place at successive points	Checking is left until the end of a phase
The checker is thoroughly experienced in construction techniques	The checker is not experienced in construction techniques
The checker is independent of the design team	The checker is part of the design team
The team leader believes checking is critical to a good project, and ensures it happens	The team leader thinks checking is a good idea, but allows progress to use up the time for checking
Inter-discipline checking requirements are established and rigorously maintained	The team leader presumes that other disciplines are responsible for their own checking

The fourth of these points may require explanation. The person most likely to miss an error or omission is the person who made the error or 'created' the omission. Conversely, the less a person knows about a project, the more likely it is that they will question things that don't seem quite right or quite complete.The most common excuse given for failing to carry out intended checking programs is that the team 'ran out of time'. Over the last ten years, in my workshops at National AIA Conventions, I have been asking audiences about their experience with checking. The results, approximately:

Table 7.6.2 *Incidence of pre-bid checking*

Question:	10 years ago		Today (2005)	
Answers >	Yes	No	Yes	No
Do you believe that pre-bid checking is essential?	100%	nil	100%	nil
Do you actually carry out the checking most of the time?	35%	65%	75%	25%
Do you include time for checking in project plans and schedules?	20%	80%	75%	25%

While I certainly do not claim that asking the question has caused the change, these results indicate that:

- US architects today are far more likely to plan and schedule checking than they were ten years ago, and
- the success in their intention to carry out checking is tightly related to planning and scheduling it.

Powerful stuff!

Checking methodologies

Most successful practices have evolved checking methodologies, which (as noted above) work when they are planned and scheduled as part of the project process. Two examples stand out:

The **Redicheck** system, developed by William Nigro, an architect who was a Lt. Commander with the U.S. Navy, responsible for construction of naval facilities during the 70's and early 80's. Nigro was the first person to develop a system of validating the usefulness of checklists, and his controlled experiments will stand a long time as having established the value of checking.

Redicheck includes the use of spot checks, final checks and comparing plans drawn by various disciplines, over-laying them on a light-table. Nigro's conclusion from having tracked the results of pre-bid checking on hundreds of NAVFAC projects is that savings are typically 3% of cost of construction.

More information on **Redicheck** is available from the **Redicheck** web site: http//www.redicheck-review.com.

The Heery International model: **'Red-Green-Yellow'** method of checking is a well-developed, fairly rigorous, 9-step checking process.

It identifies 'potential' changes in green pen, signalling other checkers that there is a problem that must be solved through coordination. 'Definite' changes are marked in red. Green items are reviewed and gradually converted to red as interdisciplinary solutions are found.

Finally, an independent reviewer checks the changes and marks corrections in yellow. More information on this method is available on the handbook website [www.mqia.com].

Checklists

Checklists are formalized checking aids; prompts about things that should be checked.

The single most important fact about checklists is an inherent paradox in our perspective on them: *We all really believe in using them, but we staunchly resist doing it.* You can't build a successful system of checklists in your practice without resolving this paradox.

In the last two decades, I have had a lot of experience building and promoting checklists systems, first for the Royal Australian Institute of Architects (RAIA) and later as a part of the model quality management systems my business marketed. This experience has been instructive. Here are the key lessons from it, which I hope will be useful to readers who are engaged in producing firm checklists:

- Checklists must be easily practice-definable, e.g. able to be customized to suit the practice.
- Checklists must be project-definable.
- Checklists must be easy to complete, without too much thinking or writing.
- Project checklists should not include non-applicable items (to the specific project).
- One set of checklist forms should work for multiple checking periods, rather than being re-cast for each checking period.

These lessons caused me to re-evaluate the whole design of our checklists, because what those findings really mean is that the checklist has to be an interactive database if it works the way users want it to work. Easily stated; not so easily achieved. More on that below.

Checklist theory: memory-jogger vs. process-based

For all their popularity, checklists are not easy to get right. Most checklist system developers use the 'memory jogger' approach, which tends to eventuate into such massive structures as to be practically useless. [1]

The memory-jogger checklist is simply a long list of items – nouns – that should be considered in evaluating a set of documents or a situation. The problem with the memory-jogger checklist is that it doesn't actually tell you what to look for or what to do when you find it. For that you need a process-based checklist, so designed that if you do what the checklist tells you to do, you will have satisfied the quality requirements. For example: A memory-jogger checklist item might be 'Light switches'. The corresponding process checklist item might be 'Check that light switches are not behind door swings'.

The CHECKIT! system

> CHECKIT! is similar to Nigro's pioneering efforts, in that it is process-based rather than a memory-jogger. However, it covers the entire design, documentation and contract administration process, rather than just validation of contract documents.

The CHECKIT! system was developed in 1987-95 for the RAIA National Practice Division. Prior to publishing the first of the series, working with the RAIA Practice Division and a select team of seasoned practitioners, I did some research that established that a major reason why architects did not use checklists was that they were too long and took too much time. At that time, the only checklists that RAIA members had were the British RIBA checklists, which were very comprehensive. *Too* comprehensive, in fact, for Australian users!

So we worked on the 85% theory – that it was better to have an easy-to-use system that got 85% of things right most of the time than to have a system that would get 100% of things right, but be too lengthy to use. I didn't know it at the time, but what we were doing was applying Juran's Pareto principle of the 'vital few'.

We decided that the checklist for each checking function should be limited to what would fit on one A4 page, which, by allowing two lines of standard typing on a matching fill-in form, turned out to be 28 items. We used an alphabetical system, so we ended up with the 'vital few' being 26 functions by 28 items – which, being process items, represented the '85%' of quality checking an architect had to do. One of these checklists is shown on the following page, in reduced size, to illustrate the arrangement.

E

CHECKIT! PROJECT QUALITY REPORT
(US English)

Schematic Design

No.		Check Box *
01	Prepare summary of detailed brief (program) including all up-to-date information; confirm with client. Include ADA and/or LEED requirements as appropriate. Distribute to office team.	
02	Develop list of questions affecting schematic design pertinent to each engineering discipline. Circulate with requested target date for answers.	
03	Prepare schematic phase work and staffing plan and time schedule. Review with PIC.	
04	Verify progress to work plan in current period. Note deficiencies.	
05	Prepare functional diagrams including relationship to existing structures; develop viable functional arrangement options; review with client. Select preferred arrangement(s).	
06	Study siting options and climatic influences; develop massing models; evaluate relationships to site context.	
07	Test massing options against preferred functional arrangement and brief; review with client. Select model.	
08	Evaluate provisional concepts for accommodation of economic structural systems with SEng.	
09	Evaluate provisional concepts for accommodation of parking requirements.	
10	Receive SEng's preliminary report on structural system options; review with Cost Estimator and client. Select provisional system(s).	
11	Receive BSEng's preliminary report on building services options; review with Cost Estimator and client. Select provisional systems, using LEED guidelines where/as appropriate.	
12	Develop plan for presentation materials, renderings, models and written materials. Confirm with client.	
13	Select and appoint other consultants or subconsultants for presentation materials; confirm costs and delivery schedules. Advise client.	
14	Confirm any revisions to project cost estimate; request updated cost plan from Cost Estimator.	
15	Prepare preliminary schedule of internal & external finishes; confirm with client & submit to Cost Estimator; request confirmation of any cost plan changes and costs for alternatives.	
16	Check concept plans for conformity with fire and egress (including ADA) requirements.	
17	Establish provisional egress space requirements.	
18	Establish provisional lift shaft sizes, air duct sizes, raised floor requirements, plant room sizes and other mechanical requirements.	
19	Establish provisional beam depths, duct crossovers and floor-to-floor heights.	
20	Establish disabled access requirements, including applicable ADA requirements.	
21	Establish energy conservation design criteria (E11).	
22	Confirm compliance with plot ratio requirements and bonuses.	
23	Determine if shading studies are required; if so, prepare and submit.	
24	Check schematic design against all GROUP C requirements. [GROUP C is Surveys and Planning Approvals]	
25	Review scheme with planning authority personnel for informal advice and comment.	
26	Submit schematic design to Cost Estimator for review of preliminary cost plan.	
27	Review schematic design with client's marketing/real estate advisors.	
28	Obtain client's approval of and sign-off on schematic design, or obtain authority to proceed to next stage.	

* Tick if applicable to this project

Readers can download free sample copies of these checklists in pdf format [www.buildingtech.com > Building Technology > Management Systems & Tools].

Checklists as interactive database tools

As noted above, an interactive database is really the way to go if the goal is a truly user-friendly system. I did that, developing CHECKIT! as an automated FileMaker Pro™ database tool, bundled with the model QM system we sold to Australian architects and engineers. Its features included tagging checklist items such that when setting up a project checklist, the user could select the state the project was in and the type of construction contract to be used, and the software would auto-configure all of the checklists for that location and contract type.

These powerful aides, and other features, made the checklists very easy to use, and overcame all of the problems of the paper-based systems. Alas, it was an instructive experience! This elegant system required that all the project architects in a practice would need a FileMaker Pro™ site license – an expense many practices felt they couldn't afford no matter *how* good the system was!

You can use the above methodology to create excellent checklists for a variety of purposes, For example, I was hired by a major construction firm to develop a checklist system for subcontractor QC. In developing the solution, I realized that standards typically are about 80% on *materials* quality and 20% on *installation* quality. *One* checklist item can cover the first 80%: 'Check that all supplied materials are as specified or are approved substitutions.' I found that, using Australian standards, one could easily extract the installation requirements from the standards and organize them into highly efficient checklists – no more than 3 pages long for some critical assemblies such as precast or in-situ concrete, and typically less than a page for most trades.

General contractors love this system, because it brings hundreds (if not thousands) of pages of standards down to something very manageable. The subcontractors have a short, simple guide to the standards that really do affect them (compared to the long laundry list found in most specifications) and they can go straight to the clauses they have to comply with.

Your next question might be: Wouldn't the standards associations be interested in a tool like this? Why would they? Think about it: would it sell more standards?

The future of checklists

Returning to the point about how best to deliver checklists: I am convinced that tomorrow's checklists will be web-based and web-delivered, and my current efforts are in that direction. See the end of this Part 7 for more information and resources on that. See also the next chapter: 7.7 *Document management*.

Let's return to the idea of quality management (QM) vs. quality control (QC). Checking is a QC activity. Its main purpose is to identify and fix errors before they return to bite you in the hinder.

The reason is that insurance is primarily there for errors and omissions, so it becomes a sitting duck for claims that have other causes (such as client unhappiness). There is anecdotal risk management evidence that strongly suggests that the bulk of legal claims alleging errors and/or omissions are only smoke-screens, designed to crank the lumbering legal apparatus into operation, setting up for a commercial settlement on the courthouse steps.

We've all been there. All too often, claims management can be a giant game of bluff, and the firm with the best records wins.

Checklists can be very important in this game of bluff. Failing to have them can be seen as a sign of weakness. Using them but failing to detect errors the checklists might have revealed is worse, tantamount to dereliction of duty. Using them, and detecting and fixing errors is a thick coat of Teflon. This is a tricky situation. You have two realistic choices: (a) have and *use* them, or (b) don't do either.

This doesn't excuse errors, of course. But are errors best avoided by more QC, or by better planning and other quality management methodologies? Hopefully, you will find the answer to that question elsewhere in this handbook!

7.7 Document management

Coordination is the project manager's toughest task – and lack of coordination, the biggest source of problems. A system that shortens and clarifies the connections between pieces of information is certain to reduce mistakes and delays.

Jonathan Cohen

Readers of this handbook know that even modest design projects can be very complex in terms of document and communication control; in major projects, managers have to deal with thousands of drawings, each containing hundreds of bits of information; and tens of thousands of messages. Loss or misinterpretation of any piece of this information can cause problems for the practice.

Document quality issues

ISO 9001 requires control procedures for documents *required by the quality management system* (cl. 4.2.3), and for *records*, which are a 'special' kind of document (cl. 4.2.4). The standard also requires a written procedure for document control.

Quality document management means:

- Having a user-friendly system for coding and filing documents that facilitates retrieval.
- That you check documents and approve them prior to issue.
- That you review and updated them as necessary, and ensure that the latest (current) version is so marked.
- That you check that users have the current versions or have been notified of the current version or any revisions.
- That documents are legible and properly identified, and that obsolete documents which are kept as records are so marked.
- That you have a system for archiving documents, and disposing of them when no longer required.

Note that the above list doesn't say anything about documents being error-free! That is the responsibility of the design/document functions, not document management.

Paper-based document control

If your paper-based document management processes are in disarray, a good place to learn the basics is Elena Marcheso Moreno's Chapter 13.2: *Information Management*, in the *AIA Handbook.*

There is a matrix format that represents the ultimate evolution of paper-based document control, used by more design firms than any other method of tracking document issues, and it could not be more efficient. You can download an example of this model from the handbook website (www.mqia.com > Projects > 7.7a). As control systems move away from paper, as they must, and are, however, we find that the elegant simplicity of this paper model can't practically be re-invented as a database template.

Even practices that are database-savvy find that it is not easy to develop user-friendly computerized document management systems.

Electronic document control

For more information on EDM and shared project systems, see Cohen, pp 169-203. Refer ***Resources*** at the end of this Part 7.

Email Management Tips

Email gets around. Never put anything in an email you would not want to appear in the newspaper.

Legally, deleting an email is the same as shredding a paper document.

Email whose subject matter is project **Cost, Time, Scope, Risk** or **Quality** should be printed and filed.

Putting the project number as first put of the subject line automates organization of email files.

Aconex is manufactured by Aconex Pty Ltd; home office in Melbourne, Australia with 15 offices around the world, including London, Dubai and Hong Kong (www.aconex.com). The fastest growing IT company in Australia, Aconex at this writing is used by 20,000 companies in 20 countries on US $45 billion in project value.

dv TDM is manufactured by Practical Programs Inc., with offices in Adelaide, South Australia and Houston, TX. (www.practicalprograms.com) dv TDM is currently sold in 31 countries and is available in eleven languages.

So, we are, increasingly, putting document management under the care of standardized systems providers. There are several options:

- Intranet systems: Proprietary software running on the firm's server. Documents going outside the firm are handled in the traditional way, but can be transmitted via email to others or to reproduction/distribution houses.
- Internet-based electronic document management (EDM); of which there are two types:
  - Centralized registry; where all project information is stored and maintained on a single server. This server can be housed in the office of one member of the project team, or can be housed and maintained at a remote location.
  - Decentralized registry, housed on multiple servers, maintained by an independent information broker.
- Shared project model, or object model integrated database. This approach is the object of a lot of research and experimentation.

The latter is probably the 'way of the future', but today, EDM models have reached sufficient developmental maturity to be viable solutions for firms and projects of all sizes.

Developers of EDM systems have sprung up, died, combined, morphed, mutated and evolved considerably over the last two decades. At this writing, the 'heavyweights' in a field of a dozen or so suppliers probably are Autodesk's Buzzsaw™, and Bentley Systems' ProjectWise™. If you are a user of AutoCAD™ or MicroStation™, there are obvious benefits to using the same provider for EDM.

EDM systems are far from equal in their features, ease of use and costs to set up and maintain (and it is ***not*** easy to get good comparisons), so it might be well worth your time to investigate other providers and products, regardless of the tools you use.

There are two relatively new suppliers with approaches that, in my opinion, warrant close review before making decisions in this area: Aconex™ and dv TDM™; both the result of Australian innovation.

The table on the next page compares the features of these two products, and can be used as a checklist when evaluating another document management system (DMS). There is lot more to DSM selection than features, obviously: First cost, ongoing cost, cost and availability of training and support services, and compatibility with other systems and tools are key issues.

Another factor to consider is that the lead consultant, or lead contractor in a contractor-lead DB project, necessarily controls the EDM system for the project team – and will likely dictate that used by all parties. Of course, web-based document management can only work when everybody on the team uses it!

Table 7.7 *EDM feature checklist*

Features	Description	Aconex	dv TDM	Others?
Document control	Create, share, track, and archive all documents, drawings, plans, and contracts	■	■	
	Access security to document and user level	■	■	
	Audit trail: Track who printed, edited the index, edited the document, or viewed the document	■	■	
	Email files in their native format or in PDF; record who received what, when and what version they received compared with what is the current version	■	■	
	Document version control	■	■	
Correspondence management	Create, send, search and filter all forms of correspondence	■	■	
	Content search on any word/phrase	■	■	
	Bar-coding, scanning and OCR technology		■	
	Capture documents created in MS Office; ensure the correct templates and file name always used		■	
Email / fax integration	External email generation, automatic importing & linking, incoming faxes are automatically entered into the system	■	■	
Project management	Task/action lists, outstanding & overdue items, time-based tracking	■		
	Workflow: Automate standard processes, monitor resources and people	■	■	
	Access 24/7 from anywhere in the world	■	■	
Contract management	Track committed and estimated costs through budgets, contracts, variations, claims, and potential cost impacts	■		
	Auto-generate bills of materials		■	
Bidding/tendering	Creation, distribution, collation, management, assessment	■		
Reporting	Comprehensive search functions, accurate report generation	■	■	
	Customize output formats for different users/groups		■	
Document printing	Print all documents, plans, and drawings through your reprographics centre of choice	■	■	
Handheld device integration	Collate data and manage defects. create, send, search and filter all forms of correspondence	■		
Hosting	Choice of remote (ASP) server or in-house server	■	■	
Built in Viewer	View CAD and MS Office documents without the need of the application	■	■	
	Redline documents, compare documents and web conferencing	■	■	
Customisation of Menus	The ability to completely remove menu items from the application to make use easier.		■	
Compatibility	Cross-platform (Windows, UNIX, Macintosh)	■	■	

You can use this table as a checklist to evaluate EDM systems you are considering implementing.

7.8 QM & performance specifications

Today, the prime reason for litigation against architects is 'failure of function'. Behind that worrying wide classification usually lies either poor control over workmanship or an inadequate specification. And there is a direct, inverse relationship between the rise in specification-linked litigation and the profession's tendency to off-load this vital area of design control.

Louise Rogers, Deputy Editor, *RIBA Journal*

The performance specification method describes the results a building component must achieve in use, rather than describing what it is built from.

Why use performance specifying?

Performance specifying can have great advantages for certain building systems. It also presents the possibility of heightened risk to all parties involved in a project.

Performance specifying is being used increasingly for the following reasons:

- To optimize value: The specialist subcontractor has the freedom to design systems as competitively as possible as long as the performance is met.
- To transfer risk: By centralizing the responsibility for the design and execution, the design risk passes to the subcontractor.
- To reduce construction time: The subcontractor can choose from components most immediately available.
- To resolve the problem of the designer not understanding systems sufficiently to be able to write a good proprietary specification.

When a little bit of knowledge is dangerous

It is my view that the design professional specifying performance needs to know more about the way the system works than she would if writing a proprietary specification. When the specification is performance based, you do not know what you will get back, but you must understand it. The designer who does not is putting the client at risk, regardless of the language of the contract.

The first three reasons above are valid, the last is not. If this last reason is part of why performance specifying is used – whether or not admitted by the designer – then all parties are put to increased risk, including the client.

If the designer does not understand a building system well enough to write a proprietary specification, it is not likely that she will understand how to determine whether or not the system as proposed by the specialist subcontractor is going to meet the performance requirements.

You might argue: What difference does that make? If the specialist subcontractor, backed up by the builder, has taken responsibility for the performance of the system, it isn't the designer's problem.

Research into design risk shows that it is *not* possible to transfer *all* of the risk to some other party; that at the very least designers must understand the workings of a building system well enough so they can reliably advise the client as to whether a proposed solution will in fact meet the performance requirements.

Most performance specifications are not solely performance based, but some mixture of proprietary and performance requirements. This can pose a particular problem for the inexperienced specifier. In a mixed specification there is always the possibility that some of the performance requirements could be mutually exclusive with the proprietary requirements.

This is a formula for trouble for all concerned. It also can create particular legal problems, as we will see below.

A prototypical nightmare

A narrative poem in American folklore describes how, for the want of a horseshoe nail, a decisive battle was lost. This is the situation here: a failure to check the performance characteristics of a selected (proprietary) component has set the scene for delay, cost blowout, frustration to all parties, and a loss of money or reputation, or both, to the architect.

Some architects and engineers try to get around the problem by writing specifications containing elaborate statements that say, in effect, 'Mr. Builder, by tendering on this project, you are certifying that you have understood everything in the contract documents, that you agree that it all will fit together the way the architect intended, and if it doesn't, it's your job to make it right at your own expense.'

Such 'murder clauses' are a waste of words, and cannot be counted on to exonerate the designer who fails to check contract documents.

To take a simple example, let's say that a facade was specified to have certain conductivity and reflectivity performance requirements, but the drawings called up a type of colored glass that could not meet those requirements.

Let's say the client had selected the glass from samples shown by the architect, and the engineer had designed the air conditioning system based on the performance characteristics. Let's also assume that the project was fast-tracked, and the columns were going in before the air conditioning subcontractor was selected.

Let's assume the client insists on having the glass that was originally selected, and tells the architect that any resulting problems are up to her to resolve. The engineer says, terribly sorry, but the air conditioning system will have to be re-designed, and someone will have to pay for it. Without agreeing to pay for it, the architect tells the engineer to redesign the system.

The redesign shows that the ducts have to be made larger to handle the increased heat gain of the building. This means raising the floor-to-floor height by 50 mm (2 inches) as it was designed right to the limit in the first place.

All of the pre-made column forms are now too short, and the builder submits a claim for delay and extra cost. Then it is discovered that the main return air plenum in the core will also have to be increased, which will either require relocating some existing footings and columns, or putting in a big, expensive transfer beam which in turn will require a re-routing of main trunk ducts on the ground floor level, which are already fabricated.

You may be thinking that no architect would be so stupid as to overlook such a simple matter as to make sure the selected glass met the performance requirements specified. True, most petty oversights do not end up as horror stories. Nevertheless, in every case where one part of the instructions conflicts with another part of the instructions, risk to all parties increases.

A real example

Let us consider another, more complex case, which occurred on a major Melbourne office tower a few years ago. The architect carefully researched facade systems.

The point of these examples is that the ability to change some aspect of a building system – a central concept in performance specifying – can trigger a whole set of consequential changes which may be hard to appreciate at the outset.

This is not to warn you away from performance specifying – but to warn you to be careful when considering doing it!

Boston specification writer Mark Kalin commented to me that with the tremendous growth of green building, more architects are being very proprietary as they sort out the claims of the different manufacturers. He says when the architects review submittals during construction administration, he almost always gets a call when another manufacturer is suggested. The architect has a greater responsibility when a proprietary spec is used, he says.

The specification was scrutinized by all involved. The system was designed as a proprietary system of the 'stick-built' type: e.g. the erection of a metal framework into which would be set the vision and spandrel glazing sheets.

The builder could propose alternative systems. The winning bid included such an alternative system; on which was based on a 'panelized' system: e.g. the glazing sheets factory fitted to metal frames that were then fixed to the structure. This system represented the cutting edge of technology and offered significant advantages. However, few firms had the technology to produce this kind of system, so it was not suitable as a base bid design.

The specification provided for a joint width of 15 mm (5/8 inch), with tolerance limits.

Well into the facade contractor's design, it developed that in certain locations, building deflections would require a 20 mm (3/4 inch) joint. This set the width of the joints for the entire facade at 20 mm. The architect accepted this change. However, the 20 mm joints were significantly more expensive than the 15 mm joints, and the facade contractor sought a large claim for the increased cost.

The architect was able to demonstrate that the 15 mm joint would have sufficed quite well in the original stick-built design, and pointed out that the facade contractor had failed to advise in their proposal that the way the panels moved under deflection loading was different than the way a stick-built system moved.

In this case, the architects had done their homework and it was the facade contractor who had to absorb all of the risk of the alternative system.

Performance specifications and ISO 9001

ISO 9001 was developed for manufacturing industries, and presumes a seamless responsibility between design and production. In this model, the designer has an obligation to track *all* changes in the design, and verify that they comply with design input requirements.

If you consider that the people to whom this secondary design responsibility gets passed on to – mostly building services subcontractors – have no control or sometimes even knowledge of how their design inter-relates to other building systems, then the matter of responsibility gets murky indeed.

What happens when responsibility for the *completion* of design is transferred to some other party? No one knows, and it hasn't been tested in court to my knowledge, but I can readily imagine that the courts would find that the 'master' designer had a responsibility to the end-users to ensure that the secondary designer also complied with all design input requirements.

The only way around this, in my view, would be an agreement, not unlike a deed of trust, where the secondary designer accepted this responsibility and agreed to hold the first designer harmless from any downstream problems. I've not seen such a clause yet in my travels.

The situation in Europe

> Information in this section is abstracted from an article by Louise Rogers in the November 1993 *RIBA Journal*. Although 12 years old at this writing, to the best of my knowledge, these conditions are unchanged.
> See www.ribajournal.com

Under present European legislation, the architect is banned from thwarting free competition by demanding that a named brand is used. So traditional, prescriptive specification is difficult. The answer is to recommend one specific, preferred product accompanied by the option for the contractor to allow an alternative *only* as long as it meets up to the detailed performance specification.

A well-written performance specification will ensure that substitutions later on will have to stand up to the criteria set by the architect.

Current guidance on the writing of adequate performance in design specifications is hard to come by. An unpublished report by John Veal, formerly RIBA Assistant Director for Practice, points to the distinct lack of information in this area. The report, which monitors the available design and performance specification guidance says:

> It requires patience, but without certainty, to locate design standard information, a commodity which is in short supply in the majority of design offices, especially if a quality management system is not in operation.

What happens if the contractor changes the specification without getting permission from the architect? The news from the U.K. is not encouraging. An industry-wide survey by Barbour Index found that only about half of specifiers are aware of changes made to their specifications. The RIBA says that many architects labor under the illusion that if the end product fails and is not the one specified, the blame will fall elsewhere, but that the truth can be very different:

> From the many cases of specification law in court across the country, the message is clear. *The architect's design duty continues right up to practical completion and that includes detecting and putting right any diversion from the specification of design.* It may not be fair, but architects should take note. (My italics – Ed.)
>
> The key judgment in this area, Richard Roberts Holdings Ltd v Douglas Smith Stimson Partnership, took place in 1989. The case involved the switching of a specification made by the architect. The judge in the case found the architect to be at fault when the substitute specification failed despite the fact that the architect had not recommended it. The judge decided that the architect, as the expert in the process, had a duty of discovery.

The situation in the U.S.

An aspect of the Federal procurement reform law that affects design professionals is the call for greater use of performance specifications, in contrast to design specifications.

The Schinnerer *Liability Update* newsletter notes:

> It will be important for architects and engineers to be aware of how the courts have been defining the differences in terms of how contractor claims are handled when it is alleged that the contractor failed to comply with the different specification approach.
>
> Whether the specifications are ruled to be either performance or design is critical in resolving contractor claims because under an old and still-prevailing doctrine known as the 'Spearin Doctrine', if the specification is deemed to be a design specification there is an implied warranty from the owner that if the specification is followed an acceptable result will be produced.

The designer who mixes prescriptive and performance criteria in the same specification will thus significantly complicate the resolution of claims. This may be primarily a risk management issue, but it has ramifications for quality management as well, especially when coupled with the ISO 9001 implied responsibility for ensuring that design complies with design input requirements.

7.9 Measuring documentation quality

Even in the most quality-oriented firm, there is still a chance that plans and specifications may contain discrepancies or deficiencies which will cause change orders to be written.

DPIC Companies

Every design practice I have ever seen undertakes some level of quality checking of their output documents, for all the obvious reasons. Moreover, most use more-or-less standard methods of doing so – typically by 'red-lining' of incomplete or conflicting information, which is then corrected by the person who prepared the documents.

In the vast majority of cases, that sums up the intent clarification/ error detection process. There is rarely any organized feedback process that helps the firm learn from this checking. Here is precisely where the idea of *continual improvement* comes in, and where QM-conscious practices differ markedly from QM-unaware practices.

How hard is it to measure documentation quality?

I suspect that at least 90% of readers of this handbook will at one time or another have done this red-lining. Think about this for a moment: Suppose that you kept a list of the sort of items that you saw repeatedly, and put a mark against each items when it came up again. After checking a few sets of drawings, you could have created an experience-based checklist of common red-lining issues, specific to your practice.

What could you do with this tool? First, you could assign each 'issue' a code number, and use that simple code number to explain the issue when doing your red-lining – saving hours and hours writing the same notes on project after project.

Second: Each time you check a set of drawings, you could check the frequency (by making a tick mark against the check item) of those issues. Now you are *measuring document quality*. Then, with this record of issue frequency caused by the documentation process, every four, or six, or twelve months you could look at the cumulative record, and see exactly which were the endemic issues, and which were the random issues. That is process *feedback*.

Finally, you could start to make changes in the way your documentation teams work, so as to start to reduce these endemic issues. That is *quality improvement*. You might, for example, realize that your induction program (training of new employees) needed to focus on these items. Or you could convene a meeting of your documentation team, and 'kick around' these results, taking suggestions on how to improve on them.

You might discover that several of your staff were really interested in these kinds of ideas, and would volunteer to form a working group to implement changes to really reduce the need for red-lining. Now you have the start of a *continual improvement* program.

What is the cost of doing this? Almost nothing – perhaps another 1 or 2 percent on top of the red-lining time – which would be returned immediately by simplifying the red-lining! And the potential benefits? Limitless! *Is it worth trying?*

Other ways to measure ...

Paul Tilley, whose research we discussed in Chapter 6.6, has researched the RFI (request for information) process as a potential indicator of design/documentation deficiency.

Tilley notes: *When contractors are supplied with project documentation that is incomplete, conflicting or erroneous, the RFI process is used to formally request the clarifications required. By investigating the reasons for the issuance of RFIs, the extent of RFIs issued and the time taken for RFIs to be responded to, we can develop a system which will enable the quantification of both the extent of the deficiencies in the documents and their relative severity.*

His research focused on two Australian projects with a combined value of about AUD $30 million; one delivered in the traditional 'design-document-bid-build' and the other in a more flexible, PM-managed format with more fluid communication paths. Analysis of drawing registers for both tracked drawing revisions and new drawing issues after bidding.

Space does not permit providing you with the details of his 23-page analysis, so I'll jump to the conclusions. Tilley found that both projects had serious deficiencies, as measured by the number of RFIs, the number of revisions and additional drawings, and by the time required to issue responses. An outcome of his research was the development of a mathematical model called Information Clarification Severity (ICS).

Most architects would not opt for the rigor of adopting Tilley's research model to their projects. However, it is fairly easy and not time-burdensome to track RFIs as to cause and response time, and with whether drawing revisions were required by the response. This is a highly valid measure of documentation adequacy.

What this discussion does **not** cover is the problem of 'fake' RFIs, that happens when a contractor seeks extra cost and/or prolongation claims and attempts to make a case for blaming it on the designer by 'burying' the designers with floods of RFIs, mostly spurious.

This is a risk management issue, far more than a QM matter.

Critical to this approach is agreeing with the contractor of the maximum time for RFI response without impeding the project – this requires pre-contract negotiation. It well may be reasonable to agree that there is more than one class of RFI 'urgency', to help facilitate timely responses.

Why is this important? For the simple reason that time and money *are* quality issues in design and construction – and if the designer's level of documentation and/or ability to respond to RFIs impedes construction (always thereby increasing costs) it amounts to a service quality breakdown. And the contractor will have every right to seek additional time and compensation, to the detriment of the designer's reputation, and, probably, pocketbook.

Finally, such record-keeping will provide you with a most valuable guide as to how much time adequate design really takes!

7.10 Quality in project management

An able project manager can increase the profit of the firm beyond anyone's imagination.

Paul W. T. Pippin, AIA

Architecture is a project-based business. The unique characteristic of projects – unlike most commerce – is that they have finite beginnings and endings. Teams form, do projects, and disband. This 'start and stop' characteristic is important in that it mitigates against the concepts of feedback and resultant continual improvement that are integral to QM and absolutely essential to the notion of a 'learning organization'.

For this reason, any study of QM in architecture must examine current PM thinking, in order to evaluate PM models for their ability to deliver on, or be adapted to deliver on, this key issue of continuing improvement.

The big three models

PMBOK™ is a Trademark of the Project Management Institute, Inc.

PRINCE2™ is a Trademark of the Office of Government Commerce, UK.

There are three main, publicly available PM models:

- *The Project Management Book of Knowledge* (PMBOK) produced by the Project Management Institute (PMI).
- PRINCE2 (**PR**ojects **IN** Controlled **E**nvironments). '2' is the second version; published by The Office of Government Commerce, UK.
- The *Ultimate Project Management Manual* (UPMM) published by PSMJ Resources, Inc., Newton, MA.

Next in line are the proprietary, in-house PM bodies of knowledge created, maintained, and carefully guarded by the global PM companies such as Bechtel, The Austin Company, Parsons Brinkerhoff and the like. Some government construction agencies have highly developed PM systems; Australia's NSW Department of Public Works is an outstanding example.

Finally, the professional architectural societies, such as the AIA, the RIBA and the Royal Australian Institute of Architecture (RAIA) have extensive collections of PM-related information; although this information is not really organized into 'systems'.

PMBOK

PMI is the fastest growing professional society on the planet, with – at this writing – more than 160,000 members in 146 countries (see endnote, Part 5).

The PMI PMBOK is the de facto world standard for PM. The current (2000) version is a concise, well-organized 216 pages. PMBOK is generic; that is, it applies to any kind of project, which means it needs some adaptation to fit architectural projects. As its structure is flexible, this is generally not seen as an issue by users.

PMBOK is supported and complemented by dozens of high-quality guide books published by PMI, and by a world-wide network of organizations who train people to certification to its methodology. QM is core to the PMBOK approach; one of its 12 main sections.

PRINCE2

Some of the information in this section has been provided by Key Resource Peter Whitelaw, Director, Rational Management Pty Ltd, Melbourne, an accredited PRINCE2 training organization. Whitelaw has prepared a full comparison of PRINCE2 and PMBOK, available on the handbook website. (www.mqia.com > Projects > 7.11a and 7.11b.)

PRINCE was developed in the United Kingdom in 1975 and underwent several enhancements after acquisition by the UK government in 1979. A consortium of 150 European organizations contributed to the revision, and PRINCE2 was released in 1996. It is now (also) a de facto world standard, in use in approximately 34 countries and many thousands of organizations.

Like PMBOK, PRINCE2 is a generic PM model. It is more rigorously structured than PMBOK, which is either an advantage or disadvantage depending on your perspective. This structure is scalable from very small to major projects. It is more an operational model than a 'body of knowledge'. See the next chapter for Whitelaw's notes on the comparison of these two systems.

QM is core to PRINCE2, one of its 19 processes, components and techniques sections.

UPMM

Each of these models could learn a lot from the other – but each has to protect its intellectual property as well, which means a certain amount of fortress-buttressing around its concepts.

PSMJ Resources' UPMM is, in contrast to PRINCE2, far more a body of knowledge than a PM operational system, although the UPMM contains all the tools and techniques needed to deliver projects in architecture. First published in 1993, it is a rich 700+ page compendium of best PM practice assembled from the project manuals of dozens of PSMJ's A|E|C clients. Unlike PMBOK and PRINCE2, it is specific to architecture.

Like PRINCE2, its structure is linear, starting at the start of a project, and ending with project closeout. Unlike PRINCE2, UPMM 'starts' a project with marketing, so it crosses over into what are generally considered to be 'pre-project' activities. QM is core to the UPMM; one of its 19 main sections.

Which is the best model?

I have compared these three leading models of information on PM, and conclude that none is 'best', at least for architecture. Each has strengths and weaknesses. My opinion:

- UPMM' s strengths are its non-generic application to architecture and the richness of its tools and techniques; its weaknesses are a lack of a management structure and not extending QM principles through all aspects of PM.
- PMBOK's strengths are in the simplicity of its flexible structure and its compactness as a model.

Its weaknesses are in being a generic model and certain specific deficiencies identified by Whitelaw in his paper for this chapter.

- PRINCE2's strengths are in its completeness and stage controls; its weaknesses (from an A|E|C perspective) are in being a generic model and complex, highly prescriptive control processes that amount to a steep learning curve for mastery.

Further, I think (although proponents of each would argue against this) that all three are lacking in adequate mechanisms to learn from project experience and to move the project-generating practices toward being true learning organizations – obviously a goal I deem important.

Is there a better model?

With these thoughts in mind, over the past year I have been looking at how one might combine the best features of these three models as well as to incorporate an answer to the point raised in the previous paragraph. Although still in a stage of development, I propose the general structure shown below. You can see a color version, and learn more about it, on my website at www.practman.com.

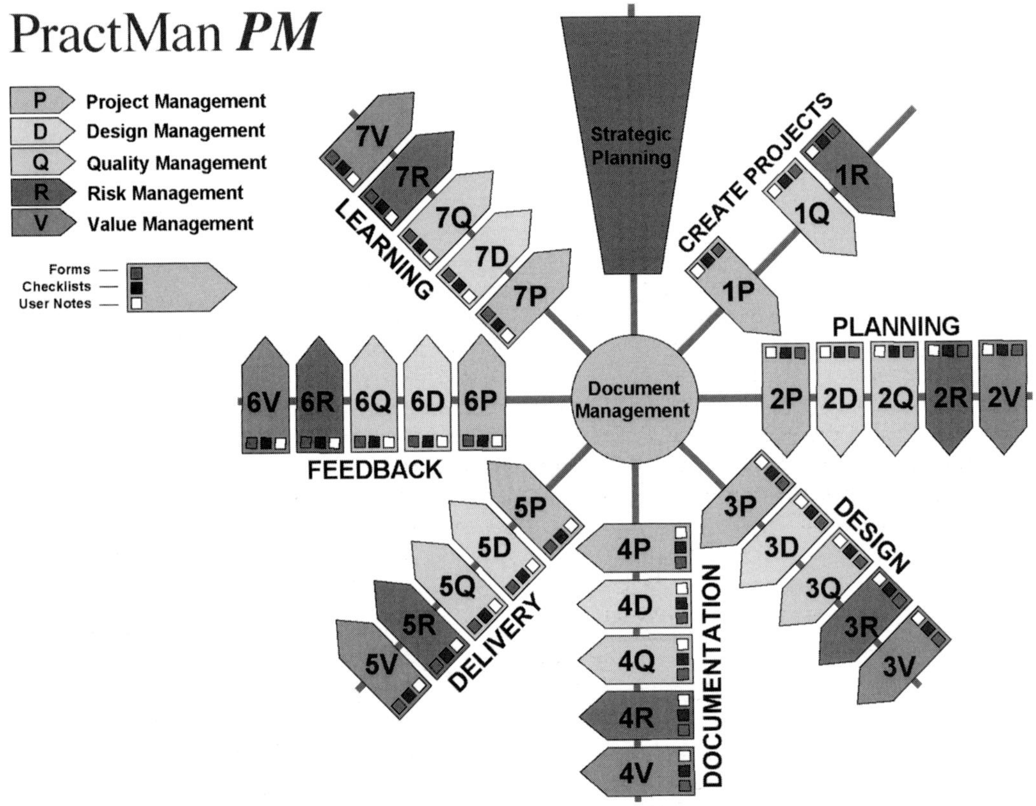

Figure 7.10 *Proposed project management delivery model*

This model links, by project phase, the five main built environment management disciplines: project, design, quality, risk and value management. Depending on project requirements, any of the last four can be included or not included. All relate through the 'hub' of the wheel, document management (or information management, which includes document management and communication).

This is a learning organization model, where Phase 6 feedback is used to learn from project performance, which then critically informs the strategic planning process. Learning and strategic planning are corporate activities, not project activities. But they are mission-critical to PM in that strategic planning sets project goals and provides guidelines for client and project selection, as well as other learning organization functions.

Each of the five components is a workflow model, and each node is closely linked to the others by project phase. Note that each node can (but does not necessarily) have forms, checklists and/or user notes. The latter are essentially brief process descriptions.

7.11 Quality in project management: PRINCE2 vs PMBOK

People, more than any other resource, make the difference in quality for a project.

Lewis R. Ireland

PMI and PRINCE2 restrict reproduction of their intellectual property, so I have not quoted from their documentation.

Accordingly, the comments on this page are my own overview interpretation of the comparative quality approaches of PMI's *PMBOK Guide* and PRINCE2, and do not attempt to convey the richness or detail of either. – Ed.

The PMBOK Guide requires QM as an integral part of PM, as does PRINCE2. PMBOK identifies three main headings under Project Quality Management; *quality planning, quality assurance,* and *quality control.*

Like almost everything else in the PMI approach, and reflecting PMI's process model, information below these categories is organized under headings of *inputs, tools and techniques*, and *outputs*. As you might expect, planning inputs include quality policy, project scope and standards; outputs include the QM plan and identification of suitable QC measures such as checklists.

The QM plan becomes a key input to QA, whose output is quality improvement. It is also a key input to QC, where the outputs include further quality improvement, rework, verification records, and adjustments to processes.

By comparison, the PRINCE2 structure deals with quality in several ways. First, *Quality in a project environment* is one of the eight basic components of the method, which embrace QM, QA, quality planning and QC. In a project, these elements are managed within a *quality path*, which begins with client expectations and results in a quality log, which is checked at each stage of the project.

Besides the eight components, PRINCE2 defines six processes, including IP: Initiating a Project. There are six sub-processes to IP, the first of which is IP1, Planning Quality. Similar to the PMI methodology, inputs to this sub-process are quality standards, the project brief, and the project approach. The principal output is the project *quality plan*; other outputs are templates for the *quality log*, an *issues log*, and a *lessons learned report*.

Process QC is managed through the maintenance of the quality *log*. Corrective action is handled as a separate function, not part of QM.

PRINCE2 revisits all key documents at each project stage, updating them as required. Hence, there is a *Stage* Quality Plan, which is an update of the original Quality Plan.

***A comparison of PRINCE2 against PMBOK*, by Peter Whitelaw**

The following table is excerpted From Key Resource Peter Whitelaw's paper for this chapter. You can download his complete report, in two documents, from the handbook website: www.mqia.com > Projects > 7.11a *PRINCE2 and ISO 9000* and 7.11b *A Comparison of PRINCE2 Against PMBOK.*

Table 7.11 *Comparison of quality management provisions*

Function	PMBOK Summary	PRINCE2	Comments
General	Includes the processes required to ensure that the project will satisfy the needs for which it was undertaken. Covers the quality policy, objectives, responsibilities, QA, QC and QI within the quality system. Intended to be compatible with ISO 9000, TQM and Continuous Improvement.	Quality considerations are embedded in all of the eight processes and many of their sub-processes. There is also a component providing guidance on quality in a Project Environment and a technique describing a Quality Review procedure. PRINCE2 is fully ISO 9001 compatible.	Both methods recognise customer expectations, prevention over inspection and management responsibility.
Quality planning	Involves identifying what quality standards are relevant to the project and determining how to satisfy them. The main output is a quality management plan.	Fully covered in IP1, Planning Quality. PRINCE2 also offers a process, SU4, where the customer's quality expectations are sought and recorded. The Project Quality Plan is the equivalent of the quality management plan.	PMBOK does not formalise the customer's quality expectations.
Quality Assurance	PMBOK uses the phrase to cover 'all the planned and systematic activities implemented within the quality system to provide confidence that the project will satisfy the relevant quality standards.' It covers reviews of quality results and audits of the other quality management activities.	Separates the organisation-wide quality assurance role – setting and monitoring the use of standards – from aspects of the Project Assurance role, the planning of resources for quality work and monitoring the results for a single project. PRINCE2 offers a quality file for all quality documents, which can be used for quality audits.	PRINCE2 accepts that there may be audits from an organisation-wide quality assurance group, independent of the project, but also offers a role for this group as part of Project Assurance.
Quality Control	Involves monitoring specific project results to determine if they comply with relevant quality standards.	Covers the need in products and techniques such as the Quality Log and quality reviews.	Both cover the quality of products and project management. PMBOK includes a description of Pareto diagrams.

7.12 Value management for designers

Think of value *as quality with a price-tag.*

Ed.

> VE is defined (by the Society of American Value Engineers) as *a professionally applied, function-oriented, systematic team approach used to analyze and improve value in a product, facility design, system or service – a powerful methodology for solving problems and/ or reducing costs while improving performance/ quality requirements.*

> The Japanese expect that VE/VM will be a standard part of every construction project, and say that *good* VE/VM is completed by the end of design development. This approach is fundamentally different from cost-slashing exercises after documentation is complete.

Value management (VM) is a term that is gradually replacing its predecessor, value engineering (VE), as the concept broadens in scope and application. VE has a bad name with architects who've endured 'cost-slashing' exercises misnamed as 'VE'.

VM works because every project – large or small – is based on a large number of assumptions: assumptions about what the project should look like, how it should be constructed, the techniques, materials and systems used, what should be prefabricated and what should be site-constructed, and so on. These assumptions, based on previous experience, are necessary in order to move projects forward – but they also often result in hidden inefficiencies that unnecessarily push up costs.

VM is an important PM tool, used particularly where scope and cost are not aligned. The technique essentially involves challenging project assumptions, to see if there is a more cost-effective way of approaching the assumptions – one by one. All phases of VM involve a search for answers to the question: 'What else will accomplish the function of a facility, system, process, product, or component at reduced cost?'

Ideally, VM is an on-going discipline throughout the design process. The earlier in the project VM is used, the better will be the results obtained, as the diagram below demonstrates.

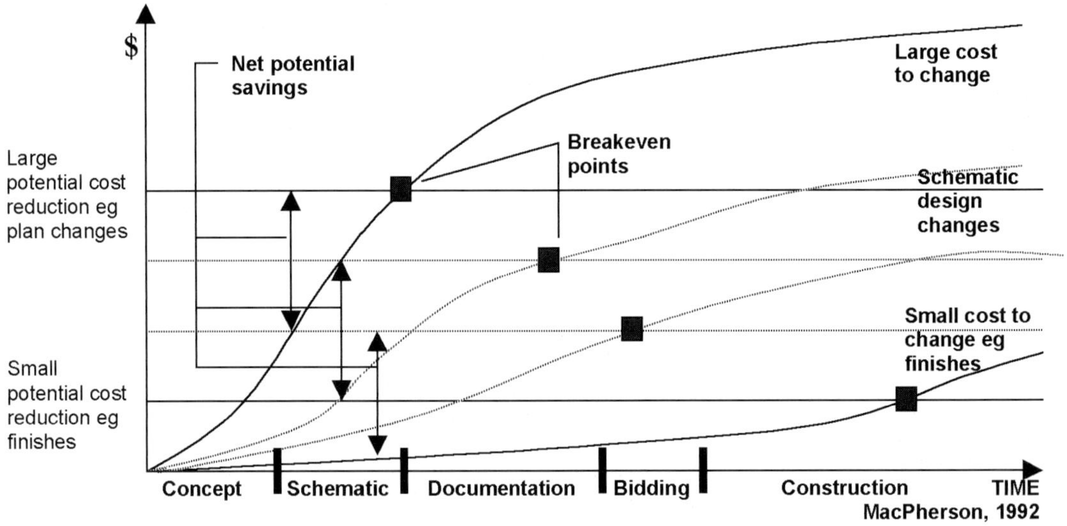

Figure 7.12 *Value Management opportunities for savings*

When project criteria are being established and design concepts are being formulated, roadblocks to cost-effectiveness are more easily removed, and new approaches more readily taken, without adversely affecting design cost and project programs. The matrix diagram below suggests areas for applying VM techniques by design/development phase.

Table 7.12 *Value Management study matrix*

Study Areas	Concept design	Schematic design	Design development
General	Design concepts Program interpretation Access, circulation Net-to-gross ratios	Floor plans & sections Approach to systems System integration Floor-to-floor height Functional space	Floor plans & sections Typical details Integrated systems Space circulation Specifications
Structural	Performance requirements Framing systems Initial framing review Structural loading criteria	Structural system selection Framing plan outline Sizing of elements	Details Floor & roof framing plans Sizing of major elements Outline specifications
Architectural	Interior design Configuration of key rooms Circulation Impact of key equipment	Concept elaboration Selection of wall systems Selection of partition types Circulation sizing Impact of key equipment on room design	Materials selections Materials sourcing Key details Initial finish schedules Interior construction elements Outline specifications for equipment items
Mechanical HVAC Plumbing Fire protection	Impact of mechanical concepts Initial systems selection Performance requirements for plumbing, HVAC, fire protection	Mechanical systems selection Refinement of service & distribution plan Input to schematic plans Energy conservation	Detailed systems selection Initial system drawings & details Distribution & riser diagram Outline specifications for system elements Equipment supply sourcing
Electrical Service & distribution Lighting & power	Power supply Performance requirements for lighting Special electrical systems	Selection of lighting & electrical systems General service, power & distribution concepts	Detailed systems selection Distribution diagrams Key space lighting layouts Outline specification for electrical elements Equipment supply sourcing

Maybe it's obvious – but I'll state it just in case it's not: Design professionals who learn how to – and regularly practice – VM as part of the design discipline are not likely to have it imposed on them later!

All criteria should be examined at an early project stage. This review should include technical guidelines, regulations and other instructions, including those in the scope of work or mandated by regulatory authorities and agencies, and approximate life-cycle cost savings if proposed criteria changes are accepted.

The purpose is to identify and question anything that inhibits completion of a required task at the lowest overall cost consistent with desired performance.

7.13 Quality issues in international materials procurement & logistics

If it hasn't happened already, globalisation is about to upset your materials-supply apple-cart. Are you on top of the issues?

Ed.

Key Resource Alan Travers has prepared a definitive paper on this chapter's topic, which can be downloaded in full from www.mqia.com. This chapter is a condensed extract of his paper.

Quality in international materials procurement and logistics by Alan Travers

Alan Travers is Managing Director of Civil Construction Products, Melbourne, an international business with manufacturing facilities in China.

This chapter focuses on the issues that surround international procurement, e.g. organizations in developed countries purchasing product from developing countries. These international and intercultural issues mirror, albeit in an exaggerated fashion, the difficulties of procurement in any arena.

The ISO 9001 organizational approaches are generally considered highly desirable. Often the underlying principles of controlled, documented processes are treated with a less cynical attitude than in businesses in some Western countries. In China, in particular, the Japanese presence in business and the significant influence of international auto manufacturers has had a major influence.

Procurement, internationally, is at an interesting developmental stage. Globalization is now a hot topic politically, and opinions are sharply divided as to the whether the opening of world markets are the best or worst current trend in world economies. Whatever the outcome of this debate, an increasingly unhindered flow of goods and services between countries is inevitable.

Only how we, as an international society, can limit the potentially adverse impacts of globalization is worthy of debate. Even on a local trade basis, the focus of the last decade's enthusiasm for the procurement or outsourcing of almost all business functions has spawned as many failures as successes. Some fundamental developments have occurred in recent times, which have facilitated international procurement activities.

Not long ago, manufacturing organizations in developing countries that maintained management systems to ISO 9001 or other international recognized standards were a rarity. ISO 9001-accredited organizations are now commonplace.

The impetus for many companies adopting these systems was to seek a marketing advantage. Maintenance of system standards and market-driven achievement of third-party certification have systemized manufacturing in countries where traditional methods of managing businesses was the norm. That's not to say that aspects of long-standing traditions do not remain. As a Chinese friend in Hong Kong once explained, when it comes to hiring in his organization, they use the 'FBI' principle – Family, Brothers and In-laws.

A pervasive factor in recent times in international business has been the Internet. As a starting point for research on what others are doing in the world, the Internet has no equal. Whether the information being sought concerns competitor activity, potential suppliers, customers, business or cultural background information, the Internet's only drawback is coping with the bulk of information and making judgments on its veracity. Ultimately, the Internet brings communication with little cost, but with high quality and depth – especially the ability to transfer files between businesses.

Communication and travel have brought an increased commercial sophistication to the approach of third world suppliers. This is particularly the case in architectural supplies.

Suppliers from China and India initially entered Western markets with products designed to meet the tastes of their own internal markets, but now work with importers to present products which reflect the requirements, both aesthetically, and in terms of certification issues, of their target markets.

In most cooperative ventures, the transfer of spreadsheets, drawing files or other digital data is now almost a daily issue – that this is now so simple, immediate and inexpensive brings an ease to communications that could not have been achieved just a few years ago.

As clichéd as it may seem, the single most important precursor to success in procurement are the *people* involved. As in marriage, the choice of a partner is critical. Thanks to the Internet, any organization with orders to place is likely to be inundated with potential vendors. Sorting through candidates and making sourcing decisions is a difficult and fraught exercise, but usually the problem is not a lack of potential partners. A planned approach is imperative, and an ideal supplier profile must be developed and applied in the evaluation process.

Much of the exporting in third world countries is carried out through trading houses. Although this structure appears to add an extra layer of cost to purchasing, the right trading house can bring considerable value to the transaction. Apart from financing transactions these facilitators often bring specific technical as well as language and organization skills that all international business requires.

Early interactions between buyer and potential supplier, unfortunately, are negotiations, and – with the focus being almost entirely on price – an impression can be formed in the supplier's mind that price is the most significant issue.

Communication at every stage needs to give a *balanced view of the full needs of the purchaser and the supplier.*

Visits to potential suppliers' facilities must be part of the process, and such visits need to be carried out by both technical and management staff. Although a thoroughly skeptical approach is called for initially, one of the pleasures of such visits is the way that a common interest and experience in technical issues overcomes what initially appear to be major communication barriers. Often translators are left well behind, to a comical degree, in conversations regarding technical issues, and a 'language' consisting of sketches, jargon and gestures allows a surprisingly fluent and productive level of communication.

Suppliers, assuming the correct partner is chosen, can bring a great depth of experience and know-how; and a good supplier should be considered a valuable resource.

In cultures where traditionally relationships were the deciding factor between success and failure, the importance of social networks remains. This view of business still has great relevance in international business relationships today.

The social interactions in international business are also an important part of the communication mix and should not be overlooked or fast-tracked. A particular aspect of intercultural communication that is important in this context is the manner in which quality issues surrounding supplied product are expressed. In some cultures, admitting an error can be difficult and damaging to the standing of an individual, and 'loss of face' may result. A proven method of dealing with these sensitivities regarding quality issues is to systemize communication.

When a focus is maintained on the most important aspects of the supply process, incidents and trends – backed up by data – are dispassionately discussed, communication is less likely to be inhibited.

Quality feedback, non-conformance information and supplier responses (positive and negative) need to be an ongoing dialogue. In this context, images from a digital camera, sent by email, are a powerful communication tool.

De-personalizing and systemizing in this way inevitably brings a level of professionalism and an understanding by both parties of the core issues.

Organizations seeking to source product must be aware of the manufacturing environment in which a potential supplier operates and the limits of the capability of suppliers. Many do not give this area sufficient attention. A manufacturer in a developed country may wish to duplicate their current range in a country with lower labor costs, but, in many cases, this tactic is far less likely to bring success than *re-engineering* a product for production in a different industrial environment.

Often the area of specifying difficult-to-meet tolerances can highlight quite different views in the minds of buyer and seller.

Whereas the buyer may assume that tighter tolerances can be achieved with improvements in manufacturing techniques or more attention to detail, often the seller sees tighter tolerances as only indicating a potentially higher level of rejects.

Negotiations should encompass an understanding on both sides of the manufacturing techniques and outcomes expected rather than a focus entirely on price.

An obvious example is manufacturing tolerances. Notwithstanding a vendor's natural tendency to promise anything; antiquated, highly modified, non-automated manufacturing equipment is unlikely to consistently achieve the same results as purpose-built, computer numeric controlled machinery. Recognition of this fact in the tolerances specified in designs, and – specifically expectations regarding the interaction of components – is important to reducing issues with final products.

An interesting and beneficial outcome of a more comprehensive understanding of manufacturing in a low labor cost environment is the recognition of opportunities that arise from a reassessment of your product. Conventionally product design evolves under the influence of market forces, commercial issues and available manufacturing techniques. Once labor, as a cost item, diminishes, incremental increases in labor usage can be used to add features or otherwise improve products.

In the research phase, *location* of a potential supplier is an element to be considered. In developing countries there are a number of factors, related to location, that will determine your supplier's ability to be a long-term reliable and cost-effective supplier. Research, independent of the supplier's advice, is required to assess the factors noted below:

- Proximity to available, appropriate, raw materials supplies can have an important influence on your supplier's reliability. Inland transport in many countries is potentially uncertain and internal trading in cash poor economies is difficult enough without the added dimension of inland logistical issues.
- Skilled labour in certain industries is often only readily available in regions where these industries have a historical base. The cost of labour can also vary significantly from one district to another.
- The supplier's closest port can also influence the efficiency of your supply arrangements. Ports differ widely in the regularity of international shipping; and goods leaving certain ports, depending on destination, are subject to transhipping, a potential cause of delays and longer lead times.

Delays can result and extra costs incurred if containers are not prepared in ways that are acceptable to the customs authorities in the receiving port.

Australia, for instance, requires (amongst other things) fumigation of wooden items including pallets – and this fumigation must be carried out and certified by an organization acceptable to Australian authorities.

- Packaging in international business is an important, often-neglected area, requiring the development of agreed specifications. Once goods are shipped, the purchaser will have plans in place for utilization of the goods, and replacement of items that arrive unfit for use is problematic and expensive. Many importers have experienced receiving a container load of goods only to have items tumble out of the container door as it is opened. The protection of items stowed in a container is one issue. The material utilized in packaging is another.
- Location can be a factor in where and how items are packed. Factories without easy access to shipping containers, due to their distance from commercial centres, may send goods by road to be repacked in containers at the port. This re-packing by a third party is often unsatisfactory and should be avoided if at all possible, as it adds both delays and a higher potential for damage arising from inappropriate packaging.

In simplified form, the process of commencing international procurement is shown in the table below.

Table 7.13 *Summary of international procurement steps*

Steps	Points for consideration	Resources
1 Develop a profile of ideal offshore supplier	• Supplier's experience • Skill base • Location • Accreditation level • Communication skills	• Experience of other importers • Specialized consultants
2 Research into potential suppliers	• Compare candidates with profile • Visits to supplier's sites • Review supplier's history with similar products • Prices and terms offered	• Internet (for finding suppliers) • References from supplier's existing clients
3 Re-engineering of product where necessary	• Ensuring tolerances are within manufacturing capability • Opportunities for product improvement considering lower labor costs	• Technical assistance from potential supplier • Purchaser's technical staff
4 Negotiation with supplier	• Sustainable pricing • Payment terms • Shared view for the future • Include formal review periods	• Use personnel with experience, empathy and patience
5 Commence transactions	• Start with small quantities and grow as confidence increases	
6 Monitoring of performance	• Feedback to be systemized – regular and non-accusatively	• Data gathered from both suppliers and purchasers

7.14 Design quality issues in construction management

While the tools used in delivering quality product may differ between first and third world projects, the principles driving quality management techniques remain constant.

Stanley Mehlhoff

Key Resource Stanley Mehlhoff has prepared a definitive paper on this chapter's topic, which can be downloaded in full from www.mqia.com. This chapter is a short extract of his paper.

Quality in Construction Management by Stanley Mehlhoff

Stan Mehlhoff, AIA, is President of PM/CM Japan KK, a Tokyo-based project/construction management consulting group.

Quality is a definable and measurable variable, but it is only one of the many project objectives to be achieved. It is important to recognize these distinctions when dealing with differing stakeholders, who frequently have differing perspectives on the hierarchy of the numerous project goals and objectives. Because of these differing perspectives, quality objectives should be defined and ranked as a first step in developing a quality management system that is responsive to a client's expectations.

The failed projects where this simple principle was ignored are legion.

Achieving a defined level of quality in the built environment is contingent on achieving quality in the management delivery system. If the management delivery system is flawed, quality results will be serendipitous and random, and a successful project will be the result of luck rather than of a cognitive and predictable process.

The definition of quality should be expanded to include schedule and cost performance. A project's construction phase is simply the final act in a long implementation process. Achieving the desired level of quality in the construction management (CM) process is rooted in the QM and decision-making processes undertaken during the programming, planning and design phases. If quality issues were not addressed during prior phases, there is little chance of achieving a client's quality objectives during this final implementation phase.

Preconditions for successful QM in construction

Successful quality management during the construction phase is rooted in the prior performance of the following design management activities:

- Preparation of a ***Baseline Report*** which defines specific goals and objectives (including quality), program of spaces, conceptual designs, detailed budget, milestone schedule, and implementation plan including procurement packages and contracting approach.
- Periodic ***plan checks and quality audits***: During the design phase the design should be 'frozen' at the 30%, 60% and 95% complete stage, and both cost and quality reviewed against the Baseline Report.

♦ **Constructability analysis:** Throughout the design process, the project's constructability is reviewed to ensure that logical, efficient and locally acceptable construction practices are incorporated in the design.

The core quality tools in CM

There are four core QM component elements in CM that are required to deliver a successful project:

♦ **Cost Control** is of prime importance in meeting owner expectations. Ideally, the project has been designed to budget, tendered and awarded at or below the approved budget.

The budget and the contract award amount are broken down into a code of accounts and incorporated into a master cost control document referred to as a Cost and Commitment Report, which includes the following essential cost information in spreadsheet format: Original budget; original contract price, approved change orders, amended contract price, outstanding change orders, disputed change orders (potential claims), and forecast completion cost.

♦ **Schedule Control:** The purpose of a project schedule is to create a workplan (in terms of activities, duration and logic), which defines and organizes project and construction activity and provides a basis to measure performance.

On complex projects it is advisable to break the master schedule down into ever increasing levels of complexity and detail, based on user needs. At the highest level, the schedule is generally a simple milestone summary schedule showing start, completion and key interim events for major project elements and contracts.

The next level is usually a detail summary schedule showing, in increasing detail, the work breakdown structure for the total project. The next level is the master schedule which breaks the major construction elements/activities down into craft and trade level activity, showing start and completion dates and constraints and interfaces with other craft and trade activity.

On large, complex projects there is a final level of scheduling that is of critical importance in QM of schedule performance – it is generally referred to a four (or five) week rolling schedule where the past week's activity and actual performance are indicated and the next three (or four) weeks' planned activities are scheduled.

The schedule is at the very heart of QM, in that it not only defines what activities and durations will be performed, but how the project will be implemented.

Zero defects?

In design and construction, zero defects, while theoretically possible, is in reality not achievable or possibly even desirable.

The goal of reducing defects to some minimal level, consistent with the cost of reducing defects to this theoretical level, is very much the goal of quality construction management and the cost control / change control process.

This is acknowledges the Law of Diminishing Returns, which states that at some point the cost of further defects reduction will exceed the value derived from such a reduction.

In theory, plan checks during the design phase of work have a goal of zero defects. These checks have a significant cost, and at some point the cost of continuing a plan check will exceed the 'premium cost' of correcting the errors during construction. It is preferable to document field change order costs and correlate them against the cost of plan checks to determine historical trends and the value added of additional plan checks versus reduction in premium construction costs due to change orders.

The Japanese construction industry is renowned for delivering world-class quality on time – for an admittedly high price. In an essentially closed society/economy, the owners, contractors and suppliers have developed a relationship-based delivery system, in response to their unique needs and culture.

Owners typically work with select architects and contractors who in turn work with a stable of specialty subcontractors, and suppliers – the system is vertically integrated and no one works outside of their 'Zaibatsu' family, usually a large holding company centered on a 'family' bank.

The system has obvious faults, in that it limits competition and liquidity in the marketplace, and is an ultimate manifestation of the 'old boy' network with all its classic deficiencies.

The advantages of this traditional relationship-based delivery system are perceived to outweigh the disadvantages, and as a delivery system, it does not require a control system focused on documenting performance (or non-performance) and contract changes.

Performance in Japan is almost a given, and changes rarely, if ever, occur.

While achieving physical quality in the Japanese market is a given, this is not the case for most of Asia and the underdeveloped world. Reducing the cost of construction is now of paramount importance in the Japanese market, while cost tends to be secondary to improved quality in most of the underdeveloped world.

It will include and define the acquisition of land, permitting and approval processes, design and contracting strategy and durations, procurement and long-lead material acquisition requirements, agency interfaces and inspection requirements, and finally, commissioning and turnover activity.

The project schedule is truly a map defining the project's development strategy and implementation process. Schedule management is essential to delivering quality product and to meeting client expectations.

- ***Quality Control:*** Along with cost and schedule, meeting required QC objectives completes the 'trinity' of key project objectives that are central to achieving overall client expectations. The QM techniques required to achieve five star quality, or lesser levels of physical quality, focus on detailed attention to micro planning, design to internationally recognized concepts and standards and implementation to these same standards.

  In achieving a specific level of quality during construction, the focus will be on the contractor's development and implementation of a QC program that defines the number and type and tests, calculations, reports and shop drawings to be performed by the contractor to achieve the desired level of quality, and then to perform, submit and receive approval by the architect, as the interpreter of contract intent and achievement of the contractually required level of quality.

- ***Document Control:*** While not included with the traditional quality objectives (cost, schedule, and physical quality) associated with a project's success, a comprehensive document control process is *central* to achieving quality objectives. It is the glue that holds the QM process together, thereby contributing to, if not guaranteeing, project success and achieving client objectives.

  Typically, each piece of correspondence or unique document is sequentially identified and controlled; including a code defining both the originator and the recipient. Each document is then recorded in a log dedicated to the specific type of document.

  Currently, this is increasingly accomplished using document control software included within a family of PM software, which typically includes compatible cost and schedule control components.

  Whatever the degree of sophistication used in setting up a document control process, whether an integrated software program, a simple Excel spreadsheet, or a manually maintained log and retrieval system, the principle is the same – each project ***must*** have a controlled system of document identification, storage and retrieval.

  Do you have that function ***really*** operating in ***your*** practice? Reality check time, right now.

Part 7: Sources, resources & notes

NOTE: *The Architect's Handbook of Professional Practice 13th Ed., Joseph A. Demkin, Exec. Ed., published by John Wiley & Sons,* is referred to as *AIA Handbook.*

Sources

7.8 Rogers, Louise (November 1993) *RIBA Journal.* See www.ribajournal.com

Victor O. Schinnerer & Company (October 1994) *Liability Update* newsletter.

7.9 Tilley, Paul A. (2002) *Indicators of Design and Documentation Deficiency*, unpublished.

7.12 The Society of American Value Engineers (SAVE) has become SAVE International. Many excellent, related resources can be downloaded free of charge from their website: www.value-eng.org.

Resources

7.1 Mears, Peter (1995) *Quality Improvement Tools & Techniques*, McGraw-Hill. This is the ultimate, classic guide on the topic.

Nelson, Charles (1996) *TQM and ISO 9000 for Architects and Designers*, McGraw-Hill, pp 141-79. This chapter, which can be downloaded from the handbook website, contains extensive references to other resources for QM tools.

7.2 Ashford, J. L. (1989) *The Management of Quality in Construction*, E. & F. N. Spon, p 90.

Hershberger, Robert G. (2001) *AIA Handbook,* Ch. 17.1: *Planning – Predesign Services*, pp 519-25.

Salisbury, Frank (1990) *Architect's Handbook for Client Briefing,* Butterworth-Heinemann Ltd. Still the best source available on this important topic.

7.5 Ashford, J. L., pp 144-58.

Burgess, John A. (1984) *Design Assurance for Engineers and Managers*, Marcel Dekker, Inc., pp 259-74.

Juran, Dr. J. M. (1992) *Juran on Quality by Design*, The Free Press, pp 313-16.

Stebbing, Lionel (1990) *Quality Management in the Service Industry*, Ellis Horwood, pp 106-34.

Taylor, J. R. (1989) *Quality Control Systems*, McGraw-Hill, pp 277-97.

7.6 CHECKIT! system: www.buildingtech.com > Building Technology > Management Systems & Tools.

Fred Stitt is the world's most prolific checklist generator. Many of his checklists are excellent, but most are of the memory-jogger type; exhaustively voluminous. Refer GUIDELINES, PO Box 456, Orinda CA 94563. 800-634-7779.

Excellent checklists on specific topics can be found in any of Frank Stasiowski's books.

7.7 Cohen, Jonathan (2000) *Communication and Design with the Internet*, W. W. Norton & Co., p 168-203.

Moreno, Elena Marcheso (2001) Information Management, *AIA Handbook,* p 380-91.

7.10 *A Guide to the Project Management Body of Knowledge (PMBOK Guide)* (2000) Project Management Institute, ANSI 99-001-2000.

Atkins, James B. and Grant Armann Simpson (2005) Lessons in Project Management, *AIA Handbook Update 2005*, pp 39-50.

Ireland, Lewis R. (1991) *Quality Management for Projects & Programs*, PMI.

Managing Successful Projects with PRINCE2 (1998) CCTA, The Office of Government Commerce, UK.

Stasiowski, Frank and David Burstein (1994) *Total Quality Project Management for the Design Firm*, John Wiley & Sons, Inc.

7.11 *A Guide to the Project Management Body of Knowledge (PMBOK Guide)* (2000) PMI.

Managing Successful Projects with PRINCE2 (1998) CCTA, The Office of Government Commerce, UK.

7.12 Dell'Isola, Michael D. (2003) Value Analysis, *AIA Handbook Update 2003*, pp 133-42.

7.14 Mutchler, Robert C. and Christopher R. Widener, Construction Management, *AIA Handbook,* Ch. 18.7: pp 589-96.

www.mqia.com:

7.1a Nelson, Charles, *The Designer's TQM Toolkit.*

7.7a Building Technology Pty Ltd: *PF10: Project Document Register & Transfer.*

7.11a Whitelaw, Peter, *Quality in Project Management: A comparison of PRINCE2 and PMBOK.*

7.11b Whitelaw, Peter, *Quality in Project Management: PRINCE2 and ISO 9001.*

7.13a Travers, Alan, *Quality in Materials Procurement and Logistics.*

7.14a Mehlhoff, Stanley, *Quality in Construction Management.*

Epigrams

7.1 Mears, Peter, p 18.

7.2 Salisbury, Frank, p ix.

7.3 Juran, Dr. J. M., p 13.

7.4 Cornick, Tim (1991) *Quality Management for Building Design,* Butterworth-Heinemann Ltd, p 177.

7.5 Juran, Dr. J. M., p 314.

7.6 DPIC Companies; citation not located. Quoted in Nelson, Charles (1996) p 202.

7.7 Cohen, Jonathan, p 168.

7.8 Rogers, Louise (November, 1993) *RIBA Journal.*

7.9 DPIC Companies (1988) *Lessons in Liability: A Notebook for Design Professionals*, p 75.

7.10 Pippin, Paul W. T. (1992) *Design Office Management Handbook*, Arts & Architecture Press, p 342.

7.11 Ireland, Lewis R., p VI-1.

7.12 Nelson, Charles.

7.13 Nelson, Charles.

7.14 Mehlhoff, Stanley.

Endnotes

1 Nelson's First Law of Checklists: Checklist usefulness is inversely proportional to length.

8 Pushing the Envelope: The Future of Practice

Last Friday of the month again – Party Time!

8.1 Post-occupancy evaluation

By including postoccupancy evaluation services as part of the owner-architect agreement for building design and construction, the designer is able to discover and correct any functional concerns before complaints emerge.

Larry Lord and Margaret Serrato

Architects, especially, are famous for calling in the star photographers to capture the 'essence' of their pure designs before the messy human project users arrive to, *yes*, mess it all up. Although this elitist tendency is on the wane, it still persists in a few mega-centric pockets of the profession.

Designers who commission these pristine pictures are the ones just too busy to revisit the 'scene of the crime' after reality sets in. They forget that projects (even including zoos) are for *people.*

Post-occupancy evaluation (POE) is all about continual improvement through feedback from the results of past projects. It can have a *very* powerful secondary benefit, which is client relationship building, but that is some other chapter; in some other book.

POE can be most humbling. Wasn't how you thought it would be! Your brilliant design for glue-on, floating stainless steel baseboard has failed, and the janitor has re-affixed the baseboards with random-located TEC screws. Not a pretty sight!

The main reason that many design professionals fail to take advantage of the huge benefits of POE is that they have a project-based mentality, rather than a client-based mentality. This may sound funny, but most of us see our output in physical terms, rather than subjective terms – despite our insistence on promoting motherhood statements like 'designing to improve societal values' or the like.

In my previous book on quality, I included several diagrams illustrating how feedback and organizational learning varied from one project delivery model to another. They are on the handbook website for your review if you want to explore those ideas: www.mqia.com > Future > 8.1 *Going in Circles vs. Feedback Loops.*

POE is not rocket science. Simply, find out – in detail – how the *users* of your projects see the results of your design, and from that, think about how your design processes could be improved. Of course, you will need some tools to help you. There are a couple of first-rate guides available – see the Resources section at the end of this Part 8.

POE steps

POE generally has the following steps:

- Planning the evaluation, including assessment of records, energy audits and other information that may be available.
- Facility walkthrough; meeting and discussing the functioning of the facility with selected users, including security and maintenance functions.

- ♦ Survey of selected users on the adequacy of various aspects of the building, such as:
    - Overall design; site design
    - Health and safety; security; accessibility
    - Internal and external appearance
    - Spatial relationships and activity spaces; circulation
    - Climate control; plumbing systems
    - Electrical systems; acoustics
    - Materials: suitability, ease of maintenance

  Survey items are generally scored as being Excellent, Good, Fair or Poor, to aid in ease of tallying results.

- ♦ Analysis of the walkthrough and survey results, which can lead to results benefiting all parties:
    - Building users: Items that can be addressed directly in the facility, such as improving certain aspects of the facility, including safety and maintenance items.
    - Designers: Items that can inform and improve the design of future similar projects.
    - Facility owners: Items that can inform and guide future development of like facilities.
- ♦ Input to the design organization's strategic planning processes, which brings increased clarity to project briefing, design planning, and design management functions.

8.2 Assertive practice: Designing your way to excellence

Assertive practitioners consciously choose which risks they want to take on and which they do not. They do not slide into projects they are truly ambivalent about.

Ava Abramowitz

This chapter was prepared by Key Resource Ava J. Abramowitz, Esq., Hon. AIA – Ed.

Assertive practice by Ava J. Abramowitz

Ava Abramowitz, Esq., Hon. AIA, is the author of *The Architect's Essentials of Contract Negotiation.* She teaches negotiations at the George Washington University Law School and lectures across the United States on risk management and project negotiation.

In today's world, society rewards people who provide value. Assertive practitioners find themselves much sought after as a result. Assertive practitioners hold to the premise that they can design their practices as effectively as they can design a building. To that end, they are committed to maintaining their skill levels and knowledge bases so that when a new business opportunity presents itself, they are ready for it.

They are prepared to evaluate it and consciously determine whether they want to seek that opportunity and how. And, if they determine that the opportunity is in their interests, they go for it, giving their all to the pursuit. Wait a second. Did you read 'whether they want it?' Absolutely.

Assertive practitioners know they owe nothing less to themselves and their clients than un-ambivalence. They know better than to waste time chasing after projects that, even if completed successfully, will get them nowhere. Remember: these people *design* their practice. They know that design excellence only results from the shared commitment of client and architect to that excellence.

Assertive practitioners figure client selection is the first step toward enhancing their chances of design success, of repeat business, even of new business. And research data confirms their instincts. Not only is client selection a prerequisite for design excellence, it is one of the best protections against claims. Simply put, clients and architects who work well together, like each other at the outset and grow in respect for each other over the course of the project do *not* sue each other.

So they pick their clients well, choosing to work with only the ones with whom communication is easy and open, values are shared, and project goals and objectives are clearly stated and understood by all.

Assertive practitioners and good clients share this attribute: Both know that risk is inherent in a design project. That is why good clients retain assertive architects in the first place – because assertive architects are not afraid of risk. They understand and accept it. They know how to recognize risks and manage them well. They even like that part of the process. It is one of the many reasons they get paid the big bucks.

Assertive practitioners know that those who take on reasonable risks and manage them reasonably will make money. Those who shy from risk will not. So assertive practitioners come to grips with risk, 'making friends' with it in the process.

A principal from one of the fastest growing architecture firms, known for its designs, said, 'We are growing because of projects we turned down, as much as because of projects we accepted.'

These practitioners evaluate each opportunity that comes their way and ask themselves, 'What risks are facing us if we take this project on?' They then stack those risks up against their capabilities, their skills, and their resources and ask themselves, 'Is this one that we want to take on?' Only when the answer is a resounding 'yes' do they pursue the offering.

When assertive architects accept a commission, they do not stop there. They quickly seek out responsibility for every service they need to manage the risk effectively. Then they go after the power that will help them manage those responsibilities efficiently and effectively, and *only* when capabilities, responsibilities, and power are fully aligned with the exposures at risk, do they take on the project.

What powers do assertive architects seek? First is authority. Assertive architects know all too well that the easiest way to doom a project to failure is to misalign responsibilities and authorities. There is nothing worse than being given responsibility for something over which you have no authority or seeing both responsibility and authority being assigned to someone without the expertise to handle either. Assertive practitioners look out for their clients when they work with them to make sure that neither situation occurs on the project.

Do these arguments mean that assertive architects never take on losing propositions? Of course not. These practitioners, though, make conscious decisions to take on loss leaders, expecting to expand their practice and skill sets in the process. It is one component of designing their practice.

Second, assertive architects want fees sufficient to empower them to implement the responsibilities and authorities they took on. Yes, they want to make money, but that is not how they approach fees. Their thinking first and foremost is, how much money do we need to activate our forces to produce for our client the project the client seeks. They know their client has a bigger purpose in mind when they commission a building than just having a new building, and it is that purpose they hope to help the client achieve through their design services. Helping clients accomplish their business objectives is one of the assertive architect's own objectives. Sufficient fee is a prerequisite to that.

It is that caring for themselves and for others that bolsters their success. Assertive practitioners nurture their practices as much as they nurture their client relationships. And they extend this caring to their consultants and the contractors with whom they work. They know from experience that only when each of the parties to the construction process is assigned the responsibilities and powers they need and can effectively handle does a project stand the chance of being brought in on-time, on budget and claims-free.

The value proposition they bring to their clients is their ability to design a process and a project that starts out aligned and ends up on track with all who see it and experience it thinking the world a better place for it.

8.3 Transformative practice: What is it? Do I need it?

Clearly the need for transformation is great and the stakes are high.

James Franklin

James Franklin was one of the first in architecture to use the term 'transformative practice'. It was the working subtitle of his 2000 book *Architects Professional Practice Manual* (McGraw-Hill), but his publishers talked him out of it – presumably because it was not a subtitle that would sell books!

A few cogent thoughts from Davy and Harris:

A continued failure to adapt will lock many into a future that offers, at best, marginal returns and, at worst, loss of independence and identity as professionals. (p 11)

For all its simplicity, the billable hour and its corresponding emphasis on utilization have pushed architecture and engineering firms into a vicious cycle of declining performance. (p 28)

A professional domain has a sacred quality. To suggest that a domain needs updating is thus a sort of brazen act, the more so if the profession in question has a long and illustrious history. (p 115)

The current business model itself poses a significant challenge. It has reached the mature point in its life cycle in which commoditization will force a wave of innovation followed by a wave of extinction. (p 47)

The names of Clayton Christensen, Arie de Gues, Ronald Heifetz, Peter Senge and Stephen Shapiro won't ring bells with the great majority of readers. However, these thinkers – and others – have, over the past few years, been laying the intellectual groundwork for a solution to the mental trap that professional consultants have found themselves in.

More recently, two people in our industry, helped by a brilliant and dedicated group of two dozen volunteer practices, have taken the work of these pioneers and extracted from it a landmark set of guidelines for rethinking, and re-engineering, the way we practice. These two people, Kyle Davy, AIA, and Susan L. Harris, PhD, have recently published a book on their research: *Value Redesigned: New Models for Professional Practice.*

I've written a brief review of their book; it is available on the website: www.mqia.com > 8.3a. Relevant to this handbook, Davy and Harris discuss the 'types of work' formulated by Heifetz, interpreting them in terms of design practice. They call these three types *technical, collaborative* and *transformative*:

- *Technical* work, the traditional mainstay of architecture, is 'selling hours': technical solutions to client problems where strong leadership is not required.
- *Collaborative* work is that where strong leadership is required. Davy and Harris posit that our failure to meet the challenges of this type are directly responsible for a loss of influence and the increasing commoditization of design services.
- *Transformative* work means that the clients need not just project leadership, but bigger-picture organizational help and leadership, to guide them through difficult, rapidly changing environments – more like redesigning the *client* than the project.

It would be easy – and an error – to conclude that this typology is a re-jigging of the business models developed by The Coxe Group and others, as discussed in Chapter 6.1.

Regardless of the business approach a practice takes, or what name it is called, there is always some combination of two foci: a *product* focus and a *client* focus. Sometimes the balance of these needs are expressed by the client, as part of the brief – but more typically it is assumed by the designer, based on the designer's approach to his craft.

One way of thinking about these ideas is to contrast the Coxe/Maister model with the Heifetz – Davy/Harris model in a matrix, as shown below.

	Heifetz' Work models as interpreted by Davy & Harris		
	Technical work is that which 'an organization knows how to do'	Solutions known, but learning is required to address and resolve clients' values conflicts	Technical solutions don't exist – work consists of guiding stakeholders through difficult change processes
Coxe/Maister work models (in italics)	***Strong idea*** **Technical**	See notes	See notes
	Strong service **Technical**	**Collaborative**	**Transformative**
	Strong delivery **Technical**	See notes	See notes

Table 8.3 *Work type matrix*

Note: Technical work, in the Heifetz – Davy/Harris model, can be any one of the Coxe/Maister types. Although the strong idea and strong delivery models can be extended to collaborative and transformative situations, both tend to focus more on the physical products of design rather than the service aspects. Hence, the transition to collaborative and transformative work will be easier for practices with a strong service mentality.

Davy and Harris note (pp 46-7):

> Like any living system, a profession must continue to develop and adapt to changes in its environment. Over time, these professions' lack of creative response to the extraordinary forces that have transformed our society has wrought a very fundamental form of damage.
>
> Even where firms and individuals were otherwise equipped to lead, these professions' domains and, thus, their fields, have not provided a viable base from which to exercise leadership. This loss of leadership capacity is a problem not only for the professionals themselves, but for society as a whole.
>
> Responding defensively rather than creatively to the market and social forces transforming their world, they have caused their services to be seen as less important and less relevant to the world's emerging issues and challenges.

I haven't given you any of the historical background that underpins the work of Davy and Harris, or of the thinkers whose work they draw on. In the next chapter, I will give you my own version of that history, and why my own conclusions from it – coming from a different perspective – agree with them.

So, do I need this?

Do you need this kind of thinking? It depends on whether or not you are satisfied with your current situation and believe it'll go on being that way for the next few decades. And, lest my description seem like this is an academic or theoretical discussion, the authors illustrate every stop on the journey with real-time examples.

8.4 Catching the next big wave

A learning organization is a place where people are continually discovering how they create their own reality. And how they can change it.

Peter Senge

A metaphor for success is sensing the next big wave, getting up on your surfboard, and riding it to the end; then finding the next, and so on.

To segue from the last chapter to the idea of wave-catching, I give you my own perspective on the last half-century of architecture; 1955-2005. The last big wave, the building of industrial America, had come to a crashing end in 1929. That wave was the last hurrah of the profession of architecture as the vocation of gentlemen – although that wasn't apparent for some time.

In 1941, New England architect Royal Barry Wills (see the epigram to Chapter 6.1) lamented the loss of professionalism to the forces of business. WW II exhausted the world, but its aftermath created the conditions for the next (medium-sized) wave in architecture: a huge pent-up demand for construction, the baby-boomer generation, and a sense of hope, confidence, and invincibility in being 'American'.

I write this from the perspective of one raised in the American educational system, with standard American values, but with the perspective of having spent two decades abroad. This expat view allows me to see the American experience a bit more like the rest of the world sees it; rather than the myopic, self-reflective view that still characterizes some pockets of American thinking.

We welcomed the poor and starving of the world before the war, we fought and won two wars at the same time on behalf of our friends, and we were rebuilding Europe with the Marshall Plan. I don't say this to brag; it was just the way it was seen, and I submit that it reinforced in Americans an ultimately unhealthy sense of self-righteousness that periodically returns to haunt us.

Architecture was already going through a kind of globalization; the Bauhaus had been transplanted to Harvard, and Wright was being edged out of favor by adoration of van der Rohe, Corbusier, Aalto, and others, by the time I was in architecture school in the 50's. There was plenty of work for everybody, and we pursued it with all the zeal of new-age master builders, with Beaux Arts-inspired training and craftsman guild pride.

We ensured high ethics: no architect could get her hands dirty in construction and be a member of the professional society.

The origins of QM

In the dark days after WW II, the US government dispatched an obscure statistician with experience in census-taking to Japan. This solitary piece of highly disruptive technology, in the form of W. Edwards Deming, changed the world forever. Deming returned to Japan, and taught the Japanese his views on quality. They were humbled by occupation, desperate to rebuild their shattered lives, and they listened, and followed his instructions. Within three decades, by 1980, they were eating Detroit's lunch, bringing the mighty US auto industry to its knees.

The world-wide TQM movement had started, and Detroit automakers embraced it as the only way to stave off an otherwise inevitable demise.

I'm simplifying the story somewhat, but accuracy in detail wouldn't change the outcome. In fact, Dr. J. M. Juran was already working in quality in industry in the late 1920's and 1930's.

The TQM movement quickly changed manufacturing approaches worldwide. Service industries, like architecture, tried out these ideas, where it was widely seen as a failure and dismissed as a passing fad. However, some governments, big developers and major clients in other countries saw potential in these new ideas, and forced professionals to start using the principles. TQM devolved to QM, which wasn't quite such a total shock to the practice systems. The first international quality standard was published in 1987 – less than two decades ago.

Paralleling the QM 'coming of age' were two other critical trends in American architecture: the growth of business models to design, applied both from within and without the industry, and the growth of claims and litigation against design professionals.

The seeds of commoditization

Outside the profession, and as a direct consequence of America's swing toward improving productivity as a way to fend off the early Asian moves to capture market share of the world's commodities, the purchasers of design services began to abandon any pretence of treating their architects and engineers as the gentlemen of an elite profession. They starting putting value squarely on the line – largely by challenging hourly rates, percentage fees, and lump sum offers. Commoditization of A|E services had begun.

Within the profession, in the 80's, Weld Coxe, FAIA, gathered together some of the brightest business-oriented minds of the time into a sort of *atelier* of business practice, setting in motion a widely-read and followed rethinking of practice around different ways of dealing with the trend Wills had identified 40 years earlier. These efforts were aimed at making sense of and responding to the commoditization pressure from services buyers – and in many ways, they succeeded. These models and some of their variants are noted in Part 6. See also www.mqia.8.3b: *Thoughts on the Coxe/ Maister Model vs. the Heifetz Model of Work* (Kyle Davy).

The rise of claims against professionals

Litigation, as measured by the number of claims per 100 projects, as well as the 'severity' of payouts, had been moving steadily upward for many years, hitting a high point of 44/100 about 1983. The reasons for this growth have been debated at great length. The favorite reasons given are (a) greedy, avaricious lawyers, taking advantage of the ability of US lawyers to work on a success basis, and (b) a growth in errors and omissions caused by clients' insistence on reduced fees and impossible deadlines.

Research by Victor O. Schinnerer & Co. concluded that only about 2% of claims against architects are 'frivolous' (see Sources at the end of Part 8).

Do I buy this? First, research by US professional indemnity insurers shows that only about 30% of errors and omissions claims are caused by errors and omissions – the other 70% have other causes. And I have met very few greedy, avaricious lawyers! While these factors may have had some influence, I believe there is another, far more powerful cause.

Here I return to the quintessential American post-war mindset noted above: presumption of invincibility, pride and self-righteousness. People with this mindset typically do not see failure as a learning experience. Because they are *right*, when something goes wrong, it has to be somebody else's fault, and the right course of action is to find and punish them by seeking compensation.

Whatever the cause (and I don't expect much agreement on this thesis inside the US), the profession, the AIA, and US professional indemnity insurers were deeply worried about the escalation of claims and the corresponding rise of premiums. In the middle 80's, the two largest insurers (Victor O. Schinnerer & Co. and DPIC), working with the AIA, began intensive risk management training programs across the country.

How have we responded to marginalization? I hear quite a bit of plaintive, futile whining about how the AIA should do more to get clients to have more respect for design. I also see a lot of practices cutting their way out of these Gordian knots; creating new opportunities. Davy and Harris' book is full of examples of the latter.

And, incredibly, I have heard architects voice the suspicion that the idea of quality was some 'dark side' trick to get us all practicing the same, to facilitate our commoditization.

These programs worked, and they gradually brought down claims incidence to about half of previous levels (22/100) where they stabilized. While solving the instant problem, these moves did not identify or address the real reasons that clients, as a group, were losing confidence in their design advisors.

There was a dark side to these 'wins'. Productivity up, risk down. Forces outside us, *but with our unwitting full accommodation*, were moving big chunks of the profession surely but steadily toward a maginalized, globalized, commoditized, risk-adverse workforce, away from the idea of an esteemed profession long respected for its ability to think beyond the imperatives of running a risk-averse business.

But does it matter? Despite all the outsourcing and off-shoring, most firms with any moxie are *very* busy at the moment. Despite continuing downward pressure on fees, there is more work around than there are qualified people to do it. Seller's market, but the buyers hope you won't realize it.

What wave are we on; what next?

I'm not a pessimist, but I know some very intelligent, thoughtful people who believe that we are riding close to the end of the last wave. My take is that we live in very uncertain times, with a dangerous stew of man-made and natural disruptive and destabilizing forces, any of which could tip the world economy on its head. And swamp our professional canoe in the process.

Still-active, first-world generalist design professionals who don't meet this test will be baby-sitting outsource CAD drafting departments in what we still think of as third-world countries.

Studying the portents has not so far revealed to me the shape of the next big wave, or when it is likely to form. Nevertheless, I think that the Davy/Harris blueprints for surfboards are the right ones, and that it is *now* time for tomorrow's master surfers to decide which model to build, and to get started. This takes me around the loop, back to their three future business models.

Technical practice: There will always be a technical role to play, but it will be increasingly commoditized. Successful first-world players will have one or (preferably) more of the following:

- Well-developed specialist, high-value skills in niche markets.
- Learned to produce high quality work with *extreme* efficiency.
- Convincing demonstration of QM-based management principles.
- Embraced the assertive practice methodology proposed in 8.2.

Collaborative and transformative practices: Very sorry, but I can't develop this without giving you more of the Davy/Harris logic than there is room for here. You'll have to buy their book if you want to go there. The firms already doing it are at the cutting edge of future practice. But it isn't for everyone. Davy/Harris point out that each is built on the last. You can't get to *collaborative* without mastery of *technical*, and the majority of present practices haven't done that yet. And you can't get to *transformative* without mastery of *collaborative*.

What has all this to do with *quality*?

OK, there are no arguments for QM in Davy/Harris's work. That is an enhancement that I am adding to their formula. It goes like this, and reflects the structure of this Part 8:

Post-occupancy evaluation (Chapter 8.1)

POE, as an idea, has been around a long time, languishing on the back burner of the architecture stove. Most architects don't want to do POE; they'd rather get on with the next project, and chance losing money on it rather than searching for clues to better practice in the detritus of yesterday's projects.

I am reminded here of that defining scene in the movie Zorba the Greek, where Anthony Quinn rips open his shirt to show the scars on his chest, telling Alan Bates, 'There are no scars on my back'.

However, POE is a direct doorway to continual improvement, one of the central tenets of QM. POE is *also* a key pathway to some of the critical mind-shifts that Davy/Harris discuss. POE is easy for us because it is at once *project*-centric (which is where most of our heads are at) and *client*-centric (which is where we need to go).

Assertive practice (Chapter 8.2)

One hallmark of the current, prevailing *technical* focus of the great majority of practices today is risk-aversion. In 8.2, Ava Abramowitz, past Deputy Legal Counsel for the AIA and a past Vice President of Victor O. Schinnerer & Co., invites us to stop running away from risk; and turn around and deal with it.

Assertive practice, while apparently embracing risk, in fact lowers it through changing the basic nature of the architect/client relationship; increasing the quality of the relationship and therefore the consultative possibilities within it.

Risk and quality are opposite sides of one coin, tightly related. Following quality principles inevitably lowers practice risk.

New models for practice (Chapter 8.3)

Scary as Abramovitz' advice may be, it is little baby steps compared to the sheer mountain walls of new-think that Davy/Harris advise us to climb. By bringing in the thinking of Clayton Christensen and others on this subject, they have done us a huge service in outlining the parameters of three new models for practice. Of course, these models are ideas on a continuum. Every project will be somewhere on it. But their goalposts signal the need for critically different ways of thinking, and of client relationships, as we (some of us, anyway) move from *technical* to *collaborative* to *transformative* work.

At the heart of QM is the idea of aligning 'supplier' goals with 'customer' goals – another way of expressing the conclusions of Davy/Harris with respect to new practice models.

Facilities management (FM) (Chapter 8.5)

FM has been around the edges of architecture for decades, and many practices have departments that carry out facilities management assignments. Quality in FM means that we look beyond the end of the defects liability period, and design from a perspective that includes the whole of a project's useful life.

Key Resources Gerald Davis and Françoise Szigeti, President and Vice President of the International Centre for Facilities, make the case for quality – and involvement – in FM.

Asset management (AM) (Chapter 8.6)

Unlike FM, the idea of having a role in asset management is foreign to most design professionals. In asking Dr. Penny Burns, a founder of AMQ International, to prepare a paper for this handbook, I hope to extend reader's imagination past FM, out into the mindsets of those who ultimately create our projects. This represents a further, possibly ultimate, 'alignment' of the quality of the design focus with our end users' needs.

Workplace design & performance (Chapters 8.7 and 8.8)

Finally, the intent of this Part 8 is completed with a brief summary of the work of Key Resource Gérald de Kerchove, in the areas of how design of the workplace relates to profit and productivity; a specific measure of design quality for certain building types.

8.5 Quality in facilities management

Your designs need to respond not just to the needs at move-in, but to the likely changes in use, taking into account even the eventual disposal of the facility.

Françoise Szigeti and Gerald Davis

Key Resources Françoise Szigeti and Gerald Davis have prepared a definitive paper on this chapter's topic, which can be accessed in full from www.mqia.com. This chapter is a summary of their paper.

Quality in facilities management by Françoise Szigeti and Gerald Davis

Françoise Szigeti and Gerald Davis are, respectively, Vice President and President of the International Centre for Facilities (IFC), Canada

Quality in facilities management (FM) relates to how architecture and interior design work in practice, since FM is responsible for the Whole Life Cycle Management (WLCM) of the facility. The value of architecture to an enterprise relates to the capability of a facility to meet the stated and implied requirements at the time of delivery and over the period of use, at an affordable cost that the client is willing to pay.

How does this get done? By ensuring that all the requirements for the project are well documented, include on-going costs and performance-in-use, not just first costs and move-in requirements, and are presented in such a way that the design team can validate and verify that the design and the facility respond to these requirements. This is the core of the QM process for project delivery and for 'quality' in FM.

FM is described by the International Facility Management Association (IFMA) as ... *a profession that encompasses multiple disciplines to ensure functionality of the built environment by integrating people, place, process and technology.*

Core FM competencies include: Communication, Finance, Human and environmental factors, Leadership and management, Operations and maintenance, Planning and project management, Quality assessment and innovation, Real Estate, and Technology.

The FM group looks after the assets during use. It is the group that takes delivery of the facility from the design and construction team. The FM group deals day-to-day with the user groups. It is in the front line. It gets the complaints. It is asked to cut on-going costs, energy consumption, and the use of other resources. It has to provide more with less. It deals with code-compliance and environmental matters. It knows what works and what does not work because of its hands-on experience.

Even so, the FM group is seldom asked for its advice at the front end of projects. The Operations and Maintenance day-to-day problems and costs are often forgotten when first costs and designs are reviewed. Therefore, architects who want to pursue a quality management approach should get interested in FM and make sure that those stakeholders are in the loop.

Describing requirements as ends and results, rather than specifying solutions, is called a Performance Based Building approach (PBB). It should be an essential part of an FM quality process. A PBB approach presupposes that the client understands quality concepts, and is in line with ISO 9001.

The core of PBB is the dialog between the client group and the supplier, in this case, the design and construction project team. (Figure 8.5.1)

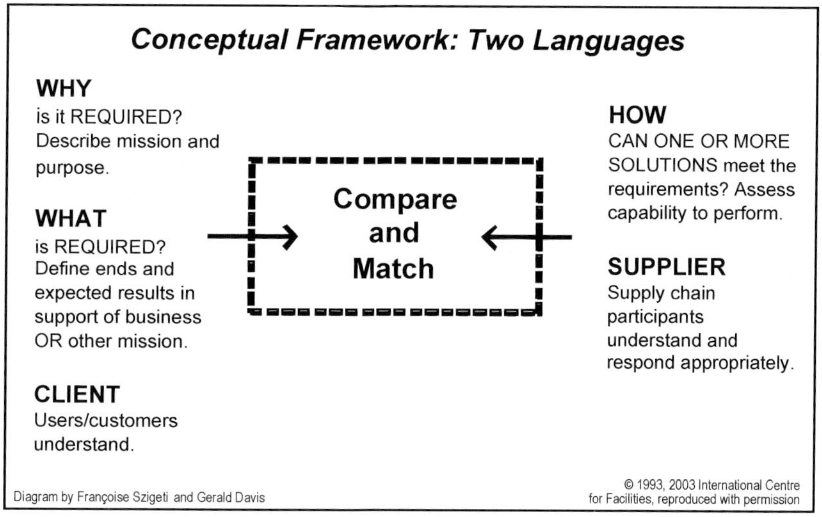

Figure 8.5.1 *Two Languages: 'client/user' and 'supplier/provider'*

CRE vs. FM

The CRE group is transaction-oriented. It sets the corporate strategy for portfolio and asset management, negotiates the financing and usually acts as the buyer or renter on behalf of the enterprise.

Some large organizations have both a Corporate Real Estate (CRE) group and an FM group. On most major projects, the CRE and/or the FM functions are the architects' client on behalf of the enterprise. In many large organizations, they work independently of each other. This can cause problems for all service providers, and for architects in particular, because the CRE and FM groups often have conflicting views of what is needed.

Architects need to avoid getting caught between the two groups, yet since it is the responsibility of the design team to *confirm* their understanding to the client, to ensure that the requirements of all stakeholders have been taken into account. To make explicit the implied requirements, you'd better be sensitive to the power plays among these two groups and the rest of management!

Quality in FM is the *appropriate* level of service

The QM people in the FM group of a large organization called us once and asked that we explain what 'quality' is to their outsourced operations and maintenance service provider. So we met with the senior manager responsible for providing the services.

He said that 'he knew' what an *excellent* technical performance and level of service was – so why had he been asked to talk to us? We told him that his client did *not* necessarily want *excellent* services across all their facilities, but *appropriate* services, tailored to each situation.

For instance, we said, it was part of his job to find out which facilities were obsolete, or housing a unit that would soon be shut down, or expected to be vacated for any reason. If owned, the facility might be renovated, sold or disposed of. If rented, the lease might be coming up for renewal and the time would be right to decide whether to renew or move. In such cases, the level of service for that facility might be to do just enough to keep it maintained 'to code' until the organization was ready to act.

As part of his primary job, he knew the condition of the facilities and the needs for physical repairs and maintenance. By getting an understanding of functionality and what the users needed, he would be able to advise the FM group more comprehensively, and by being more responsive, he would provide added value. We also told him that there were a number of tools that could be used to gather information for all the facilities, so that he could help the in-house FM group assemble a WLCM plan for each facility. This is the focus of forward-thinking FM groups.

Did we get what asked and paid for?

> Clients often say 'How can I verify that what I get is what I asked for and paid for?' Qualitative and quantitative metrics are key. Then, the client and the design team can measure whether the resulting facility meets those requirements.

Quality needs to be *measurable* in a coherent, structured, transparent, objective, auditable way, so that the appropriateness of the results can be measured, validated, verified, and compared to the stated requirements. This can be done at many points during the life cycle of a facility; starting during planning, design, construction, at commissioning, periodically when the facility is in use, and before disposition. Taking an evaluative stance, FM gathers the *actual* quality and performance of the facilities and services that support occupants, their mission and their enterprise.

There are many different ways to accomplish this. One way is to use calibrated scales that allow direct, objective comparison between requirements of the users (demand) and the capability of the design or facility (supply) to respond. Then, the fit between requirements and capability can be measured, and the gaps, in any, can be presented to senior management in support of requests for decision and funding. (Figure 8.5.2)

Design can make or break it for FM

> Quality is part of a management process that also involves continuous improvement, lessons learned and feed-forward, throughout the WLCM of facilities. Design has a major influence on the entire life cycle of facilities.

Quality and Value, as applied to architectural products and services, can be affected by:

- more precise definitions of what these are at the stages of portfolio and asset management, planning and design;
- more accurate tools to measure them; and
- an FM process that takes these concepts into account.

Conversely, decisions made during design affect the constructability, accessibility, adaptability, maintainability, serviceability, energy effectiveness, waste management, use of resources, costs-in-use, etc., of the facility.

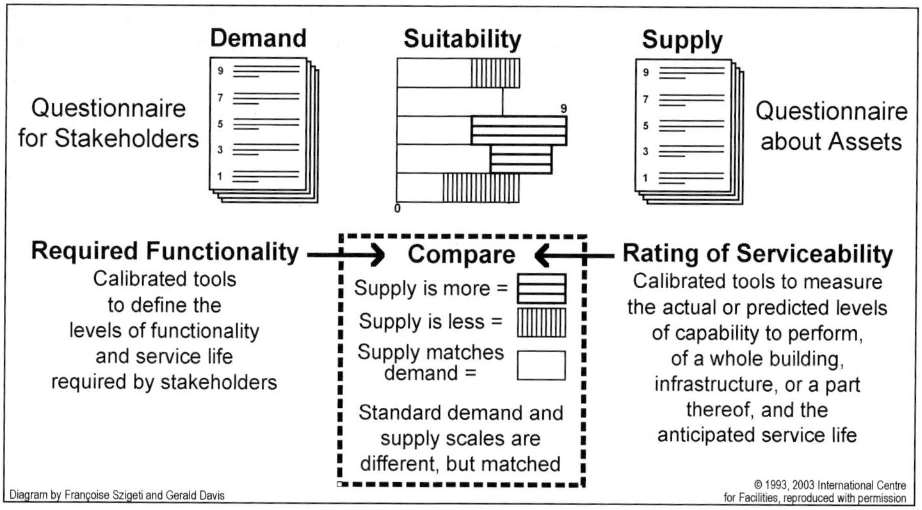

Figure 8.5.2 *Matching demand and supply to prepare gap analysis*

To keep track of all these aspects of a project, a good information base is essential. It goes a long way to ensure good communications. On this front, help is on the way. Interoperability of data bases, comprehensive building information models, and other electronic devices, will make it possible for all stakeholders to use a single pool of digitized information at each stage throughout the WLCM of facilities. (Figure 8.5.3)

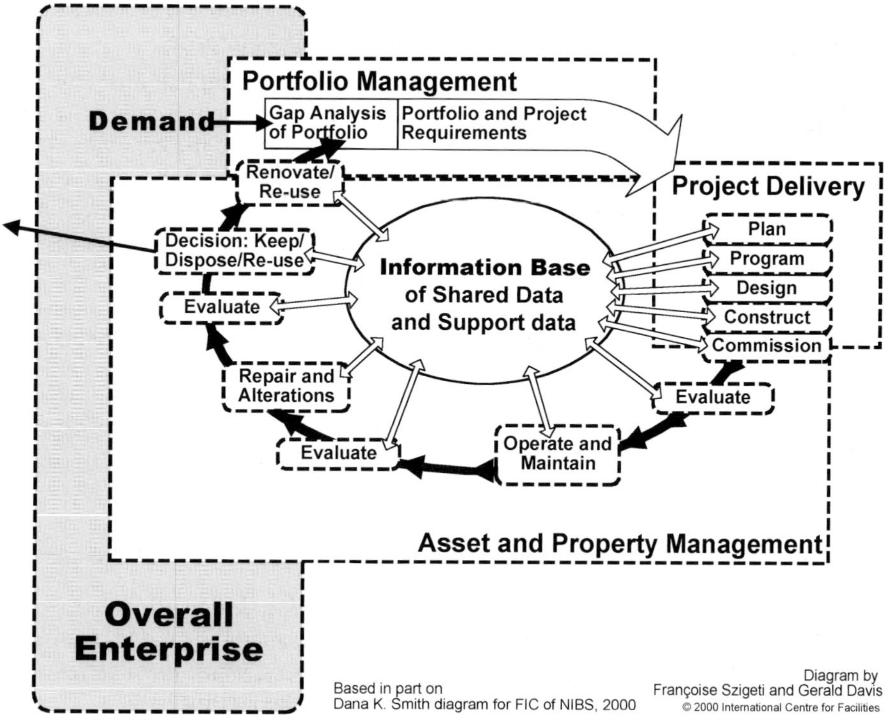

Figure 8.5.3 *Life cycle management of facilities and its information base*

Learning from project to project

FM groups striving to improve their QM have been paying attention to the lessons they can learn from each project, to best practices, to Key Performance Indicators (KPIs), and to benchmarking, whether using qualitative or quantitative metrics.

These terms are now part of the vocabulary of most, if not all, major FM groups, and are very much in evidence at FM conferences such as IFMA's World Work Place. Evaluations are becoming an on-going activity that is part of the budget cycle. Information from such activities feed forward to the next project and budget cycle. (Figure 8.5.4)

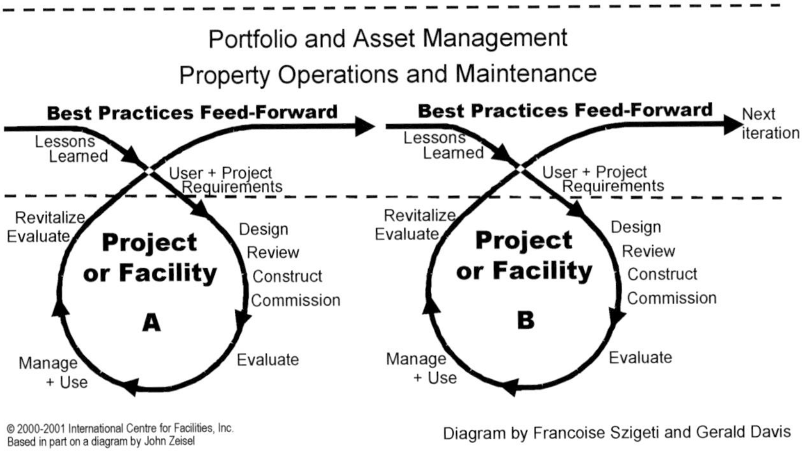

Figure 8.5.4 *Feed forward*

8.6 Quality in asset management

Quality is not just quality now or the way the building looks and functions on delivery, but rather 'quality for a lifetime'; this is where the asset management requirements of the brief become important.

Penny Burns

Key Resource Dr. Penny Burns has prepared a definitive paper on this chapter's topic, which can be downloaded in full from www.mqia.com. This chapter is an extract of her paper – Ed.

Asset Management - - Quality for a lifetime by Penny Burns

Dr. Burns is the editor of *Strategic Asset Management*, and a founder of AMQ International.

Asset management is choosing, using, maintaining and disposing of an asset in a manner that optimises benefits for the owner and stakeholders. It concerns the decisions made before the asset is acquired, and those decisions that continue throughout the life of the asset. In essence it is about maximizing benefits over the entire life of the asset, be that ten, twenty or 100 years or more. *Is such a 'life cycle' approach relevant for the designer whose involvement in the project is a pretty short one?*

'Asset management' is an umbrella term that is used to cover the *integration* of all the steps in the life of a building asset from concept, through design, construction, maintenance, use and its eventual disposal. It looks at the links between these hitherto largely separate functions, for the purpose of producing the lowest life cycle cost for the desired function. The technical fields dealing with this include 'life cycle analysis' and 'post-occupancy evaluation'. *Surely the responsibility of the designer cannot extend to maintenance, use and disposal?*

But asset management is concerned with maximizing the cost effectiveness and quality delivery of *the total asset portfolio* of the business, rather than with maximizing the output or quality of any one individual building. In other words, each asset, each building is evaluated not as a 'stand-alone' but rather in terms of what value it will add to the owner's total asset portfolio. The technical fields dealing with this include 'corporate asset management' and 'portfolio management'. *What does this wider management function have to do with the designer?*

Why asset management is important to architects

Actually, all of the above points apply to the designer – and thus to excellence in design documentation. While the actual construction is the responsibility of the builder, and the maintenance and use of the building is the responsibility of the facilities and maintenance managers, the *integration* of these elements has its basis in the way the asset is designed.

I said in Chapter 1.2 that quality assurance was about making express or implied promises to the client. Dr. Burns quite rightly expands the recipients of QA, noting:

Quality promises are implicitly made to the client, the wider community and the profession.

The quality promise to the wider community is that the building will add value to the total urban landscape – or, at the very least, that it will not diminish it! Building designs that do not consider the management of the asset through time can quickly become urban eyesores rather than highlights.

The promise to colleagues is that this design is one that will support, even enhance, the reputation and credibility of the profession. – Ed.

Incorporating the explicit, or implicit, asset management requirements of the brief is not an 'extra' requirement; it is part of effective communication with the client, of meeting and exceeding the client's expectations and also of meeting international standards for quality. It is fundamental to quality in design and delivering on the quality promise.

Building owners, especially in the public sector, are now developing specific asset management requirements. For many, the asset management requirements of the brief may be implicit rather than explicit. But this does not diminish the responsibility of the designer; it just makes it more of a challenge!

Design concepts are tested, not only by the way the building looks, but by the way it behaves through time; whether it leaks or does not, whether it suits the needs of the occupants now and into the future, whether it is easy to maintain and adds value to the owner's total building portfolio.

The client wants a good end result, and unless the brief is for a monument, that result includes functionality. Clients *trust* the designer that the design will be one that the builders can actually build, that it can be maintained and will meet the functional (and emotional) needs of the users.

Until now, design, construction, maintenance and facilities management have developed as separate disciplines, paying little heed to each other. However, in all fields from science to the arts, to politics and to business, great new ideas and developments are today being wrought by collaboration. Asset management is an expression of collaboration. It is a multi-disciplinary field that brings together the building owner, the user, the designer, the constructor, facility manager and maintainer and many others.

Planning for asset management is part of the QM process

Clients' expectations extend beyond their intended period of use of the building to the resale value of the building. They expect that when the time comes to sell the building that its condition and functionality will commend the building to future buyers.

Design practices that included a requirement for all designers to review, within 2-5 years of building completion, what worked and what didn't, taking into account the views of both user and maintainer, would go a long way to re-assuring clients that their design would be one that would 'work in the longer term', and that it would really take into account the asset management requirements.

Internationally, there is now a strong movement to design buildings that are aesthetic, functional, *and* that care for the environment. For example, in the United States, energy usage in federal facilities is to be reduced (on a Btu/SF basis) by 35% by the year 2010 relative to 1985 levels, and in industrial and laboratory facilities by 20% relative to 1990 levels. All energy conservation measures have to be life cycle cost effective.

How do we bring asset management thinking into design?

Only a few elements are addressed here, but further information, illustrations and examples can be found on the asset management resource website,www.amqi.com, and in the full version of this paper in www.mqia.com.

Anagrams, anybody?

Ways that design can enhance asset management include:

- Access by design: The ease of access to services greatly impacts on the cost of maintenance and certain design trends increase these costs.
- Longevity by design: Each element within a building has its own natural life cycle, determined by both functional obsolescence and normal 'wear and tear'. Good design enables those elements that have naturally shorter lives to be easily removed and replaced. The use of non-standard sizes and fittings can double or treble the cost of renewing these shorter life components.
- Efficiency by design: Buildings vaunting 'latest technology' or trend-setting design features may be at risk if the technology or features chosen are such that operating performance is unknown, maintenance requirements are not fully understood, spare parts are difficult/expensive to find, and/or no local supplier is available/ qualified to maintain or work on it.

Life cycle cost analysis

Ongoing costs can exceed the initial capital cost by a factor of three or more. Fully two thirds of these costs are determined before the building even gets to the construction stage. This is not to say that the costs *are incurred* by this stage, but rather that the pattern of these costs is laid down at the project brief, planning and design stages.

If expected life cycle is very short, then whole-of-life issues will be about fairly rapid adaptability with a relatively short life-cycle for the building. If it's long-term, then alignment with the client's overall portfolio will be as important as the functionality of the building. It may be that cost models for a range of life-times might be needed for a client to determine the ideal life-cycle objectives for the building.

Environmental issues are now forcing use of life cycle analysis. Potential for 'designing in' lower life cycle costs will be increasingly exploited as owners are required to focus on ongoing costs, rather than capital costs, to reduce energy usage under stringent new environmental standards, and as they become more aware of the ability to use design to reduce ongoing costs in total.

Opportunities to reduce life cycle costs rest predominantly at the concept/design stage. As the building passes through the concept to the project development and design stage the cost reduction potential decreases and the costs required to make any changes increases. Once the design stage has passed, most of the opportunities have gone and change costs rapidly escalate. *This is why the designer is so critical to asset management goal of minimizing life cycle costs.*

Within each building or facility the life cycles vary with each component. The implications of varying life cycles is that the proportion that an element contributes to the first up capital cost may be very different from its contribution to life cycle cost.

Some materials and building systems are particularly reliable or durable and repay their higher initial costs with savings in future operation and maintenance efforts. Other materials or systems may be selected because their lower initial costs meet the limits of available construction budgets and, with proper use, are likely to deliver entirely satisfactory service. Sometimes safety, security, or aesthetic concerns warrant both higher initial and future costs. Designers and owners of buildings recognize that there are many such choices and trade-offs among initial construction costs, recurring operations and maintenance (O&M) costs, and building performance.

Decisions about a building's design, construction, operation, and maintenance can in principle, be made such that the building performs well over its entire life cycle and the total costs incurred over this life cycle are minimized.

Unexpected use of the building, unusual events such as storms or earthquakes, poor construction practices, changes of ownership, budgetary constraints, or financial conditions may alter the strategy for minimizing life cycle cost.

In practice, defining and controlling the life-cycle costs are difficult. The future behavior of materials and mechanical and electrical systems is uncertain, as are the future uses of the building, the environmental conditions to which it may be exposed, and the financial and economic conditions that influence relationships between present and future costs. Finding the best course of action and assuring that it is followed are challenges that continue as long as a building is in use, challenges that life cycle cost analysis can help decision makers to meet.

The future client

Within the public sector, clients are now increasingly required to take life cycle costs into account in assessing designs. Expect more of this. In particular, expect to see:

Within the private sector there is a trend to design, build and maintain contracts. Some of these contracts extend to design, build, maintain *and* operate (with the contractor providing ongoing catering, cleaning, security, etc services). As competition for these contracts increases, the need for minimizing the life cycle costs for a given level of service will become the driving force behind design.

- Client briefs that include an explicit assessment of design alternatives that influence life-cycle cost as an element of the scope of work and fees of agency designers.
- Clients requiring VE programs, construction contract incentives and other procurement mechanisms to demonstrate savings in expected life cycle cost rather than construction cost only.
- Clients that direct their designers to clearly document their design decisions made to control life cycle cost and the subsequently expected operating consequences for each facility.
- More knowledgeable clients – with a reduction in new buildings and an increase in their size, agencies will have both the ability and incentive to allocate the resources for client control.

Keeping up to date

The designer's vision needs to be combined with the field knowledge of engineering services engineers, property management people, quantity surveyors and valuers (and specialists such as façade technology consultants). Asset management is very much a multi-disciplinary field.

All professional fields are rapidly evolving – and asset management is no exception. To keep up to date in this field without investing an inordinate amount of time, visit and bookmark AMQ International's *Emerging World of Asset Management* at www.amqi.com, and make a practice of regularly catching up with the latest in the section *For designers and urban planners*. This section is managed by architects and other design professionals, for people in their professions.

8.7 Workplace design for profit

Perhaps you consider office space secondary to the nitty-gritty process of innovation. Well, at IDEO we consider it one of our premier assets. Creating great office space may be one of the hardest parts of the innovation puzzle. It doesn't happen simply by hiring forward-thinking architects or leasing cool buildings.

Tom Kelley

Key Resource Gérald de Kerchove has prepared a definitive paper on this chapter's topic, which can be downloaded in full from www.mqia.com. This chapter is an extract of his paper. – Ed.

Workplace design for profit by Gérald de Kerchove

Gérald de Kerchove founded PdK Consulting, which invented a performance measurement methodology to create performance enhancing workplaces for knowledge workers.

Tom Kelley, CEO of IDEO, in his book *The Art of Innovation*, describes ways that IDEO has adopted to create workplaces that work and look great. He talks about building neighborhoods, thinking in terms of teams, creating playful, flexible foundations that evolve, creating team icons, and telling stories about the workers and the company.

Kelley is at odds with the majority of business leaders who consider the workplace as strictly a source of costs. The prevailing workplace strategy is providing a place of work for every worker at the lowest possible cost. Workplace designers are viewed as suppliers of commodity services to be purchased at the lowest possible cost. However, there is as much as 16 times more profit opportunity from equal gains in performance than in cost reductions, because of the relative value of each component in the total cost of an employee.

In *Excellence by Design*, Michael Joroff describes the four critical dimensions of the workplace, noting that *conceiving the Workplace as a strategic element in the enterprise requires a shift in how we view the workplace itself.* He continues: *The workplace as a strategic element of the organization is more than this: it depends upon the internal compatibility – indeed, the active mutual reinforcement – of spatial, organizational, financial, and technological arrangements.* He states *these dimensions are interdependent and in a dynamic relationship with one another. A change in one demands change in others.*

Don Cohen and Lawrence Prusak in *In Good Company* make the case for the importance of 'Social Capital'. They add another key dimension to the successful workplace: *Space and time for people to gather and make connections with one another are the seedbed and sunlight of social capital.* Cohen and Prusak say *if you want people to connect, to talk, to begin to understand and depend on one another, give them places and occasions for meeting, and enough time to develop networks and communities. Social capital needs breathing room – social space and time – within work and surrounding work.*

The building of 'performance enhancing workplaces' that support innovation, encourage knowledge capital growth and stimulate social capital generation, require a multi-disciplinary approach.

Ethnographers describe the culture and analyze networks; sociologists identify communities of practice and social networks; organizational psychologists examine motivation and satisfaction; organization development consultants develop performance measures; workplace consultants sketch design strategies; and architects and designers transform the strategic designs into performance-enhancing workplaces.

All of these separate disciplines need to have their input integrated under a single, unified design umbrella.

Unfortunately, this fascinating data failed to prove that a better workplace would help people perform better – as it may only indicate that people who perform better tend to gravitate toward organizations that provide a better workplace.

Nonetheless, it provides us with the first empirical hint that the workplace might affect performance.

Does design affect the performance of knowledge workers? Empirical evidence emerges from an unlikely source. Tom Demarco and Tim Lister have focused their attention on software developers' performance as recounted in their book *Peopleware: Productive Projects and Teams*.

Starting in 1984, they ran an annual survey as a sort of public competition in which teams of software implementers from different organizations compete to complete a series of benchmark coding and testing tasks in minimal time and with minimal defects. They call these competitions 'coding war games'. Over 600 developers from 92 organizations were tested over a three-year period.

Why are Demarco and Lister's findings interesting to designers? Simply that having identified these huge differences in performance, they became curious and tried to identify the factors that correlated with performance. They isolated a number of factors, which had no effect, or minimal effect.

The factors that *did* matter were the participant's organization and the workplace. The hypothesis is that the environment and corporate culture is attracting and keeping the best people and is making it possible for them to work effectively. They also hypothesized that many companies provide developers with a workplace that is so crowded, noisy, and interruptive as to fill their days with frustration.

To test the hypothesis that the workplace may have a strong correlation to developers' effectiveness, they gathered data on the workplace by having each participant fill out a questionnaire about the physical quarters in which they worked. Comparing the environment of the performers in the top quartile with those in the bottom quartile, they found that:

- The top quartile had an average of 78 sq ft of dedicated workspace vs. 46 sq ft for the bottom quartile.
- 57% of the top quartile participants found their workplace acceptably quiet vs. 29% for the bottom quartile.
- 62% of the top quartile found their workplace acceptably private vs. 19% for the bottom quartile.
- 38% of the top quartile were able to work without needless interruption vs. 76% for the bottom quartile.

Our own research, based on workgroups as diverse as software engineers, human resources specialists, and insurance underwriters, indicates that a true measure of the impact of the workplace factors on the firms' business results is between 10% and 15% as compared to 85% to 90% for non-workplace factors such as culture, management, and economic factors.

The methodology we describe in Chapter 8.8 yields performance-enhancing criteria that, in the hand of a skilled designer, can generate 5% to 10% improvement. Stated differently, changes in workplace design can provide between 0.50% to 1.50% net improvement in business results of the workgroup or profit.

Challenges for designers

What are the design requirements for performance-enhancing workplaces? Above, we suggested acquiring skills that are not traditionally associated with design professionals. We also suggest that traditional sequential design processes familiar to most designers will not work to achieve performance-driven design. Charles Grantham, in *The Future of Work,* notes:

> The workplace is becoming more egalitarian and team-oriented and that is being driven toward collaboration as a way to get work done. The special, technological, and management practice manifestation of this 'egalitarianism' must be blended into design solutions.
>
> The workplace is no longer an element distinct from other human habitations. The workplace, school, home, and community centre are moving closer together. When we embark on a workplace design process, it becomes a much larger enterprise. In order to include these subtle social factors in the design process, one must use the participatory design process. Techniques exist that involve users in the design process itself – not as observers or bystanders but as full participants, equal with designers and developers. Ideally, users begin working with technology creators at the conceptual stage of development.
>
> The heart of the participatory process is that each step is interactive, jointly involving the designers and the end users. It is far more intrusive than bringing in end-user groups, showing them an existing product, and asking for input. Participatory design means just that: users of technology have roles as equal partners in the design process. Myriad techniques to facilitate group interaction can be used in the process, depending upon group characteristics, history of interaction, and time constraints. What designers often miss is the human interaction of the process of work.

Preparing people for organizational change is part of the process of using new technologies.

Designers need to team with technologists, process engineers, organizational psychologists and sociologists, thereby creating 'communities of practice' to provide integrated solutions linked to business results.

Fundamentally, designers need to understand the social movement and the technology drivers of the future of work to, using a favourite cliché of the last decade, re-invent the design profession in order to deliver increasing value to the knowledge age, or even do I dare say, to join the knowledge revolution.

What does this means to today's design firms? First of all they must realize that the workplace is primarily a tool supporting knowledge workers in creating and distributing knowledge.

Workplace design is one leg of a four-legged stool stimulating performance improvements together with technology, process improvements and behaviour changes.

de Kerchove's research and recommendations are similar to those reached by Davy and Harris in moving toward *collaborative* design. – Ed.

To be comfortable members of those communities of practice, designers must develop methods of learning and becoming familiar with the basics of sociology, information systems, organizational psychology, process engineering, just as they have in the past teamed with electro-mechanical and structural engineers.

To enhance that basic familiarity, they also need to establish strategic alliances with experts in those fields to provide fully complete service packages to their clients.

Designing for profit

Consider this example: A software company adopted the methodology we describe in Chapter 8.8 to design a new workplace for its 1,600 software developers. It saw its annual profit increase by $3,045 per developer, nearly $ 5 million. The ROI for the new workplace exceeded 131% with a payback of less than 10 months.

The empirical evidence linking design to performance, while convincing, requires further refinements as well as proof of replicability to be fully accepted.

We estimate the impact of high-performance workplace design in today's US economy to be as much as $150 billion annually. Is our estimate close? We think so, but to make it stand, more research is needed.

Traditional corporate real estate executives are used to managing their operations based on reduction of cost per square foot as a key metric. This won't work any longer in our new economy. Corporate real estate executives need a 'value added' metric to show how their efforts are creating value for the company – not just conserving resources.

8.8 Workplace performance measures

We challenge business leaders to demand performance-driven workplaces from the design profession, and we suggest that they pay for those services in proportion to the value received.

Gérald de Kerchove

Key Resource Gérald de Kerchove has also prepared a definitive paper on this chapter's topic, which can be downloaded in full from www.mqia.com. This chapter is an extract of his paper.

Workplace performance measures, by Gérald de Kerchove

The methodology to build a performance enhancing workplaces, while requiring a multi-disciplinary approach, should be coordinated by a skilled practitioner with strong project management experience. The methodology uses a five-step process, as shown in Figure 8.8:

- Assess the workplace and its culture.
- Identify the desired business results and the performance drivers that cause those results to be achieved.
- Quantify baseline performance.
- Synthesize data collected to optimize workplace strategies.
- Audit performance improvements.

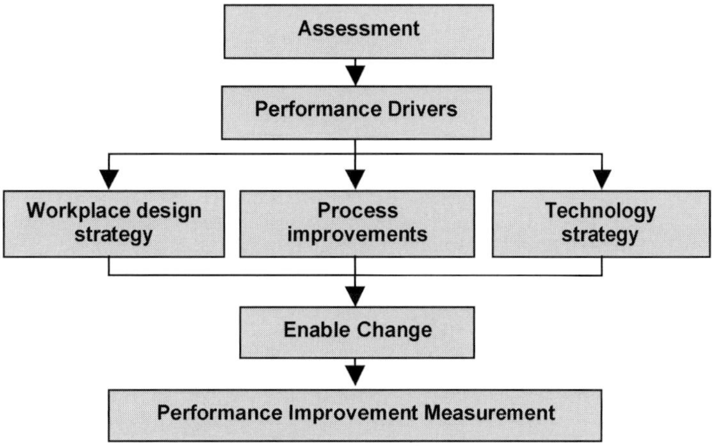

Figure 8.8 *Performance measurement process*

Workplace performance diagnostic

The Workplace Performance Diagnostic is an interactive process aimed at establishing the existing broad business objectives and strategies that the new workplace needs to stimulate in order to maximize performance improvements. Using the Balanced Scorecard approach the practitioner identifies the firm's corporate objectives, culture, vision, mission and values.

The Balanced Scorecard, developed by Harvard's Norton & Kaplan, is described in www.mqia.com > Future > 8.8b Balanced Scorecard.

Those are usually identified as part of the firm's strategic plan. If there is no explicit statement of the firm's strategic plan, the practitioner will need to interview key members of the firm's senior management in order to obtain an explicit statement of the organization strategy and objectives. The identified outcomes will need to cover the four perspectives of the Balanced Scorecard:

- *Financial* – measured by ROI and Economic Value-Added (EVA).
- *Customer* – measured by satisfaction, retention, market, and account share.
- *Internal process* – measured by quality, response time, cost, new introduction.
- *Learning and growth* – measured by employee satisfaction and information systems availability.

This top-down, bottom-up approach eventually yields the development of a deep understanding of the workgroups operational strategies through observations of workplace usage and occupancy, work processes, technology employment, and organizational structures.

Following this top-down approach, a bottom-up process is necessary to validate the alignment of the workgroup objectives with the previously identified corporate goals and strategies of the organization. This is done via a series of interviews with key members of selected workgroups, during which they translate their view of the organization's strategy into explicit objectives.

The practitioner organizes this information by creating templates with explicit statements of workgroup objectives for review and acceptance by management and workgroup members.

Identification of business objectives & performance drivers

This process results in a matrix of 12 sets of objectives for each of the combinations of Scorecard perspectives and performance dimensions. Examples, and the resulting Balanced Scorecard construction, are shown in the full version of this paper.

This step performs a detailed analysis leading to the identification of specific performance drivers for the business objectives identified in the previous step for each of the selected workgroups.

Key members of the workgroup are coached by the practitioner to identify a few specific outcomes or results that characterize the workgroup business objectives for each of the Balanced Scorecard perspectives (financial, customer, internal process, learning and growth) and of the three performance dimensions (strategic, workplace, workers).

Depending on the size of the workgroup and on the organization culture, the evolution of the template with stated objectives into a series of objectives with performance drivers is best done via: Individual or group interactive sessions, and homework.

Baseline performance quantification

The third step is concerned with the quantification of the baseline, or current level, of performance of the workplace. For each performance driver, there exists a metric and a data collection method. Several tactics are available, described in the full version:

- Time utilization study.

- Workplace performance survey.
- Focus groups and personal interviews.
- Video ethnography.
- Baseline measure.

The results identify the most prevalent activities, work styles, attitudes and structures, with an aim towards prioritising issues to be addressed in the solution strategy.

Optimize workplace development

The Balanced Scorecard completed in our second step, with its dozens of objectives and hundreds of performance drivers, lends itself to the development of specific strategies and tactics for performance improvements, forming a series of 'Action Maps'. An Action Map is developed for each of the four performance elements: workplace design, technology employment, process improvements and behavior adaptation.

Performance improvement quantification

Our last step repeats the second step of data collection and quantification. Aimed at measuring the changes in performance, this usually takes place six to nine months following the implementation of the new workplace. The time lag is necessary to allow knowledge workers to fully adapt to the new workplace.

However, an early data collection effort taking place immediately following implementation, can advantageously replace traditional POEs, by suggesting adjustment to the workplace to respond to glitches and to remedy minor flaws to the new workplace design.

The practitioner will use tools similar to those in step three. Identical data to that acquired in step 2 is collected and changes in level of performance are identified. Using the same data reduction model as the workplace performance baseline measure, improvements in the overall performance of the workgroups are quantified.

Summary

Building 'performance enhancing workplaces' requires a rigorous methodology, which acknowledges that performance increases can only result from behavior changes. The methodology fully recognizes and capitalizes on the interactions between work practices, technology, and space. A multi-disciplinary approach leads to holistic solutions with demonstrable and measurable business performance improvements.

Why do we care? Simply because 'performance enhancing workplaces' are *very profitable* workplaces.

Part 8: Sources, resources & notes

NOTE: *The Architect's Handbook of Professional Practice 13th Ed., Joseph A. Demkin, Exec. Ed., published by John Wiley & Sons,* is referred to as '*AIA Handbook*'.

Sources

8.3 Davy, Kyle V. and Susan L. Harris (2005) *Value Redesigned: New Models for Professional Practice*, Ostberg Library of Design Management.

8.4 Abramowitz, Ava, Esq. (1986) *Professional Liability from the Architect's Perspective, Guidelines for Improving Practice,* Vol. XVIII, Number 3, Office for Professional Liability Research, Victor O. Schinnerer & Co.

8.5 ASTM (American Society for Testing and Materials) (2000) *ASTM Standards on Whole Building Functionality and Serviceability*, ASTM, West Conshohocken, Pa.

Baird, G., et al. (1996), *Building Evaluation Techniques,* Wellington, New Zealand, McGraw-Hill.

Preiser, W., and J. Vischer, eds. (2005), *Assessing Building Performance: Methods and Case Studies*, Oxford, UK, Butterworth-Heinemann.

8.7 Cohen, Don and Lawrence Prusak, (2001) *In Good Company: How Social Capital Makes Organizations Work*, Harvard Business School Press.

Demarco, Tom, and Timothy Lister (1999) *Peopleware: Productive Projects and Teams*, Dorset House, 2nd Ed.

Grantham, Charles E. (2000) *The Future of Work: The Promise of the New Digital Work Society*, McGraw-Hill. Grantham can be contacted through his website: www.thefutureofwork.net.

Horgen, Turid H., et al. (1999) *Excellence by Design: Transforming Workplace and Work Practice*, John Wiley & Son.

Kelley, Tom (2001) *The Art of Innovation: Lessons in Creativity from IDEO, America's Leading Design Firm*, Currency-Doubleday.

Resources

8.1 Baird, G., et al., pp 85-92.

Lord, Larry and Margaret Serrato (2001) Postoccupancy Evaluation, *AIA Handbook,* Chapter 19.7, pp 688-92.

Preiser, W. F. E., et al (1988) *Post-Occupancy Evaluation,* Van Nostrand Reinhold.

8.2 Garber, Richard B. and Charles R. Heuer (2001) Risk Management Strategies, *AIA Handbook,* Chapter 12.1, pp 319-30.

8.4 Senge, Peter M. (1990) *The Fifth Discipline: The Art and Practice of The Learning Organization*, Random House. I recommend that you get and study this resource, and fight your way through it (not easy). The fifth discipline (systems thinking), integrates the other four disciplines, and is the rough equivalent of transformative practice.

8.5 Ellerthorpe, Robin (2001) Facility Management, *AIA Handbook*, Ch 19.4, pp 674-8. Includes an extensive reference list.

Gibson, E.J. (1982) *Working with the Performance Approach in Building,* CIB Report, Publication 64, Rotterdam, Holland.

Hammond, D., et al. (2005) *Integrating a Performance-Based approach into practice – case study of the US Coast Guard Framework for Integrated Decision-Making,* Building Reasearch & Information 33 (2) March-April, pp 128-41.

International Council for Research and Innovation in Building and Construction (CIB). See the CIB World website (http://www.cibworld.nl/website) for information on and downloads of relevant papers, including PBB reports. See also the Performance Based Building Thematic Network (PeBBu): http://www.pebbu.nl/resources/allreports/.

McGregor, W., and D. S. Then (1999) *Facilities Management and the Business of Space*, London, UK, Arnold, a member of the Hodder Headline Group.

Van der Voordt, T.J.M., and H.B.R. van Wegen (2005) *Architecture In Use*, Bussum, The Netherlands, THOTH publishers with Architectural Press, an imprint of Elsevier.

U.S. Federal Government (2004) Executive Order 13327: *Federal Real Property Asset Management*, 6 February 2004, Washington, DC, USA, The White House (U.S. President's Management Agenda).

8.6 *Post-occupancy Evaluation* (March-April 2001) Building Research & Information, Special Issue, Vol 29, No 2.

Further examples of the relationship of design to life cycle costs and aesthetic appeal over the life of the asset may be found in Strategic Asset Management, Issues 81 (Feb 8, 2002) and 82 (Feb 22, 2002) on *Maintainability*.

8.7 Cramer, James P. and Scott Simpson (2002) *How Firms Succeed: A Field Guide to Design Management*, Ostberg Library of Design Management, pp 98-102.

8.8 Kaderlan, Norman (1991) *Designing Your Practice,* McGraw-Hill, pp 87-9.

Kaplan, Robert S., and David P. Norton (2001) *Strategy Focused Organization: How Balanced Scorecard Companies Thrive in the New Business Environment*, Harvard Business School Publishing Corp., pp 22-6.

Mann, Thorbjoern (2004) *Time Management for Architects and Designers,* W. W. Norton & Company, Inc., pp 111-26.

www.mqia.com:

8.1a Nelson, Charles, *Going in Circles vs. Feedback Loops.*

8.3a Nelson, Charles, Review of *Value Redesigned: New Models for Professional Practice* by Kyle Davy, AIA and Susan Harris, PhD.

8.3b Davy, Kyle, *Thoughts on the Coxe/Maister model vs. the Heifetz model of work.*

8.5a Szigeti, Françoise and Gerald Davis, *Quality in facilities management.*

8.6a Burns, Dr. Penny, *Asset Management – Quality for a lifetime.*

8.6b Burns, Dr. Penny, *Minimising Life Cycle Costs.*

8.7a de Kerchove, Gérald, *Workplace design for profit.*

8.8a de Kerchove, Gérald, *Workplace performance measures.*

8.9b de Kerchove, Gérald, *Balanced Scorecard.*

Epigrams

8.1 Lord, Larry and Margaret Serrato, p 688.

8.2 Abramowitz, Ava (2002) *Architect's Essentials of Contract Negotiation*, John Wiley & Sons, p 73.

8.3 Franklin, James R. (2000) *Architect' Professional Practice Manual*, Introduction.

8.4 Senge, Peter, p 13.

8.5 Szigeti, Françoise and Gerald Davis (See www.mqia.com > Future > 8.5a).

8.6 Burns, Dr. Penny (See www.mqia.com > Future > 8.6a).

8.7 Kelley, Tom, *The Art of Innovation.*

8.8 de Kerchove, Gérald (See www.mqia.com > Future > 8.8a).

9 Lessons from the Leaders – Case Studies in Quality

9.1 Introduction to the case studies

We asked the city manager of a midsize San Francisco Bay Area city and the director of facilities for a large public university, 'What is the most important thing you need from the architectural and engineering firms that you work with?' Both of them answered, without a moment's pause, 'leadership'.

Kyle Davy and Susan Harris

For more information:

See the *AIA Handbook Update 2003* reference under Resources 9.2.

The profiles in Update 2003 compare three of the study practices (ADD Inc, ABA and HarleyEllis) with respect to: Vision and mission, Overcoming resistance to change, Using external quality consultants, Benefits vs. disadvantages of implementing a QM system, Staff responsibility for quality, and Thoughts about implementing QM.

Davy and Harris's many examples of design leadership include a description of a unique project, by Anderson Brulé Architects (ABA) for the San Jose Redevelopment Agency, that involved the creation of a new organization to manage a joint-use library. ABA is one of the five design practices profiled in the next chapter.

In the 1980's, a number of practices attempted to redesign themselves to live by the principles of TQM. Almost all failed. To my knowledge, ABA is the only practice that went down this path and came out the other side – and in the process gained strategic planning skills that very few design firms possess – and they use these skills to provide a very high level of service to their clients.

Three of the other design firms in this study have approached quality from the basis of ISO 9001, which are more generic than the TQM theories espoused by gurus such as Deming, Juran and Crosby, and at the same time, are much more suited to design consulting practice. The fifth practice, while placing a very high emphasis on quality, takes a more traditional approach.

As you read these case studies, think about the differences between them, compared to their approach to quality.

What is common to this diverse group of practices is that they all appreciate the value of consciously introducing quality management principles into every aspect of their practices. This fact sets these practices apart from firms who think that quality is somehow embodied in the design process and doesn't require a conscious focus.

In a world of increasing commoditization, this focus truly differentiates these practices from their competitors. It gives them a long head-start toward moving into the new practice models – and toward exercising the level of leadership – envisioned by Davy and Harris.

You can download the complete contributions from the handbook website. See the list under Resources at the end of this Part 9.

The practices profiled in Chapter 9.2 provided descriptions of how quality is perceived, and how quality systems operate, in their practices. Some provided very extensive material; others briefer descriptions. I have edited the extensive descriptions to provide a consistency and quantity of content across these contributions, limited by the space available in the handbook.

9.2 Profile: Five design practices

Define excellence in design or technical solutions to include all *concerns and aspirations of the client – including budget and schedule – as essential design or problem-solving parameters.*

Kyle Davy and Susan Harris

ADD, Inc.

ADD, Inc. has offices in Cambridge, MA and Miami, FL. The firm is also part of the E2A Global Strategic Alliance, with offices throughout Europe and Asia.

Profile by Jefferey T. Wade, AIA, Principal and Director, Project Delivery

Web: www.addinc.com

Our mission statement:

Develop resources and Quality Assurance procedures to improve the management process and technical quality of our projects and educate technical staff through direct and indirect training opportunities.

Quality management is a process that starts before a project even begins and touches all aspects of our business/internal processes. At ADD Inc we first looked at our overall company and found specific areas that required expertise. We set up groups or departments that would be responsible for certain aspects of our business. These groups are Project Delivery (PD), Information Technology (IT), Accounting (AC), Human Resources (HR), Operations (OP), and Marketing (BD). Two things had to happen to make this part of QM work:

- Put one expert/leader in each of these groups and trust in their capabilities.
- Cross fertilize between these groups to share information that will allow each leader to better serve our business needs.

Project Delivery is a fairly new group. PD may be thought of as the group that checks drawings before they go out. This is but one of the aspects of PD at ADD Inc. While reviewing drawings is very important, it comes at a late stage in a project, often too late to be able to really help a project. A true QM program needs to start much earlier in a project.

The areas that we provide at ADD Inc through PD are the following: Training, Advisory assistance (both targeted and as a resource), Resource/information management (technical & material library and research), Standards development, and Procedures and tools development.

Training is a big part of our QM program. Training comes from every department; the combined efforts are known as the ADD University. There are mandatory and elective courses. PD trains the staff for CDs, CA, and PM Training; these are mandatory.

We also provide training for specific standards (standard details, procedures, etc.) or tools (computerized database or other software) used to develop a tool that helps organize and manage a certain portion of a project. We also bring in outside experts, product reps, and industry leaders to present a range of topics. Training happens every week in one form or another.

Our ***Advisory*** Program is very important to our staff. Instead of a person sitting and spinning their wheels, they know they have a person they can contact to get help from.

> It is our belief that it is better to start out on the right path (or catch things early) rather than catching things further down the road when they are too big to fix or steer. We have joined with our other office groups, IT in particular, to set up this systematic assistance program.

Across the board, for all groups, we have initiated a list of Go-To-People. The other part of Advisory is the targeted advising. Here we identify where a project is in its process, and touch base with the PM to review in a technical and management sense where they are and what the next phase will bring.

We guide them to make their work better and more efficient. An example is to meet with the PM before the start of CDs to develop a cartoon set to organize drawing and project requirements. Our Advisory program has been one of the greatest successes for PD.

> The bottom line is you need to know what is out there and available for projects and you need to know how to use it. The Library fills both needs.

Resource management includes resource in the form of materials and technical information. We try to have the most current materials in addition to the most-used materials on our projects. We collect information about the materials/products from project feedback and through our own research to better educate all.

Standards is the development of many tools, from standard details to standard graphics to a drawing numbering system to standard components. These components are not only time-savers but also ensure accuracy and correctness. You need to have an effective feedback loop to update your details from things you learn in the construction phase.

> Infosite contains all contacts, project and contact history, and project startup forms and information, in one location.

Procedures and tools development is another aspect of standards. ADD Inc has developed a number of procedures and tools to help in every phase of a project, including Infosite, Project task analysis, Project schedule, and databases for Transmittals/directory, Actions, Programming, Furniture, Door and hardware, CA modifiers, Shop drawings and Archives. These are all described in the website version of this chapter.

The main benefit of a QM system is reduced exposure, better client satisfaction, advancements in knowledge and ways of doing things, better-educated staff, and better projects in technical and design sense. Disadvantages are small. One of the things that we have found is that people tend, when busy/rushed, to rely on the standards and think that they are 100% applicable to their project. You have to encourage/remind people to think. Also you need to encourage the senior staff to continue to mentor the younger staff. PD does not replace this, as too many people may wish.

Anderson Brulé Architects, Inc.

> ABA has offices is in San Jose and Santa Cruz, CA
>
> Profile: Pamela Anderson-Brulé, AIA, Principal
>
> Web: www.aba-arch.com

ABA believes that the quality of the process profoundly affects the quality of the product. The process we have developed is a response to the need to expand the way architects work with their clients in the creation of their environments. The key elements to the process are:

- to develop a collaborative team with the client in which the whole is greater than the sum of the parts,

Our vision statement:

Quality in the Built Environment

The vision has helped to draw individuals to the firm who are like-minded, have a tendency towards 'team-centered' cultures, are passionate, committed, and visionary in search of learning and in giving back to society in the practice of architecture and interior design.

- to begin with the end in mind by focusing on the long term success of the project,
- to remain open to creative exploration and change during the process, and
- to develop the plan based on research and qualified analysis.

ABA's vision statement was written by Pamela Anderson Brulé, and has guided the firm through more than a decade of growth and development. The firm is dedicated to personal growth and mentoring, with an emphasis on developing an entrepreneurial spirit in each staff member, allowing them the space to challenge the existing state and to explore new ways to deliver a higher value of service to our clients and to our community.

ABA's journey towards 'quality' has been a twenty-year research and development project in the creation of a 'new model' for architectural/interiors design firms. The project was initiated when Pamela began to practice in the early 80's and found that there was an incredible lack of leadership skills, systems thinking, planning tools, delivery models and project understanding, which was systemic to the industry.

The 'traditional' outcome often was dissatisfied clients, project budget and schedule overruns, and completed projects that were not actually achieving the results that the client had originally intended or needed.

There 'had to be a better way', and she was determined to find it. Her search led her to Harvard University's Graduate School of Design, where she studied with Weld Coxe, and to the Advanced Management Institute for Architects and Engineers (AMI), in San Francisco, California, where she studied TQM.

The concepts were shared with the entire staff and they were allowed to creatively explore opportunities to fully embrace the concepts. A leadership course was developed and the entire staff participated in a learning process of personal growth and mastery, communication, meeting facilitation, systems thinking, etc. Staff began to study and research the entire service delivery process and explore the complexities of rework and inefficiencies within our own industry.

These studies began the next level of development in the firm's creation. As we embraced the new technology era, the firm began to record the processes and tools, using information management systems. We were then able to formalize our tools and processes and began a new model of working in a highly interactive and collaborative manner with our clients.

We began taking our clients through a TQM exploration of their own, and crossed the line of traditional practice – hence beginning our journey into strategic planning that has grown to be one of the firm's primary focuses.

Over a decade later ABA has become a model firm for the discovery and exploration into new ways of working and thinking within our industry. ABA fully embraces the principles of TQM, with continuous learning and improvement as a culturally embedded element of our practice.

We use state of the art processes and tools to re-create the way our staff work with clients in forming the built environment. ABA is committed to assisting clients in improving their own culture, environment, operation and function, etc. through the design of their cultural and organizational needs into architectural spaces.

ABA has constantly expanded our research to include the latest in current exploration of new theory in the leadership of quality and how it can positively impact our built environment and society. To that end, we have developed a unique and innovative approach and methodology to architecture.

This methodology includes establishing a project framework, where an entire team of client representatives, architects and consultants meet early to establish the vision, goals, objectives, criteria and process for a successful project. Our Strategic Planning is founded in the facilitation, exploration and discovery of both the problems and the solutions to our client's emerging issues in our ever changing and challenging world.

Through highly evolved 'systems thinking' and critical analysis, we guide our client partners through a deep and meaningful transformation of thought, theory, planning and accelerated decision-making. We capture both the process and decisions in a final deliverable, which provides them with a foundation for the implementation and realization of their own strategic plans.

Geyer Pty Ltd

Geyer has offices in Melbourne, Sydney and Brisbane, Australia

Profile: Michael Greer, National Knowledge Manager & Partner

Web: www.geyer.com.au

Geyer has been certified to ISO 9001 since 1996.

Our Quality Policy:

Geyer aims to establish and maintain a position of industry leadership in the provision of professional interior design and related services to our clients.

To support this objective and assist our people in its delivery the management of the practice is committed to the maintenance and on-going development of quality management systems and procedures.

Quality in our services is defined as:

- The provision of services which, at a minimum, meet the expectations and objectives agreed with each client.
- The delivery of services in accordance with the consultancy agreement reached with each client.
- The provision of cost-effective services within a dynamic framework of procedures and standards modelled on AS/ISO 9001:2000.

This focus on service delivery underlines the goals and objectives of the business as defined in the business plan current for each year. It is incumbent on every employee of the firm to embrace these objectives; the procedures and standards which support these objectives; and the on-going development of the quality system within which the procedures and standards are structured.

Our QA system covers client services and related mandatory functions of training, resourcing and IT Systems. Broadening the role of QM into all areas of the business is not seen as adding value at this point as there are good corporate governance practices in place already.

Upgrade to ISO 9001:2000 in 2002 brought a change in emphasis from compliance to continuous improvement. Continuous improvement is a natural part of our business, though mainly driven by competitive markets, changing technology and development in our service offers.

> In more recent times, the increasing pressure on delivery programmes and quantum of fees have seen attempts to marginalize good risk management procedures as optional 'if there is time…' activities.

Initially, we encountered some resistance to our QM approach, which resulted from poor understanding of the value that a structured approach (process) brings to the delivery of design services. It was seen as invasive to the creative process, rather than a means of bringing order and clarity to a design form that has a direct responsibility to the clients on which it relies.

We found that to overcome the resistance (which still persists with new employees) required a multi-level response:

- ***Story telling:*** In regular meetings, our project coordinators/ managers bring their stories of problems and issues that arise through the course of running a project to a meeting designed especially for that purpose. The environment had to be one in which the individuals could trust there would be anonymity outside the room. Solutions were debated and the concept of structured risk prevention soon became a preferred response.

  The system at hand to codify this preferred response was the quality system. It also allowed us to build a support network for those in the front line of managing project risk for the business. This approach continues to be used as it helps align new employees with our approach to structured management through project systems.

> One of the most important of these tools is the Start-up Roadblock, which engages the core project team in the analysis of the project objectives, the project risks and the project opportunities; allocates responsibilities and plans the resource requirements. The completion of the Project Quality Plan is the last step in the completion of the Roadblock.

- ***Good quality tools:*** Rather than expecting to achieve a full understanding and engagement in the quality system by all that use it, easy-to-use tools that guide and support the key review points in the project compliance regime have been developed and refined to be specific to the services we provide.
- ***Staying relevant:*** Continuous development of systems that support the delivery of our quality policy, based on a combination of feedback from those who deliver our services everyday, changes in technology and evolution of our services, are important to the value those who use the system place on it.
- ***Training*** – with our clients being the point of focus. The simple example of a $30 toaster being used to elicit our people's underlying expectations of performance in an everyday object, irrespective of price, quickly brings focus to what our clients should reasonably expect of us when we are responsible for what can be millions of dollars of project value. External validation through guests in training and workshop sessions also helps to ground our expectations of ourselves in a broader reality.
- ***A small stick:*** Systemic non-compliance by a few cannot be accepted, no matter how eminent they may be; so including QM as part of the regular management reporting brings underperformance in this area into the net of the overall management of the business.

QM brought a discipline to a business built on a reputation for high-level creativity as it went through the transition to a business located in more than one state, with a growing base of international clients, in the difficult economic period of the early 1990's.

As with all cultural transitions, to reach a substantial level of true engagement (we still cannot claim full engagement as that would mean engagement by the whole design profession) took time.

One of the key cultural attributes of the firm that both supported and hindered the transition to a certified QM system was its belief in structured organization of its activities. On one hand, there was, and is, an appreciation of the discipline that the quality system brings to the delivery of our services; on the other hand the individual discipline and competence the organization seeks in those it promotes to its leadership continues to challenge the role of a centralized system of risk and quality management.

Harley Ellis Devereaux

Harley Ellis Devereaux has offices in Detroit, MI, Chicago, IL, Cincinnati, OH and Los Angeles, CA

Profile: Dennis King, FAIA, President

Web: www.harleyeliss.com

Although many business decisions are initially made on cost alone, in the end the only thing that truly matters is the 'quality' of the customer's experience with your firm. An ISO structured QM system gives you the tools to focus on exactly those issues that bring customers in and keep them for long-term relationships: Doing projects on time, at budget, and with high quality documents.

With a structured QM system, problems and errors are highlighted in documented fashion, so root causees can be identified and reoccurrence prevented. One of the elements of our success was to require that principals of the firm serve on the internal audit team. This puts the ownership of the firm on the front line of project activity and customer concerns.

The Harley Ellis Devereaux mission statement is focused on these four areas:

Our People / Our Personal Mission

Our Customers / Our Service Mission

Our Work / Our Professional Mission

Our Success / Our Economic Mission

You can read the full text of these on our paper on the handbook website.

Our Detroit office has been certified to ISO 9001 since 1999, and achieved Ford Motor Company's Q1 Quality Certification in 1996.

The 2000 edition of the ISO 9001 standard brings a requirement that the actual 'voice of the customer' be directly ingrained into your activities. This is more than getting customer input on their project, it is about bringing the customer inside your organization to be part of the process, and importantly, to be critical of those processes which are not oriented to project success and customer service.

Architects have an unfortunate professional tendency to be the 'expert', and maintain an arm's-length distance from their customers. They assume that it is their role to mine the customer input and simply fashion the appropriate response. While this may work on a commission-by-commission basis, it leaves no chance to truly understand your customers and to learn from them what is most important to your collective future and business success.

Did we encounter resistance in implementing our QM system?

We did. Change is always seen as threatening by some people and some portions of organizations. While true professionals never object to quality initiatives in their work, it must be defined for them as part and parcel of their everyday responsibilities. They must instinctively believe and literally see each quality initiative as value-added activities at all times.

Our most dramatic quality improvements were made once we developed a clear strategic vision and a strong organization with which to embrace it. Our success is based on a well defined, properly communicated, and sustained focus on aligning our processes with each other and empowering the human resources of our organization. We concentrate on creating an invigorating and nurturing corporate culture.

> An organization working in harmony delivers high levels of quality and service to its customers. Our quality-focused corporate culture means higher morale, less conflict, more innovation, and less bureaucracy.

How did we overcome the resistance? By erosion – the long, slow, consistent and persistent wearing away of those individuals and institutions that attempt to resist. If the cultural revolution undertaken is seen as truly permanent and ultimately inevitable, the necessary changes actually do occur through hard work over time. This is all about, and only about, a clear vision personally embodied and modelled by leadership, beginning at the top of the organization and outward. Over time, our efforts have been recognized with many quality awards.

In summary: Lead by example. Challenge your people every day. Give them the responsibility, then get out of their way. Create a unique value proposition for your customers and your employees. Turn your organization chart upside down, and recognize it is the ***customer on top, not the CEO.*** Strip away superfluous titles and perks. What does it truly mean to be the 'vice president' anyway?

What matters is the attention the organization brings to each customer, not the titles of those assigned the task. Don't fall prey to the 'drop everything and try this' flavor-of-the-month attitude. Selectively pursue only those aspects of business that will provide a real long-term return on investment. Inspire the supportive and voluntary efforts of your people.

Constantly repeat and assure your partners that such a 'leap-of-faith' ***will have*** positive and sustainable benefits for the organization. The race for quality has no finish line. When we began, we devised a five-year plan. When we got to the five-year point, we realized that it was more realistically a ten-year program.

Only when we got to ten years did it finally hit us that this is, quite literally, a lifelong endeavor. The pursuit of Superior **Q**uality, Unequaled **S**ervice, and Constant **I**nnovation is a journey, rather than a destination. We call it '**QSI**'.

Rehler Vaugn & Koone, Inc. (RVK)

RVK's office is in San Antonio, TX

Profile: Ken Rehler, RA, President

Web: www.rvk-architects.com

RVK is not an ISO-certified practice, and does not have a formal quality policy.

At RVK we take a different approach to quality control, although it is certainly not unique. It is a proven method used by many organizations, but not the approach normally used for QM. Our approach is based on the old saying 'do it right the first time'. Stated another way, we believe QM comes from the right person making the right decision at the right time.

We rely on continual checking to find and correct all errors. All members of the project team do 'final checking' during the entire project. We also have a full time employee who checks and coordinates our work with our consultants. However, we have no 'draftsmen' whose work we need to constantly check. Each staff member has a degree in the field of architecture, interior design or landscape architecture.

Compared to an average firm, we are considered 'top heavy' with a high percentage of registered architects, interior designers and landscape architects. But in our office, these people actually do the work. This highly experienced staff designs the buildings and produces the drawings. They do not just manage projects done by others. They are highly paid, but the total hours spent are fewer, since they can 'do it right the first time'.

The reason it works is a result of our hiring practices. We hire the very best, most experienced and talented people possible. People who want to be personally involved with a project all the way through, not people who want to have others do their work for them. We hire people who *want* to be architects, interior designers or landscape architects. And we all help each other whenever help is needed.

Everyone gets along and respects each other at RVK. Regardless of how talented a person is, if he or she does not get along with others, then that person must leave. In fact, the main reason people enjoy working at RVK is because we all work together as a team. This has not changed from when we had 6 to 8 people to when we had 60 to 80 people.

A key factor is that we do not hire when we need help; we hire when we find the very best people. We interview all year around and when we find a top quality person we hire him or her. We adjust our workload to our staff; we do not adjust our staff to our workload. This seems hard to do or impossible at times, but it has worked very well for us over the past 32 years.

My job, as the managing principal, is to do whatever is necessary to allow the staff to do what they do best. They are provided excellent working conditions and environment, the latest computer equipment and software, flexible work schedules (within reason), excellent benefits, fair pay.

It is important that everyone in the firm likes and respects each other. It is very satisfying to be surrounded by and work with talented people. In general, at RVK we hire the best and allow them to do their best. More talent and experience means fewer errors and higher quality of services for our clients.

Part 9: Sources, resources & notes

Sources

9.1 Davy, Kyle and Susan Harris (2005) *Value Redesigned*, Greenway Communications, pp 163-7. Describes ABA's San Jose Redevelopment Agency project.

Resources

9.2 Nelson, Charles (2003) A Case for Quality Management, *The Architect's Handbook of Professional Practice: Update 2003*, John Wiley & Sons, pp 45-54. This article provides more information on how quality systems work in the ADD, Inc., ABA, and Harvey Ellis Devereaux (then HarveyEllis) practices.

www.mqia.com:

9.2a *The ADD Inc. Quality story*

9.2b *The ABA Quality story*

9.2c *The Geyer Quality story*

9.2d *The Harley Ellis Devereaux Quality story*

9.2e *The RVK Quality story*

Epigrams

9.1 Davy and Harris, p 168.

9.2 Davy and Harris, p 121.

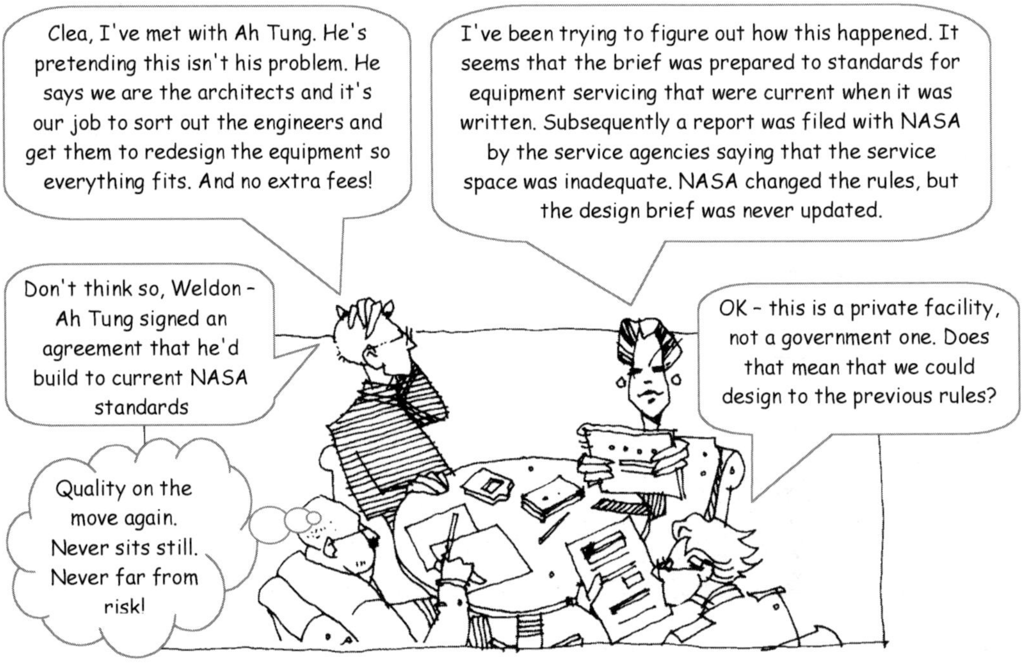

10 Problems: When Your QM System Hits the Wall – What Next?

10.1 Resistance to change

The only one who likes change is a wet baby.

Ray Blitzer

People hate change. It doesn't matter if you put it bluntly or if you develop learned theories about it (which many have done). Arie de Geus succinctly puts the case for change: 'Continuous, fundamental changes in the external world – a turbulent business environment – require continuous management for change in the company. This means making continuous fundamental changes in the internal structure of the company.'

We *do not* like that idea. Too close to home. de Geus notes 'the essence of learning is the ability to manage change by changing yourself.' Peter Senge says 'We all find comfort applying familiar solutions to problems, sticking to what we know best.' He goes on define the dynamics of trying to create a climate for change:

> Leaders who attempt organizational change often find themselves unwittingly caught in balancing processes. To the leaders, it looks as though their efforts are clashing with sudden resistance that seems to come from nowhere … So long as the leader continues to be the 'model', his work habits will set the norm. Either he must change his habits, or establish new and different models.

In the next two chapters, Key Resources David Standen and Paul Hinkley, respectively, explore resistance to change, and suggest ideas on how to use the everyday tools of design practice to effect change up and down the project hierarchy.

As you saw in Chapter 9.2, Pamela Anderson Brulé set about to create new models for her practice, and led from the front. That is exactly why she *has* succeeded, where so many others, with similar visions, fail. The quality coordinator for an otherwise brilliantly managed, very high-profile US practice wrote to me:

> As the Managing Principal is the only upper manager interested in ISO certification, and has the most demands on his time (first priority rightly being the promotion of new work for the firm), little advocacy for the quality system comes from the top level of the firm. Additionally, the Quality Coordinator is not presently a member of the 'inner circle' (a Team Leader or Associate) and is therefore out of the loop when decisions are made which interact with the QM system. This distance makes it difficult to embed the quality system into the everyday workings of the firm, it remains an 'outsider'; always playing catch-up ball in response to firm changes in procedures.

There you have a clear-cut formula for guaranteed failure. Structural change under these conditions simply cannot happen.

I've penned long-winded theories about why people won't change. I threw them all out, to keep this to one page. Be grateful!

10.2 Overcoming resistance

There is clearly a resistance to change on the part of many architects whose management practices I have witnessed in recent years. And they are still paying the price.

David Standen

This chapter was prepared by Key Resource David Standen – Ed.

Overcoming resistance to QM by David Standen AM

David Standen, mentor, guru, teacher, and for 32 years a member of the West Australian RAIA Practice Committee, was awarded the Order of Australia, is a Life Fellow of the RAIA and Honorary Fellow of the New Zealand Institute of Architects. He is the author of *If You Practice Architecture…* (1996, RAIA) and *Terms in Practice* (1981, RAIA) – Ed.

It often seems that nothing matters except the artist's goal (while acknowledging that there really are other goals, such as making money or supporting a family). George Bernard Shaw seems to have known something of this when he was writing *Man and Superman*: 'The true artist will let his wife starve, his children go barefoot, his mother drudge for his living at seventy, sooner than work at anything but his art!'

The title of this chapter takes for granted that resistance to QM is a fact. I have learnt about this resistance, in architectural circles, in years of dealing as an architectural consultant with unhappy architects, unhappy clients of architects and unhappy builders of architects' designs. It is certainly a fact.

'Unhappiness' is expressing the reaction, in many cases, much too mildly. Often the atmosphere is charged with anger, tears, hopelessness and threats of legal action. Sometimes the threat of legal action is followed up to an unpalatable conclusion for one of the parties, architect or client. Always there is a breakdown of human relations, arguments about money and a deep sense of disappointment on the part of at least one party if not both in the client-architect relationship.

Here's my point. In not *one* of those many cases was there any evidence at all of an architect's QM system in place. There was certainly no evidence of any acceptance of systematic QM of the kind that has become the published norm.

What I did see was evidence of attitudes that betrayed resistance to the very idea of management of almost anything but certainly of management of anything done by artists, as if to say that art, including art in architecture, simply cannot be managed except at the artist's pleasure.

Yet the same architects have entered into contractual relationships with others whose businesses have learnt from the standards and who have adapted their own management systems to their obvious benefit. Engineering consultants with publicly acknowledged QM systems in place provide expert consultancy services to architects who do not have that advantage.

Construction companies with acknowledged quality systems in place submit bids and tenders to architects who are less capably managed than the builders. And when the architect gets a demanding letter from a client's lawyer it is often the case that the lawyer's letter will bear evidence of a QM system in place in the legal office. Yet in the face of all such examples, there are architects who will not follow suit. Why?

It seems to me that if we were to survey architects' attitudes to both QM and information technology (IT) we would find parallels as well as paradoxes. The parallels are in the fact that good management in modern conditions require and often demand that nothing but the best in available IT will properly serve the management goals. Like the horse and carriage, you can't have one without the other. Thinking practitioners do not need to be told that.

The paradoxes can be found in architectural practices where computerization and other manifestations of modern technology are patently obvious to any visitor entering the office. This is where things often ain't what they seem to be, because the investment in technology is not matched by QM. In spite of all the visible and outward signs, the screens, the cables and the keyboards, there may be no real system of managing achievement of the office goals. There may be little management of quality and little quality of management.

Why is this so? A most obvious reason, I think, is that IT relies on visible things like hardware and handsets and is a purchasable commodity, like the practitioner's car, whereas QM is not. This is probably where resistance to QM starts. There is no sales pitch, no obvious dollar sign and no sample or specimen to stare at or to trial. In their place is an invitation to invest not inconsiderable time, to discipline the mind, to change attitudes and to undo what has been the habit, the custom and the mindset for a long time past. It is not hard to see why visible gadgets get the nod while invisible qualities are often not even the subject of interest.

The topic of this chapter is not simply resistance to QM. It is *overcoming* resistance to QM. It is about resistance on the part of architects, project managers and designers.

I have to presume that the reader who has reached this page is somewhat motivated to read on. If that is true then you are not completely resistant to change. I presume therefore that you thus far are partly converted to the need for an upheaval in management but needs push to strengthen conviction and create action of a positive kind.

So let me help by offering some idea of the practical rewards available if you go further in the direction assumed to be already taken.

In my years of consultancy services for architects and their clients I have learnt over and over again that problems they experience reflect the quality level of management at the very start of each commission for a new project. Architects who don't get the beginning right spend a lot of time thereafter in rescue mode, interfering with level of service, professionalism and, most obviously, profit, parallel with a diminishing level of client satisfaction.

The first step is learning what the client wants. Without knowing that much, it is simply not possible to form a view of what the client needs or to make any form of recommendation. Time and time again I have seen this step either ignored or taken too lightly. Either way, the low quality of management at that stage is a harbinger of a difficult road ahead. At that point a trap is set for the unwary.

The practitioners least prepared are those who do not have in place QM designed to recognise the trap. I would like a dollar for every time I have seen an architect fall into this trap, try to escape and end up falling also from the client favour. What trap is this? Let me explain.

> Take, for example, the conventional prospective new client who wants a new building and who expresses needs in terms of space, standard and cost. There is not usually, if at all, any assurance that the space and the standard can be attained within the client budget.
>
> The architect produces a design that fulfils the client's space needs and is capable of achievement at the standard of finishes required, much to the delight of the client.
>
> It all goes sour when the architect discovers that the client budget is not enough to pay for it.
>
> That is often the start of a series of program delays that sometimes lead to abandonment of the whole project, not to mention the agony that fills the client mind where ecstasy was the intention.

When a client expresses needs it is not necessarily the case that it is possible for anyone to satisfy those needs. The architect or designer who has not learnt that much has not learnt the first lesson. He or she proceeds to perform the impossible. No level of management quality can help to fulfil the impossible, but a QM regime in place at the start will raise the signal: *It can't be done*. Time thereafter is not time wasted.

The architect is the professional, the expert, the adviser, who should know either at the start or very soon afterwards, perhaps after minimal research, if 'it can't be done'. In some cases that message might be received intuitively, whatever the form of management – but you don't need to be an Einstein to see that a management system that automatically alerts the architect without reliance on intuition is the ideal, whether in terms of the client's values or the architect's values.

Quality (my own definition) is the *totality* of features and characteristics of the architect's services that bear on the architect's ability to satisfy stated or implied needs. The totality, and therefore the quality, can never be attained if it is not present in the very first stage of services.

What architects do in providing normal services of design, documentation and contract administration makes for a very long catalogue of actions, decision making recommendations, directions, judgments, investigations, and the like. It is possible that resistance to QM is born from the fear that there is so much to be done to bring about change that the time, cost and energy simply to up-grade from the status quo is too off-putting. So the resistance remains – and reigns. I *cannot* think of any other reason why an architect, having heard of the benefits of QM, resists any impulse to do something about it.

On that basis I come to my suggestion for architects who are in that category, i.e., who are partly aware of the value of QM, but who nevertheless resist every urge to adopt it.

If the enormity of the task of change is what bothers you, do not fall into the trap of thinking that QM can be implemented in part measures over the whole of your services. That is not QM at all. An alternative, if you are still resisting, is to introduce QM in full measure over part of your services. 'Give it a go', but do it *properly*. Don't reduce the commitment; simply reduce the field.

QM, of course, is not simply about management of projects. It is also about management of offices. It is possible therefore that it may be trialled in one segment of office management as equally well as trialling it in one segment of project management.

Either way, all I am suggesting, if you are still in a state of partial resistance and are still of a mind that you should do something, is that you should simply reduce the field of resistance.

Commonsense says that your resistance will be easier to overcome.

If that option appeals to you then there is no better part to start with to test the idea of QM than the very first stage. This will certainly embrace the framing and execution of the client-architect contract and in most cases the contracts for the specialist consultants, with either client or architect. Just getting those right is a big step in QM but I am thinking of more than that. I am thinking of the need to get right the briefing and the first design stages that from the start either fit in with client requirements or demonstrate to both client and architect that the goal is unreachable. This would automatically show that the client, *not the architect*, is in need of a mind shift and would do so at exactly the right time.

It seems to me that, having achieved your goal and found the benefit, you won't stop there. The resistance, having been broken in one area will continue to be broken down. If your reduced field of resistance is the project start, as I have suggested, you will also find that you have overcome one of the most persistent thorns in client-architect relations. If that doesn't goad you into going further with QM, then I don't know what will.

I have not endeavoured to catalogue reasons for resistance to QM. I cannot leave the subject without at least trying to do so, based on my observations of many architectural offices. As I have already said, there are architects who see themselves more as artists than businesspeople and who do not go in for systems. They like to be free-roaming.

They will resist anything that might spoil their *joie de vivre*. To be frank, I can't think of anything that will break down their resistance. Then there are those who say that their clients are not demanding it, so why should they worry about it? There are those also who have a deeply held faith in human nature and who say they don't need anything else. Then there are those who say 'we are a profession, not an industry'.

Standen is of the belief that the whole idea of a 'profession' has become so diluted and marginalized that it has lost all meaning. No doubt most readers will heartily disagree with this view – even though we see the same thing happening to the meaning of the word 'architect'.

Several chapters I intended to include in this handbook were dismissed due to limitations on length, including the one Standen refers to. – Ed.

I think all such architects are misleading themselves, particularly those in the last category. To them I say that the notion of professions, born in Britain in the 19th century, and fostered wherever British people had an influence in the 20th century will in this 21st century be shown to be worth nothing at all except to historians.

The notion that QM and the professions do not go together is both right and wrong: right because the professions no longer go with anything and wrong because QM goes with any category of human enterprise. A chapter proposed for an early version of this book was 'Is the profession of architecture ready for cultural change?' I am glad I am not the one answering the question, because I think the answer is both yes and no, but more no than yes.

The greatest cultural change, I believe, and therefore the greatest challenge, will be ignoring the path so-called 'the professions'. There are now so many walking that path that there is no longer any right for a particular group to be there, if there ever was, which I think is doubtful.

My telephone directory has the word 'professional' with such entries as roller shutter manufacturers, hair stylists and beauty therapists. The cultural change architects should already be facing up to is society's changing ideas about professions. Perhaps cultural *challenge* would be more appropriate. Notions such as 'the professions', however, have no bearing at all on the subject of QM. Beauty therapists could benefit from it as much as architects, but to do so there must first be an awareness of QM, and then at least a modicum of acceptance, or non-resistance.

From that point on anything can happen – but for many it might have to be one step at a time. For architects, whose services are provided in defined steps, that should not be difficult. For them, overcoming resistance of whatever kind can be staged, which perhaps gives architects an advantage over some other 'professions'.

Resistance to QM? You bet there is. Overcoming resistance to QM? Where there's a will, there's a way. I have attempted to show a way, provided only that there is a will: stage it. If the resistance is total then some other solution is needed and I confess I don't know what it is.

Tim, we have good news. Ah Tung has got a letter from the contract service people he is using that says they can work to the old standards. In that basis, NASA is allowing us to proceed on condition that we demonstrate that we have made every effort to comply with the new rules, and document that.
I've had a close look at the situation. With some rearrangement, we can probably provide about half the extra access widths required. To meet the deadline, there will be some overtime required. I'll let you know the damages.
You'll all be interested to know that I read in the paper this morning that Sir Richard Branson is taking deposits for travel on his space ship. He'll likely beat Ah Tung at this rate!

10.3 When you have to manage upward

Ultimately, the challenge of managing up is the art and technique of minding your client's or boss's QM without being told to mind your own business.

Paul Hinkley

This chapter was prepared by Key Resource Paul Hinkley – Ed.

Managing quality up – Minding your clients' QM, by Paul Hinkley

Paul Hinkley is a qualified civil engineer, Foundation Member of the Australian Institute of Project Management, Certified Management Consultant and Registered Psychologist.

Management is often seen as bosses directing subordinates, and indeed the traditional hierarchical management is characterized by bosses directing as in military command. And so QM could perhaps be mistaken for being something like this. Effective QM requires managing both 'up' and 'down'. In other words, the project leader and quality manager must concern themselves with the QM of the client, or their boss, as well as that of the design and construction teams.

The other aspect of managing quality up is trouble-shooting across organizational layers. In these situations a team member may find him or herself in conflict with his or her boss or other superior, perhaps a development manager or other executive with QM authority. In either case, managing up can be challenging with respect to interpersonal relations, as the person in the 'higher' position may feel threatened by initiatives or criticism coming from subordinates.

Understanding your client

Clients and customers: The client is the individual or organization ultimately responsible for the capital investment and overall success of the project. Alternative terms include *owner*, *principal* and *sponsor*. In other areas of business, the term *customer* is more common but in the case of buildings, the customers are the end-users of the shopping center, apartment complex or hospital, for example.

Ultimately the client *and* the customers must be satisfied. The quality objectives of the client must be met or exceeded, and customer needs must be satisfied, if the project is to be totally successful. Usually the client will have had extensive experience with its customers and thus be fully conversant with the customer issues. If not, focused research through a customer interview and feedback program may be required.

However, even if your client has this information, your client may not necessarily be able to articulate his objectives in a way that can be carried through project delivery. Thus, fully understanding and articulating your client's quality objectives and customer satisfaction issues is the first step in managing quality up.

The degree of commitment of your client to the project, at individual and organizational levels, is important to consider. There may be a high degree of commitment of the organization to the project, but key individuals may be preoccupied by other pressures; for example, the imperatives of other projects.

Insight into your client: Another common problem in QM is the assumption that clients are sophisticated or competent enough to manage their own internal quality management processes. There are several types of clients in terms of competency and ethics, for example:

- Class A; Smart, skilled, experienced, open, honest and ethical clients.
- Class B; Naive, inexperienced clients, who may or may not recognize or acknowledge their lack of skill and experience.
- Class C; Difficult clients who are frequently unrealistic about what can be achieved and want 'champagne on a beer budget'.
- Class Z; Unethical / 'rogue' clients who are skilled and experienced, but wish to maximize every possible commercial opportunity to their own advantage. *Beware.*

Practical techniques for managing up

Using the project brief: The preparation of a definitive project brief is a formal process for ensuring the client understands the QM objectives and processes of the project. The small amount of time and effort is a sound investment in ensuring success.

Developing the project brief for a major project is usually a multi-disciplinary process that must be led by a diligent and responsible project leader. He must have respect for client needs, as well as the expertise the architectural, engineering, estimating and construction disciplines bring to the project and their professional responsibilities.

After inception, building projects typically go through a phase of determining the functional and quality requirements of the client and customers. This is referred to as *programming*, or *project feasibility* stage. This usually includes the preparing of concept sketches and a preliminary project brief. This draft should preferably be circulated to all team members as well as external consultants, if appointed at this stage.

In addition to clearly defining functional and commercial objectives, the project brief must clearly define specific quality objectives and processes for the project. Developing a project brief in a Class A organization can be a relatively straightforward task. In a Class B or C organization, extra diligence and formal decision-making is required. In all cases, the final project brief should be confirmed and signed-off by a client executive.

Project team responsibilities: The consultant brief document should detail all responsibilities related to QM, which in turn are related to the project brief, design client standards, or required by statutory regulations. The formal approval of the consultant brief document is a way of assuring the client that quality objectives and requirements will be carried through to project delivery.

Decision and action: The project team should assist the client in being clear on what decisions are expected of the client organization, and the deadline for when these are required by the project schedule. All decisions needed from the client should be summarized in an *action list*.

Most projects have change management systems. However, managing quality up is assisted by having 'go and hold gates' that allow the impact on quality of each change to be properly evaluated without detriment to the schedule and budget.

Such evaluations may include a formal cost-benefit study in the case of high-impact changes. The study aims to ensure the decision is made rationally and with the right inputs.

Cost-benefit studies include not only the tangible costs and benefits, such as budget and schedule, but also the 'soft' ones that typically include quality and customer satisfaction parameters.

This includes the item number, subject, the person responsible for the decision and the deadline date by which the decision is required. In this way surprises and misunderstandings are avoided, and good client relations fostered.

Managing project changes up: Client-initiated changes need to be carefully considered for the potential impact on the project. Having succeeded in getting the client to define the quality objectives at the beginning of the project and achieving a signed-off project brief, then having the client make changes to quality requirements after the project delivery has commenced in earnest, can be disconcerting and de-motivating. Some changes can jeopardize the overall success of the project.

At the same time, project managers must be highly responsive to the needs of the client. Thus, the quality plan must include procedures for handling change. For example, the procedure may require the contemplated change to be reviewed by the main project management meeting.

Customer and client satisfaction: The success of the project can be evaluated by objectively measuring customer-satisfaction by means of a well-designed survey, preferably conducted independently. The quality of the service you have provided to your client is also important, and this too can be measured rationally and independently. Both will make managing-up the next project easier, because client confidence is increased.

The interpersonal skills of managing up

The interpersonal skills for managing up, are perhaps less obvious than those for managing down. Here are some general guidelines.

Being skilled in facilitation is particularly important with the client organization above the project manager or quality manager, as he has no formal authority over them, and making decisions on their behalf is fraught with danger and highly inappropriate – not to mention the contractual or legal implications.

Aligning all players: In the enthusiasm to get a project started, team members may launch into doing 'their own thing', uncoordinated with the overall project objectives.

Client and team members often have quite different perceptions and expectations of project objectives at the outset, resulting in compromised quality, and wasted time and effort, if not addressed. Thus the project or quality manager has to use his leadership skills and personality to align both client and his own team with the project objectives without being too confrontational, prescriptive or coercive.

Facilitating change: The approach for getting others outside your turf to act in the best interests of the project is usually called the *facilitative* approach – essentially managing up, down and across by negotiation and agreement.

Know your client or boss: Respect the human strengths and weaknesses of your client or boss. Again it is important to recognize the type of client or boss with whom you are interacting.

In a complex Class B or C organization with a degree of internal politics, the 'transparency' of process may be important. This is usually achieved by a wide degree of dissemination of information about the project, and appropriate opportunities for key players to be involved in the important decision-making processes.

Efficient managing-up in a well-organized Class A client requires commonsense and diligence, but with other types of clients, particularly those who are their own worst enemy, you may find yourself having to avoid guerrilla warfare.

A good familiarity with your client's business is essential, especially in regard to the commercial and quality drivers. These can be elicited by direct questioning – which can be confrontational – or by a more subtle approach of socializing with the client. In either case, self-confidence is necessary.

Maintaining credibility and trust: Maintaining your credibility is important when navigating in the uncharted waters of your client's organization. For example, unrealistic or unnecessarily tight deadlines erode the credibility of the project and quality manager. Attention to building the trust of the client team is very important, as some vulnerabilities may be exposed.

Avoiding naiveté: Only the more honest clients and bosses will respect a trouble-shooter. Most really do not want to admit that their organization has problems that need to be fixed. Managing up requires you to avoid being naive or cynical, and remaining attentive to the critical issues.

Just as we know the stories about the messenger being shot, trouble-shooters are often in the same danger of being shot at, rather than shooting. This is an occupational hazard.

Last resorts: After all else fails, you may need to go over the top of someone in an organization, but it is by far preferable to tell the person of your frustrations first. Whistle-blowing is a gut-wrenching business, and a last resort.

Two examples of managing upward follow.

Example 1: Precast façade quality.

The precast façade on a high-rise tower project was being cast offsite according to a specialized design. Soon after the young project engineer joined the project team, he expressed concern about the casting technique and panel design. The engineer discussed his concern with the PM, a person of some senior standing, and suggested an alternative. The PM did not welcome the initiative, saying that any change would cause schedule delays and additional cost.

Given that the panels were by this stage being fixed on the building many levels above the street, the engineer became quite concerned and considered whistle-blowing by going over the PM's head to the company Directors. Instead he prepared a cost-benefit study. The analysis showed rationally that by changing the design and construction technique, the quality would be improved.

Further, the additional cost could potentially be offset by schedule gains. The PM was finally convinced and the change implemented. A significant time saving eventuated.

It was too late to do anything about the panels already in position. Within ten years of the building being completed, small – but dangerous – pieces of concrete were separating from the building and falling to street level. The pieces were found to be coming from the lower part of the building, below the level at which the change had been physically implemented.

The client was required to construct unattractive public protection measures over the sidewalks.

The rest of this story does not need recital, except that the young engineer found that his relationship with the PM soured and his trouble-shooting was neither recognized nor rewarded.

Example 2: Major distribution facility.

The facility was housed in a large long-span portal frame warehouse building clad in metal sheeting, with an adjacent office. Internally it comprised an arrangement of multi-level stacks and a semi-automated materials-handling system of conveyors. The project start had been delayed, so the client requested an accelerated program but without quality being comprised.

As the client did not have a formal project brief document, the project manager prepared one and got client sign-off. The brief included a client decision list including all quality-related decisions, with timing based on a critical path schedule. At the same time as design commenced, the project manager jointly engaged his company's quality department and the client's to initiate a design-construct quality system.

The client decided to retain management of the procurement and installation of the materials-handling system within its own organization.

Nonetheless, the project manager attempted to include all the critical functional and detail quality issues of the system on his client decision action list, not the least to ensure that the system and the ancillary work were well-coordinated. He was told to mind his own business. And he did.

The building and engineering works were designed and constructed within the accelerated schedule and with minimal quality problems. On the other hand, problems with the materials-handling system persisted for years after the facility was completed.

We can conclude that if the same process of managing up had been applied to the materials-handling system, as had been applied to the building and engineering works, the chances of the system working efficiently would have been greatly increased.

In summary...

Managing quality up for your client or boss is much more than avoiding being the 'meat in the sandwich' and alienating both sides. Overall guidelines are:

- Understand your client, their business and quality objectives, and their sophistication and competency.
- Use the project brief as a tool to coordinate all client information required for the project – quality management as well as functional, budget and schedule requirements.
- Make the client fully aware of the quality and other decisions that are needed, who is responsible, and when these decisions are required to be properly implemented within realistic timetables, preferably using a formal action listing and review system.
- Set up a change management system that includes 'go and hold gates' so that the impact on quality of each change can be properly evaluated without detriment to the schedule and budget, and with a cost-benefit analysis if warranted.
- Apply the appropriate interpersonal skills, such as aligning all team members – up and down – to common objectives, facilitating rather than attempting to force progress, knowing and respecting your client's strengths and weaknesses, maintaining credibility and trust, and being aware of the occupational hazards of trouble-shooting.

Part 10: Sources, resources & notes

Sources

10.1 de Geus, Arie (1997) *The Living Company: Growth, Learning and Longevity in Business,* Nicholas Brealey Publishing, Ltd., pp 27, 36.

Senge, Peter M. (1990) *The Fifth Discipline: The Art & Practice of The Learning Organization*, Random House, pp 61, 88.

Resources

10.1 Nelson, Charles (1996) *TQM and ISO 9000 for Architects and Designers,* McGraw-Hill, pp 263-8; 305-7.

Epigrams

10.1 Blitzer, Ray, quoted by Stephen M. Shapiro (2001) in *24/7 Innovation: A blueprint for surviving and thriving in an age of change*, McGraw-Hill, p 67.

10.2 Standen, David, from his paper prepared for this handbook.

10.3 Hinkley, Paul, from his paper prepared for this handbook.

11 Surviving & Thriving in a Swiftly Evolving Professional Environment

11.1 Forces driving change in the design professions

Times of rapid change are rife with opportunities for architects.

The Client Experience – 2002, AIA

This chapter considers what industry thinkers are saying about change, looks at the results of available research and some expectations about quality issues globally, and seeks to construct some markers for the path ahead, as a way to usefully organize and present the rest of the handbook.

These few are not the only harbingers of change – they abound. I conclude that the change we are experiencing is dramatic, evolutionary, and that the rate of change is likely to increase.

The central premise of this handbook is that improving the way a practice manages quality is an important key to meeting the challenge of these changes – a way to 'survive and thrive'. Thus we need first to consider these forces – their causes; their effects - and what we can do to work within, around and above them.

A quality approach to practice must consider change and the forces driving it, because client perceptions and value judgments change in an environment of change. Most authorities on design practice say the design profession is undergoing serious change; some say *profound* change. Many practices are having difficulty in adapting to these changes, and are struggling with them.

As we consider and evaluate effective responses to these forces, we need to also understand how the management of quality relates to other key elements in the practice business model. It isn't necessary to define an optimum business model to usefully explore the importance of managing quality in practice, but a reference framework *is* required to facilitate discussion.

How swift is the evolution?

Noting that sometimes changes that appear to be evolutionary are in fact cyclical, Green says *the pace of change today – whether global, societal, or regional, in the home or at work – is so rapid that there may be a greater likelihood that the seeds of actual evolution are embedded in it.*

The quotation from Kevin W. C. Green is reproduced with permission of The American Institute of Architects, 1735 New York Avenue, NW., Washington, D.C, 20006

It is axiomatic to say that the greater the forces of change, the more rapid the change will be.

Kevin W. C. Green, of Green & Associates, Inc., a Virginia-based marketing and strategic planning consultant, discusses the dynamics of change in the first five chapters of the AIA Handbook. He says that evolutionary change, unlike cyclical change, is neither steady nor gradual, but is 'a series of long, quiet plateaus studded with sudden bursts of massive evolutionary redirection . . . called *punctuated equilibrium*.'

Davis and Meyer, in *BLUR: The Speed of Change in the Connected Economy*, ask:

> Has the pace of change accelerated way beyond your comfort zone? Are the rules that guided your decisions in the past no longer relevant? If so, you are just like everyone else who's paying attention. . . . The elements of change that are driving these momentous shifts are based on the fundamental dimensions of the universe itself: time, space and mass. . . . The fact is, something enormous *is* happening all around you, enough to make you feel as if you're losing your balance and seeing double.

Ways of thinking about forces of change

In 1996, the Center of Excellence for Change Management at Coopers & Lybrand (now PriceWaterhouseCoopers) identified four types of forces driving organizational change: (a) market forces, (b) rapidly changing technologies, (c) changing political institutions and societies, and (d) the internal need to improve performance and competitive situation.

Kevin Green identifies four levels of change: (a) global level, (b) societal level, (c) regional, urban and community levels and (d) household level.

Sometimes, internal events can have farreaching consequences. For example, the consent decrees between The AIA and the U.S. Department of Justice caused a permanent change in the practice of architecture in the U.S. Standard fee schedules are now history, and members of the AIA are prohibited from any discussion of fees whatsoever when they get together.

There are several approaches to analyzing change and the causes of change (see sidebar). I believe that there are three broad categories of forces affecting the professional services environment and driving change: cyclic, cultural, and events-based forces. In order:

- **Cyclic:** There has always been a cyclic pattern to construction activity, Of course, without construction, design may take place, but unbuilt design is not 'usable'. These cycles tend to be fairly long (8–10 years) and are related to business prosperity and consumer confidence generally, as well as interest rates, investment preferences and similar factors. In recent times, these patterns have grown more complex and less predictable.
- **Cultural:** Cultural change grows out of evolving attitudes in society in general and the design marketplace in particular. Cultural change can be extreme – think French Revolution; fall of the Berlin Wall; 'bursting of the bubble' in the Japanese economy – or slow and incremental – think development of computer-aided design (CAD) systems; the growing preference for design-build solutions; the rise of litigation against professionals of all kinds.
- **Events:** Events can be external or internal to the profession and/ or the practice. Single events, such as the September 11, 2001 destruction of the World Trade Center in New York City, can dramatically, instantly reshape the entire economic climate for design services, as well as alter future demand for those services. On a more localized basis, natural events, such as a volcanic eruption or tsunami, will rapidly re-align the requirements for design services. Is there an asteroid in your future?

As sometimes happens, various forces for change can occur together, amplifying the effect. At the point of writing this – mid 2005 – we are in such a period. Those who successfully adapt will survive and thrive; those who do not are an endangered species.

We appear to in the up side of cyclical change, but we are only a few years away from the point where most of the 'baby boomers' will have retired, and with their retirement, will have stopped spending and started saving. We are in the midst of several overlapping evolutionary changes. The last few years have seen the explosive expansion of the Chinese economy, comparable only to the Industrial Revolution or the early years of investment in the U.S.

We have experienced recent, dramatic events that are changing design priorities, and we understand that it will be a long time, if ever again, before we will live in the 'kinder, gentler times' we remember.

Unexpected, dramatic events are to be expected – we just don't know when, where, or what they will be. This one fact turns out to have important consequences for our professional future. The era of chaos that Tom Peters predicted in 1987 is here, only more so.

What are the forces driving change?

What follows is my own synthesis of opinions of those who have cautiously ventured into the murky arena of identifying forces, merged with my own analysis of the change drivers. Except for the first one listed, there is no order of importance for the rest. Sometimes these forces act in concert, sometimes in opposition. The greatest effects will occur when the forces act in concert.

1. ***Global connectivity:*** The primary force driving change is the dramatic, ongoing explosion of global connectivity. This force is a global 'leveller' as well as a destabilizer of traditional patterns.
2. ***Increasing the value proposition:*** Customers demand higher quality, faster, and at lower cost. This very powerful force uses competition as its lever, driving every kind of business to rethink its operation, its processes, its standards. It is worldwide. It has already dramatically changed many hard-product industries, and it is changing service industries. Architecture is *not* exempt. Any firm that cannot clearly demonstrate what Tom Peters calls its 'dramatic difference' will be treated as a commodity provider.
3. ***Risk is growing riskier:*** The design professionals, their clients, their mutual public, and their insurers are locked in a delicate dance, which is starting to come undone. Actuaries are conservative. They bet on rational, defensible probabilities; they take very calculated risks. They do not bet on the unpredictable. As risk becomes increasingly unpredictable, they raise the stakes, back away or both. It is happening now.

> Example: Australia, in 2004, was down to just two re-insurers of professional practice risk, both of which tightened requirements. It is nice that (some) governments require design professionals to carry professional indemnity insurance – but what happens when such coverage is simply not available?

4. ***Globalization of services performance:*** The firm that is poised to 'eat your lunch' may be in Bombay, or down the street – you just don't know any more. Yes, there are quality issues here – but it truly is a whole new ball game. What if the lunch-muncher in Bombay delivers higher quality than the guys down the street? Not to mention faster, and cheaper? It is already happening in the IT world. It is starting to happen in design.
5. ***Globalization of client building programs:*** Manufacturers and many other commercial businesses have no alternative but to constantly seek out the most viable mix of local labor markets, raw materials, skills base, trade incentives and trade barriers, political stability and social responsibility issues – despite high levels of world uncertainty.

6 ***Militant disruption of institutions:*** Whether predictable, serial street wars protesting globalization, or random, unpredictable chaos and violence caused by religious extremists or other disaffected members of society, this global force that will more likely increase than decrease, with implications for design businesses.

7 ***Growth-motivated wealth redistribution:*** The IT revolution created millions of new stock owners, thousands of millionaires, and – when the bubble burst – a vast army of ordinary people determined not to lose their money the next time around. There are billions of dollars searching for new homes that offer both growth and protection. Searching literally for new homes, because suddenly real estate looks like the best show going.

The real danger is that this flood of cash will both drive up real estate values to unrealistic and unsustainable levels (remember Japan), and create more housing than markets can utilize.

8 The demand for 'one stop shop', ***single point of responsibility*** is growing.

9 Normal 'up and down' ***construction activity cycles***, with which we are all familiar.

There are also other major patterns occurring that might or might not be considered to be 'forces'. For example, patterns of affluence are shifting. Not long ago, India had the fastest growing middle class in the world. It increasingly appears that China is today in a similar position. Middle classes buy housing and other kinds of architecture disproportionately to their wealth, compared to those both poorer and richer.

New markets spring up as others mature and slow. The logical consequences of these forces are shown in Table 11.1.1.

Trends

Logic says that the consequences of active forces – as the response of organic systems to those forces – will appear as *trends* in society. More is written about the nature of change taking place (or trends) than about the forces driving these changes. Three of the recent trend reports are described below.

Research by Kyle V. Davy and Susan Harris identified six major trends, produced by information technology, that are 'transforming conditions within which design firms are operating', shown in Table 11.1.2.

Table 11.1.1 *Consequences of forces for change*

Force	Type	Consequences
Explosion of global connectivity	Cultural	Dramatic repositioning of the connection between work and living locations. In many job roles, one can work effectively anywhere in the world, without being there Instant communication: project teams can function on a global basis
Increasing the value proposition	Cultural	Only a strong brand will keep design firms from being put in the commodity market trap by clients Clients will not accept any diminution of quality of service in exchange for downward negotiation of time and cost
Risk is growing riskier	Cultural	Cost of cover will rise, and exclusions to cover will increase Where permitted, some clients will waive cover requirements Project-based cover is disappearing Many smaller practices won't be insurable, driving amalgamation and rationalization
Globalization of services performance	Cultural	Work will increasingly flow to locations where quality and cost are optimized, in the same way that manufacturing does now
Globalization of client building programs	Cultural	Facilities that can be re-located to take optimum advantage of financial opportunities without undue risk will be – architects will need to demonstrate their capability to work in those locations to retain their clients
Militant disruption of institutions	Events	Clients will expect security to be 'built in' to design – signs are they won't expect to pay a premium 'Signature' buildings become liabilities; 'at risk' businesses will prefer anonymity Document control will become a significant issue
Growth-motivated wealth redistribution	Cultural	During economic downs, investment will flow to 'safe havens' such as real estate, tending to counter the influence of construction activity cycles; possible over-building Continued downward pressure on interest rates except where the funds flow is perceived as inflationary, which will exert upward pressure on interest rates
Growing demand for single point responsibility	Cultural	Design-build will continue to gain in popularity; traditional design-bid-build projects will decrease
Construction activity cycles	Cyclic	Chronic over- or under-supply of qualified staff and other resources

Key Resource James Cramer, Editor of the industry newsletter DesignIntelligence, Chairman/CEO of Greenway Consulting and keen trendspotter, sees 30 current trends, outlined below (Table 11.1.3). Note that some of Cramer's reported trends are really predictions. The full description of Cramer's trends is available on the handbook web site at www.mqia.com > Change > 11.1b.

Table 11.1.2 *Davey & Harris's six trends*

1	The shift from capital to knowledge
2	The shift from a local, geographically bounded operation to a global one
3	The shift from having to choose between 'one-of-a-kind' and 'mass production' to the new option of 'mass customization'
4	The shift from integrated practices toward the segmentation and specialization of services
5	The shift from centrally-managed processes toward empowerment, self-organization and collaboration
6	The shift away from operating as one company (one shop) to operating as a network or alliance

Table 11.1.3 *Cramer's 30 trends*

1	Research and innovation are increasingly differentiators for design firms.
2	Design in all building segments is going through transformation.
3	Overt, quantifiable benefits are increasingly expected. Providing tangible, measurable service excellence and innovation creates new playing fields for designers.
4	Medical advances, wellness and health agendas will become increasingly important to design firms.
5	The Internet is growing logarithmically and globally.
6	Training and education become re-engaged at new levels of sophistication and expand to all corporate levels and generations.
7	For all professions the signs are clear: The professions will change or die.
8	The global economy will expand despite pockets of extreme resistance.
9	Genders will achieve equality in the construction industry and in the design professions.
10	Retirement will be redefined.
11	Some associations and unions will lose power.
12	Patron architecture will expand.
13	Generation X will provide highly innovative new leadership to design firms.
14	Time will become an increasingly precious commodity.
15	Knowledge-based design organizations will replace the old guard command and control types.
16	High-performing firms will have flatter structures and more informed decision-making.
17	Trust, ethics and confidence will become a key designer selection criteria.
18	New security risks create new value propositions.
19	Environment and green movement gets increasingly strategic.
20	Technology will annihilate traditional practice.
21	Building solutions will be pre-assembled at a large scale.
22	There will be diminished labor requirements in A/E/C.
23	Design appreciation will reach new levels – as will 'uglification.'
24	Building construction will be 30 to 40 percent more efficient.
25	Architects and designers will morph and expand their relevancy – but they may also become marginalized.
26	Design-build and new integration models become 69 percent by 2010.
27	There are radical new value propositions.
28	Design firms are increasingly asymmetrical in their strategic planning.
29	Clients will see themselves as architects and designers.
30	Change will change – alert firms can anticipate wildcards.

Business management guru Tom Peters, in his keynote address to The American Institute of Architects at its 2002 annual convention in Charlotte NC, said that there were five kinds of changes confronting architects: the *world*, the *work*, the *firm*, the *talent* and the *client*. Summarized very briefly, his points were:

- *The world changes:* Peters quoted Steve Case: 'There will be more confusion in the business world in the next decade than in any other decade in history. And the current pace of change will only accelerate.'
- *The work changes:* Traditional employment models will diminish rapidly, replaced by transient, project-based team contracting.
- *The firm changes:* Providing shelter will be out; providing 'encompassing experiences' will be in. Practices will have to demonstrate their 'dramatic difference'; their brand; to clients to get work. 'Architecture firms . . . are woefully under-branded'.
- *The talent changes:* 'Brand = talent'. There will be intense competition for great talent, which women are best placed to provide (see next point).
- *The client changes:* Women increasingly dominate purchasing decision-making, and men don't know how to design for women.

Putting it all together

What do these driving forces, and the trends they are producing, mean for the design profession? I summarize all of the above into five key 'parameters of practice' that will mark the firms that will survive and thrive from those that won't.

1 Profession redesign: Perhaps Jim Cramer summarizes the prevailing attitude best in his seventh trend: 'The professions will change or die.' Probably not abruptly – those who fail to adapt will wither away through increasing irrelevancy, or slowly starve to death, exhausting themselves on the commodity treadmill.

The prevailing consensus is that those who loudly lament the passing of general client respect for the noble art of architecture, and resent being bought and sold like penned animals, have to start taking down the fences that pen them in. That is, they have to change the attitudes with which they see their professional role; they have to individually and collectively redesign their profession from the inside out. And it isn't a navel-gazing exercise: the only perspective that will work is external; the perspective held by those who buy design services. This is my summation of the prevailing opinion expressed by design industry leaders.

2 Living with change: The second prevailing view is that the issue is not about getting from where we are now to some other method of practice, it is about getting from where we are now to a practice model that is comfortable with constant change, and is structured to take advantage of change.

The driver of this heightened climate of change is the complex and constant reforming of global barriers and opportunities to business, created by combinations of evolutionary forces and unpredictable events, modulated to some degree by cyclic forces.

3 Team flexibility: The third prevailing view is that an important key to bringing constant change inside our comfort zone will involve far greater flexibility in resource management. This flexibility will include the use of project-based teams for almost all practice functions – teams that cut across traditional firm structures, which form, do work and un-form as needed.

4 Responsive value propositions: The fourth prevailing view is that the 'value propositions' – what service packages are on offer, and how they relate to clients' perceptions of needs – will, for the successful practices, become far more flexible and open to 'rapid response' solutions than most practices can manage today.

5 Life cycle focus: There is a fifth important view, but it is a minority view, expressed mostly by those whose professions who are, like facilities managers and asset managers, closely aligned with client interests. This view is that designers who successfully adapt to the new order will undertake a fundamental shift in the way they perceive their 'product' and therefore their value propositions. This view of the built environment shifts emphasis and value on the 'built' part to the 'environment' part. It puts the primary focus of creating architecture not on the design and construction process, but on the life cycle of the process results.

This focus has at least two key dimensions; the bottom-line, economic one, raised by some observers, and the 'encompassing experience' identified by Tom Peters.

Those ***five key parameters of practice*** encapsulate the consequences of the forces driving change and the trends that researchers are seeing. I haven't noted the connectivity explosion / communications revolution here: this phenomenon is present in all of these; it is the common denominator in all five; it both creates pressure to change and new opportunities to respond to the pressure.

There are also important themes present in these parameters; for example; issues of ethics, branding, risk aversion / risk management – and of course, quality, which is in everything. Like the communications issue, typically these tend to flow across and be expressed in the key parameters.

How does your practice strategic plan relate to these five key parameters?

What will the high success, 'survive and thrive' firms of tomorrow look like? Certainly not much like the traditional services structures we were educated to build and run!

11.2 Can the professions respond in time?

Rather than being good at change, most professional firms are quite the opposite: They are resistant to it.

David Maister

Some time after I wrote the previous chapter, I discovered, on the internet, a paper of Dawson's; *The Seven MegaTrends of Professional Services: The Forces That Are Transforming Professional Services Industries and How to Respond.* It reinforces my conclusions. I suggest you read it. Do a Google search on Ross+Dawson+Epicor and you'll find several sites where you can download it.

Melbourne architects Fender Katsalidis, arguably one of the most sought-after design firms in the Asia-Pacific region, regularly involves its clients in the design process on an in-depth basis (see Chapter 11.3). This is a clear example of strategic transparency.

Dawson notes that US regional law firm Powell Goldstein works with its clients that have implemented Six Sigma to meet their internal Six Sigma targets, and charges fees by how its assists its clients in achieving those objectives. I can think of only one design practice I've come across that would be able to do that, ABA (Chapter 9.2).

Ross Dawson, an expert on knowledge-based client relationships, states 'What is most valuable to clients is making them more knowledgeable, helping them to make better decisions, and enhancing their capabilities'. His advice on how to respond to the trends of our times (see the sidebar), outlined in his paper, are:

- Lead your clients into knowledge-based relationships
- Build strategic transparency
- Create a highly networked firm
- Evolve your business models

His first point underscores everything this handbook says about the need for a better understanding of our clients' businesses.

By 'strategic transparency', Dawson means letting your client see your internal delivery processes.

By a 'networked' firm, Dawson means developing better internal connections; better leveraging of the firm's talent. Architects may be better at that than some other professions, but we could be a lot better at it than we are. 'Evolve your business models' equates closely with Davy and Harris's analysis (Chapter 8.3).

To return to the question posed by the title of this chapter: *Can the professions respond in time?* I suppose it begs a second question: *In time for what?* My answer: *In time to retain remaining relevance and regain lost relevance.*

I have not seen many signs that professional societies see what others consider to be 'handwriting on the wall'. The AIA launched an initiative in 2005 to revitalize its continuing education program. The first recommendation in this program includes 'Find the best architects; Determine the skills and knowledge needed; create curricula around the best skills and knowledge needed; and Figure out how to stay on top of the news/trends/changes in best practices.' This is a noteworthy goal, but I wonder how the AIA will define 'best architects'. That seems to me to be mission-critical.

What I think will happen is that, increasingly, individual firms will move up the evolutionary ladder defined by Davy & Harris: Many will become better at *technical* work; some will advance to the level of *collaborative* work as envisioned by them, and a very few will join the likes of ABA at the level of *transformative* work.

11.3 The art of presentation

It is a fundamental rule that effective knowledge transfer to large groups must be designed to cater to a range of cognitive styles. As such, an understanding of cognitive styles should be a core skill of all professionals who communicate with clients.

Ross Dawson

This chapter was prepared by Key Resource David Sutherland – Ed.

The art of presentation, by David Sutherland

David Sutherland is Director of Planning at Fender Katsalidis Architects, Melbourne. The firm's skill at presenting their projects is up there with the best. I asked David to prepare a short paper on his approach to communication of design.

One picture is still worth a thousand words, and unfortunately, the technology to bring you Sutherland's approach in pictures isn't yet available in book form.

One day, not far away, this book will be on a chip, and it will have instant access to display all of the things I have told you to look up – including a video of Sutherland demonstrating what his words really mean. – Ed.

Architects need to explain the buildings they have created to others. We used to show our projects using drawings and models. However, drawings are not a good basis for explanation, as they are in themselves, and in the absence of a completed building, the final output. Missing is the underlying rationale. That lack could, of course, be overturned by a series of accompanying sketches which explored the logic and principles of the building design.

Such an approach may be entirely appropriate. However, it is difficult to exert influence over more than one or two people at a time in that manner. Any more than that, and someone is going to miss out on some information.

Enter the electronic presentation. While this can be used for projecting images onto a wall for more people to see, more importantly; it is a tool for analysis, for dissection, for exploration as well as illustration. The electronic presentation has the advantages of time, of accumulation, of transparency, of fade, of motion, of focus, of transition and segue, of sequence and control.

The electronic presentation allows the revealing of the building blocks of the design one at a time in a manner that can encourage discussion and collaboration and foster understanding. It allows us to reveal the art of architecture as one of consideration, analysis, synthesis, logic and emotion.

It allows us to communicate in a compelling way that architecture is far more then the skin-deep sculpting of built form. By requiring us to explicitly fashion the structure of our presentation, the act of creating an electronic presentation forces the presenter to carry out the critical task in the communication of the architectural design: to know the subject.

Which introduces us to a primary principle of electronic presentations: the person who is going to be speaking should be the person who structures the presentation. Electronic presentations need a composition, they need a flow. They need climaxes, and they need lulls. They need a dynamic that creates a focus on the critical messages.

When structuring these we need to imagine and rehearse what we will be saying as each image will be displayed.

Of course, that does imply that the presentation be interesting. An electronic approach provides us with the ability to create an intense interest through combination of said word and graphic. More people will grasp an interesting message than a dull one.

So let's ourselves grasp that opportunity. To do so means that almost inevitably we need to ignore all the opportunities to create really boring presentations that come bundled with presentation software. Quickly discard the templates; these merely create sameness. Forget about having your company name or logo or the topic of the presentation on each slide; these create boredom and the irritation of the viewer for being patronised. Use the graphics to create the visual structure of the presentation.

Having done all of this, we find now that we know what we will be talking about and therefore will be authoritative, we have structured the information so that others may understand it, and we will be able to keep them interested in how we enlighten them.

11.4 Anticipating the path ahead

Learning begins with perception. Neither an individual nor a company will begin to learn without having seen something of interest in the environment. That is why surviving and thriving in a volatile world require, first of all, management which is sensitive to its company's environment.

Arie de Geus

de Geus defines *environment* as 'the sum total of all forces that affect a company's actions'.

Possibly, we have a flawed, selective memory; reflecting the princely domains conjured up by the Beaux Arts traditions that still lurk within most of our formal design training centers.

One of the Superman movies had a sequence where Superman zoomed around the world, in the opposite direction of rotation, so that he could turn back time to right some horrible wrong. Well, we aren't Supermen, and there is no scientific evidence that this technique would work even if we were.

I don't think we can turn back time. We are *here*, it is *now*, and it is time to study the signals from the outside world – and to create some memories of a new, different and *better* future that fits with those signals.

de Geus's epigram opens a chapter entitled *The Memory of the Future*, a wonderful idea and a reference to his research that demonstrates 'We will not perceive a signal from the outside world unless it is relevant to an option for the future which we have already worked out in our imagination. The more memories of the future we develop, the more open and receptive we will be to signals from the outside world.'

The six plus years of research that have gone into preparing this handbook convince me that the design professions have had some powerful signals blinking at them from the outside world for some time, and that they have gone largely unnoticed.

Why? de Geus's research suggests that we haven't allowed our imagination to construct 'memories' of how our professional life could be better *and* different. This sounds right to me; the vast majority of the many hundreds of design professionals I've talked with over the last decade seem to want it to be better *and basically the same* as their collective memory of 4,000 years of practice.

If that idea is right, why haven't we imagined these alternative futures? Is it because we are so intent on spinning the wheel in the rat-cage ever faster and faster in our goal to beat back the inevitable marginalization of design practice that we haven't any time to think outside the rat cage?

I don't know. What I *do* know is that there are two, and only two, common demoninators of the whole of design practice, inseparable from every function we do, common to every design discipline in the built-environment industry, and they are ***communication*** and ***quality***.[1]

With the help of the Key Resources, I have tried in this handbook to show the pervasiveness of quality in design and the need for recognizing it in a more structured way – and tangentially kept bumping into communication, quality's lockstep dance partner.

I suggested at the end of Chapter 11.2 that we would see movement toward the business models proposed by Davy and Harris; their conclusions are too compelling to be ignored.

There is also a lot of recent, heartening movement in other key aspects of quality in design practice – areas that I wish I had the time and space to explore and present here in more detail. They will be in the next version of this handbook. Some of these are:

- ***Lean design.*** This is an idea straight out of the TQM tool lean manufacturing, adapted to our industry, and making great inroads in our thinking. For a good introduction to the concept, visit the Albert Kahn website (www.albertkahn.com).
- ***BIM,*** an acronym for Building Information Modelling. The basic idea has been around for a long time, but it has recently gained a lot of gravitas, as computing power and ease-of-use has caught up with theory. For an overview, see www.aia.org/tap_a_0903bim.
- ***LEED*** (Leadership in Energy and Environmental Design) is the 'green building' structure. For information, see the U.S. Green Building Council website (www.usgbc.org).
- ***ISO 14000 Environmental Management.*** This international standard for excellence in environmental issues is slowly but surely becoming the worldwide baseline document for same. It is designed to be used with ISO 9001.

Some current Key Resources, and others who really *should* be Key Resources, and who are knowledgable about (or instigators of) these developments, have been agitating for their inclusion in this project. Expect that the handbook website will, over time, include articles and links to knowledge sources in these areas.

Wrap-up home truths

This is my last chance to write something brilliant, to bring it all together in a cosmic burst of communication. Sorry, but there are no lightning flashes that will split your corporate tree asunder; no silver bullets; no magic wands.

Quality is core to excellent practice. Ignore the static about meaningless paperwork; that's not it at all; that is *faux* quality.

Best quality is ***hard*** work, ***real*** discipline. It is about connecting *all* the dots all the way around the learning cycle, and ensuring that everybody in your practice is on the same bus; singing from the same hymnal. That is *not* as easy as it sounds.

The practices that have 'been there; done that' are different, and better, in ways you can't imagine until you've done it. They are eating your lunch – and, increasingly – running your cafeteria.

One of my clients, whose current role is Manager, Project Delivery, for a vibrant 2100-strong engineering practice with 33 offices from Manila to Abu Dhabi, wrote me last week, 'Most of our staff do not remember life pre-QA.' They ***are*** there. Are you?

Part 11: Sources, resources & notes

NOTE: *The Architect's Handbook of Professional Practice 13th Ed.,* Joseph A. Demkin, Exec. Ed., published by John Wiley & Sons, is referred to as '*AIA Handbook*'.

Sources

11.1 Green, Kevin W. C. (2001) Clients and the Forces of Change, *AIA Handbok*, pp 15–18.

Davis, Stan and Christopher Meyer (1998) *BLUR: The Speed of Change in the Connected Economy*, Warner Books, p 6.

Peters, Tom (2002) AIA 2002 Convention keynote address, www.tompeters.com > slides > 2002.

11.2 AIA Continuing Education (2005) *Comprehensive Strategic Plan, Summary*, p 4.

Dawson, Ross (2000) *Developing Knowledge-Based Client Relationships: The Future of Professional Services*, Butterworth Heinemann. p xvi.

Dawson, Ross (undated) *The Seven MegaTrends of Professional Services: The Forces That Are Transforming Professional Services Industries and How to Respond*, Epicor.

11.4 de Geus, Arie (1997) *The Living Company: Growth, Learning and Longevity in Business*, Nicholas Brealey Publishing, p 46.

Resources

11.2 Cohen, Jonathan (2004) Beyond Flat Earth: New Horizons in Design Practice, *AIA Handbook Update 2004*, pp 43–54.

Maister, David H. (1997) *True Professionalism*, The Free Press. Chapter 16: *The Adaptive Firm* (pp 156–63) is a succinct description of what firms must do to adapt to new ways of working.

Ross Dawson's book, noted above, is an excellent, highly readable source for increasing your understanding of the dynamics of client relationships.

www.mqia.com:

11.1a Cramer, James, *The Innovative, Visionary Practice.*

11.1b Cramer, James, *30 Trends to Watch Today.*

Epigrams

11.1 *The Client Connection – 2002*, AIA, p 7.

11.2 Maister, David H., p 157.

11.3 Dawson, Ross, p 73.

11.4 de Geus, Arie, p 30.

Endnotes

1 These two aspects of practice cannot logically be shoe-horned into any one of the four main topic areas of the AIA's *The Architect's Handbook of Professional Practice*; Client, Business, Delivery and Resources. Quality and communication are equally common to all those areas.

12 Appendices

12.1 Quality acronyms & terminology

Acronyms

Acronyms used in this handbook, listed below, do not include abbreviations of practice names or acronyms used within firms and defined in chapters about them.

ACEC	American Consulting Engineers Council
A|E	Architect/Engineer
A|E|C	Architect | Engineer | Contractor (or) Architecture | Engineering | Contracting
AIA	The American Institute of Architects
AIPM	Australian Institute of Project Management
AM	Asset management
AMI	Advanced Management Institute for Architecture and Engineering
ANSI	American National Standards Institute
ASQ	American Society for Quality
BHAG	'Big, hairy, audacious goal'
BIM	Building information modelling
CA	Contract administration
CAD	Computer-aided design/drafting (also CADD)
CDs	Contract documents
CEO	Chief Executive Officer
CIB	International Council for Research and Innovation in Building and Construction
CM	Construction manager / Construction management
CRE	Corporate real estate (group / function)
CRM	Client relationship management
CSI	Construction Specifications Institute
CSIRO	Commonwealth Scientific and Industrial Research Organisation (Australia)
EDM	Electronic document management
D/B	Design/Build (also DB)
FAIA	Fellow of the AIA
FM	Facilities management
GC	General contractor
GMP	Guaranteed maximum price
HR	Human resources
IFC	International Centre for Facilities
IFMA	International Facility Management Association
ISO	International Organization for Standardization
IT	Information technology
LEED	**L**eadership in **E**nergy and **E**nvironmental **D**esign
KPI	Key performance indicator
MBAQ	Management by asking questions
MBWA	Management by walking around
PBB	Performance-based building (method)
PI	Professional indemnity (insurance)
PM	Project manager / Project management
PMBOK	Project Management Book of Knowledge
PMI	Project Management Institute
POE	Post-occupancy evaluation
PQP	Project quality plan
PRINCE2	**PR**ojects **IN** **C**ontrolled **E**nvironments **2**
QA	Quality assurance
QC	Quality control
QI	Quality improvement (aka Continual improvement)
QM	Quality management
QMS	Quality management system
RAIA	Royal Australian Institute of Architects
RFI	Request for information
RFP	Request for proposal
RIBA	Royal Institute of British Architects
RM	Risk management
SI	Site instruction
TQM	Total quality management
UPMM	*Ultimate Project Management Manual* (a publication of PSMJ Resources, Inc.)
VM	Value management (also called VE – Value engineering)
WLCM	Whole life cycle management

Terminology

The following terms, as used in this handbook, are defined below. Page location of the point of definition in the handbook, or other source, is indicated in brackets eg [p 24] or [ISO 9000]. In some cases, I also add some of my own informal definitions, which are in italics following the source definition. All ISO 9000 definitions are downloaded from the *Quality Glossary*, an online resource hosted by the quality consulting group 1stNClass (www.1stnclass.com).

Balanced Scorecard	[p 264]	A management system that enables organizations to clarify their vision and strategy and translate them into action. It provides feedback around both the internal business processes and external outcomes in order to continuously improve strategic performance and results. When fully deployed, the balanced scorecard transforms strategic planning from an academic exercise into the nerve center of an enterprise. (Source: The Balanced Scorecard Institute – www.balancedscorecard.org)
Continual improvement	[ISO 9000]	Recurring activity to increase the ability to fulfil requirements.
Keystone species	[p 244]	In biological eco-systems, keystone species are major contributors to the health and vitality of the eco-system; such that without their contribution, the existence of the eco-system would be threatened. (Source: Davy & Harris, p 187)
Quality	[ISO 9000]	Degree to which a set of inherent characteristics fulfils requirements. *Quality is whatever the client says it is – Ed.*
Quality assurance	[ISO 9000]	Part of QM focused on providing confidence that quality requirements will be fulfilled. *QA is the sum of your promises to your client – Ed.*
Quality control	[ISO 9000]	Part of QM focused on fulfilling quality requirements.
Quality improvement	[ISO 9000]	Part of QM focused on increasing the ability to fulfil quality requirements.
Quality management	[ISO 9000]	Coordinated activities to direct and control an organization with regard to quality. *QM is everything you do to honor your promises to the client – Ed.*
Transformative practice	[Ch. 8.3]	Davy & Harris's term for adaptive work, defined by Heifetz as the learning required to address conflicts in the values people hold, or to diminish the gap between the values people stand for and the reality they face. Adaptive work requires a change in values, beliefs, or behavior. Davy & Harris extend this idea to include technological/social innovation.
Validation	[ISO 9000]	Confirmation, through the provision of objective evidence, that the requirements for a specific intended use or application have been fulfilled.
Verification	[ISO 9000]	Confirmation, through the provision of objective evidence, that specified requirements have been fulfilled.

12.2 MQIA website | AIS epilogue

MQIA website

This closing chapter is really just a reminder to suggest a visit to this handbook's website, where I, and the handbook's Key Resources, intend to keep these efforts from becoming obsolete. In case you skipped the Introduction, skip back to page xiii and read the short guide to using the site, then fire up your browser and head for www.mqia.com.

We welcome your comments and questions; suggestions for improvements and criticisms. A number of the Key Resources have asked not to have their direct email links up on the web, to avoid spam, so if you want to write to one whose link isn't there, send it to me at info@buildingtech.com, and I'll forward it on.

AIS epilogue

A little epilogue to the cartoon at the end of Chapter 10.2: On the very last day of writing this book, I read an article in *The Australian* that seemed to validate the AIS project: It reported that Sir Richard Branson had selected Roswell, AZ as the site for his Virgin Galactic tourist space station, and had already collected $14.7 million in deposits from 38,700 people who had registered for the 20-minute space experience.

Public toilets in space can't be far away! I expect to use one in my lifetime, and I'll be thinking of the folks at AIS when I do. See you there!

PS: Want to sign up? Go to www.virgingalactic.com/en/.

Quality journeys inevitably encounter all the obstacles in the path that our friends in AIS have dealt with, and more. Starting with being dragged, more or less reluctantly, to the idea by a client, or sometimes a principal who wants to improve the practice but not 'lead the charge', project teams struggle to reconcile the theory of quality and the reality of practice.

Often they see the potential, but see their efforts undercut by conflicting management priorities and the deadlines of projects. Hidden agendas and personality and generational clashes get in the way, and cloud good communication. Project briefs are found to have critical gaps, damaging schedules and creating rework the client doesn't want to pay for.

The details of project work become urgent, and overtake the important-but-never-urgent systems development. Learning opportunities are lost because corporate knowledge trapping mechanisms are inefficient, not implemented, or permitted to drift into the background. All this happens, despite the best intentions of all concerned. No real learning occurs, and the cycle repeats again. And again. Each repetition without forward motion puts the practice further into the past, less relevant to the changing world.

The easy response, that most practices adopt, is that the whole quality idea is unsuited to design practice and not worth continuing with. This is a 'shoot-the-messenger' solution. A few practices, like those noted in chapters 2.9 and 9.2, take the less-easy answer, and forge ahead, however they choose to identify their quality programs. If you are not in that latter group, I hope that the story of Vern, Les and Clea, and the arguments of my Key Resource colleagues from around the world, will convince you to rethink your commitment. Thank you for staying with us to the end!

Index